This rich collection of Australian and B_____ _____ _____
attention on the instrumental role played b__ _____ , ___ ___
of teaching/learning - ranging across secto__ _____ ...ing social semiotic
approaches and across individual and social perspectives as it does so.

        Professor J R Martin, Department of Linguistics,
        University of Sydney, Australia

This volume brings together a timely and useful set of chapters that reveal many of the challenges for children in learning to write before school and in the primary and secondary years. As such, the volume offers valuable insights for teachers at all ages.

        Frances Christie, Emeritus Professor of Language & Literacy
        Education, University of Melbourne, Australia

This multi-national edited collection is the work of experts in the field who understand the relationship between research, policy and practice, and will be an authoritative guide for years to come.

        Professor Richard Andrews, University of Edinburgh, UK

This edited volume of classroom research provides a needed resource that expertly addresses the complexity of supporting children becoming writers across time. Chapters offer accessible accounts of interdisciplinary research with clear implications for pedagogical practices across the years of schooling.

        Maureen Boyd, Associate Professor, Department of Learning
        and Instruction, Graduate School of Education,
        University at Buffalo, USA

This book is an important contribution to the literature of writing development. It deals with fundamental requirements for developing good writing education: it presents a nuanced understanding of the concept of writing development. It combines perspectives from both linguistics and psychology in a rich array of research, and throughout the book implications for classroom practices are discussed.

        Synnøve Matre, Professor in Nordic Languages and Literature,
        Department of Teacher Education, The Norwegian University of
        Science and Technology (NTNU) Trondheim, Norway

Developing Writers Across the Primary and Secondary Years

Writing development and pedagogy is a high priority area, particularly with standardised testing showing declines in writing across time and through the years of schooling. However, to date there are relatively few texts for teachers and teacher educators which detail how best to enable the children to become confident, autonomous, and agentic writers of the future.

Developing Writers Across the Primary and Secondary Years provides cumulative insights into how writing develops and how it can be taught across years of compulsory schooling. This edited collection is a timely and original contribution, addressing a significant literacy need for teachers of writing across three key stages of writing development, covering early (4–7 years old), primary (7–12 years old), and secondary years (12–16 years old) in Anglophone countries. Each section addresses two broader themes – becoming a writer with a child-oriented focus and writing pedagogy with a teacher-oriented focus.

Together, the book brings to bear rigorous research and deep professional understanding of the writing classroom. It offers a novel approach conceiving of writing development as a dynamic and multidimensional concept. Such an integrated interdisciplinary understanding enables pedagogical thinking and development to address more holistically the complex act of writing.

Honglin Chen is an Associate Professor in TESOL (Teaching English to Speakers of Other Languages) and Language Education at the University of Wollongong, Australia. Her research focuses primarily on three interconnected areas in language and literacy education, including writing development, English curriculum and policy, and teacher knowledge and pedagogy.

Debra Myhill is Professor of Education at the University of Exeter, and Director of the Centre for Research in Writing. Her research interests focus principally on aspects of language and literacy teaching, particularly linguistic and metalinguistic aspects of writing, and the composing processes involved in writing.

Helen Lewis is a researcher and sessional lecturer at the University of Wollongong, Australia. Her research interest centres around literacy development at primary, secondary, and tertiary levels, and pedagogic practices that support the development.

Developing Writers Across the Primary and Secondary Years
Growing into Writing

Edited by
Honglin Chen, Debra Myhill and
Helen Lewis

Routledge
Taylor & Francis Group
LONDON AND NEW YORK

First published 2020
by Routledge
2 Park Square, Milton Park, Abingdon, Oxon OX14 4RN

and by Routledge
52 Vanderbilt Avenue, New York, NY 10017

Routledge is an imprint of the Taylor & Francis Group, an informa business

© 2020 selection and editorial matter, Honglin Chen, Debra Myhill and Helen Lewis; individual chapters, the contributors

The right of Honglin Chen, Debra Myhill and Helen Lewis to be identified as the author[/s] of the editorial material, and of the authors for their individual chapters, has been asserted in accordance with sections 77 and 78 of the Copyright, Designs and Patents Act 1988.

All rights reserved. No part of this book may be reprinted or reproduced or utilised in any form or by any electronic, mechanical, or other means, now known or hereafter invented, including photocopying and recording, or in any information storage or retrieval system, without permission in writing from the publishers.

Trademark notice: Product or corporate names may be trademarks or registered trademarks, and are used only for identification and explanation without intent to infringe.

British Library Cataloguing-in-Publication Data
A catalogue record for this book is available from the British Library

Library of Congress Cataloging-in-Publication Data
A catalog record has been requested for this book

ISBN: 978-0-367-89373-6 (hbk)
ISBN: 978-0-367-89375-0 (pbk)
ISBN: 978-1-003-01885-8 (ebk)

Typeset in Bembo
by Taylor & Francis Books

Contents

List of figures ix
List of tables xi
List of boxes xii
List of contributors xiii
Foreword xvii

1 Developing writers in primary and secondary school years 1
  DEBRA MYHILL AND HONGLIN CHEN

2 Children learning to write in early primary classrooms 19
  LISA KERVIN, BARBARA COMBER AND ANNETTE WOODS

3 Writing before school: The role of families in supporting children's early writing development 40
  CATHY NUTBROWN

4 Bringing more than a century of practice to writing pedagogy in the early years 60
  SUSAN FEEZ

5 Teaching writing in digital times: Stories from the early years 78
  CLARE DOWDALL

6 Developing textual competence: Primary students' mastery of noun groups in two factual text types 94
  HELEN LEWIS

7 Apprenticing authors: Nurturing children's identities as writers 113
  TERESA CREMIN

8 Developing confident writers: Fostering audience awareness in primary school writing classrooms 131
  HONGLIN CHEN AND EMMA RUTHERFORD VALE

Contents

9 Developing a pedagogy of empowerment: Enabling primary school writers to make meaningful linguistic choices   154
SUSAN JONES

10 Writing their futures: Students' stories of development and difference   173
ERIKA MATRUGLIO AND PAULINE JONES

11 Wordsmiths and sentence-shapers: Linguistic and metalinguistic development in secondary writers   194
DEBRA MYHILL

12 Growing into the complexity of mature academic writing   212
BEVERLY DEREWIANKA

13 Articulating authorial intentions: Making meaningful connections between reading and writing in the secondary classroom   237
HELEN LINES

Index   256

Figures

1.1	A cognitive model of writing based on Hayes and Flower (1980)	2
1.2	Integrated representation of cognitive and socio-cultural models of writing	3
1.3	Integrated representation of cognitive, socio-cultural and linguistic models of writing	5
2.1	Learning clusters and the writing process	24
2.2	Learning intention and success criteria	25
2.3	Star assessment	26
2.4	Hayden's drawing of his Year 1 writing classroom	29
2.5	Hayden's plan and writing	30
2.6	Hayden's drawing of his Year 2 writing classroom	31
2.7	Caitlyn's drawing of her Year 1 writing classroom	33
2.8	Caitlyn's planning and writing	34
2.9	Caitlyn's drawing of her Year 2 writing classroom	35
3.1	Gregg's writing	43
3.2	Jigsaw of Early Writing Development	46
3.3	'Mummy work' – age 2:2	48
3.4	'Bear got parcels' – age 2:6	49
3.5	'Mrs Moore – next door' – age 3:0	49
3.6	Shopping list – age 3:10	50
3.7	Puppy. Mummy. Daddydog – age 4:7	51
3.8	Speech and thought bubbles – age 4:7	52
3.9	Puppy list – age 4:8	53
3.10	Cat, mat, mat – age 4:8	54
7.1	Rachel's drawings of Holly's oral story	121
12.1	NAPLAN writing results of student cohort over time	214
12.2	Teaching and learning cycle (after Rothery 1994)	215
12.3	Initial building of knowledge of the field	216
12.4	Ongoing incorporation of new learning into evolving draft	217
12.5	Supporting students to read relevant texts	218
12.6	Graphic organiser for consequential explanation	219
12.7	Teaching the organisation and language features of the genre	219

12.8 Supporting students' writing 221
12.9 Independent use of the genre 222
12.10 'Text organisers' in student text 226

Tables

6.1	Univariate view of the noun group	98
6.2	Uni- and multivariate views of the noun group	98
6.3	Structure of noun group with extended quantifier (Focus)	99
6.4	Types and subtypes of Focus	99
6.5	Embedded clauses as/in noun groups	100
6.6	Noun groups in Reports	101
6.7	Univariate view of noun groups in Reports (percentage)	102
6.8	Use of pre-modification in Reports	103
6.9	Examples of use of Focus in Reports	103
6.10	Describers and Classifiers in Reports	104
6.11	Use of post-modification in Reports	104
6.12	Use of embedded clauses in Reports	105
6.13	Noun groups in Expositions	105
6.14	Univariate view of all noun groups in Expositions (percentage)	106
6.15	Use of pre-modification in Expositions	106
6.16	Examples of use of Focus in Expositions	107
6.17	Describers and Classifiers in Expositions	107
6.18	Use of post-modification in Expositions	108
6.19	Use of embedded clauses in Expositions	109
8.1	An overview of audience expectations mandated in the Australian Curriculum: English	148
9.1	Summary of case-study findings	165
10.1	Overview of classroom observation data	175
10.2	Writing in the ALARM lesson	177
10.3	Scaffolding poetry writing in Year 7	183
12.1	Moderately complex > sophisticated texts	224
12.2	Given and new information focus	226
12.3	Resources for expressing causality	229
12.4	Instances of student's nominalisations	230
12.5	Creating a causal relationship between nominalisations	231
13.1	Student interview sample	244

Boxes

11.1	The boat incident	201
11.2	The opening of Gemma's narrative	203
11.3	Establishing a setting	205
11.4	Establishing character	206
11.5	Showing a character's inner reflection	207
12.1	First draft	216
12.2	Later draft	220
12.3	The impact of the discovery of gold	222

Contributors

Honglin Chen is Associate Professor in TESOL (Teaching English to Speakers of Other Languages) and Language Education at the University of Wollongong, Australia. Her research focuses primarily on three interconnected areas in language and literacy education, including writing development, English curriculum and policy, and teacher knowledge and pedagogy. She has a keen interest in the roles of metalinguistic understanding, talking about writing, thinking and reasoning, and intersubjectivity in promoting writing development.

Barbara Comber is Research Professor in the School of Education at the University of South Australia. Her research interests include teachers' work, critical literacy, place-conscious pedagogy, and social justice. She has conducted longitudinal ethnographic case studies and collaborative action research with teachers working in high poverty and diverse communities. Her research examines the kinds of teaching that make a difference to young people's literacy learning trajectories and what gets in the way. Her ongoing research explores transdisciplinary curriculum development and pedagogies of reconnection. Books include *Literacy, Place and Pedagogies of Possibility* (Comber, 2016) and *Literacy, Leading and Learning: Beyond Pedagogies of Poverty* (Hayes, Hattam, Comber, Kerkham, Lupton & Thomson, 2017).

Teresa Cremin is Professor of Education (Literacy) at the Open University. An ex-teacher, then staff development co-ordinator and ITE tutor, Teresa now undertakes research and consultancy in the UK and abroad. Her sociocultural research focuses mainly on volitional reading and writing, teachers' literate identities and practices, and the relationship between teachers' identities and the identity positions afforded and enacted by younger literacy learners. For more than two decades, she has led research projects in these areas, also examining creative pedagogical practice in English. She has also undertaken advisory roles for Foundations, charities, and policy-makers.

Beverly Derewianka is Emeritus Professor, retired after a career of classroom teaching and teacher education, including some three decades at the University of Wollongong, Australia, where she taught and researched in the fields of language education and TESOL (Teaching English to Speakers of

Other Languages). She has contributed to language and literacy policy development in Australia and elsewhere and is a regular plenary speaker at international conferences. She currently works with a number of school clusters in improving students' writing.

Clare Dowdall is Lecturer in Education (Language and Literacy) at the University of Exeter where she works in the Graduate School of Education. Her own research focuses primarily on children and young people's meaning making, writing, and text production in 21st-century contexts. She has a particular interest in the possibilities for pedagogies and practice in relation to digital textual communication and the factors that influence this.

Susan Feez is Associate Professor in the School of Education at the University of New England (UNE). She worked for many years as a classroom teacher of English language and literacy, specialising in the teaching of English as an additional language (EAL). She holds Association Montessori Internationale (AMI) diplomas for children aged from three to six years and for children aged from six to twelve years, and has taught for several years in Montessori classrooms. Susan is currently a teacher educator and researcher in the fields of English language, literacies, and EAL education with particular interest in social semiotics, educational linguistics, and Montessori education.

Pauline Jones is Associate Professor, Language in Education at the University of Wollongong. Her research interests include educational linguistics/semiotics, literacy development, and disciplinary dialogue. She has recently completed the Transforming Literacy Outcomes (TRANSLIT) project, a local study of literacy development from preschool to junior secondary. She is also chief investigator on an ARC grant investigating the use of multimodal texts in science classrooms. A current project (with colleagues from UOW and Charles Sturt University) investigates the nature of creativity and critique in English, history, and science, with a special emphasis on the dialogic basis of students' creative and critical capacities in these curriculum disciplines.

Susan Jones is Senior Lecturer at the University of Exeter and a member of the Centre for Research in Writing, a successful research team that has conducted a series of publicly funded research projects in the UK exploring contextualised grammar teaching and writing development with a particular focus on metalinguistic understanding. This research has been undertaken in both primary and secondary schools and seeks to engage teachers in the research process.

Lisa Kervin is Professor in Language and Literacy Education in the Faculty of Social Sciences at the University of Wollongong, Australia where she also serves as the Associate Dean Research. Lisa leads the 'Play, Pedagogy, and Curriculum' research group for Early Start Research. Her current research interests are focused on young children and how they engage with literate practices and she is currently involved in research projects funded by the Australian Research Council focused on adult and child interactions when using technology, young children and writing, and digital play. She has researched her own teaching and has collaborative research partnerships with teachers and students in tertiary and elementary classrooms, and prior-to-school settings.

Helen Lewis is a researcher and sessional lecturer at the University of Wollongong, Australia. Her research interest centres around literacy development at primary, secondary, and tertiary levels, and pedagogic practices that support the development. She has a particular interest in analysing students' textual competence, drawing on analytical tools informed by Systemic Functional Linguistics.

Helen Lines is a research fellow at the University of Exeter's Centre for Research in Writing. She has worked on a number of large-scale projects in primary and secondary schools, investigating the impact of contextualised grammar teaching on children's writing and the development of their metalinguistic understanding. She has particular interests in writing pedagogy and the assessment of writing, and in contributing to teachers' professional development through conference workshops, projects with schools, and online resources.

Erika Matruglio is Senior Lecturer in TESOL at the University of Wollongong Australia. Her research explores the complexities of the connections between language, knowledge, and values and is driven by the need to understand how these connections differ according to discipline. Erika draws on complementary theories of Systemic Functional Linguistics and Legitimation Code Theory in her research on literacy practices in schooling to engage with topics such as the nature of classroom discourse, conditions which enable cumulative knowledge building, disciplinarity, and the demands of writing in the disciplines.

Debra Myhill is Professor of Education at the University of Exeter and director of the Centre for Research in Writing. Her research interests focus principally on aspects of language and literacy teaching, particularly linguistic and metalinguistic aspects of writing, and the composing processes involved in writing. In 2014, her research team was awarded the Economic and Social Research Council award for Outstanding Impact in Society. Over the past 20 years, she has led a series of research projects in these areas, in both primary and secondary schools, and has been involved in commissioned research or advisory roles for policy-makers and examination boards.

Cathy Nutbrown is Professor of Education at the University of Sheffield, School of Education, and president of the UK charity, Early Education. Cathy's research focuses on young children's learning and development, how they develop as readers and writers in their earliest years, and how parents and early childhood educators can collaborate to further support young children's learning and development. Over the last two decades she has developed and run a series of family literacy projects, most notably the Raising Early Achievement in Literacy project for which, in 2013, she was awarded the Economic and Social Research Council award for Research with Outstanding Impact in Society. Cathy's most recent work has been in developing a family literacy project with imprisoned parents.

Emma Rutherford Vale is a doctoral candidate researching in the area of writing development in science across the primary to high school transition at the University of Wollongong. An ESL teacher by training with ten years' classroom teaching experience in language diverse schools, Emma's research interests include writing pedagogy, the role of grammar and meta-language in classroom instruction, and literacy development across the years of schooling. Emma has a particular interest in building teacher knowledge about language to support writing development across the curriculum.

Annette Woods is a professor in the Faculty of Education at Queensland University of Technology. She teaches and researches in the areas of literacies, social justice, curriculum, pedagogy and assessment, and school reform. Her current research projects include a sociomaterial investigation into learning to write in the early years of school; a study of the implications of bringing literacy and sustainability together as children in kindergarten name their worlds; and research with teacher researcher partners on bringing imagination as a concept to the curriculum. She was a teacher across early childhood, primary, and adult literacy contexts for many years before entering the academy. In 2018–2019 she was the president of the national research body, Australian Association for Research in Education (AARE).

Foreword

As a writing researcher and teacher educator, my work focuses on writing as a complex ecology. By this I mean that different personal and contextual conditions are always emerging in relation to each other as they shape the writer, the writing and the context in which writing happens. The writer is always 'present' in their writing – their identities, emotions, linguistic and cultural resources, skills, knowledges, and motivations. The context also shapes the writer and writing – the physical and technological environment and tools, the discipline, the curriculum expectations, the platform, the political landscape, the cultural and social values, and 'norms'. These kinds of complex and interrelated conditions are interrogated in this wonderful collection, which provides research-informed advice for educators.

In the schools with which I work, there is no single strategy that is enacted in the same way or indeed produces the same outcomes. It is impossible to standardise our approach to writing even though we work in conditions of standardised testing in many countries around the world. We know that writing is uneven in its attainment and in the importance ascribed to it by individuals. Drawing on the work of many of the authors in this book, I see writers as reflexive designers of text. That is, they need to be able to make purposeful choices that work for them in different conditions. Teachers, then, can consider how they enable different writers to thrive and to develop a love of writing.

We often focus on the product of writing because that is what is usually assessed – particularly in accountability landscapes. I'm delighted that this collection considers, in different ways, the person, the context, and the product in writing development and pedagogy. The focus on writer identities, perspectives, and experiences is beautifully interwoven with insights about contextual influences of materiality, disciplinarity, genres, and cultural forms, and the values and epistemologies that we promulgate around writing.

I'm passionate about moving away from reductionist views of writing as a mechanical exercise. We must, instead, celebrate the personal and contextual nuances that make every writing experience different. This book challenges us to consider different perspectives and importantly provides insights and affordances for classroom practice. It is a must-read collection for both novice and experienced teachers of writing.

Mary Ryan
Writing researcher
Professor and Head of Education
Macquarie University, Sydney, Australia
August 2019

1 Developing writers in primary and secondary school years

Debra Myhill and Honglin Chen

Introduction

In the 21st century, writing remains a ubiquitous mode of human communication. Indeed, the rapid technological changes witnessed over the past 25 years have actually *increased* the amount of writing that most of us routinely engage with, at the same time as altering the nature of the writing we do. In this period, email, Twitter and various forms of texting applications have decreased our use of oral communication through phones and made written communication an intrinsic (sometime invasive) part of our everyday lives. In parallel, the multimodal possibilities afforded by the web have also changed how we can communicate across time and space, and through creative combinations of text, hypertext and image.

Arguably, the new technological possibilities for writing have democratised it as a mode of communication, with more people than ever before using written forms as an everyday tool for connecting with others. Political activism, for example, has been significantly enhanced by the affordances of rapid digital written communication: revolutions, election campaigns, and protest movements are sustained by it. Think of the Arab Spring revolutions in 2010–2013, or the #MeToo campaign in 2017, or American President Donald Trump's preference for Twitter as a means of mass communication. But writing is more than democratic engagement. Through writing, we can express our most private thoughts, our deepest fears, and our greatest hopes. And through writing, we can reflect on the past, critique the present, and generate new ways of seeing the future.

And yet, despite the evident power of writing, our understanding of being a writer and the teaching of writing lags behind our understanding of the teaching of reading. In this chapter, we provide an introductory overview of research on writing, including the different ways writing has been theoretically described; what we know about becoming a writer, and about development in writing; and empirical evidence about pedagogies for writing. The chapter closes by presenting the rationale for this book and the chapters which follow.

Interdisciplinary perspectives on writing

Research which investigates how we learn to write and become writers is much younger than its sister field of reading, and it has been approached by researchers who come from very different theoretical perspectives – and they rarely talk to each other! From the point of the classroom teaching of writing this is not helpful, and in this section, we will explain the three major theoretical ways of thinking about writing and look at how they all have something valuable to offer in understanding growing into and becoming a writer.

The first theoretical models of writing were *cognitive*, in other words, they focus on the mental processes we use to produce written text. Cognitive models of writing frame writing as a problem-solving process, in which we have to work out both *what* to say it and *how* to say it (Bereiter and Scardamalia 1987). The Hayes and Flower model (1980) was the first cognitive model (see Figure 1.1), and although there have been many variations and adaptations since, the core components have remained largely the same. This model identifies three principal components of the writing process – planning, generating text, and reviewing. The planning process is not what we often think of in school settings as planning, that is, writing an outline plan of the text we are about to write. Rather cognitive models conceive of planning as a much broader process of thinking about and preparing to write, which includes, for example, researching a topic; generating ideas through activities such as freewriting, concept-mapping, notetaking; and thinking about the goals for writing – what is the purpose for writing the text. The drafting process relates principally to getting text from ideas in the head into words on the page and may involve the production of multiple

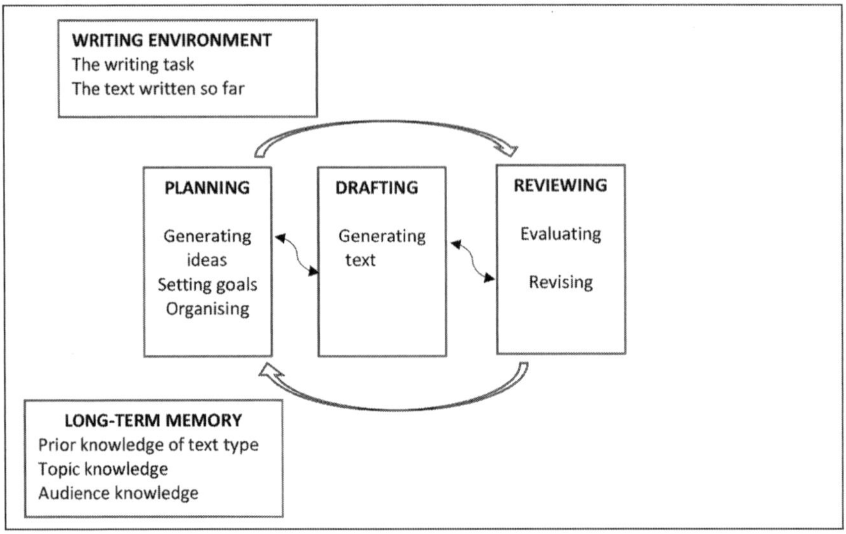

Figure 1.1 A cognitive model of writing based on Hayes and Flower (1980)

drafts before a final piece of writing is completed. The reviewing process is principally about judging the effectiveness of the text and revising it to make it more effective. Crucially, these three processes interact during the writing process: it is not a stage model of plan-draft-revise as is typical of many pedagogical approaches. It recognises the messy recursiveness of writing, and that when we are drafting we often generate new ideas, and that when we are planning we are often evaluating and selecting, as well as generating.

In addition, cognitive models recognise that the process of producing written text also involves our long-term memory as this is the 'resource bank' from which we draw out ideas and experiences to inform the content of our writing. The long-term memory also encompasses our knowledge of different kinds of texts and how they are structured – this is why it is harder to write unfamiliar texts, because we have limited existing knowledge of how they are constructed. Finally, cognitive models note the importance of the environment in which the writing is occurring, though this relates very much to the writing task itself, and how as we write the text, we re-read the text to inform what we write next.

Cognitive models essentially position writing as a solitary activity, and focus on the lone writer and what is happening in the writer's head. In contrast, *socio-cultural models* position writing as a social activity (Prior 2006, Dyson 2009), which is learned through interactions with others, and which is situated within communities of writers (see Figure 1.2). Socio-cultural thinking draws heavily on Vygotsky (1978) who challenged solely cognitive views of learning by arguing that learning is both cognitive and social. He placed particular emphasis on how we learn with and through others, particularly more knowledgeable

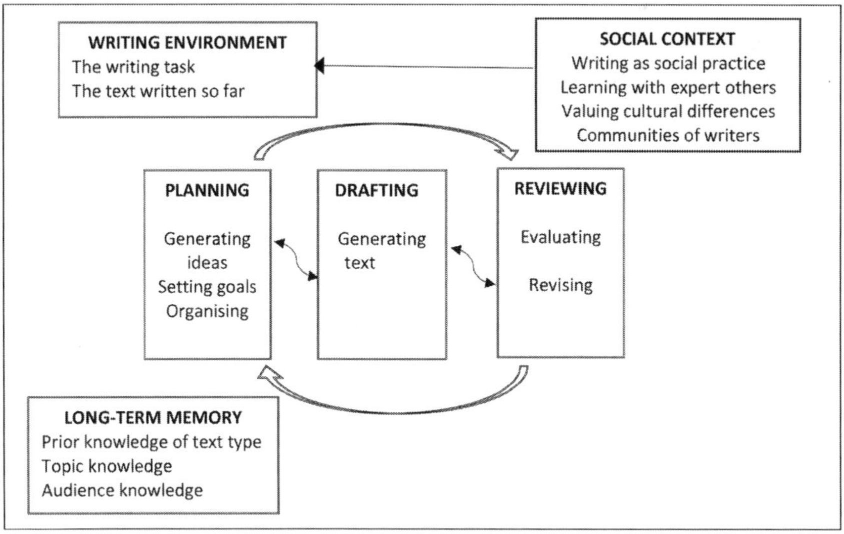

Figure 1.2 Integrated representation of cognitive and socio-cultural models of writing

others, and how a learner can begin to succeed with new learning with the right kind of support and scaffolding. Socio-cultural models are particularly important in recognising that written texts are social texts, and that what counts as 'good' writing is socio-culturally determined: what is valued as good writing in an English classroom in the UK may be different from what is valued in an Australian classroom, or a Chinese classroom. So when we teach children to write, we are inducting them into the social practices of writing in that community.

The socio-cultural emphasis on learning to write through social interactions with others has pedagogical implications, particularly in creating classrooms where children can collaborate in writing, rather than working alone. One influential interpretation of the socio-cultural model of writing was the *process approach*, advocated by Graves (1983) and Murray (1982). A process approach classroom would typically adopt a workshop approach to writing, where young writers are given stimuli or starting points for writing, and where experimentation, drafting and editing, and sharing work are encouraged. Teachers and peers play roles as more knowledgeable others, and contexts are created for children to learn to write through social interactions with others, learning together before learning as an individual. The writing conference is a cornerstone of this approach and involves an oral conversation between the teacher and the child about their writing, where the teacher gives feedback, but also gives primacy to the child's voice and experiences. However, there have been critics of the process approach (Smagorinsky 1987, Lensmire 1994, Beard 2004) and there are socio-cultural models of writing realised in many ways in contemporary classrooms, such as through careful modelling and scaffolding of writing; acknowledging the home literacy experiences of learners; creating culturally inclusive writing classrooms; and addressing the multimodality of many 21st-century texts.

A third theoretical perspective on writing is that it is a process of increasing *linguistic mastery*.

Linguistic perspectives overlap with both cognitive and socio-cultural models (see Figure 1.3). Language production and comprehension involve the mental processing of language, and writing involves decision-making (Kellogg 2008), both of which are cognitive functions. At the same time, socio-cultural perspectives emphasise how language is learned through social interactions in meaningful contexts, and that genres are socially determined text types with clear communicative purposes (Swales 1990). But the key aspect of a linguistic model of writing is that it focuses very sharply on the language of text composition, and children's increasing mastery of it. Whilst one body of research in this area looks at linguistic mastery in terms of the *presence* of different grammatical structures as markers of increasing mastery (Hunt 1965, Harpin 1976), this approach does not sufficiently take into account the *effectiveness* of the grammatical structures present in a text. It is more useful in describing how writing emerges in young early-years writers, from mark-making and scribble writing through to being able to capture ideas fluently in written form (Ferreiro and Teberosky 1982); but it is less useful in describing how children become writers increasingly able to shape their texts for a range of purposes and audiences.

Developing writers in school years 5

```
┌─────────────────────────────┐         ┌─────────────────────────────┐
│  WRITING ENVIRONMENT        │◄────────│  SOCIAL CONTEXT             │
│  The writing task           │         │  Writing as social practice │
│  The text written so far    │         │  Learning with expert others│
│                             │         │  Valuing cultural differences│
│                             │         │  Communities of writers     │
└─────────────────────────────┘         └─────────────────────────────┘

    ┌──────────┐   ┌──────────┐   ┌──────────┐   ┌────────────────────┐
    │ PLANNING │   │ DRAFTING │   │ REVIEWING│   │ Genres as social   │
    │          │   │          │   │          │   │ practice,          │
    │Generating│◄──│Generating│◄──│Evaluating│   │ characterised by   │
    │  ideas   │   │   text   │   │          │   │ particular linguistic│
    │Setting goals│ │          │   │ Revising │   │ structures         │
    │Organising│   │          │   │          │   │                    │
    └──────────┘   └──────────┘   └──────────┘   └────────────────────┘

┌─────────────────────────────┐         ┌─────────────────────────────┐
│  LONG-TERM MEMORY           │         │  LINGUISTIC MASTERY         │
│  Prior knowledge of text type│◄───────│  Functional grammar: making │
│  Topic knowledge            │         │  meaning in context; grammar│
│  Audience knowledge         │         │  as choice                  │
└─────────────────────────────┘         └─────────────────────────────┘
```

Figure 1.3 Integrated representation of cognitive, socio-cultural and linguistic models of writing

However, the work of Halliday in re-framing grammar as social semiotic, a resource for meaning-making (Halliday 1975, 1978, Halliday and Mathiessen 2004), represents a significant shift in how linguistic mastery is conceived. By linking grammar and meaning, linguistic mastery can be more helpfully aligned with how grammatical structures shape meaning in texts. Taking Halliday's Systemic Functional Linguistics as a theoretical frame, research has demonstrated the salience of pedagogical attention to the interrelationship of grammar and meaning (Christie and Unsworth 2005, Derewianka and Jones 2010, Macken-Horarik and Morgan 2011, Jones and Chen 2012) and the importance of explicit teaching of the typical grammatical structures of different genres (Rose 2009). Halliday's influence also shapes the body of complementary research which foregrounds the idea of grammar as choice (Schleppegrell 2012, Myhill et al. 2012, 2018), particularly in contradistinction to traditional representations of grammar as principally concerned with accuracy and rule compliance. This research foregrounds how linguistic choices fulfil the function of a particular text, the needs of the implied reader, and the writer's own authorial intention. In a somewhat different vein, more recently, cognitive linguistic perspectives have been used to inform research on linguistic mastery (Giovanelli 2014, Giovanelli and Clayton 2016), although this research has tended to devote more attention to the teaching of literature and analysing the linguistic characteristics of published texts (Cushing 2018).

Both cognitive and linguistic perspectives draw attention to the role of thinking about writing, both metacognitive and metalinguistic, in writing development. Metacognition in writing – the capacity to think about your own writing and how you write – has been shown to be a characteristic of more mature and developed writers (Martlew 1983), although research has shown that very young children are capable of metacognitive thinking about their writing (Jacobs 2004). The self-regulatory aspect of metacognition, in other words, a writer's capacity to manage the writing process and regulate how they respond to their emerging text is viewed as significant in raising writing attainment, and programmes to support self-regulation in the writing classroom have been developed and shown to be effective (Harris et al. 2010). In parallel, more recent research has investigated metalinguistic understanding for writing, conceptualising metalinguistic understanding both as thinking about language choices, and using metalanguage to discuss writing (Myhill and Newman 2016, 2019). Although there is a significant body of research on metalinguistic understanding as a general concept, it has focused more on early years writers, second language learning, and the more technical aspects of spelling and orthography, the research on metalinguistic understanding for writing across the age phases and in first language writing is very much an emergent field, with considerable scope for further research.

This necessarily concise overview of different disciplinary perspectives on writing is important in showing that writing research is not a coherent and unified body of research, but has tended historically to divide into these different disciplinary camps. Bringing them together into a more integrated interdisciplinary perspective enables pedagogical thinking and development to address more holistically the complex act of writing. In general, the cognitive model of writing focuses on the writer as an *individual*; the socio-cultural models of writing locate the writer within *a community of writers* with culturally ascribed practices and preferences; and the linguistic model positions the writer as *a creator of text*. All are important for the teaching of writing and at different points in a teaching sequence it is likely that a teacher may be emphasising one more than the other, but over the timeframe of a teaching sequence all need to be addressed.

Development in writing

Understanding what constitutes development and what developmental trajectories look like is pivotal to pedagogical and instructional designs (Myhill 2009). In this volume we conceive of writing development as a dynamic and multidimensional concept, evolving and changing, and consider children's mastery of linguistic features, genre forms and purposes, their thinking and understanding, and their increasing sense of audience and self.

Linguistic and metalinguistic development

Children develop emergent understandings of writing long before they begin schooling where writing is formally taught, from first drawings and markings, to understanding of print in the environment, to knowledge of letter and sound correspondence, and to understanding of the function and shape of writing (Tolchinsky 2014, Nutbrown this volume). These understandings, nurtured and fostered in a rich home and pre-school literacy environment, lay crucial foundations for later development of sophisticated knowledge about the form, function and conventions of writing (Nutbrown this volume).

Linguistic descriptions of development in primary school writing have been centred around children's mastery of syntax and structures which are typical of writing at a certain age range. This structural conception associates writing development with successive mastery of certain linguistic constructions varying in structural complexity, sentence length, expanded vocabulary use, and clause types (Harpin 1976, Perera 1984). However, writing is not simply about production, but also about choice and control. Recent studies have found that differences in linguistic development correlate more significantly with different levels of writing abilities than with age maturation (Myhill 2008, 2009). For example, high-attaining older writers have been reported to deliberately choose short simple sentences for rhetorical effect (Myhill 2009). The use of deliberate design choices suggests that development in writing should be measured by not only the mastery of linguistic constructions but also the quality and effectiveness of those choices. From this functional perspective, writing develops as students expand their repertoire of design choices in moving from speech-like to written-like writing; from simple declaration of statements to more elaborated writing for the reader; and from direct expression of thought to deliberately crafting and shaping sentences with an authorial intention (Myhill 2009).

Metalinguistic understanding – the writer's understanding of meaning-making and decision-making at a metalinguistic level – is one important element of this control (e.g. Chen and Myhill 2016, Myhill and Newman 2016). Writing itself is a form of metalinguistic activity – an act of selecting, shaping, reflecting and revising (Myhill 2011). This conscious monitoring and manipulation of language to create meanings has come to be seen as central to writing processes. Metalinguistic understanding is traditionally conceived as a cognitive concept, drawing on research in cognitive psychology. Recent studies investigate the concept from both cognitive perspectives and through the lenses of linguistics and of socio-cultural theory (e.g. Chen and Jones 2012, Chen and Myhill 2016). This work focuses in particular on the nature of metalinguistic understanding as manifested in children's metatalk, their reflection of their choices in their own writing, as well as others (Chen and Myhill 2016, Myhill and Newman 2016). Different forms of metalinguistic understanding go beyond naming or labelling grammatical concepts but include the capacity to explain or exemplify the concepts, to link understanding to writing, and to apply the concepts to shape own writing (Chen and Myhill 2016). It is this metalinguistic mechanism that students must develop, in the same way as their mastery of linguistic forms and structures, if they are to grow into designers of choices (Myhill 2009).

Genre and disciplinary literacy development

Within any cultural context, there are different ways of meaning making and producing texts that have evolved and adapted for different social purposes. These cultural ways of meaning making are construed and configured by genres (Martin and Rose 2008). Becoming writers necessarily entails learning to appropriate genre forms and use them effectively to achieve social communicative purposes in a range of social contexts (Rose and Martin 2012).

The emphasis on genres, purposes, and functions draws on broadly a social semiotic view of language that takes account of the social nature of meaning making, connecting linguistic forms to their contexts of use (Halliday 1978). A major impetus of this body of work has been to make visible the kinds of texts students are expected to read and write in order to be successful in the school contexts. The work has included mapping a range of school genres (e.g. Narratives, Recounts, Descriptions, Reports, Explanations, Procedures, and Expositions), and analysing schematic structures and recurrent patterns of language features typical of each genre form (Martin and Rose 2008).

Developing as writers thus involves learning to make choices at both clause and discourse levels within the same genre and across different genres. Previous research into genre development has provided insights into children's capacity to differentiate between different genre forms (Beers and Nagy 2011); growth of knowledge of genres (Donovan and Smolkin 2006); different degrees of control over different forms of genres (e.g. Narratives vs Persuasion) (Kamberelis 1999, Lewis this volume).

However, learning to write does not relate to mere acquisition of genre forms. Recent studies have come to see genres as social practices, particular forms of discourses that are regulated by disciplinary ways of knowledge making – activities to discover, know, and make meaning (Shanahan and Shanahan 2014, Goldman et al. 2016). The underlying perspective is that writing is largely a tool for constructing and negotiating knowledge claims – knowledge making activities specific to disciplinary fields (Bazerman 1981, MacDonald 1994). Mastering 'disciplinary distinctions' – specialised genre forms and language patterns – is thus pivotal to academic success across the middle years (from Years 4–9) and the senior years of secondary schooling (Years 10–12) where students are increasingly expected to display learning and understanding of disciplinary knowledge through language (Feez and Quinn 2017, p. 193, Humphrey 2017). Lack of explicit teaching of disciplinary literacies can constrain students' participation and success in disciplinary learning in the secondary context (Matruglio and Jones this volume). The importance given to disciplinary literacies (Shanahan and Shanahan 2008) reflects a broader literacy agenda that calls for a reconceptualisation of 'literacy teaching and learning as being about teaching young people purposeful and meaningful literacy practices engaged by people within and across disciplinary domains' (Moje 2015, p. 255).

Studies grounded in Systemic Functional Linguistics (SFL) have examined textual qualities that distinguish discourse practices in a range of disciplinary contexts (Coffin 2006, Christie and Derewianka 2008, Fang and Schleppegrell 2008). These studies have shown that language for representing, explaining, and organising scientific knowledge differs substantially from the more commonsensical story-telling, or responding and evaluating language commonly found in English texts in terms of abstraction, technicality, density, and multimodal meanings (Christie and Derewianka 2008, Fang 2013), which contrasts distinctly with historical discourses of recounting, explaining, and arguing privileged in history texts (Coffin 2006). The development of writers thus resides in an expanding and adaptive capacity to marshal and manipulate increasingly complex repertoires of genres forms and a broad range of meaning making resources (Christie and Derewianka 2008). Genre development in the middle years hence derives from an expansion of meaning making potential and is mapped as three learning trajectories shifting from the use of common sense language to an increasing control of abstraction and technicality (Christie and Derewianka 2008); from construal of the more descriptive 'categorial meaning' to the more interpretative 'perspective meaning' (Coffin and Donohue 2014, pp. 56–57); and from the everyday domain use of language to specialised discipline specific academic language (Humphrey 2017).

Growing sense of audience and self

Consideration of the important role of genres and disciplinary distinctions is predicated on the assumption that our ability to make meaning is socio-culturally defined and shaped (Halliday 1978). From a Bakhtinian social cultural theory, our knowledge of and the ability to use the meaning making resources are mediated not only by the social and cultural norms but also by the situated uses of language mediated by writers' interpretation of the context and audience, and social identities they bring to the writing (Hall 1995).

To consider the cultural norms and conventions is to engage dialogically in a 'rhetorical world of abstract authorial conversation' (Geisler 1994, p. 240). It is in the act of addressing and invoking audiences to account for them in writing that meaning is negotiated and created. The concept of audience has often been narrowly defined as a real, concrete person outside the text (Magnifico 2010). Yet a full conception of audience and how we make meanings to address persons rhetorically engaged in the situation, to support the reader in reading, and to invoke an implied audience is complex and has significance for a wide range of linguistic choices in the writing process (Chen and Vale this volume). This interactive quality of the text conveyed through the writer's rhetorical, cognitive and social awareness of an audience has come to be considered as an important indicator of maturation in writing (Chen and Vale this volume). Chen and Vale (this volume) argue that such nuanced and increasingly sophisticated understandings about audience develop over the years of schooling and are apparent in the curriculum, yet often remain largely implicit in the classroom.

Writing is inevitably 'an act of identity' (Ivanič 1998, p. 32). To write is to enact identities that writers bring to the process of writing – their history, interests, values, beliefs, and previous literacy practices (Ivanič 1998). Learning to write necessarily entails a process of identity formation – forming and redefining one's identities, and adopting a particular identity position in light of the adopted practice (Chen 2001, Cremin this volume). Students' ability to write thus expands as a consequence of participating in a range of literacy events and practices (Ivanič 1998, Lea and Street 1998). The writing itself becomes a vehicle through which a writerly self is created to fulfil certain social roles and meet the expectations of the audience (Ivanič 1998, Chen 2001).

From the perspective of writer identity, appropriating genres does not mean replicating generic structures or normative standards, but resides in the writers' efforts in getting to know both the expected use and the underlying meaning embodied in the practices.

Writing pedagogy

This volume brings together multiple theoretical perspectives on the matter of teaching and learning of writing. It does this by combining linguistic, cognitive, and socio-cultural perspectives to offer an integrated understanding of writing development that connects writers' expansion of meaning making potential to mastery of genre and linguistic forms and functions, seeing understanding, audience awareness, and the writer's engaged agency as central aspects of the development.

This multidimensional perspective of writing development requires theoretically informed pedagogies that support learners' social, cognitive, and linguistic development. This integrated understanding provides an account of learning as a social process occurring in a situated context and mediated through metatalk in which learners are assisted to explore, understand, and reflect on how language makes meaning; to make connection to the audience; and to understand social identities they bring to and are redefined in these practices (Hall 1995). These conditions are key considerations underpinning the pedagogical approaches discussed in this volume.

In Australia, much of the work in the area of teaching writing has explored an SFL genre-based literacy pedagogy which emerged in the 1980s as a response to concerns about unequitable access to language of schooling by students from disadvantaged backgrounds (Martin and Rose 2008). This influential genre-based pedagogy has evolved and been adapted broadly to a diverse range of educational contexts to bring about improved educational outcomes (e.g. de Silva and Feez 2012, Rose and Martin 2012, Shi et al. 2019). Informed by a semiotic theory of language and a Vygotskian socio-cultural theory of language learning (Vygotsky 1978, Halliday 1993), the pedagogy exploits explicit and scaffolding pedagogic practices with instruction oriented towards making visible patterns of language in texts that are privileged in a range of disciplinary contexts through social interaction in the context of shared experience (Martin and Rose 2008, Fang and Schleppegrell 2008, Derewianka and Jones 2016).

At the heart of this scaffolded genre-based pedagogy is textual scaffolding designed in a four-stage teaching and learning cycle aimed at assisting students to understand ways in which language is used to realise social purposes and thereby to develop their gradual control over schematic structures and linguistic resources (Humphrey and Feez 2016). The four-stage teaching sequence adapted from Callaghan and Rothery (1988) begins with *building the context* to develop shared understanding of the social purpose and context of use. This is followed by teacher *modelling* of an exemplar text to guide exploration of patterns of language in the text. The degree of expert support is gradually withdrawn as the teacher and students are engaged in *joint construction* or guided writing of a similar text. The final stage of *independent construction* allows students to apply learned knowledge and demonstrate mastery of genre forms. Crucial to this scaffolded teaching sequence is the development of a shared, functionally oriented metalanguage through which patterns of language are made visible to students (Humphrey 2017). Derewianka in this volume provides an in-depth, contextualised examination of how a carefully designed genre-based pedagogy can be integrated to teach about advanced and specialised ways of meaning making in the writing in history.

In the early years context, it is widely acknowledged that children learn to master a wide range of discourse types or genres and develop into a mature member of the community through their constant engagement in the dialogue structures and processes of meaning making activities (Hasan 2004). Effective writing pedagogy in this context should create conditions in which a particular kind of scaffolded dialogue about language use can be fostered (Painter 1999). This would mean using home environment or classroom as the sites, creating opportunities for children to explore and learn about conventions of writing and become emergent writers (see Nutbrown this volume).

Rose (2009) argues that for pedagogies to foster competences within the writer there needs to be an environment that encourages guided engagement in practice. The Montessori writing pedagogy discussed by Feez (this volume) provides a fine example of such an environment. Feez illustrates ways in which the teacher can engage young children actively with a purpose-built material environment carefully designed to promote the development of social and intellectual skills necessary for becoming writers. In a similar vein, Kervin et al. (this volume) highlight the affordances of material environments in supporting young children to become confident writers.

Becoming writers involves 'the constant engagement in and reflection upon our and others' interactive contributions' (Hall 1995, p. 226). Myhill, Jones, and Lines (all in this volume) illustrate how this reflective awareness can be fostered through a research-informed pedagogical approach, the LEAD model. This pedagogical model provides a powerful tool for students thinking and reflecting on meaning making decisions through four pedagogical strategies: making a *Link* between grammar and writing; *Explaining* the grammar through examples; using *Authentic* texts; and building in high-quality *Discussion* about grammar and choice. The significance given to the reading and writing connection and metalinguistic discussion has pedagogic advantages in facilitating conscious learning of linguistic forms and practices in a meaningful context.

Students' responsive understanding of a genre is derived from their active participation in situated interactions (Bakhtin 1978, Chen 2001). Harnessing the affordances of digital technologies can create authentic opportunities for students to engage in the real situated meaningful activities and thereby facilitate their gaining of an active understanding of genre forms for their deployment (Chen 2001). Dowdall (this volume) contributes to an expanded view of writing that capitalises on the potential of technologies to support children to become engaged and competent writers in the early years setting.

Effective writing tasks make salient linguistic, cognitive and social factors embodied in language use and practices. As such writing pedagogy should create 'the conditions of language use' that facilitate understanding of the practices and enactment of 'the social identities of the participants' (Hall 1995, p. 221). Cremin (this volume) demonstrates that particular writing practices such as storytelling and writing for enactment provide a powerful tool for fostering children's understanding of themselves and writing practices. Similarly, Chen and Vale (this volume) provide examples of pedagogic activities that encourage deeper engagement with the rhetorical situation – the needs and expectations of the audience. In both examples, guided engagement in practice creates essential conditions for students' social, cognitive, and linguistic development necessary for their creative deployment of language resources.

Taken together, the collective insights provided in this volume contribute to an interdisciplinary understanding of the development of writers across different years of schooling and an innovative reconceptualisation of effective pedagogic practices. Each of the chapters has suggested that developing into writers traverses different learning trajectories with each requiring different pedagogical conditions that enable and support the development. Perhaps there needs to be a *pedagogical continuum* that recognises the nature of these learning trajectories and the concomitant pedagogic practices to sustain the systematic and cumulative development of writers (Christie and Derewianka 2008, Goldman and Scardamalia 2013). Such a *pedagogical continuum* will offer a scaffolded framework for planning and assessing the development of writing across different years of schooling and disciplinary contexts.

Rationale for this book

As noted in the introduction, the capacity to write well is a fundamental accomplishment. Writing remains the principal mechanism for communicating, assessing and preserving knowledge, and in our modern world of mass communications and digital media, more people than ever before are involved in writing. At a societal level, 'writing skill is a predictor of academic success and a basic requirement for participation in civic life and in the global economy' (Graham and Perin 2007, p. 3). At a personal level, writing has a humanising power: through writing, we can develop understanding of ourselves and our world, express our most salient fears, and articulate our own most private feelings. In the words of Malala Yousafzai, 'let us pick up our books and our pens, they are the most powerful weapons. One child, one teacher, one book and one pen can change the world' (Yousafzai 2013).

And yet there is an international concern about standards in writing, perhaps particularly in Anglophone countries. In England, data from national testing shows that attainment in reading exceeds that in writing at age 7 and 11 (DfE 2017). A similar pattern is evident in Australia, where only 82% of 13–14 year olds achieving the national minimum standard in writing, compared with 92% for reading and 96% for numeracy (ACARA 2017, p. 255). Indeed, in Australia, by the age of 14, there is still a significant number of students who are struggling with basic writing skills. The results show that 16.4%, that is, nearly one in six Year 9 students, performed below the minimum national benchmark. National data from the United States of America (NCES n.d.) and New Zealand (MoE 2017) suggest similar patterns are evident there. This is concerning given becoming an effective writer is critical both for individual and for economic well-being. This is not a new problem as research and government reports over the past 25 years have pointed to what appears to be a persistent lag in writing attainment (e.g. Winch and Wells 1995, Persky et al. 2003, Crooks et al. 2007, Dugdale and Clark 2008).

Of course, it is important to be circumspect about the standards in writing issue. The standards themselves are socio-culturally determined, often by policy-makers and there is no absolute internationally agreed set of standards for writing. What counts as 'good' writing varies from culture to culture and from jurisdiction to jurisdiction, and children's writing is beholden to the 'culture-specific norms and expectations for writing at school, and values and beliefs in the societies the writers inhabit' (Smidt 2009, p. 117). An analysis of four different national curricula or programmes for writing found that the construct of writing was represented very differently in each, expressed through different discourses about writing (Peterson et al. 2018). Add to this the known unreliability in assessing writing (e.g. Cooksey et al. 2007, He et al. 2013) and it becomes clear that national assessment data may not have either the validity or the reliability that one might expect it to have.

Nonetheless, it is hard to argue against the importance of developing better understanding of writing development and effective pedagogies for teaching writing. This book sets out to address this issue through looking at development and pedagogy across three key stages of writing development in compulsory education, covering early (4–7 years old), primary (7–12 years old), and secondary years (12–16 years old). The authors are all from England or Australia, but each chapter draws not only on the author's own research but on the international research literature on writing. At the same time, each chapter considers the implications of the research for the writing classroom, bringing together practice and research in three broad themes: *fostering emergent writers in the early years, supporting social, cognitive, and linguistic development in the primary years*, and *growing into complexity in the secondary years*. Our hope is that this book will stimulate thinking, across national boundaries, about how we can learn from each other, and enable those young people we work with to become competent, fulfilled, and engaged writers of the future.

References

Australian Curriculum and Assessment Reporting Authority (ACARA). 2017. *NAPLAN achievement in reading, writing, language conventions and numeracy: 2017 national report*. Available from: www.nap.edu.au/results-and-reports/national-reports [Accessed 17. 06. 18].

Bakhtin, M. M. 1978. *The formal method in literary scholarship: a critical introduction to sociological poetics*. Baltimore: The Johns Hopkins University Press.

Bazerman, C. 1981. What written knowledge does: three examples of academic discourse. *Philosophy of the Social Sciences*, 11(3), 361–387.

Beard, R. 2004. *Developing writing 3–13*. London: Hodder & Stoughton.

Beers, S. F. and Nagy, W. E. 2011. Writing development in four genres from grades three to seven: syntactic complexity and genre differentiation. *Read Writ*, 24, 183–202.

Bereiter, C. and Scardamalia, M. 1987. *The psychology of written composition*. Hillsdale: Erlbaum.

Callaghan, M. and Rothery, J. 1988. *Teaching factual writing: a genre based approach*. Sydney: Disadvantaged Schools Program (NSW) Literacy Project.

Chen, H. 2001. *Ways of knowing, ways of citing: a study of Chinese ESL graduate students' citation behaviour in thesis writing*. PhD thesis. La Trobe University, Australia.

Chen, H. and Jones, P. 2012. Understanding metalinguistic development: a functional perspective. *Journal of Applied Linguistics and Professional Practice*, 9(1), 81–104.

Chen, H. and Myhill, D. 2016. Children talking about writing: investigating metalinguistic understanding. *Linguistics and Education*, 35, 100–108.

Christie, F. and Derewianka, B. 2008. *School discourse: learning to write across the years of schooling*. London: Continuum.

Christie, F. and Unsworth, L. 2005. Developing dimensions of an educational linguistics. In: Webster, J., Matthiessen, C. and Hasan, R. eds. *Continuing discourse on language: a functional perspective*. London: Equinox, 217–250.

Coffin, C. 2006. *Historical discourse: the language of time, cause and evaluation*. London: Continuum.

Coffin, C. and Donohue, J. 2014. A language as social semiotic-based approach to teaching and learning in higher education. *Language Learning Monograph Series*, 64(s1), 1–308.

Cooksey, R., Freebody, P. and Wyatt-Smith, C. 2007. Assessment as judgment-in-context: analysing how teachers evaluate students' writing. *Educational Research and Evaluation*, 13 (5), 401–434.

Crooks, T., Flockton, L. and White, J. 2007. *Writing: assessment results 2006 (NEMP Report 41)*. Wellington: Ministry of Education.

Cushing, I. 2018. 'Suddenly, I am part of the poem': texts as worlds, reader-response and grammar in teaching poetry. *English in Education*, 52(1), 1–13.

de Silva, H. J. and Feez, S. 2012. *Text-based language literacy education: programming and methodology*. Putney, NSW: Phoenix Education.

Derewianka, B. and Jones, P. 2010. From traditional grammar to functional grammar: bridging the divide. *NALDIC Quarterly*, 8(1), 6–17.

Derewianka, B. and Jones, P. 2016. *Teaching language in context*. 2nd ed. Oxford: Oxford University Press.

Department for Education (DfE). 2017. *National curriculum assessments at key stage 2 in England, 2017 (SFR 69/2017)*. Available from: www.gov.uk/government/uploads/system/uploads/attachment_data/file/667372/SFR69_2017_text.pdf [Accessed 18. 05. 18].

Donovan, C. A. and Smolkin, L. B. 2006. Children's understanding of genre and writing development. In: MacArthur, C., Graham, S. and Fitzgerald, J. eds. *Handbook of writing research*. New York: The Guilford Press, 131–143.

Dugdale, G. and Clark, C. 2008. *Literacy changes lives: an advocacy resource*. London: National Literacy Trust.

Dyson, A. H. 2009. Writing childhood worlds. In: Beard, R., et al. eds. *The SAGE handbook of writing development*. London: SAGE, 233–245.

Fang, S. and Schleppegrell, M. J. 2008. *Reading in secondary content areas: a language-based pedagogy*. Ann Arbor: University of Michigan Press.

Fang, Z. 2013. Disciplinary literacy in science. *Journal of Adolescent and Adult Literacy*, 57 (4), 274–278.

Feez, S. and Quinn, F. 2017. Teaching the distinctive language of science: an integrated and scaffolded approach for pre-service teachers. *Teaching and Teacher Education*, 65, 192–204.

Ferreiro, E. and Teberosky, A. 1982. *Literacy before schooling*. Oxford: Heinemann.

Geisler, C. 1994. *Academic literacy and the nature of expertise: reading, writing, and knowing in academic philosophy*. Hillsdale: Lawrence Erlbaum.

Giovanelli, M. 2014. *Teaching grammar, structure and meaning: exploring theory and practice for post-16 English Language teachers*. Abingdon: Routledge.

Giovanelli, M. and Clayton, D. 2016. *Knowing about language: linguistics and the secondary English classroom*. Abingdon: Routledge.

Goldman, S. R. and Scardamalia, M. 2013. Managing, understanding, applying, and creating knowledge in the information age: next-generation challenges and opportunities. *Cognition and Instruction*, 31(2), 255–269.

Goldman, S. R., et al. 2016. Disciplinary literacies and learning to read for understanding: a conceptual framework for disciplinary literacy. *Educational Psychologist*, 51 (2), 219–246.

Graham, S. and Perin, D. 2007. *Writing next: effective strategies to improve writing of adolescents in middle and high schools. A report to Carnegie Corporation of New York*. Washington, DC: Alliance for Excellent Education.

Graves, D. 1983. *Writing: teachers and children at work*. Portsmouth, NH: Heinemann.

Hall, J. K. 1995. (Re)creating our worlds with words: socialhistorical perspective of face-to-face interaction. *Applied Linguistics*, 16(2), 206–232.

Halliday, M. A. K. 1975. *Learning how to mean: explorations in the development of language*. London: Edward Arnold.

Halliday, M. A. K. 1978. *Language as social semiotic: the social interpretation of language and meaning*. London: Edward Arnold.

Halliday, M. A. K. 1993. Towards a language-based theory of learning. *Linguistics and Education*, 5, 93–116.

Halliday, M. A. K. and Mathiessen, C. M. I. M. 2004. *An introduction to English grammar*. 3rd ed. London: Routledge.

Harpin, W. 1976. *The second R: writing development in the junior school*. London: Allen & Unwin.

Harris, K. R., Santangelo, T. and Graham, S. 2010. Metacognition and strategies instruction in writing. In: Waters, H. S. and Schneider, W. eds. *Metacognition, strategy use, and instruction*. New York: Guilford Press, 226–256.

Hasan, R. 2004. The concept of semiotic mediation: perspectives from Bernstein's sociology. In: Muller, J., Davies, B. and Morais, A. eds. *Reading Bernstein, researching Bernstein*. London: Routledge, 30–43.

Hayes, J. and Flower, L. 1980. Identifying the organisation of writing process. In: Gregg, L. and Steinberg, E. eds. *Cognitive processes in writing*. Hillsdale, NJ: Lawrence Erlbaum, 3–30.

He, Q., et al. 2013. An investigation of the reliability of marking of the Key Stage 2 National Curriculum writing tests in England. *Educational Research*, 55(4), 393–410.

Humphrey, S. 2017. *Academic literacies in the middle years: a framework for enhancing teaching knowledge and student achievement*. London: Routledge.

Humphrey, S. and Feez, S. 2016. Direct instruction fit for purpose: applying a meta-linguistic toolkit to enhance creative writing in the early secondary years. *Australian Journal of Language and Literacy*, 39(3), 207–219.

Hunt, K. W. 1965. *Grammatical structures written at three grade levels*. Champaign: NCTE.

Ivanič, R. 1998. *Writing and identity: the discoursal construction of identity in academic writing*. Amsterdam: John Benjamins.

Jacobs, G. M. 2004. A classroom investigation of the growth of metacognitive awareness in kindergarten children through the writing process. *Early Childhood Education Journal*, 32(1), 17–23.

Jones, P. and Chen, H. 2012. Teachers' knowledge about language: issues of pedagogy and expertise. *Australian Journal of Language and Literacy*, 35(2), 147–168.

Kamberelis, G. 1999. Genre development and learning: children writing stories, science reports, and poems. *Research in the Teaching of English*, 33, 403–460.

Kellogg, R. T. 2008. Training writing skills: a cognitive developmental perspective. *Journal of Writing Research*, 1(1), 1–26.

Lea, M. and Street, B. 1998. Student writing in higher education: an academic literacies approach. *Studies in Higher Education*, 23(2), 157–172.

Lensmire, T. J. 1994. *When children write: critical re-visions of the writing workshop*. New York: Teachers College Press.

MacDonald, S. 1994. *Professional academic writing in the humanities and social sciences*. Carbondale and Edwardsville: Southern Illinois University Press.

Macken-Horarik, M. and Morgan, W. 2011. Towards a metalanguage adequate to linguistic achievement in post-structuralism and English: reflections on voicing in the writing of secondary students. *Linguistics and Education*, 22(2), 133–149.

Magnifico, A. M. 2010. Writing for whom? Cognition, motivation, and a writer's audience. *Educational Psychologist*, 45(3), 167–184.

Martin, J. R. and Rose, D. 2008. *Genre relations: mapping culture*. London: Equinox.

Martlew, M. 1983. Problems and difficulties: cognitive and communicative aspects of writing. In: Martlew, M. ed. *The psychology of written language*. New York: Wiley & Sons, 295–333.

Ministry of Education (MoE). 2017. *New Zealand education profile 2015–16*. Available from: www.educationcounts.govt.nz/__data/assets/pdf_file/0010/181981/NZ-Education-Profile-2016.pdf [Accessed 06. 08. 18].

Moje, E. B. 2015. Doing and teaching disciplinary literacy with adolescent learners: a social and cultural enterprise. *Harvard Educational Review*, 85(2), 254–278.

Murray, D. M. 1982. *Learning by teaching: selected articles on writing and teaching*. Portsmouth, NH: Boynton/Cook.
Myhill, D. A. 2008. Towards a linguistic model of sentence development in writing. *Language and Education*, 22(5), 271–288.
Myhill, D. A. 2009. Becoming a designer: trajectories of linguistic development. In: Beard, R., et al. eds. *The Sage handbook of writing development*. London: SAGE, 402–414.
Myhill, D. A. 2011. 'The ordeal of deliberate choice': metalinguistic development in secondary writers. In: Berninger, V. ed. *Past, present and future contributions of cognitive writing research to cognitive psychology*. New York: Psychology Press, 247–274.
Myhill, D. A. and Newman, R. 2016. Metatalk: enabling metalinguistic discussion about writing. *International Journal of Education Research*, 80, 177–187.
Myhill, D. A. and Newman, R. 2019. Writing talk: developing metalinguistic understanding through dialogic teaching. In: Mercer, N., Wegerif, R. and Major, L. eds. *International handbook of research on dialogic education*. London: Routledge, 360–372.
Myhill, D. A., Lines, H. and Jones, S. M. 2018. Texts that teach: examining the efficacy of using texts as models. *L1-Educational Studies in Language and Literature*, 18, 1–24.
Myhill, D. A. et al. 2012. Re-thinking grammar: the impact of embedded grammar teaching on students' writing and students' metalinguistic understanding. *Research Papers in Education*, 27(2), 139–166.
NCES n.d. *The Nation's report card*. Available from: www.nationsreportcard.gov/ [Accessed 07. 08. 18].
Painter, C. 1999. *Learning through language in early childhood*. London: Continuum.
Perera, K. 1984. *Children's writing and reading: analysing classroom language*. Oxford: Blackwell.
Persky, H., Daane, M. and Jin, Y. 2003. *The nation's report card: writing*. Washington, DC: U.S. Department of Education, National Centre for Education Statistics.
Peterson, S., et al. 2018. Conceptualizations of writing in early years curricula and standards documents: international perspectives. *The Curriculum Journal*, 29(4), 499–521.
Prior, P. 2006. A sociocultural theory of writing. In: Macarthur, C., Graham, S. and Fitzgerald, J. eds. *Handbook of writing research*. New York: Guilford, 54–65.
Rose, D. 2009. Writing as linguistic mastery: the development of genre-based literacy pedagogy. In: Beard, R., et al. eds. *The Sage handbook of writing development*. London: SAGE, 151–166.
Rose, D. and Martin, J. R. 2012. *Learning to write, reading to learn: genre, knowledge, and pedagogy in the Sydney School*. Sheffield: Equinox.
Schleppegrell, M. J. 2012. Systemic functional linguistics: exploring meaning in language. In: Gee, J. P. and Handford, M. eds. *The Routledge handbook of discourse analysis*. New York: Routledge, 21–34.
Shanahan, C. and Shanahan, T. 2014. Does disciplinary literacy have a place in elementary school? *The Reading Teacher*, 67(8), 636–639.
Shanahan, T. and Shanahan, C. 2008. Teaching disciplinary literacy to adolescents: rethinking content-area literacy. *Harvard Educational Review*, 78(1), 40–59.
Shi, L., Baker, A. and Chen, H. 2019. Chinese EFL teachers' cognition about the effectiveness of genre pedagogy: a case study. *RELC Journal*, 50(2), 314–332.
Smagorinsky, P. 1987. Graves revisited: a look at the methods and conclusions of the New Hampshire study. *Written Communication*, 14(4), 331–342.
Smidt, J. 2009. Developing discourse roles and positionings: an ecological theory of writing development. In: Beard, R., et al. eds. *The SAGE handbook of writing development*. London: SAGE, 117–125.

Swales, J. 1990. *Genre analysis: English in academic and research settings*. New York: Cambridge University Press.
Tolchinsky, L. 2014. The emergence of writing. In: MacArthur, C. A., Graham, S. and Fitzgerald, J. eds. *Handbook of writing research*. New York: Guilford Press, 83–95.
Vygotsky, L. S. 1978. *Mind in society: the development of higher psychological processes*. Cambridge, MA: Harvard University Press.
Winch, C. and Wells, P. 1995. The quality of student writing in higher education: a cause for concern? *British Journal of Educational Studies*, 43(1), 75–87.
Yousafzai, M. 2013. *Malala's speech*. Available from: www.un.org/News/dh/infocus/malala_speach.pdf [Accessed 14. 04. 17].

2 Children learning to write in early primary classrooms

Lisa Kervin, Barbara Comber and Annette Woods

Introduction

Writing is a social literacy practice. It is always highly contextual, riven with competing purposes, various in form and responsive to the ideological complexities of time and place (Heath 1983, Barton and Hamilton 1998, Brandt 2015). We understand writing to be a learned, sociocultural practice constituted by the interplay of person, product, and context. In schools, what constitutes writing is also subject to policy and assessment practices. For instance, when teachers are aware a particular genre will be assessed in standardised tests, understandably they are likely to prioritise this type of text in terms of time and explicit teaching offered to their students. Or, if teachers understand that handwriting, punctuation, and spelling are the immediate goals that they and/or their children will be judged against, they may emphasise these aspects of writing in the classroom. Or, if a system prioritises particular pedagogical strategies or makes specific resources available, these enter into classroom spaces and practices. Not surprisingly, the teaching of writing has long been subject to debate. Yet, teachers must make specific pedagogical decisions as they implement routines and interactions with the intention of facilitating students learning valued academic practices. Leander (2004) describes this as 'a set of discursive and material practices and resources that actively engages in the production of power relations and ideology' (p. 127). In other words, the teaching of writing in schools involves layers of decisions, choices, and resources, which have complex histories beyond the individual teacher, yet are contingent upon the individual teacher to orchestrate.

To understand the diversity of writing pedagogies and practices utilised within English-speaking early childhood classrooms, there is a need to compile and examine instances of classroom practice to showcase the interrelationships between the material and immaterial influences on young children's writing development. Leander and Rowe (2006) challenge us to consider and interpret the 'public performances' (p. 428) played out in classrooms as we examine the ways various texts are used, how bodies are moved, and the interactions that take place around learning to write. To understand classroom writing pedagogies involves acknowledgement of the influence of space in facilitating interactions and the selection and use of resources (material and semiotic) as well as the products produced by young children as they learn to write. Classrooms are spaces where learning events unfold, and ultimately shape the experience of the learning (Warf and Arias 2009). Classrooms are spaces that accommodate and house materials as well as people, the 'stuff' (Burnett et al. 2014, p. 92) such as artefacts, walls, texts, and screens available to text producers in their classrooms. It is this intricate interplay between the material and immaterial that creates discursive and material spaces.

Writing, or text production, is recognised as an essential component of early childhood education. However, writing is arguably the most difficult literate practice to learn, requiring high cognitive load to mediate complex psychological, linguistic, physical, social, and cultural elements (Fisher 2012). Indeed, some would argue that learning to write is a lifelong process (Ivanič 2004). When young children learn to write in the school context, they need to navigate this complexity. They need to assemble the elements of text production at the same time as they learn what the teacher expects here and now and of course those expectations are dynamic and likely to change in relation to the task, the teacher, and over time. The institution of schooling defines what counts as normal development in designated areas, including 'writing development' and children come to know what matters in this regard and how this changes over time and in different spaces (Dixon 2010).

Children engage with materials as resources within their environment, and as they become more proficient with literate practices, they gradually talk, handle materials, and participate in activities in ways that are expected of them by teachers and school (Rogers 2003). In classrooms children negotiate tensions between and among individuals, material, and social relationships as they work within their social classroom context (Wohlwend 2007). As early childhood writing researcher, Dyson (2019), powerfully demonstrated, children are constantly negotiating the social and materials worlds of schooling, as they learn to write.

> Part of being a critical ethnographer is being alert to how assumptions about contemporary childhoods, and resources for school learning, push categories of children to the academic margins, surfacing primarily as the 'different' or 'problem' children … If researchers are to offer an alternative view, and gain access to children's agentive actions, they must include ethnographies done upside down, situated within the children's world.
>
> (Dyson 2019, p. 78)

Guided by Dyson (2019), in this chapter, we begin by giving a sense of the kinds of contradictions early childhood teachers face in planning and enacting their writing programs. We then show how two different children report their experiences of learning to write over a two-year period, to illustrate what is involved from the child's viewpoint. We identify the kinds of markers of success in writing that children identify and how these shift as the two children move from Year 1 to Year 2. The children's reports indicate they are aware of teacher criteria for 'good writing'. This chapter seeks to problematise normative definitions of 'writing development', by laying out the complexity of children's material and discursive work in early childhood classrooms. We aim to make the familiar strange, by listening closely to children's reported experience and their interactions with the material and discursive practices (Leander 2004) of classrooms. This kind of research may well help to address the lack of 'a satisfactory understanding of early composing' by placing 'greater emphasis on children's ideas and language during writing and less on their ability to encode' (Quinn and Bingham 2019, p. 229).

The 'Learning to write' project

This chapter draws from a three-year federally funded, Australian multi-site ethnographic project where case studies have been compiled in low Socio-Economic Status (SES) schools to provide a broad understanding of how the teaching of writing is enacted in these contexts (Woods et al. 2015–2018). In this chapter we draw our data from one of our purposefully selected schools. This school is situated in an urban suburb of the South Coast of New South Wales, formerly a hub for heavy industry that provided employment for the population. The area has been significantly impacted by more recent changes to industry in the area. When we began our research project, the school's Index of Community Socio-Economic Advantage (ICSEA), a scale representing educational advantage, was a low 930 with 52 per cent of students in the bottom quartile (ACARA 2016). The Indigenous population of the school is 13 per cent (ACARA 2016), and this marks an increase over the past few years.

The school is a co-educational government primary school with a student population of 196 at the time of our research. The school had experienced a 19 per cent drop in enrolments from five years before (ACARA 2016), the result of unemployment (at 9 per cent at the time of inquiry) and increased housing prices which made the area unaffordable for many families who had been in the community for many years (ABS 2011). The school's annual report at the time indicated that the average class size in K-3 was 16 students. During our research, the school engaged 11 teachers and six non-teachers (ACARA 2016).

The larger study employed an exploratory qualitative design to enable us to respond to the following question: *How, when, where, with what, and with whom are children writing in early childhood classrooms?*

Informed by a socio-material approach we worked to understand how concepts of writing knowledge were represented in everyday classroom action from the perspectives of both teacher and student. This approach acknowledges that literacy is a situated and culturally specific practice (Heath 1983, Rowsell and Pahl 2011) and enabled us to focus on the intricacies of classroom writing in order to explore how materials, ideas, practices, and pedagogies 'come together, and manage to hold together' (Fenwick and Edwards 2011, p. 2). The everyday teaching and learning practices, the materials, tools, and texts used, and spatial arrangements that constitute writing pedagogy in classrooms reveal much about the 'situatedness' (Fenwick 2014). Taking the classroom as an example of a 'material culture', we examine the types of experiences it comprises, resources it offers, and the physical space. This view of 'material culture' acknowledges the interrelationships between the time, scale, space, resources, people, and interactions as we examine the interplay between the physical, temporal, and spatial elements that contribute to a young child's writing practice. It appreciates that learning to write is affected by a range of assemblages (Fenwick 2014).

Children in the first three years of primary school were interviewed individually to gather their perspectives on writing. Specifically, they were asked about when they write, where they write, who they write with, and the resources they use when writing. Interviews were recorded and transcribed. The children also drew a representation of what learning to write looked like in their classroom. This interview was repeated the following year with the same children.

As part of data collected across the larger project, all teachers and leaders at all of the schools involved were surveyed.[1] The point of the teachers' survey was to audit the current practices of teaching writing in each school, but also to gain insights into teachers' perspectives about what opportunities for learning to write were provided in their classroom spaces as they made pedagogical, curriculum, space, and material decisions. We were also interested to think theoretically with the teachers – to ask them to name the important influences upon their thinking about teaching writing and learning to write, and to compare these with teacher reports about their classroom practice, values, and beliefs. For our purposes in this chapter we use the teacher and leader responses to the survey questions to provide some context to the learning spaces and approaches being provided to young learners of writing.

After completing this survey, teachers who taught in the early years of schooling were invited to create a video tour of their classroom as they filmed and annotated key decisions they made about the organisation of the space and inclusion of resources. Then these same teachers identified suitable times for initial observation of writing experiences in their classroom. During the observations, the children engaged in classroom writing experiences that were planned and implemented by the participating teacher. These experiences were video recorded, supported by field notes and student text samples. Teachers participated in focus groups in their planning groups, facilitated by the researchers and focused on the teaching of writing. And throughout the duration of the project writing samples were collected for all participating children. We begin by using the teacher survey data from this school to provide some detail about teachers' perspectives of what opportunities were available to young children as they learn to write.

The story of the school within the national and state context

The school we draw data from in this chapter is in the Australian state of New South Wales where literacy teaching is guided by an English syllabus (based on the Australian Curriculum: English). The research occurred during a time of considerable curriculum reform – both at national and state levels. The teachers, and students, were in the very early stages of using a new English syllabus. In 2015 the decision to develop national literacy and numeracy progressions was made to enable teachers to identify specific behaviours of students that demonstrate literacy skills and understandings to help them plan teaching, assess, track, and monitor student progress. The Australian Curriculum, Assessment and Reporting Authority (ACARA) and the New South Wales (NSW) Department of Education led development of these over 2016–2017.

Alongside this, state-based initiatives contributed to the work of teachers as they navigated the national reform. The development of the state-based Literacy and Numeracy Strategy 2017–2020 became available during our three-year project and identified key elements for literacy teaching, including early intervention for students in the early years, explicit teaching, and diagnostic assessments. Central to the uptake of this strategy was targeted teaching and learning decisions, informed by the NSW literacy continuum K-10 and the national literacy and numeracy progressions. Further, NSW also introduced the 'Best Start Kindergarten' assessment to enable teachers to understand the literacy and numeracy knowledge that children have as they begin school.

The inquiry school is identified as a priority school given the number of students in the bottom quartile through the National Assessment Program – Literacy and Numeracy (NAPLAN) assessment results (ACARA 2016). This meant that the school attracted some additional funding to ensure early intervention for students in literacy and numeracy. For this school, this meant increased reporting of student progress to state authorities. At the same time, the school embarked on a system-wide professional learning program targeted on the teaching of reading and writing – L3. This program is a classroom intervention that focuses on systematic and explicit teaching within classroom-based daily literacy sessions.

Classrooms in this school clearly indicate the presence of these initiatives. To illustrate this, we draw upon three images. While these images are from the one classroom, representations of these were evident across all classrooms in this school.

Figure 2.1 depicts a noticeboard divided into three central areas. At the top left the learning clusters appropriate for children in the class are identified and explicated through the use of 'I can' statements. This display has been designed to clearly identify the criteria the teacher is looking for to indicate success in that cluster. Above the clusters are individual rocket ships with a child's name on each. This provides a visual representation of the teacher's plotting of individual children. At the bottom of this image we see a visual representation of the writing process. Surrounding each stage is an adhesive strip where children have placed their names to indicate what they are doing in their writing. In this

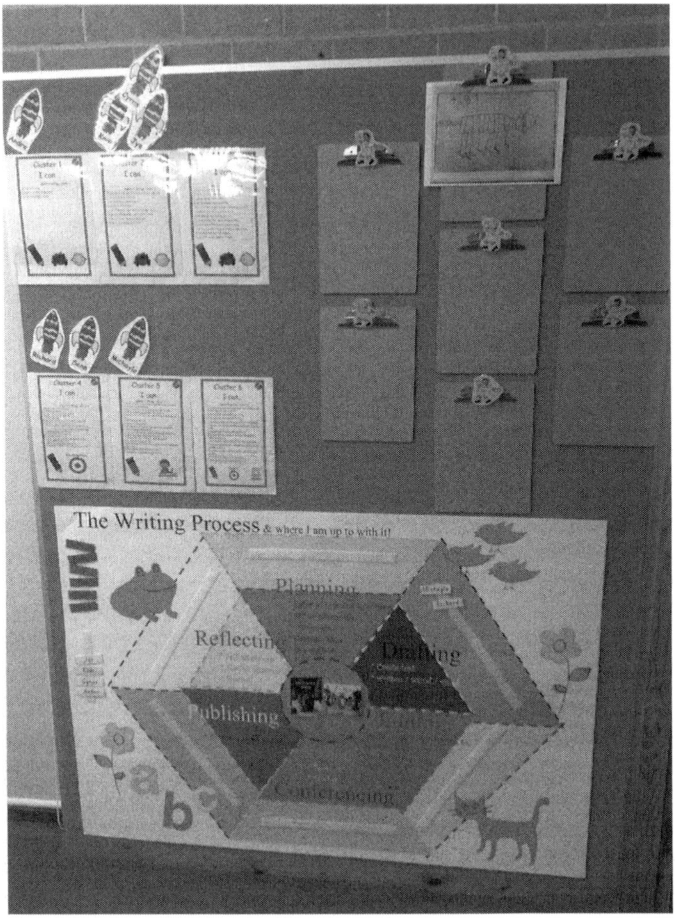

24 *Lisa Kervin et al.*

Figure 2.1 Learning clusters and the writing process

example, we can see some names at both drafting and reflecting stages. At the top right, we see some empty clipboards. The teacher of this classroom explained these are spaces where children can attach a work sample that they think shows their achievement of an 'I can' statement within their learning cluster for teacher review.

Figure 2.2 identifies a learning intention and associated success criteria. In focus groups, the teachers explained the importance of 'making learning visible' for children. There was an understanding across the staff of the importance of being clear about what any lesson's focus was and ensuring the children were aware of this and knew what they needed to do to demonstrate success. The last point in the success criteria directs the students back to their learning cluster (discussed in Figure 2.1).

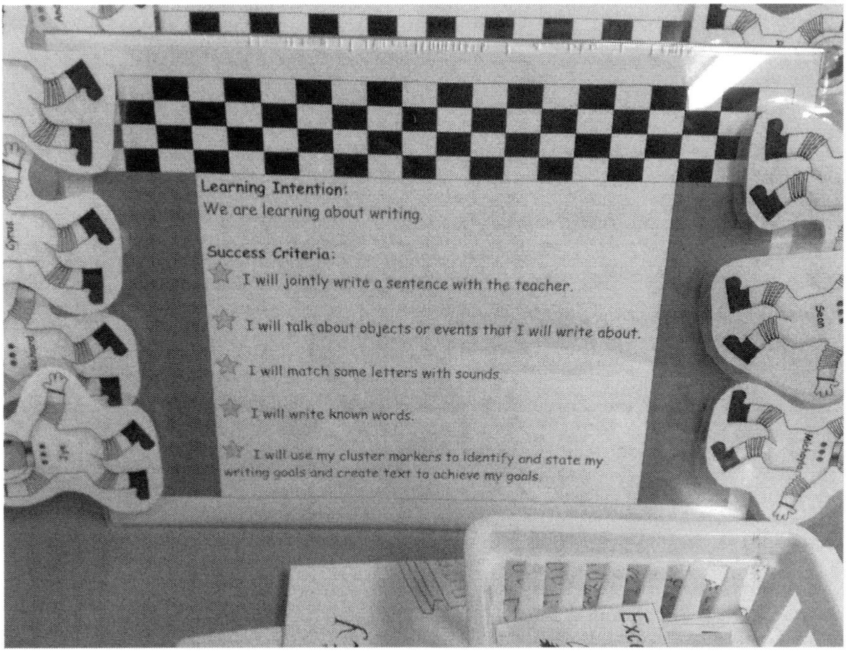

Figure 2.2 Learning intention and success criteria

Figure 2.3 visualises the teacher's assessment of success. Three stars are depicted – keep trying, almost there, and well done – to provide feedback about how individual students are going in connection with their learning goals. These individual learning goals are written onto cards and placed on the star that matches the teacher's assessment, providing as one teacher described 'a clear picture of how they're going and how close they are to achieving their goal'.

Teachers' reports about learning to write

At this school, 14 staff members identified themselves as being involved in teaching students to write. These staff ranged from classroom teachers (kindergarten, Year 1/2, Year 3/4, Year 5/6[2]), intervention or Special Education teachers including Reading Recovery teachers, instructional leaders, and school leaders including principal and an assistant principal. All of these 14 staff members completed the survey, providing a picture of the opportunities available for students across the school. The teaching staff were all speakers of English as their first language, most (n=12) had completed their teacher training at the same university, which was located less than 10kms from the school, and there was a balanced range of ages across the staff (range = 22 years to 56 years with four teachers between 20–30, four teachers between 30–40; four teachers between 40–50; and two teachers older than 50 years). Despite this,

Figure 2.3 Star assessment

more than half of the staff had less than ten years' experience as a teacher (n=8), with the most experienced teacher having 26 years' experience and the least experienced teacher in their first teaching position having only one school term experience as a teacher.

The strong shared approach to teaching writing at this school was founded on progressive ideas about language and language learning. Twelve of the 14 teachers reported that they were most influenced by ideas related to whole language approaches where modelled and shared reading and writing, drafting and publishing were given priority as teaching activities, along with a notion that context, purpose, and audience are important elements of producing text. One of the teachers who taught the children featured later in this chapter made the importance of meaning and purpose evident when asked about key issues for teachers of writing:

students need to understand why they are writing. They need to have a purpose for writing. They need to have a grounding in early abilities such as letter formation and sight words. If they don't have these, they can utilise other avenues such as iPad composing, detailed planning in the use illustrations, and bringing it back down to planning and writing one short message clearly rather than having their minds full of message they can't write down at once.
(Early career teacher of Year 1 and 2 students)

For this teacher, and others at the school, knowing about meaning and having a purpose and audience in mind were important elements of learning to write. A prioritising of process over product is also evident in the qualitative responses of teachers. As one of the teachers explained when asked about the most important issues related to teaching writing in current times:

Children need to initially plan and then it is very important that they compose ... and then they start drafting their message. Editing on the run is also a very important thing that our children do.
(Experienced teacher in a leadership role)

Notions about providing students time to plan, write, and redraft are evident in many of the responses of teachers across a number of questions in the survey. Many teachers also discussed the need to provide supportive models of writing for learners, and often used language like modelled and guided writing, draft, editing, and proofreading when discussing what is important for teaching writing in their classroom. These terms fit well with progressive, whole language approaches to literacy. In the example below one teacher explains the types of support provided to students in his class:

Students need to see writing modelled correctly. They should be involved in the guided writing process once they have viewed the steps the teacher takes when producing a modelled example.
(Early career teacher of Year 5 and 6 students)

According to the teachers, children at this school wrote regularly, and wrote a variety of texts with the help of a variety of resources and materials. Perhaps not surprisingly given the strong progressive traditions that teachers across the school hold, materials of print production are featured across the responses to queries related to what children use as they learn to write and produce texts. We know from our field work that the school was well resourced with tablets and laptop computers available for use in the classrooms, and yet only half the teachers reported that they used iPads to teach writing, and when asked to report on materials used by children as they learn to write, print-based technologies such as pencils and paper were mentioned far more often, and reported as being used far more regularly in classrooms than their digital counterparts such as laptops or image and audio recorders.

Thinking about learning to write as a discursive practice spotlights the priority given by teachers at this school to planning, writing, and discussing text production with others – whether teachers, support personnel, or children. As one example all of the teachers involved in the survey reported that children learning to write under their instruction talked before, during, and after writing. The teachers through interviews, focus groups, and collaborative planning sessions, emphasised that learning to write was considered to be a social, discursive, and material process. Further, material evidence in the charts displayed in classrooms and shared teacher spaces, policy and official school interactions, emphasised that learning to write also required other people to collaborate with, and access to materials and opportunities for children to choose where, when, with what, and with whom they would learn to write. It appears there are elements of the teachers' reports that seem to run counter to these espoused and collective perspectives. We don't consider that this counter evidence suggests that the teachers' understandings of teaching writing well are not based in ideas about providing opportunities and time for children to write regularly, using different materials and with opportunities to liaise and interact with peers and helpful adults. Instead we believe that these counter extracts demonstrate the complex messiness of teaching writing in early years classrooms. For instance, a teacher who was involved in teaching the children presented as cases in the latter parts of this chapter reported that children wrote every day in his early years classroom, and across several questions of the survey discussed points related to providing a variety of experiences, materials, and supportive modelled, guided, and independent contexts for his young learners.

Children's reports about learning to write

In this section of the chapter we focus on two children's reports concerning their understandings of writing from one year to the next. The cases provide some insights into children's reading of writing classrooms, its routines, its spaces and paraphernalia, teacher expectations, children's self-perceptions, and how they operated within the context. These children were chosen as their accounts are illuminating in signalling shifts from one year to another in terms of 'good writing' and 'good writers'. Importantly, we are interested in (following Dyson 2019, p. 76) viewing school writing 'from the vantage point of children' as they work with the material and discursive resources available to them in their classrooms.

Hayden: reading the writing classroom as a discursive and material space

When Hayden was six years old and in Year 1, he identified himself as a 'good' writer. Hayden's teacher identified that he was in one of the lower clusters for writing. Hayden was able to identify writing times in his classroom – 'we usually write before lunch'. Hayden identified the writing session within the morning literacy session as the time of the school day when he wrote. From the onset, Hayden was able to define 'good' writing. He explained, 'good writing is like publishing and reflecting. Publishing is when you have to do your neatest work'. He identified the support he got from Lucy, Caitlyn, Cohen, and Beau – his 'footy team mates' (children he played football with at lunchtime) – and his teacher. Hayden drew himself standing alongside a seemingly large desk, with a piece of paper on it with the high frequency word 'the' written on it with large letters (Figure 2.4). Hayden's face is smiling, appearing to indicate his enjoyment of writing time.

In the first writing sample we collected for Hayden he demonstrated his attempts to plan before he wrote. In this writing task, Hayden was asked to write about what a day is like in his classroom. In his planning (the left of Figure 2.5), he identifies the teacher as a key character within his classroom. He then continues to write a sentence about the teacher in his planning space.

This sentence was transferred to his written text (the right of Figure 2.5) and elaborated upon to include another character (a student) and a conclusion to the time period being written about. Analysis of Hayden's writing shows us that he is able to include ideas related to the writing topic. He demonstrates some structural features within his writing (for example the inclusion of tense) and the text has some coherence as there is an attempt to sequence his ideas. He is able to use a range of simple, everyday words and phrases with a number

Figure 2.4 Hayden's drawing of his Year 1 writing classroom

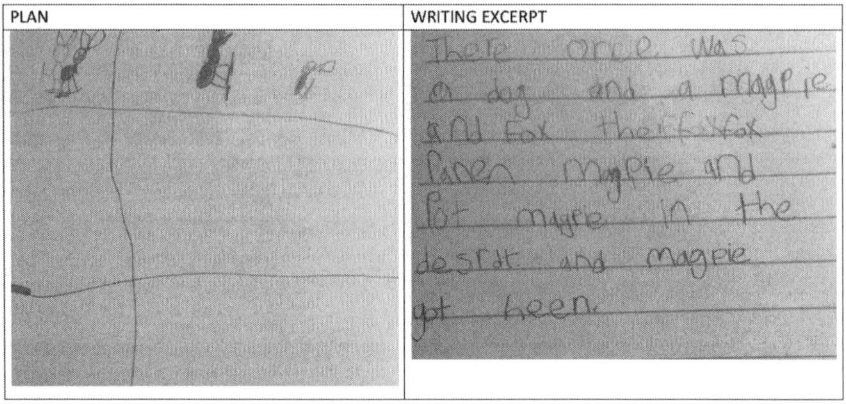

PLAN	WRITING EXCERPT
	There once was a dog and a magpie and fox the fox chasen magpie and bit magpie in the desrit and magpie got been.

Figure 2.5 Hayden's plan and writing

of high frequency words, demonstrating understanding of phoneme–grapheme relationships and word chunks.

A year later, when Hayden was in Year 2, he was ambivalent about his ability as a writer: 'depends what writing we do …[I'm] sometimes good, sometimes bad'. When we discussed this further with him, it became evident that writing fluency and accuracy with spelling, grammar, and punctuation were the major determinants for Hayden (and, he believed, his teacher too) for 'good writing'. At this point, Hayden believed good writers were those that 'hardly make mistakes … [and] one thing they do is write fast'.

Hayden again draws his writing classroom (see Figure 2.6). There are both similarities and differences between this illustration and that represented in Figure 2.4. There are similar elements in this drawing – with the inclusion of himself, the desk, something on the table to write on, and the inclusion of writing. However, there are notable differences too. The desk is bigger, and the piece of paper has now become a book. The depiction of himself is smaller, and what was once a smile has been replaced by a straight line for a mouth. Hayden has written more words on the book. Around the table we can see two windows above and a door to the right. What was also interesting to us was Hayden's talk as he drew this second picture, he described, 'we sit at our table but if we get distracted by other people then we have to move down the back'.

While it's important not to over-claim on the basis of children's self-reports, it is equally important to take their accounts and representations seriously, in terms of the possible implications for teaching and assessing. One part of the conversation between Lisa and Hayden seems to be particularly telling.

LISA: And what sort of writing are you doing today? What's Mr H asking?
HAYDEN: Narrative.
LISA: Tell me about that. What are you doing?
HAYDEN: I have no clue what narrative is.

Figure 2.6 Hayden's drawing of his Year 2 writing classroom

LISA: You don't know? Is narrative like a story?
HAYDEN: Yeah, like a story, but with commas and like adjectives, that what Mr H is telling us.

In this brief exchange, Hayden readily produced the answer to Lisa's question about 'the sort of writing' the class is doing, in that he knows the term 'narrative', but then denied that he knew anything about it. However, a little later in the conversation, when outlining 'good writing', Hayden appeared to identify a number of features of writing narrative.

LISA: … What do you think good writing is?
HAYDEN: Well like, like saying information, like the beginning starts off good and there has to be a problem in the middle. Like you have, in the middle, there's a problem but at the end they solve it. Like good adjectives …
LISA: OK. Sounds to me that you know what a narrative is because you just told me all about a narrative. Did you realise that? There you go; you do know what narratives are. Are you a good writer?
HAYDEN: It depends on what writing we do.

In this exchange, Hayden reveals a good deal of knowledge regarding school writing, or, at least he is well able at age seven to appropriate vocabulary from the teacher's professional discourse. Yet, he is more equivocal about his own status as a writer – 'sometimes good, sometimes bad' – and later explained to Lisa that he was good at writing recounts. The more Hayden knows about school writing genres, the more indifferent he becomes about his own abilities. In making these observations, our intention is not to critique Mr H, but rather to demonstrate the extent to which Hayden is interpreting and taking on board his teacher's explanations of generic structure and features and how aware he is of the contingent nature of 'good writing'. He goes on to explain that the people in his class whom he believes to be 'good writers' 'hardly ever make mistakes' and 'One thing they really do is write fast'. Yet he's not sure they accomplish this, because 'I cannot get close enough to see'. So from Hayden's view, good writers are readily identified and visible for what they do, but not within his sphere of classroom space to observe closely.

This idea of classroom space is important for Hayden.

LISA: Where do you do your writing? I saw you come out of your classroom. Whereabouts do you do your writing?
HAYDEN: Um just at the back ...

For Hayden, writing time was when he was offered support from a specialist teacher who worked intensely with a guided group. For Hayden, this meant that he was asked to work at a table at the back of the classroom space, removing him from the majority of his peers during writing time; including those he identified as being 'good' writers. Working in a designated space constitutes Hayden as a particular kind of writer needy of specific kinds of help, even as it removes him from some of his peers who he knows have ways of avoiding mistakes and writing fast.

Caitlyn: reading the writing classroom as a discursive and material space

We first met Caitlyn when she was six years old and in Year 1. Caitlyn came to our attention as a student identified by five of her peers as a good writer who 'had good ideas'. Indeed, her teacher too identified that Caitlyn was in one of the 'top' clusters for writing. Caitlyn appeared quite networked within her classroom. Caitlyn was able to identify specific strengths her classmates displayed with writing and how she brought these into her own practice. For example, she identified that she 'edited' with Emily and she called on Beau or Cohen if she needed to know 'how to spell some words'. This networking was reinforced when Caitlyn was invited to draw what her class looked like during writing time (see Figure 2.7). She took time to draw two of the table groups within her class and identified particular classmates that sat around these tables. It was these classmates who also identified Caitlyn as a 'good' writer.

For Caitlyn, good writing came about through practice. She explained, 'I like writing and I practice a lot'. Writing was something that Caitlyn did a lot at home too and she shared, 'I like to write stories that I make up ... I like to

Figure 2.7 Caitlyn's drawing of her Year 1 writing classroom

write stories about unicorns. In every one of my stories there's unicorns'. Caitlyn revealed that she often talked to her mum or her brother at home about her writing, sharing that her mum really loved her stories.

The type of writing Caitlyn reported that she did at school was quite different. She explained, 'I write different kinds of stories … [Teacher] chooses the stories I write at school'. Already, Caitlyn is aware of her teacher's authority to select what she will write at school. She did identify two times when she wrote during the school day – the daily literacy session and the time for 'drop everything and write' which was done on two afternoons of the week.

In conversation with Lisa, Caitlyn spoke about 'good' writing.

LISA: What do you think good writing is?
CAITLYN: ummm [13-second pause] it is when you get three stars all over …
LISA: How do you get stars?
CAITLYN: umm for good writing! I make them good because I use adjectives.
LISA: Oh, ok. And what sorts of things does your teacher look for in good writing?
CAITLYN: Ummm, he looks for if you do your learning goals and if you do some of your clusters.

Like Hayden, Caitlyn also appropriated her teacher's professional discourse around writing and was attuned to the reporting structures he uses to frame the writing capabilities of his students. Caitlyn demonstrated her awareness of the state-wide approach to the organisation of the cohort of students according to their achievement of specific learning goals. In Caitlyn's classroom, these abstract concepts were made material on the walls as points of reference for students to begin self-monitoring their own development (see Figures 2.1, 2.2, and 2.3).

The first writing sample we collected from Caitlyn was a story she had written about a cat called Maisy. In this particular task, Caitlyn was asked by her teacher to write a story about friendship in response to a picture book they had just read as a class. Caitlyn was able to interpret this task to enable her to bring in some of the features of her home writing that she enjoyed – made-up characters within a more extended story. Like Hayden, Caitlyn had spent time planning her story before she began writing. Caitlyn's plan was a series of six images divided into individual frames on her planning page (see the left side of Figure 2.8). The progression of the story for Maisy the cat and a witch character became evident. Maisy had different facial expressions which even at this planning stage provided indication of how the story might progress.

Using the plan, Caitlyn produced a story that was 56 words and written on three pages of her writing book. An excerpt of Caitlyn's story is provided on the right of Figure 2.8. Caitlyn's writing showed some complexity as relevant ideas were connected together to create her story. Caitlyn was able to use a range of words in her story, and she drew upon her knowledge of language to add some descriptive detail. She showed some variety in sentence structure and experimented with punctuation.

Even in Year 1 Caitlyn was aware that different writing activities came with different rules, explaining that when it was 'drop everything and write time', that 'you can write anything you want and you don't need a margin'. Like

Figure 2.8 Caitlyn's planning and writing

Hayden, Caitlyn is well attuned to how things work in her classroom and very aware of what's allowable when.

A year later, Caitlyn is in Year 2 (a different Year 2 class to Hayden) and we connect with her again to talk about writing in her classroom. While Caitlyn still identified herself as a good writer, there was quite a notable shift in the way Caitlyn talked about herself in the writing classroom. In this discussion, Caitlyn told us about her teacher who 'helps me think about ideas and they help me spell correctly'. When asked about her peers, she identified she didn't really have time to talk to them about writing. At this point it is worth remembering that Hayden identified Caitlyn as someone he spoke to about his writing. Caitlyn revealed her focus in the classroom was to 'write super fast' and 'use good punctuation'. Caitlyn described a process for herself in the classroom – 'usually I finish my writing in the first day and then I usually edit and revise the second day'.

Again, Caitlyn was invited to draw what writing time looked like in her classroom (see Figure 2.9). Caitlyn began by drawing her table group. This time though it was only herself that she drew at the table group with her teacher standing beside her to 'check' her work. Caitlyn appeared to understand the role of her teacher was to assess her writing, in line with her comments around achievement of the success criteria for the learning clusters. To the side of this, she drew two children sitting on chairs with another teacher, identifying they needed extra help. This resonates with Hayden's comments

Figure 2.9 Caitlyn's drawing of her Year 2 writing classroom

around the space he occupied during writing time. It also reminds us of Caitlyn's awareness of the different ability groups – the clusters – that existed in her classroom.

Caitlyn's enthusiasm for text production increased markedly when she talked about producing songs and plays with friends and family at home.

CAITLYN: We don't really talk about writing at all, but we just talk about what, what the story's going to be about and … or what the song's going to be about.
LISA: Oh so you're like song writers together?
CAITLYN: Mhmm. And we make shows and show my brother Lochlan and her brother Jackson. Like shows and we show my baby sister and we also show my mum and dad.

Caitlyn then checked with Lisa whether she can represent this in her drawing about writing.

As Caitlyn described her writing at home, her energy is palpable as her responses lengthen and she elaborates. This writing with her friend Lucy from across the road involves improvisation, singing, drama, and ultimately performances. It was clearly goal driven, social, and resulting in 'fun'.

Discussion and conclusion

This chapter has argued that approaches to writing and their translation into classrooms are part of a broader policy landscape – ensembles of national and state authorised curriculum, programs, and assessments – that are then worked upon within the school as a site of practice and ultimately their manifestations evolved in classrooms. Authorised normative versions of literacy development are then specified in the writing continuum and ultimately find their way onto classroom walls as learning goals and clusters. Regardless of seemingly positive attitudes at the beginning of school, children learn to identify themselves as members of particular clusters and thereby are assigned particular goals for their writing. Hayden learns to see himself as a student at the back of the classroom; Caitlyn sees writing as her favourite subject.

The impact of teachers' professional discourse is evident in the ways that children talk about writing and see themselves as writers. While this is not surprising, we need to be alert to questions about which children have access to which kind of writing experiences. For example, McCarthey and Mkhize (2013), in a study conducted across four states in the United States, found that teachers in high-income schools appeared to have more autonomy than teachers in low-income schools. While teachers in low-income schools focused on mandated curriculum, aiming at grammar and mechanics, teachers in high-income schools offered authentic, meaningful, and challenging writing experiences. Caitlyn and Hayden were both aware that school writing in Year 2 emphasised correct spelling, punctuation, generic style, and length.

Opportunities for creativity did not feature in their reports of their experiences in Year 2 as they had in Year 1.

Children's perspectives of and experiences within classroom writing experiences pose important pedagogical considerations for educators. Classroom pedagogies, and their implementation through selection of resources and access to interactions, contribute to the types of texts children produce during writing time, the kinds of help they can access, and their self-assessments. In stark contrast to Hayden's experience of not being able to access how his peers wrote so fast and avoided mistakes, Caitlyn was able to call on extra practice at home and the neighbourhood through self-selected writing occasions, as well as numerous capable peers in her classroom. It is important to recall that these children are only seven years of age at this point and already their sense of themselves as learners in relation to others is beginning to shape up. While Caitlyn was confident enough to accept her teacher's selection for school writing, she was not limited by this and continued to write about her passions at home. Hayden preferred to write about certain topics in certain ways, but knows that he is meant to write narratives. It was no accident that narrative was emphasised that year as teachers worked hard to begin to prepare these children for the NAPLAN tests they would face early in Year 3. At this stage of their educational trajectories Hayden and Caitlyn were already assessed by their teachers as belonging in different developmental clusters which resulted in quite different access to writing pedagogies.

Given that writing is so central in displaying learning throughout formal education, how these children identify as writers is important. While teachers may see the 'clusters' as formative and as a device for guiding children towards certain kinds of developmental goals, children may begin to see certain kinds of writing and classroom status as not for them. We can only wonder what might happen if Hayden was able to get access to the mystery that some of his peers can write so fast and avoid mistakes. We can only hope that his remaining confidence for certain kind of writing sustains his efforts in other genres. The point here is to understand that there are no 'natural progressions' that all children will make in learning to write. Yet frequently literacy-learning models constitute the ideal child learner writer as developing in a particular sequence, regarding genres and skills. As Dyson (2019, p. 76) reminds us, children who do not follow these ideal progressions can be assessed in ways that are highly problematic:

> Their 'differences' from the assumed 'mainstream' may become 'lacks'; their actions as agents, and their repertoire of experiences and resources, may be disappeared.

The children's accounts and representations of the processes and practices of classroom writing pedagogies begin to indicate relationality and positioning in the writing classroom. In the first year, Caitlyn depicted herself as one of a group of high-achieving children who share a table and assist each other. A year later, she illustrated herself writing with her friend and having fun, while her brother and his friend play on PlayStations. After drawing himself smiling in Year 1, in Year 2 Hayden portrayed himself as alone or with a teacher, often 'down the back'. To return to Leander's point about power relations and ideologies being inherent in the very fabric of classrooms and the micropolitics of everyday life, we can see the dangers with particular normative developmental grids separating children into 'clusters' whose learning goals are literally prescribed and differentiated. Such developmental diagnostics do not play an innocent role in where children sit or how they see themselves in relation to others.

However, teachers clearly need to have a sense of direction as they support children learning to write. Informing frameworks might be more productive if they were to take an additive approach where children could learn to document the ways in which they are assembling repertoires of practices over time, rather than frameworks where specific genres and their features are taken as appropriate for people of a certain age or stage. The selection and display of materials in classroom spaces makes evident to different children where they stand academically in relation to peers. Yet such posters could be more inclusive and dynamic, rather than comparative and divisive.

The challenge for educators and educational researchers is to consider more positive and productive ways of representing children's learning over time that attend to what they can do and are learning to do, rather than naming what they cannot do in comparison to peers. Our conceptualisation of writing needs to be rich and expansive enough to make visible to teachers and to children key complex dimensions of composing, so that they spend time on the big picture and what counts for developing writing as part on an ongoing formative learner identity.

Notes

1 The 'Learning to write in the Early Years teacher Survey' was designed as part of work completed in DP150101240. Annette Woods, Lisa Kervin, Aspa Baroutsis, and Barbara Comber were involved in different stages of design, trial, administration, and initial analysis of data.
2 In the NSW public education system the primary school years are organised into four stages. These include Early Stage 1 for children in kindergarten or the first year of formal school (children aged 4.5–6 years), Stage 1 for children in Years 1 and 2 (children aged 5.5–8 years), Stage 2 for children in Years 3 or 4 (children aged 7.5–10), and Stage 3 for children in Years 5 and 6 (children aged 9.5–12).

References

Australian Bureau of Statistics (ABS). 2011. Available from: www.abs.gov.au/.
Australian Curriculum, Assessment and Reporting Authority (ACARA). 2016. My school. Available from: www.myschool.edu.au/.

Barton, D. and Hamilton, M. 1998. *Local literacies: reading and writing in one community*. London: Routledge.

Brandt, D. 2015. *The rise of writing: redefining mass literacy*. Cambridge: Cambridge University Press.

Burnett, C., et al. 2014. The (im)materiality of literacy: the significance of subjectivity to new literacies research. *Discourse: Studies in the Cultural Politics of Education*, 35(1), 90–103.

Dixon, K., 2010. *Literacy, power, and the schooled body: learning in time and space*. London and New York: Routledge.

Dyson, A. H. 2019. Composing childhood cultures: ethnography upside down. In: Kucirkova, N., Rowsell, J. and Falloon, G. eds. *The Routledge international handbook of learning with technology in early childhood*. New York: Taylor & Francis, 74–87.

Fenwick, T. 2014. Sociomateriality in medical practice and learning: attuning to what matters. *Medical Education*, 48(1), 44–52.

Fenwick, T. and Edwards, R. 2011. Introduction: reclaiming and renewing actor network theory for educational research. *Educational Philosophy and Theory*, 43(s1), 1.

Fisher, R. 2012. Teaching writing: a situated dynamic. *British Educational Research Journal*, 38(2), 299–317.

Heath, S. B. 1983. *Ways with words: language, life, and work in communities and classrooms*. New York: Cambridge University Press.

Ivanič, R. 2004. Discourses of writing and learning to write. *Language and Education*, 18(3), 220–245.

Leander, K. M. 2004. Reading the spatial histories of positioning in a classroom literacy event: spatializing literacy research and practice. In: Leander, K. and Sheehy, M. eds. *Spatializing literacy research and practice*. New York: Peter Lang, 115–142.

Leander, K. M. and Rowe, D. W. 2006. Mapping literacy spaces in motion: a rhizomatic analysis of a classroom literacy performance. *Reading Research Quarterly*, 41(4), 428–460.

McCarthey, S. J. and Mkhize, D. 2013. Teachers' orientations towards writing. *Journal of Writing Research*, 5(1), 1–33.

Quinn, M. F. and Bingham, G. E. 2019. The nature and measurement of children's early composing. *Reading Research Quarterly*, 54(2), 213–235.

Rogers, R. 2003. *A critical discourse analysis of family literacy practices: power in and out of print*. New York: Routledge.

Rowsell, J. and Pahl, K. 2011. The material and the situated: what multimodality and new literacy studies do for literacy research. In: Lapp, D. and Fisher, D. eds. *Handbook of research on teaching the English language arts*. New York: Routledge, 175–181.

Warf, B. and Arias, S. 2009. *The spatial turn interdisciplinary perspectives*. London: Routledge.

Wohlwend, K. E. 2007. Reading to play and playing to read: a mediated discourse analysis of early literacy apprenticeship. In: *Fifty-sixth yearbook of the National Reading Conference*. Chicago: National Reading Association, 377–393.

Woods, A., Comber, B. and Kervin, L. 2015–2018. *Learning to write: a socio-material analysis of text production*. Australian Research Council Discovery Grant, DP150101240.

3 Writing before school

The role of families in supporting children's early writing development

Cathy Nutbrown

Introduction

This chapter first considers writing as understood through theories of emergent literacy. This leads to a consideration of how family literacy programmes can usefully share theory and practice with parents, to help them further facilitate their children's writing development as they begin to recognise and represent writing in everyday contexts, before they begin formal schooling. Drawing on examples of emergent writing by one young child, Evie, at home, the chapter offers an example of how a young child can begin to explore writing as a means of communication and power. This offers some insight into her personal theories of how writing works and what it can be used for. Finally, a reflection on curriculum policy in England highlights a mismatch between current policy and young children's more natural curiosity about, and understanding of, writing and implications for policy on teaching writing in the early years of school and the involvement of parents.

Theories of emergent literacy

What became known as *emergent* literacy stems from research in the 1980s (e.g. Goodman 1980, Harste et al. 1984, Ferreiro and Teberosky 1989) and provides the underpinning for understanding children's 'real life' encounters and learning about writing at home and how Early Childhood Education practices can build on such theories. As Whitmore et al. (2004) suggest, when children begin to engage with written texts, they can experience a 'tension' between their own constructions of literacy and how society (in terms of education policy) has defined literacy conventions.

An emergent literacy movement began with research in the 1980s – initially carried out in the United States – which has inspired early years educators to be curious about, and enthusiastic to develop, pedagogy to support the emergent literacy of children around the ages of two to five years. This stimulated a field of enquiry and practice around early literacy development that had – up to that point – been effectively disregarded.

In the United States, Goodman (1980, 1986) encouraged recognition of what she called the 'roots' of literacy which developed in young children; these 'roots' included: awareness of print in the environment (Hassett 2006); understanding and awareness about written language; being able to talk about written language; understanding of what writing was for and what writing looked like. Goodman's work in the 1980s brought a new perspective on how young children come to know about and create their own writing, and it is this foundation which now means early years practitioners see what was previously dismissed as 'just scribble' as early foundations of writing. In many countries in the late 1980s (particularly in the United States, United Kingdom, Australia and New Zealand) preschool teachers were discovering an enthusiasm about young children's literacy capabilities, which was stimulated by research. They derived an energy from what they learned to support children's development by using literacy in everyday contexts, as children imitated adult literacy practices. Nurseries and preschools changed. Where words were once largely banished, and writing was not encouraged (to protect young children from the worries generated by learning to read and write too early), signs, symbols, and writing areas began to proliferate. Coat pegs that once identified children with a picture label – so that, for example, children identified the place for their belongings with a ball, a cat, a flower – now bore children's names. Displays were labelled, and role play contexts which encouraged early attempts at writing were established with writing tools such as note pads and pens, clipboards, and order forms, and playing *at* and *with* writing were encouraged. There was a move towards identifying and nurturing the emergent elements of literacy that young children seemed spontaneously to exhibit, and settings encouraged parents to do the same. Preschool teachers themselves developed a new confidence in their literacy pedagogy as research about how writing developed in the earliest years found its way to the preschool.

It was studies, often by academic mothers and grandmothers, of individual children's early literacy achievements (Bissex 1980, Baghban 1984, Payton 1984, Schickedanz 1990) which led to the development of an 'emergent' perspective on early literacy that showed how much very young children knew about writing. With the dawn of these new understandings the *emergent writing* approach heralded changes to thinking about several areas: connections between learning to read and learning to write; the part that children's parents play at home in their early writing development; how play contributes to children's engagement in and learning about writing; the everyday contexts which children experience through which they derive meanings about writing. That is to say, if we adopt an emergent (or what some call a developmental) approach to writing, we see young children as active in developing their own writing skills, knowledge, and understanding, and this begins to take place long before they begin school or are formally taught them. Simply, because young children's early writing seems to be so spontaneous, and seemingly something they enjoy doing, we can say that, in literacy rich contexts, children's writing development *emerges* as a *socio-cultural* experience because the conventional rules about writing do not inhibit children from making writing their own as they take risks and try out their ideas about writing without fear of 'getting it wrong' (Harste et al. 1984).

Perhaps one of the most exciting studies about children's developing understanding of how literacy works was published by Ferreiro and Teberosky (1989) who proposed the notion of children's self-generated hypotheses about writing rules. For example, they found that many children expected written strings of letters for people's names to be proportional to the size (or age) of the person rather than the actual length of their name:

> David thinks that the written representation 'papa' is longer than the one for 'David Bernardo Mendez' (his own complete name) ... a girl who has just turned five ... says 'Write my name'. But you have to make it longer because yesterday was my birthday.
>
> (pp. 180–184)

The example by Gregg (Figure 3.1) – age four years and one month – illustrates Ferreiro and Teberosky's research into this hypothesis. Whilst the strings for 'my dad' and 'my mum' both contain nine characters, Gregg has made the first look much bigger. Similarly, some children expect a word for a large object (say a car) to be bigger than the word for something tiny (such as a kitten). Sometimes the theory works – an aeroplane has a longer name and is bigger than an ant – but sometimes it does not. It is the generation and testing out of such personal theories about writing that eventually enable children to understand that it is important that everyone holds similar theories about writing to aid shared understanding.

Summarising children's writing activity in relation to the hypothesis that a bigger object must have a big word Ferreiro and Teberosky (1989) note: 'They ... use greater numbers of graphic characters, larger characters, or longer graphic stories if the object is bigger, longer, older, or if a great number of objects are referred to' (p. 184). Ferreiro and Teberosky argued that literacy evolves through a developmental process spanning the pre-school years, from initial understandings about print to the sophisticated understandings about the function, form and conventions of writing. They suggest:

> To understand print, pre-school children have reasoned intelligently, elaborated good hypotheses about writing systems (although they may not be 'good' in terms of our conventional writing system), overcome conflicts, searched for irregularities, and continually attached meaning to written texts. But the logical coherence they impose on themselves disappears when faced with what the teacher demands from them. They must worry about perception and motor control instead of the need to understand. They must acquire a series of skills instead of coming to know an object. They must set aside their own linguistic knowledge and capacity for

Figure 3.1 Gregg's writing
Source: REAL project, www.real-online.group.shef.ac.uk/docs/writing-opps/early-writing-development.pdf.

thought until they discover, at a later point, that it is impossible to comprehend a written text without them.

(Ferreiro and Teberosky 1989, p. 279)

Discussing research from the 1970s and 1980s which led to the growth of an 'emergent literacy' perspective, Hall (1985) wrote:

> While educationalists have always been aware that some children learn to read early in life most school activities related to beginning reading seem to presuppose that children, in general, do not know anything about literacy. Thus, implicitly the judgement of teachers appears to be that children have to be taught from scratch all that they need to know about becoming literate.
>
> (p. 7)

Adopting an emergent literacy perspective means that preschool teachers can build on their sense of what children already know about aspects of literacy, before they begin formal education. Such theory can then be shared with parents in order to enhance understanding of how young children acquire some literacy knowledge and behaviour from their families, without any formal teaching. Growing up in a literate environment, where adults read and write, where they can play with the 'tools' of literacy, pens, paper, books, digital technologies, and where literacy is part of everyday life is an important grounding for learning to write when formal schooling begins.

It has been suggested that emergent writing could be thought of as one of four strands: environmental print; sharing books; early writing; and key aspects of oral language (Nutbrown and Hannon 1997), where emergent writing arises through children's involvement in everyday writing activities, including watching and imitating adults who write in everyday contexts such as letters, shopping lists, text messages, and emails, and identifying and representing print in the environment such as street signs, door numbers, shop signs, advertisements, digital transport signs, and food packages.

Early, emergent writing begins with the first tentative marks children make. Often given negative connotation when referred to as 'scribble', these early marks eventually evolve into conventionally recognisable writing. Research into emergent writing shows that as children get to know more about writing, and try things out in the early years, they begin to develop their own rules about how writing works. This important foundation comes long before trying to form letters correctly or copying words and later spellings (Niessen et al. 2011). Oral language is crucial to children's literacy learning and development, speaking being foundational to written language and eventual understanding that writing is often speech in the form of conventional symbols. When young children understand that speech can be written down, they can progress successfully in reading – because at that point in their development, children know that the marks which make up words have some meaning and can be spoken.

Family literacy programmes and children's writing development

Studies of the role of family literacy programmes (Hannon et al. 2019) and of the importance of the home environment (Ross and Bondy 1987, Hannon 1995, Deguara and Nutbrown 2017) show how young children can be supported in home and group settings in their writing development. Many have tended to focus on mothers' involvement in their children's literacy (DeBruin-Parecki and Krol-Sinclair 2003). Edwards (2014) studied the way that 15 American ('upper class and white', significantly) mothers of 18–36-month-old toddlers engaged in emergent literacy, concluding that the mothers were involved in supporting aspects of written language development. Weigel et al. (2006) explored home–preschool connections in terms of the literacy environment, identifying two perspectives:

> 'Facilitative' mothers believed that taking an active role in teaching children at home would provide opportunities for their children to gain vocabulary, knowledge, and morals. 'Conventional' mothers expressed the

belief that schools, more than parents, are responsible for teaching children and tended to report many challenges to reading with children.

(p. 191)

Recently, more effort has been made to understand and support fathers' involvement (Baker 2013, Anderson et al. 2015), with Morgan et al. (2009) reporting of one family literacy project:

> Although largely invisible to outsiders, in many families the fathers' presence in their children's literacy became apparent to teachers in the project. As one teacher commented: *Whatever Beth makes or does, she likes to show dad (although I have never met him). He obviously takes a keen interest in activities she has done.*
>
> (p. 16)

Focusing on the need for partnership between home and school and the importance of sharing theory and practice with parents, the Sheffield REAL (Raising Early Achievement in Literacy) Project, a large, longitudinal preschool family literacy study in the UK (Hannon et al. 2019) used the ORIM Framework (Opportunities, Recognition, Interaction, Model) to think about ways in which families can help children's early literacy development (Nutbrown et al. 2005). Families are powerful influences on children's early literacy and Hannon et al. (2019) showed how family literacy programmes can be effective when parents provide Opportunities, Recognition, Interaction, and Models of literacy for their children, specifically around environmental print, books, early writing, and aspects of oral language.

As Hannon et al. (2019) have shown, research into theories of emergent literacy can be shared with families and can meaningfully inform how parents support children's development as capable and confident young writers. Family literacy programmes can usefully share theory and practice with parents to help them further facilitate their children's writing development as they begin to recognise and represent writing in everyday contexts, before they begin formal schooling. One practical tool for sharing aspects of early writing development with parents is a 'Jigsaw of Early Writing Development' (Figure 3.2) which parents can refer to, to identify specific steps they know their children have taken towards writing.

Using this simple tool with parents helps them to develop their recognition skills and to understand the small steps which together make up a child's developing writing repertoire.

The REAL project shared theory about emergent writing with parents and discussed with them how they could provide more opportunities for writing, how they might recognise the steps their children were making in writing, how they could interact with their children around writing, and how they could make a point of writing for real purposes when their children were around to provide a model of how adults use writing in everyday life. This gave participating parents insights into how writing developed and confidence to do more. Parents said:

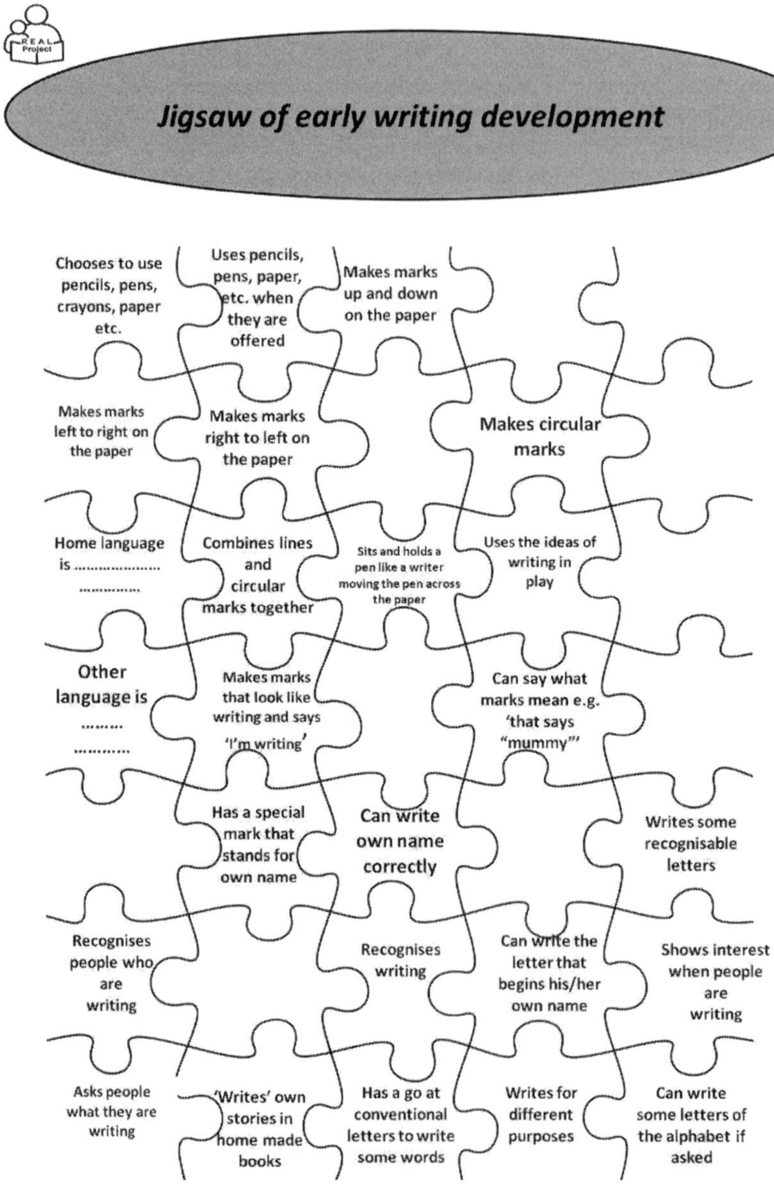

Jigsaw of early writing development

- Chooses to use pencils, pens, crayons, paper etc.
- Uses pencils, pens, paper, etc. when they are offered
- Makes marks up and down on the paper
- Makes marks left to right on the paper
- Makes marks right to left on the paper
- Makes circular marks
- Home language is ....
- Combines lines and circular marks together
- Sits and holds a pen like a writer moving the pen across the paper
- Uses the ideas of writing in play
- Other language is ....
- Makes marks that look like writing and says 'I'm writing'
- Can say what marks mean e.g. 'that says "mummy"'
- Has a special mark that stands for own name
- Can write own name correctly
- Writes some recognisable letters
- Recognises people who are writing
- Recognises writing
- Can write the letter that begins his/her own name
- Shows interest when people are writing
- Asks people what they are writing
- 'Writes' own stories in home made books
- Has a go at conventional letters to write some words
- Writes for different purposes
- Can write some letters of the alphabet if asked

Figure 3.2 Jigsaw of Early Writing Development
Source: http://www.real-online.group.shef.ac.uk/docs/writing-rec/writing%20jigsaw%20edited%20JB.pdf.

It's been a big help actually. I do think Alan has learned a lot. It makes parents aware of the things they can do with children, because to be honest, especially when you have your first child, you're a little bit unsure.

To me it were like helping her to learn, but not like learning in school.

[Her] dad has brought her an old diary from work which she's enjoying writing in.

On holiday he drew letters in the sand with dad.

… dad often writes with Suzy.

These few comments indicate how parents value learning more about their children's early writing development (and other aspects of literacy) and, as Hannon et al. (2019) show, a family literacy programme can be effective in helping parents teach their children: 'There were literacy gains for children in the programme. Children further disadvantaged in terms of their mothers' lower levels of education had greater, and longer lasting, gains' (p. 23).

Evie: an emergent writer

This section presents a case study of some of Evie's writing. It draws selected examples of her writing between the ages of 2:2 and 4:8 years in a home context. This shows how a young child can begin to explore writing as a means of communication and power and illustrates her personal theories of how writing works and what it can be used for. It argues that the 'everydayness' of writing for real purposes, which many young children experience at home, with their parent models, can be used to create meaningful writing encounters for young children in preschool settings.

Methodology

The case study here of Evie is drawn from 60 such cases which were part of a longitudinal study of early literacy development which focused specifically on children coming to literacy in their home and family contexts. Children were selected according to birth date only, from ten schools which had agreed to participate in a family literacy intervention. Parents were fully informed of, and consented to participation in, the study and children were free to engage in ways which they were comfortable with. All participating families were aware and consented to sharing and publication of their contributions including copies of children's writing samples with the originals usually staying with the child. Because much of young children's mark-making takes place spontaneously, and the context of the writing is important to understanding its meaning, parents were involved in collecting and dating the children's writing and sharing something of the context in which it occurred. The case study using of Evie's writing which is reported in this chapter was selected because it was fairly typical of many others from the sample.

Evie developing as a writer 2:2–4:8

At home one day with her carer, Evie, knowing her mummy was at work, wrote to her saying 'mummy work' (Figure 3.3). Written on the outside of an envelope, we do not know whether it was intended as a note to her mummy or whether it simply represented something Evie wanted to say. We can infer that her mother being at work was an important part of Evie's life and so she wanted to represent this in the symbols she used to write at the time – a series of left to right marks. Such 'lines' of writing are often an early representation of 'being a writer'. Evie (2:2) knows that writing can convey meaning.

Some four months later – looking at the picture on a Christmas card showing a teddy with a sack of presents, Evie made a series of seven separate marks, all somewhat circular. These are still in a line – but there are distinct and individual symbols. This, she said, read 'Bear got parcels' (Figure 3.4).

Books, poems and rhymes can stimulate children's oral language and their writing. Aged 3 years, and after sharing Shirley Hughes' (2000) poem 'Toes' with her mother, Evie wrote her own version (Figure 3.5). The layout of her writing – with separate lines for each line of the poem she recorded – shows her developing insight into how writing works and how marks hold meaning.

Adult models of writing, and the opportunity to write in play and for real tasks, can stimulate children to write. The shopping list created between Evie and her mother (Figure 3.6) shows that Evie is beginning to learn about how lists are usually composed, with an item on each line. Evie first dictated 'corn, chocolate, crisps, carrots' which her mother wrote down. Evie then took over, using her developing repertoire of letter-like marks to fill the page as she made her list of items to buy from the supermarket.

Figure 3.3 'Mummy work' – age 2:2

Figure 3.4 'Bear got parcels' – age 2:6

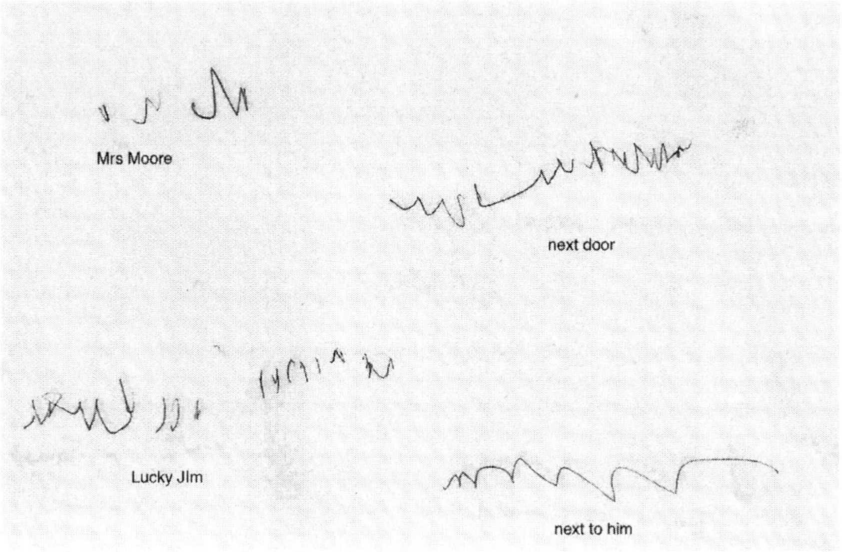

Mrs Moore

next door

Lucky Jim

next to him

Figure 3.5 'Mrs Moore – next door' – age 3:0

corn

chocolate

crisps

carrots

Figure 3.6 Shopping list – age 3:10

At this point, Evie seems to like lists and is beginning to know what they look like, and how they can be used. At 4:1, Evie has copied words that she asked an adult to write for her about her puppy (Figure 3.7). In doing so, she had adapted the writing to incorporate her own theories about writing. This list has a large full stop at the end of each word. Full stops seem to have become important in Evie's writing, so she uses them at the end of every line; it seems to be a writing rule that she has created and follows in her list writing. She also has a clear theory about how letters can be made larger or spread across the paper according to the size or importance of what they represent, similar to the theory put forward by Ferreiro and Teberosky (1989). The word for the 'mummy dog' is smaller – less spread out than that for 'daddy dog', and 'puppy' is the smallest word.

Figure 3.7 Puppy. Mummy. Daddydog – age 4:7

Evie, now 4:7, drew a picture of a girl thinking and talking about her friend (Figure 3.8). It was drawn and written at home after reading a comic which featured many speech and thought bubbles. There is clear indication here that Evie now knows much about how writing can represent not only words, but also ideas.

A month later the family were going on holiday and a family friend would care for the puppy. Evie (4:8) was concerned about this – worried that the friend would not know what the puppy needed. So, showing her understanding of the power of writing – and her knowledge of a key word ('and') and her emerging phonetic understanding – Evie wrote a list at home (Figure 3.9). The list has the title 'Puppy' at the top and reads 'Breakfast. and dinner. and tea. and toy and BEd'. A neat and knowledgeable list of what her puppy needs during the day.

Figure 3.8 Speech and thought bubbles – age 4:7

Puppy
Brefs.
and
diny
and
tiy
and
tiy and BEd

Figure 3.9 Puppy list – age 4:8

Again, the full stops are an important feature and her emergent spelling comes into its own as she writes independently. Evie's considerable knowledge about the power and importance of writing and what she can do independently is clear in this list which she wrote one evening at her kitchen table after eating tea with her mum and dad.

Opening her book bag that evening, her mother found an example of the writing Evie had done at school that same day (Figure 3.10). The sticky note attached – written by her teacher – read, 'Evie is practising words ending in "at" and working on letter formation'. Seeing her mother looking at the writing from school Evie said, '*I hate writing – it's rubbish*'. This example, and Evie's comment, is in stark contrast in terms of the meaning, power, capability, and pleasure of writing present in Figure 3.9.

These two examples provoke the questions as to how we can understand Evie's two writing worlds and how they inform each other. Looking at the two

Figure 3.10 Cat, mat, mat – age 4:8

examples together it is not apparent that writing in school offers her opportunity to bring what she las learned about writing from her family context. The narrow emphasis in current curriculum policy in England on correctness in spelling and writing form does not appear to encourage the development of a child's personal writing theories and their growing knowledge about the power and usefulness of writing. This is not to say that there does not come a time when the conventions of writing – including spelling and efficient and consistent letter formation – need to be taught and rehearsed, but it is important to teach writing in schools in ways which do not turn children off such that they perceive themselves as writers no longer and – as in Evie's case – lead them to feel that they 'hate' writing. It is a fine balance to strike, but achievable when teachers have time and opportunity to learn from parents what their children can do at home and can build on the writing pleasures which some children experience at home and can bring to school.

Current policy on teaching early writing in England

This chapter raises a number of questions about policy on teaching writing in the early years of school which need to be addressed. Taking policy in England as an example, the separation of home and school writing can set expectations for preschool learning which are alien to how young children come to writing. Though practice varies, there are examples in US and Australian contexts where this is the case. For many young children in England, there seems to be a mismatch between current education policy and their more natural curiosity about, and understanding of, writing. As we have seen with Evie, the writing worlds which many young children experience at home and school can be poles apart. Current policy should consider how teaching and assessing writing in early years settings and in formal school classrooms take account of theories of emergent literacy to understand and support children's early writing development on entry to school.

In England, it is the Early Years Foundation Stage (EYFS) (DfE 2017) which sets out 'standards for the learning, development and care of your child from birth to 5 years old'.[1] 'Communication and language' is one of three *Prime Areas of Learning*, with 'literacy' identified as a *specific* area of learning and development. However, there is very little mention in the EYFS of children's early writing development, so little, in fact, that it is possible here to quote the two short extracts in full:

> **Literacy** development involves encouraging children to link sounds and letters and to begin to read and write. Children must be given access to a wide range of reading materials (books, poems, and other written materials) to ignite their interest.
>
> (DfE 2017, p. 8)

There is no real indication here of the extent to which children's home writing is understood and valued in curriculum practices. Nor is there any suggestion that teachers should understand and work with children's personal theories about how writing works. The policy continues with a comment on writing:

> **Writing:** children use their phonic knowledge to write words in ways which match their spoken sounds. They also write some irregular common words. They write simple sentences which can be read by themselves and others. Some words are spelt correctly, and others are phonetically plausible.
>
> (DfE 2017, p. 11)

The stress on 'simple sentences' gives little recognition to how early schooling might support children's understanding and use of writing as a means of communication and power. Of course, in many preschool settings and schools, where educators are informed and forward-thinking, their practice values what children bring with them, but this is not because policy guides them in such a pedagogic direction.

In addition, under 'Physical development – Moving and handling' it states that:

> children show good control and co-ordination in large and small movements. They move confidently in a range of ways, safely negotiating space. They handle equipment and tools effectively, including pencils for writing.
>
> (DfE 2017, p. 11)

These are the elements of writing learning and development which are currently assessed under the guidance of the EYFS Profile (DfE 2018). Consider this description of what the English school inspectorate regards as outstanding practice with four- and five-year-old children, in their first year of formal schooling:

> In schools visited where writing was of a high standard, the children were able to write simple sentences and more by the end of Reception. They were mastering the spelling of phonically regular words and common exception words. These schools paid good attention to children's posture and pencil grip when children were writing. They used pencils and exercise books, while children sat at tables, to support good, controlled letter formation.
>
> (Ofsted 2018, p. 5)

In children's home writing worlds, they often write spontaneously wherever they find themselves when they need to write. This is not always sitting at a table with good posture. In the real world people write in all kinds of places: sitting on the floor, standing up, leaning against a wall, hunched in an armchair, and so on. A mismatch between present policy on writing and the potential for spontaneity of writing at home needs to be addressed to provide coherent home–school approaches to the development of young children's writing at four years old. In many cases there seems to be a lack of recognition of children's home writing world experiences. Where schools emphasise only good control, posture, and correctness, this can mean that writing becomes an alien process for children and that parents are not offered vital information and encouragement to support their children's emergent writing in everyday contexts at home.

The emphasis in the extract above is on specific measurable skills and abilities, conveying a somewhat narrow view of writing practice, mostly devoid of meaning, purpose, and creativity. It places skills before meaning, 'simple' form above complex understanding, and prioritises correctness over expression. There is no mention in policy or inspection reporting of how children come to *feel* like writers.

Yet many of the four-year-olds who encounter a curriculum which is highly prescriptive and skills oriented have had, and continue to have, everyday encounters with literacy which emphasise the pleasure, power, and meaning of writing. They have learned that they can use writing to communicate. Must they leave this rich understanding at the classroom door? Or can we look forward to a time when England's schools inspectorate and national curriculum embrace what children know and can do at home as starting points for helping children to become writers, learning necessary skills in the context of having something to say? Given the strength and persuasion of the research available about how writing develops when children learn in the company of other writing models, it is a puzzle as to why curriculum policy is developed at odds with that we know.

In many homes where early writing is encouraged, an account of their learning about writing could be quite different from that from Ofsted cited above. In families where children use writing spontaneously, examples of writing can proliferate. Children write for a range of purposes, believing themselves to be writers, and using what they know of letters and sounds to convey meaning and purpose. They can demonstrate what they have learned from watching other writers in their family, about the shapes and sounds of letters, and why people write. Using their own uniquely developing theories of writing – developed through interaction with other writers – their writing shows children's understanding of the usefulness and power of writing. Spellings are not always conventional, but often show some understanding about writing. Letters are often in upper case; many children find this easier at first, and sometimes a single mark represents a whole word. Parents who have some understanding of how early writing develops know that they need to provide opportunities for children to write, and that writing can happen anywhere, particularly in playful and real life contexts. Impromptu writing – whilst resting on a box or leaning on a kitchen table – for real purposes and in play – indicate that children know that they can use a range of tools to make their marks. In well-resourced homes, where families understand their role in supporting early writing, young children will, over time, move towards conventionally recognisable writing of meaningful stories, lists, and accounts.

There is a danger that home and school learning environments could be unrecognisable to the other, but it is not inevitable that two potentially different settings are in opposition in terms of young children's learning. Where early years settings support parents in learning more about how writing develops and their role in supporting their children, and where schools shun formality too early, and take account of individual children's development and build on their capabilities and interests, the home can complement the school and the school can work with the informal learning events that children have at home. Given that we know that family literacy programmes can have a positive impact on children's literacy, it is important that schools offer parents such programmes which share theory and practices with parents to help further facilitate their children's writing development.

If children can develop as willing and enthusiastic writers at home, it is important that education policy supports teachers by embracing young children's capabilities when introducing more formal aspects of writing including letter formation and spelling. This way, children who come to school believing that they *are* writers, continue to believe the same as they learn the conventions of writing and move from emergent writers to conventionally capable and confident writers.

Note

1 www.gov.uk/early-years-foundation-stage.

References

Anderson, S., et al. 2015. Helping us find our own selves: exploring father-role construction and early childhood programme engagement. *Early Child Development and Care*, 185(3), 360–376.

Baghban, M. 1984. *Our daughter learns to read and write*. New York and Delaware: International Reading Association.

Baker, C. 2013. Fathers' and mothers' home literacy involvement and children's cognitive and social emotional development: implications for family literacy programs. *Applied Developmental Science*, 17(4),184–197.

Bissex, G. 1980. *GNYS AT WRK: a child learns to write and read*. Cambridge, MA: Harvard University Press.

DeBruin-Parecki, A. and Krol-Sinclair, B. eds. 2003. *Family literacy: from theory to practice*. Newark: International Reading Association.

Deguara, J. and Nutbrown, C. 2017. Signs, symbols and schemas: understanding meaning in a child's drawings. *International Journal of Early Years Education*, 26(1), 4–23.

Department for Education (DfE). 2017. *Statutory framework for the early years foundation stage: setting the standards for learning, development and care for children from birth to five*. London: Department for Education. Available from: www.gov.uk/government/publications [Accessed 20. 05. 18].

Department for Education (DfE). 2018. *Early years foundation stage profile 2019 handbook*London: Department for Education. Available from: www.gov.uk/government/publications [Accessed 20. 05. 18].

Edwards, C. M. 2014. Maternal literacy practices and toddlers' emergent literacy skills. *Journal of Early Childhood Literacy*, 14(1), 53–79.
Ferreiro, E. and Teberosky, A. 1989. *Literacy before schooling*. Oxford: Heinemann
Goodman, Y. 1980. The roots of literacy. *Claremont Reading Conference Yearbook*, 44, 1–32.
Goodman, Y. 1986. Children coming to know literacy. In: Teale, W. H. and Sulzby, E. eds. *Emergent literacy: writing and reading*. Norwood: Ablex, 1–140.
Hall, N. 1985. When do children learn to read? *Reading*, 19(2), 57–70.
Hannon, P. 1995. *Literacy home and school: research and practice in teaching literacy with parents*. London: Falmer Press.
Hannon, P., Nutbrown, C. and Morgan, A. 2019. Effects of extending disadvantaged families' teaching of emergent literacy. *Research Papers in Education*.
Harste, J. C., Woodward, V. A. and Burke, C. L. 1984. *Language stories and literacy lessons*. Portsmouth, NH: Heinemann Educational Books.
Hassett, D. D. 2006. Signs of the times: the governance of alphabetic print over 'appropriate' and 'natural' reading development. *Journal of Early Childhood Literacy*, 6(1), 77–103.
Hughes, S. 2000. *'Toes': the Shirley Hughes collection*. London: The Bodley Head Children's Books.
Morgan, A., Nutbrown, C. and Hannon, P. 2009. Fathers' involvement in young children's literacy development: implications for family literacy programmes. *British Educational Research Journal*, 35(2), 167–185.
Niessen, N. L., Strattman, K. and Scudder, R. 2011. The influence of three emergent literacy skills on the invented spellings of 4-year-olds. *Communication Disorders Quarterly*, 32(2), 93–102.
Nutbrown, C. and Hannon, P. eds. 1997. *Preparing for early literacy education with parents: a professional development manual*. Nottingham: NES Arnold/REAL Project.
Nutbrown, C., Hannon, P. and Morgan, A. 2005. *Early literacy work with families: policy, practice and research*. London: SAGE.
Office for Standards in Education, Children's Services and Skills (Ofsted). 2018. *Bold beginnings: the reception curriculum in a sample of good and outstanding primary schools*. Manchester: Ofsted. Available from: www.gov.uk/ofsted [Accessed 20. 03. 19].
Payton, S. 1984. *Developing awareness of print: a child's first steps towards literacy*. Birmingham: Educational Review.
Ross, D. D. and Bondy, E. 1987. Communicating with parents about beginning reading instruction. *Childhood Education*, 63(4), 270–274.
Schickedanz, J. 1990. *Adam's righting revolutions*. Portsmouth, NH: Heinemann.
Weigel, D. J., Martin, S. S. and Bennett, K. K. 2006. Mothers' literacy beliefs: connections with the home literacy environment and pre-school children's literacy development. *Journal of Early Childhood Literacy*, 6(2), 191–211.
Whitmore, K. F., Martens, P., Goodman, Y. and Owocki, G. 2004. Critical lessons from the transactional perspective on early literacy research. *Journal of Early Childhood Literacy*, 4(3), 291–325.

4 Bringing more than a century of practice to writing pedagogy in the early years

Susan Feez

Introduction

In a world dominated by rapidly evolving interactive communication technologies, educators are faced with the complex challenge of supporting young children, many of whom (though not all) are immersed in digital technologies, to develop the multiple literacies it is predicted they will need for success in the 21st century. This challenge is compounded by the increasingly common requirement that children from as young as six be prepared for high stakes testing of literacy skills considered to be the foundation of future success. For 21st-century children, whose emergent writing is as likely to be composed on an electronic tablet as on paper (Ewing et al. 2016, Palaiologou 2016), it seems implausible that a pedagogy designed more than a century ago would contribute to their writing development. The focus of this chapter is, nevertheless, just such a pedagogy, a pedagogy designed in the first decade of the 20th century in Rome by Dr Maria Montessori for the benefit of street children too young to be at school but who nevertheless showed interest in writing. In response to the children's interest Montessori created an extensive repertoire of materials and activities designed not only to develop the mechanical skills needed for writing, but also the intellectual foundation that underpins what Gee (2012, p. 418) describes as 'premium grade' literacy.

For more than a century Montessori pedagogy has endured largely unchanged in Montessori schools all over the world, while conventional schooling has been adjusted in response to the ebb and flow of competing ideas and approaches. Although the Montessori approach in its original form has endured for so long, largely ignored by 20th-century educational researchers, in the 21st century Montessori schools are increasing in popularity across the world and in recent decades scholarly interest in Montessori education has also increased (Lillard 2018, Marshall 2017, Whitescarver and Cossentino 2008).

Reasons offered by Lillard (2019) for the durability of Montessori education include the social and educational advantages it offers children, the greater job satisfaction and enjoyment experienced by Montessori teachers, and parental demand. In addition, Lillard draws attention to evidence from developmental psychology that highlights the benefits to the human child of the principles underpinning the Montessori approach. These principles include the freedom to choose from an array of activities made interesting because the materials both embody learning and are interconnected. Children choosing activities they find interesting leads to concentrated attention, development of self-regulation, and intrinsic motivation uncontaminated by external rewards and punishments. Children in Montessori classrooms are also free to engage with peers across a three-year age range, supported by warm and supportive relations with teachers in an ordered and organised environment (see also Lillard 2017).

Issues in Montessori research

The implementation of Montessori pedagogy can vary from classroom to classroom. In some classrooms Dr Montessori's original blueprint is implemented with fidelity by fully trained Montessori teachers, while in others the Montessori program might be supplemented with conventional materials such as commercial puzzles or workbooks, or it might be delivered by a teacher without specialist training. In a study in the United States preschool children from a comparable demographic were enrolled in classic, high-fidelity Montessori programs, supplemented Montessori programs, and conventional highly regarded schools. These children were tested at the beginning and end of the school year for executive function, theory of mind, social problem-solving, reading, vocabulary, and mathematics. In this study Montessori pedagogy implemented with fidelity was linked 'with significant gains in student achievement and development relative to supplemented Montessori and highly regarded conventional school programs' (Lillard 2012, p. 397). High-fidelity Montessori classrooms feature prescribed sets of distinctive concrete learning materials designed and manufactured to meet exact specifications and arranged in a carefully prepared environment in which a teacher interacts with children in ways that 'promote children's self-directed engagement with those materials' (Marshall 2017, p. 2).

Evidence of gains in learning and social development made by children in high-fidelity Montessori programs relative to gains made by children in more conventional programs is accumulating in international studies (Lillard and Else-Quest 2006, Diamond and Lee 2011, Diamond 2012, 2014, Lillard 2012, 2017, 2019, Culclasure et al. 2018, Lillard and Heise 2016, Lillard et al. 2017, Ruijs 2017, Rioux et al. 2019). One finding of relevance to the theme of this volume is that by the end of elementary school when children admitted at the age of three by random lottery to high-fidelity public Montessori schools in the United States were given the same writing test as children admitted to non-Montessori public schools in the same lottery, 'Montessori children wrote more creative essays with more complex sentence structures' (Lillard and Else-Quest 2006, p. 1894). Nevertheless, it is difficult to determine experimentally which aspects of Montessori education contribute to such positive outcomes, and in what ways, because the complexity of the pedagogy makes it difficult to isolate variables (Marshall 2017).

Despite growing evidence of the positive outcomes for children in Montessori settings, measured in terms of achievement, well-being, and executive function, Lillard (2019) notes that the Montessori approach tends to be 'ignored in discussions of school reform' (p. 17). This, she argues, is because it is not commensurable with conventional schooling; when researchers try to identify elements of Montessori education that make a difference, they are asking the wrong questions, because the Montessori approach can only be understood as 'an interconnected, self-reinforcing whole' (p. 18). This perspective is pertinent to the account below of the way children learn to write in Montessori classrooms. Features of high-fidelity Montessori classrooms which contribute to their incommensurability with conventional classrooms include the three-year age range and uninterrupted three-hour work periods, the interconnected and materialised curriculum, individual and small group lessons, and children's freedom to choose their own activity and to work where, with whom, and for as long as they wish on their chosen activity. Moreover, learning in such environments is oriented towards meeting challenges through effort and persistence, a mastery orientation, rather than to impressing others, a performance orientation (Lillard et al. 2017). In summary, Montessori learning environments are designed to support the development in children of social and intellectual independence.

While the lack of longitudinal and randomised control trials continues to be identified as a limitation of Montessori studies from within the disciplines of cognitive and developmental psychology (Marshall 2017), Lillard (2012, p. 397) suggests that 'more closely observing the micro-level interactions of teachers and students' in high-fidelity Montessori environments might also be a means of gaining insights into what makes Montessori pedagogy effective. This is likely to be especially true in the case of writing development in an educational context in which children freely choose their own activity when we consider the argument made in relation to language development in general that 'what children do linguistically under experimental conditions is very little guide to what they are doing naturally, and it is necessary to back up the vast amount of experimental ... studies of children's language with ... intensive observations' (Halliday 2007, p. 184).

Researching the development of writing in a small suburban Montessori school

Building on prior social semiotic analyses of the materials and the associated lessons and activities that comprise the materialised and interconnected Montessori pedagogy designed to teach writing and reading (Feez 2007, 2008, 2010, 2011, 2019), a study of the use of these materials, with particular emphasis on the role of the materials used to teach young children about grammar, was undertaken in three high-fidelity early childhood Montessori classrooms at a small suburban Montessori school in an Australian capital city. Two classrooms at the school were Montessori preschool environments for three- to six-year-old children, with 17 children in each class, while the third was a primary school class of 20 children aged from six to nine years.

Each classroom was equipped with Montessori apparatus designed for the age group and was directed by a teacher with specialist Montessori training and one or two decades of experience working in high-fidelity Montessori settings. The school principal, a trained Montessori specialist, had more than two decades experience as a teacher in high-fidelity early childhood Montessori classrooms in both the United Kingdom and Australia before her appointment as principal. The principal noted that in the 18 months since the three teachers participating in the study had been employed, 'free choice and purposeful work is much more evident', with more emphasis on observing children and following their needs and interests, thus, enhancing the fidelity of the classrooms.

The principal, the two preschool teachers, Julie and Jane, and the primary school teacher, Kirsty, were interviewed at the beginning and the conclusion of the study over Terms 2 and 3 of the four-term school year.[1] Lessons were recorded and students' freely chosen work with the materials, and samples of student work related to the lessons were collected. While Montessori teachers are trained to observe and record children's activity before deciding when to offer a child a new lesson, the participating teachers' experience collecting classroom data for research purposes highlighted how challenging it is to record micro-interactions between children, materials, and teachers in Montessori settings. Julie, working with the three- to six-year-old age group, reported:

> The thing I've found difficult is just because the classroom is so dynamic, it's really hard, you'll be seeing something going on and then you think oh gosh I've got to take a photo of that and then you get waylaid by something else.

Where Jane could not record interactions, she 'tried to remember the conversation and quickly wrote it down'. Despite these challenges and the limitations of the small sample and short time frame, the study findings align with the accumulating evidence of the effectiveness of the Montessori approach but oriented in this case to written language development.

In each classroom, the Montessori curriculum was embodied in the classic array of distinctive objects initially designed by Maria Montessori. The objects are combined with movement and language in sequences of lessons and activities that interconnect to become a web of detailed instructional pathways through which children are apprenticed into both everyday and educational knowledge (Feez 2011). The pathways are materialised; each object, or set of objects, has a specified location on a shelf, the physical location reflecting its location in a child's progression through each domain of knowledge.

All three teachers had trained in the pedagogy over a year of full-time study for the three-year age range they are now teaching. They were trained to organise and display the objects in ways that appeal to children and to engage children with the objects in precise, captivating lessons matched to each child's age, stage of development and interests, and to observe children's freely chosen use of the objects in order to make judgements about what to teach next. During training, the teachers also interpreted, recorded, and illustrated the Montessori repertoire for the three-year age range in personalised multimodal 'albums' assessed by internationally certified trainers. To investigate writing development in a Montessori setting, it was necessary to locate the teaching of writing in the web of Montessori instructional pathways and to understand the precise, almost choreographed ideal delivery of the lessons recorded in the albums, while also monitoring the implementation of these lessons and the activity they generated in the participating classrooms.

Learning to write in a Montessori setting

Overview

Montessori writing lessons and activities offer children two separate but parallel developmental pathways for learning to write: one mechanical and one intellectual. In Montessori preschool classrooms these two pathways lead children to writing before they learn to read. The mechanical pathway comprises two parallel developmental trajectories: learning how to hold and control a pencil, and (for alphabetic writing) learning to distinguish individual sounds in the stream of spoken language and to match the sounds with letters. The intellectual pathway also has two parallel developmental trajectories: learning to use letters to (re)compose the sounds of the language as written words, and learning to organise the words into written text.

Montessori writing lessons and activities are matched to children's sensitive periods, periods of heightened interest which signal the opening of 'windows of [developmental] opportunity' (Lawrence 1998, p. 15). The notion of sensitive periods was credited by Vygotsky (1986/1934) as a precursor of his theory of the zone of proximal development: 'For each subject of instruction, there is a period when its influence is most fruitful because the child is most receptive to it. It has been called the *sensitive period* by Montessori and other educators' (p. 189; emphasis in original).

Vygotsky continues by describing Montessori's success in teaching four-year-old and five-year-old children to write as 'a striking example of the strong influence that instruction can have when the corresponding functions have not yet fully matured'. In the Montessori tradition, the child is in a sensitive period for learning spoken language from birth, for organising the sounds of the language from about three and for attending to written language from about four.

Foundation knowledge and skills

When children at about age three enter high-fidelity Montessori preschool environments such as those prepared by Julie and Jane, they encounter two foundation knowledge domains: the exercises of practical life and the exercises of the senses (for an introduction, see Feez 2010).

The practical life domain is the domain of everyday knowledge. Familiar everyday routines in the surrounding culture are recontextualised in lessons, sometimes called 'how-to' lessons, and in self-chosen follow-up exercises through which children learn elements of social interaction, control of movement, self-care, and care of the environment. When a child shows interest or readiness, the teacher models the exercise, and children then practise for as long and as often as they wish, with the teacher adding points of interest, incrementally more challenging variations, and further complexity, to sustain interest. These exercises not only build children's social independence and confidence, they also build executive function (Diamond and Lee 2011, Diamond 2012, 2014), hand-eye coordination, fine-motor control, and powers of concentration, a configuration of skills and dispositions that prepare for learning to write. Practical life lessons modelled explicitly to the smallest children include how to choose a book from the class library, how to carry a book with two hands, how to turn the pages of a book, and how to return the book to the shelf. Many practical life activities extend into craft activities, including making small books and binding them with ribbon. In Kirsty's class a group of six-year-old children produced little books about animals which they would bind 'and put in the library for everybody to read'.

The sense exercises involve children solving sensory puzzles using sets of manipulable objects Montessori (1967/1948, pp. 176–177) described as 'materialised abstractions'. Each set of objects isolates and varies one sensory quality, such as sound, texture, colour, shape, size, or volume, in equal incremental intervals from one object to the next, while all other properties are held constant. The teacher models precise movements for manipulating the objects, such as accurate tracing around shapes or gripping tiny knobs or cubes with finger and thumb. Usually the puzzles are solved by matching or grading to build arrays harmonious to the sense being exercised. Through subsequent exercise sequences, children learn to perceive and later recall increasingly fine distinctions. At the same time, children are given precise language to label their perceptions in terms of culturally meaningful categories (e.g. volume, taste, shape, size, colour, musical notes), categories which are interesting at an age when children are striving to classify their experience (Painter 1999, p. 78).

The refinement of movement, perception, and memory enabled by the sense exercises further refines the fine-motor skills and hand-eye coordination needed to control a pencil and prepares children for distinguishing between the phonemes of spoken language and the shapes of the letters. The sense exercises also develop intellectual tools that can be applied to imaginative and creative tasks, such as visual arts, music, dramatic play, and creative writing.

While the foundation knowledge domains described above were not discussed by the two participating preschool teachers during interviews, the practical life and sense exercises were observed in constant use in their classrooms. In Montessori settings, the contribution of children's work in these domains to the development of writing is assumed. In Kirsty's classroom for six- to nine-year-olds, instead of practical life exercises, children solved practical and social challenges through discussion, role-play, and research, and the sense exercises had evolved into lesson and activity sequences used to teach educational knowledge, including mathematics, science, history, geography, and language. Traces of the sense exercises were especially visible in the materials children in this classroom used to build knowledge about grammar and spelling.

Spoken language preparation

Also assumed in Montessori settings is the role spoken language development plays in young children learning to write and then read. From the time children first enter the preschool, they are engaged in games designed to enrich vocabulary, to build knowledge about the different ways people use language, and to distinguish individual phonemes in the stream of spoken language. These include energetic naming games in which small children are asked to find named objects and stand beside them. The games are extended by adding adjectives to the names of objects or contrasting the names of objects with words representing actions.

A popular vocabulary enrichment activity in Julie's classroom is an activity that prepares for later learning about adjectives. Julie reported how much the three-year-old children enjoyed this game, as illustrated in this interaction:

JULIE: Can you bring me a horse from *The Farm* [a miniature farm used in language games]

The child brings a horse.

JULIE: It's a lovely horse – *shakes her head* – but it's not the one I want. Would you like a clue?

The child nods.

JULIE: The *white* horse.

Julie described how the children soon ask her for the adjective clue straight away. When they play the game independently with their friends, she hears them asking 'Would you like a clue?'. She concluded:

> It's like a joke they all share. So even though they don't know it's the adjective that they're wanting they're ... looking for the word that will give them the clue that will describe the animal ... like the white horse or the black horse.

Further language enrichment activities involve collections of pictures of different types of things in their environment, for example, fruit, furniture, cutlery, clothing, or transport. Children name the images they recognise, learn the names of the others, and mix and sort the collections, which are changed regularly to maintain interest. Some picture collections prepare for later learning, such as sets of different types of animals, plants, musical instruments, and tools, or images of an object, such as a flower or a tree, and its parts.

Picture collections were popular in Jane's class during the study. She described two young boys looking at the collection of pictures of African animals unable to decide which was the cheetah and which the jaguar. Jane helped them research the animals, showing them pictures and reading text aloud; 'then they went off to do their own work about it and we had a big discussion about rosettes which are the circles on the leopard skin'.

In Montessori preschool classrooms, children are introduced to different ways people use written language. The teacher reads aloud factual accounts of real people, things, and events, perhaps illustrated by an object or photograph, including recounts or biographies related to familiar or famous events or people, or accounts of the lives of animals or plants, or where products such as milk, glass, or paper come from. Younger children have many opportunities to listen to and learn rhymes and poems, with their attention drawn to the sound patterns, while older children are introduced to imaginary stories, the teacher often reading children's literature out loud in serial form, for example, in the afternoon while children either listen or choose quiet work such as drawing, sewing, or handwriting.

All the teachers in the study read regularly to the children, both factual texts and children's literature. All three credited reading aloud to the children with kindling interest in writing that was not there when they first started teaching these classes.

The sound game is a daily activity in Montessori preschools, including in the two participating preschool classrooms. This game and its many variations build phonemic awareness; children learn to discriminate between and manipulate phonemes in sequences of increasingly challenging games. The teacher first asks a small group of children to listen to a sound, which she carefully articulates before they say it for themselves. She thinks aloud of words that use the sound, inviting the children to help, first initial consonant sounds, and later median and final sounds including vowels, as well as digraph sounds. For very young children, the teacher might limit the game to two or three objects chosen because their names begin with contrasting sounds, ensuring success before more challenging variations are introduced.

In all three participating classrooms, children were encouraged to share important objects or stories with the teacher and one or two classmates in small groups. In an activity known as the 'Question Game', the teacher uses questions to help children structure their talk effectively: *What is it? What is it made of? Where did it come from?* or *Who is the story about? Where did it happen? What happened first?* Children are shown how to display objects or organise photographs on a story board to guide the describing or retelling. A variation of this approach was used by Jane when a group of children arrived with news of a leopard seal washed up on the beach near the school. The children spontaneously brought in newspaper cuttings about the event to share, and drew pictures of what they saw. Jane used a question game to help the children retell what happened, foreshadowing a subsequent shared writing activity.

The development of mechanical writing skills

In Montessori settings, children learn the mechanical writing skills, holding and controlling a pencil, and sound-letter correspondence, by interacting with two sets of materials: metal insets and sandpaper letters. The metal insets, metal geometric shapes set into metal frames, are used in a sequence of increasingly precise tracing, colouring, and design activities during which children build the motor skills needed for handwriting. This work further extends children's concentration while building the pencil control needed for both handwriting and drawing.

The sandpaper letters are (traditionally) cursive letters cut out of fine sandpaper and glued onto smooth coloured cards in contrasting colours, typically blue cards for vowels and red cards for consonants. After playing the sound game successfully, children aged about three years are presented with sandpaper letters in sets of three or four letters at a time. Each letter is traced with a flowing continuous movement, the sound pronounced as the movement finishes. Initially, children are introduced to letters with contrasting shapes and sounds, but gradually more letters are added to the child's repertoire followed by a set of key digraphs, which are also introduced as sandpaper letters, each digraph glued on a green background. Children later trace the outlines of the letters they know in a variety of media, including chalk, crayon, and sewing cards.

The sandpaper letters have been introduced to three-year-old children in Montessori settings ever since Maria Montessori observed in her first classroom that children of this age chose to work with sandpaper letters out of interest and acquired knowledge of sounds and letters easily but that this interest waned, making learning sound-letter correspondence more difficult as they grow older (Montessori 2012). For both Julie and Jane, children learning sound-letter correspondence between the age of three and four is critical if they are to make progress with the many Montessori activities that involve writing and reading. Older children yet to pass this milestone were particular concerning for Julie: 'I haven't been able to move on just yet because … my older children (aged five) are just learning their sounds.' She elaborated her concern in terms of sensitive periods:

> I found that when I came, the children were barely knowing their sounds and were doing them past the sensitive period so sandpaper letters weren't [so helpful] … I was actually having to pull out all stops [for] these children to learn their sounds … most of them went up to Kirsty knowing their sounds thank goodness but this new group … they're sort of driven so the sandpaper letters they've picked up like that so most of my three-year-olds are probably three quarters of the way through.

In a study of one child's 'natural' language development from two to five years, Painter (1999) found that from the age of three-and-a-half, the child began to attend to the letters in words and to display interest in how the letter shapes are formed. At this stage, however, although the child was 'talking about symbols, he was considering them as material entities' (p. 115). With the sandpaper letters, and later moveable alphabet, children of this age in Montessori settings manipulate the letters of the alphabet in material form, while the parallel metal inset work builds pencil control that children apply to handwriting when they are ready.

The development of the intellectual skills needed for writing

The development of the intellectual skills needed for writing in Montessori settings begins with preschool children (re)composing the sounds of their own language with a moveable alphabet. They also take part in activities that reveal how words are organised as text.

When children in Montessori settings have learnt, by playing the sound game, to analyse and decompose their own spoken language into constituent sounds, and have learnt, using sandpaper letters, the correspondence between up to ten vowel and consonant sounds and letters, they are introduced to the moveable alphabet, a set of loose letters stored in a box. The letters of the moveable alphabet are the same size as the sandpaper letters, colour-coded to sustain the vowel-consonant distinction, a distinction not taught to the children explicitly until they are about six. Parallel to their work with sandpaper letters, children use the letters of the moveable alphabet to recompose words as writing on a mat on the floor. Work with the moveable alphabet is described by Montessori (1967/1948, p. 216) as 'an exercise of the intellect freed from mechanical activities and not held down by the need to imitate letters in writing'. Using the moveable alphabet, children in Montessori classrooms write before they read; they compose their own meanings in writing, before interpreting the meanings written down by others. 'The ability to write [is] the result of the analysis of the words [the child] possesses' (Montessori 1955, p. 97).

If graphophonic awareness and pencil control are developed by the age of four, an age when children experience a sensitive period in written language, according to the Montessori tradition, the transition to writing (and reading) occurs with ease. At the age of four, the child studied by Painter (1999) echoes this trajectory, when he became interested in analysing words for sounds. He thus made the transition from conceiving of letters as material objects to using them as representations of phonemes used to make meanings.

> As a graph, a letter is a material object to be discriminated and decomposed ... But as a representation of a phoneme, a letter construes something much less tangible – not just a sound qua sound, like a bark or a crash, but a sound as a form of semiotic realization.
>
> (Painter 1999, p. 125)

The traditional sequence of Montessori activities involving the sound game, sandpaper letters, and moveable alphabet was followed with fidelity in the preschool classrooms participating in the study, with children by the age of four transitioning from tracing sandpaper letters as material objects to composing words on mats with the moveable alphabet, using the letters to represent meanings. Julie described how at one stage in her classroom the interest of four-year-old children in writing with the moveable alphabet was further sparked by her reading to them and 'they just kept writing and writing … mats and mats'. On another day there was a burst of moveable alphabet she described as 'fabulous' when three boys who 'didn't know a lot of their sounds' moved onto the moveable alphabet 'with the help of the older one … spurring themselves on'.

By the age of six, the age when children in the study moved from the preschool to Kirsty's class, they begin to find composing with the moveable alphabet too laborious to maintain the flow of meaning, especially when they want to write longer texts. The parallel metal inset work develops pencil control so handwriting can take over as children in their own time abandon the moveable alphabet. In Montessori's words, 'written language is acquired and improved through exercises which are *akin to*, but which are *not*, writing' (1964 [1909/1912], p. 292; emphasis added).

In Maria Montessori's first classroom, after the children used sandpaper letters, metal insets, and moveable alphabet for a few months, they began covering the walls and floor with words written in chalk (Montessori 1964 [1909/1912]). News of this explosion into writing by such unlikely children who appeared to be teaching themselves propelled Montessori and her pedagogy into the international spotlight. Montessori's use of indirect preparation to teach the mechanical skills of writing was endorsed by Vygotsky (1978/1935, p. 118) who described it as 'organised development rather than learning'. He advocated the same approach to teach 'the internal aspect of written language', criticising Montessori for not taking this step. Montessori, however, apparently unknown to Vygotsky, did take this step, by using grammar as a means for organising the next phase of literacy development, a phase in which children's attention is turned to meaning-making in connected discourse and the intellectual demands this places on writers.

In Jane's class, the children initially labelled objects and pictures with the moveable alphabet but with little interest in reading them back. They later began reading printed single word labels and matching them to objects and pictures organised in sets, an activity the children 'loved to do', while many began reading small books. Montessori teachers interpret children's interest in reading back words composed on a mat with the moveable alphabet as evidence of their readiness to move beyond 'mechanical' writing to preparing for the intellectual demands of written composition.

Five-year-old children in the Montessori preschool explore the composition of written language in an extended series of grammar games foreshadowed in the spoken vocabulary enrichment games enjoyed by three-year-olds. These games continue as children make the transition from pre-school to primary school. The grammar activities begin with lessons illustrating the 'function', of each type of word, including the function of words in the 'noun family' (noun group: *article, adjective, noun*) and verb family (clause: *verb, adverb, pronoun*), as well as the 'servant' words (*conjunction, preposition*) and *interjection*. Noun groups are handwritten onto slips of paper, initially by the teacher and later by the children themselves, to label moveable objects arranged in a miniature environment, such as a model farm or a dolls' house. Verbs and adverbs are handwritten onto paper slips to compose commands for the children to act out. Children ask questions to distinguish each word or group of words on the basis of function, for example, the word that tells you 'which one', or the word that tells you the action. Next they tear apart the words on the paper slips, and 'transpose' them to experiment with word order, often finding the results hilarious.

As well as engaging children in extended writing and reading practice, the grammar activities enable them to *play* with written language, just as they play with spoken language. All the teachers in the study spoke about how much they enjoyed watching the children discover that changing word order in grammar structures changes the meaning, and can even turn sense into nonsense. Julie video-recorded a particularly boisterous transposition game played by a group of five-year-old boys, the peals of laughter attracting the fascinated attention of much younger children. The games conclude when the children re-order the words meaningfully, and label each one with a moveable 'grammar symbol'.

Each grammar symbol, one for each part of speech, is a geometric shape varying in colour and size in ways which draw attention to the function of the word and its relation to other words. A large red circle symbolises the energetic verb contrasting with the large black equilateral triangle symbolising the stable noun. Smaller orange circles symbolise adverbs, while articles and adjectives, part of the noun's family, are smaller blue triangles. When the symbols are placed over the words in a word group, phrase, clause, or sentence, the grammar pattern is materialised. In this way the children use the moveable grammar symbols to analyse the stream of meaning in written language, just as they used the moveable alphabet to analyse the stream of sound in spoken language.

By the age of six, when children transition to the primary school, they are introduced to technical terms such as *article, adjective, noun*, and *noun family*. They also embark on a set of activities in which the grammar symbols re-appear as moveable wooden circles, triangles, and arrows. These are used to analyse sentences, often taken from favourite books or composed by the children themselves, handwritten or printed on slips of paper. For example, in Kirsty's class, a seven-year-old child wrote the following sentence on a paper slip:

Tim and Cody ate their lunch slowly.

Kirsty then guided the child through the following questions:

KIRSTY: What is the first question we ask?
CODY: What is the verb?
KIRSTY: And what is the verb?
CODY: ate [tearing the verb out of the sentence and placing the verb slip on the red wooden circle in the array]
KIRSTY: Next question we ask?
CODY: Um … who ate?

At the end of the activity, the sentence parts are arranged like satellites around the verb on the red circle, with the colour-coded wooden symbols highlighting the function of each sentence part.

Parallel to the work with functions of words and sentence analysis, children engage with activities that build vocabulary and spelling skills using small coloured moveable alphabets, charts, and booklets to learn about digraphs, morphemes, and sight words. In the participating classrooms, this work extended across the preschool and primary classrooms.

When children enter the primary class, Kirsty tells the 'great story' of writing, a story told in all Montessori settings to children of this age. Children are shown pictures of early rock art and are asked to imagine how humans might have invented spoken language, before being told the story of writing and the alphabet we use today. They are told that while speech makes us human, writing makes us immortal. The story is told dramatically but economically to spark children's interest in finding out more about this history for themselves. From this point, when new sight words or technical terms are introduced in any curriculum area, children are told stories about the etymology of the words, thus layering knowledge of morphemes over knowledge of sounds.

Between the ages of seven and nine children are introduced to the grammar boxes, a series of colour-coded boxes, each with a large compartment holding reading cards plus small compartments holding small single word cards colour-coded according to function. Children read the text on the large cards, acting it out to experience differences in meaning. In Kristy's class, Cody, aged seven, was recorded reading and acting out the following two sentences written on a large adverb grammar box card:

Walk to the window *constantly* clapping your hands.
Walk to the window *occasionally* clapping your hands.

He then used colour-coded individual cards to reconstruct the sentences and place grammar symbols over the cards to reinforce the grammar pattern. By such means, grammar becomes, in Dr Montessori's (1965 [1916/1918], p. 7), words, 'the amiable and indispensable help to the construction of connected discourse'. This help is exemplified in the following comment from Kirsty about the work with the grammar boxes of seven- and eight-year-old children in her class:

> I think they really connect with grammar and language a lot more because of the concrete materials and that ability to be able to take it off the shelf and create the sentences and have their hands reaching for hopefully the right compartment where they're going to find the word and then putting the symbols on.

In the later primary years, the grammar symbols are used to study and appreciate the writing styles of favourite authors.

A culture of writing

During the interviews the teachers did not always find it easy to articulate how the different strands of the learning pathways outlined above contributed to the writing culture so visible to an observer in all three Montessori classrooms participating in the study. One exception was the storyboard about the leopard seal found on the beach. The storyboard was taped onto a window at the entrance of Jane's preschool classroom. After the spoken language retelling, Jane asked questions to help the children reconstruct what happened in writing. She wrote the sentence they jointly composed onto the storyboard.

> A leopard seal lay on the beach. A cookie-cutter shark bit it.

The children drew grammar symbols over each of the words in the text. Jane linked this work to prior grammar lessons: 'In this work are all the symbols learned so far: the noun family (noun, adjective, article), the verb, and now including the preposition.' The children had not yet learned about pronouns so the word 'it' did not have a symbol.

The goal of the parallel Montessori pathways to writing – the mechanical and the intellectual – is that children will integrate both to become independent writers of literary as well as factual texts. Julie reported that she had taken a long time to encourage writing in her preschool class but that she felt that reading the children chapter books and factual books, and asking them to recall what they read had sparked interest. She added: 'I also had a couple of girls who were really interested in writing songs so they started to write these songs … it was like an opening really.'

A culture of writing was particularly visible in Kirsty's early years primary classroom. Writing work samples collected in Kirsty's classroom included imaginative stories comprising multiple chapters, poetry, factual texts, and extended written self-chosen project work following up topics from across the curriculum areas. Some samples were handwritten in cursive handwriting; others were typed and printed on computers. Kirsty maintained that the writing culture emerged because 'they have that freedom' in an environment that allows children to communicate 'about all manner of things that you wouldn't have in an environment that was more controlled'. This culture Kirsty admitted 'took a while to establish – but now they just love it'.

Like Julie, Kirsty felt she had built children's interest in writing by reading to them 'a whole variety of literature', including classics, chapter books, poetry, and factual books. Nevertheless, it seems clear that the proliferation of writing was also a function of multiple strands of the interconnected Montessori curriculum coming together in the children's work. These included the repertoire of lessons and activities along both developmental pathways, the mechanical and the intellectual that support writing development directly, as well as other areas of the Montessori curriculum, as illustrated in Kirsty's explanation of the writing samples produced in her classroom:

> they're writing, they're really writing, they're producing volumes of information, project writing, story writing, poetry … that's just kind of what's expected … there's just these kinds of outpourings of information and story writing going on at the moment. A lot of the older ones have done invertebrate zoology and vertebrates … they've a good knowledge of that whole animal classification … so that's the knowledge that's underneath so doing the research though is very much generated by what animals they are interested in and so they just set up to do a project … they know they're not allowed to plagiarise that they have to paraphrase the information so I showed quite a few of them how to take notes when they were reading information and then some of them just read it and just write down the bits they're interested in … I mean – I haven't done much … I've done some more structured report writing with the older children but this is stuff that they just generate and they just do because they want to and have an interest in and then they illustrate them all and you know they love it they absolutely love it.

Traces of earlier grammar lessons can be heard in these interactions recorded when a seven-year-old child was discussing with Kirsty an imaginary story he was writing:

KIRSTY: When you write 'pointy hat' I can imagine the hat much better and it immediately makes me think of a witch.
TIM: Yes, it's a describing word. If you just wrote 'hat', it would be any old hat.
TIM: (later in the discussion): What is 'great' in the grammar boxes?
KIRSTY: Give me a context.
TIM: He took the great ruby from the sword.
KIRSTY: What is 'great' describing?
TIM: Oh yeah! It's describing a noun. It's an adjective.

In other examples, children used colours to identify the function of a word, for example, 'It's the blue one' to identify an adjective, and Cody was heard saying in passing to a six-year-old newly arrived in the class taking part in a first grammar box lesson: 'Grammar helps you write stuff.'

Since the conclusion of the study, participating children have sat the mandatory Year 3 Australian National Assessment Program Literacy and Numeracy (NAPLAN) tests. While the demographic of the children's families is mostly middle-class and comparatively affluent, the small cohort includes children learning English as an additional language as well as a group of children with learning difficulties. Nevertheless, the cohort achieved results on the NAPLAN writing test well above the national average, echoing the results recorded in the study conducted by Lillard and Else-Quest (2006) in the United States.

Conclusion

In Montessori early years classrooms around the world the teaching of writing draws on a pedagogy that can lay claim to more than a century of practice. Because this same pedagogy is still in use today, it provides a rare opportunity to investigate an enduring educational practice through which children for more than a hundred years and in more than a hundred countries have become writers.

The account presented in this chapter of writing development across Montessori preschool and early years classrooms suggests that children educated in these settings are provided with opportunities to develop not only foundation mechanical sound-letter correspondence and handwriting skills but also the intellectual skills needed to control the written language 'used in research, empirical reasoning, and logical argumentation' described by Gee (2012, p. 418) as 'premium grade' literacy. That those who master 'premium grade' literacy also master 'premium grade digital literacy' (p. 419) perhaps explains growing interest in the Montessori approach in the 21st century. This chapter's brief excursion into the areas of the Montessori curriculum that support writing development in the early years represents endorsement of Lillard's proposal that the Montessori approach 'warrants a close look and more research to determine whether it could be a useful alternative model for schooling in the twenty-first century' (2019, p. 21).

Note

1 These names are pseudonyms.

References

Culclasure, B., Fleming, D. J. and Riga, G. 2018. *An evaluation of Montessori education in South Carolina's public schools*. Greenville: The Riley Institute at Furman University.

Diamond, A. 2012. Activities and programs that improve children's executive functions. *Current Directions in Psychological Science*, 21(5), 335–341.

Diamond, A. 2014. Understanding executive functions: what helps or hinders them and how executive functions and language development mutually support one another. *Perspectives on Language and Literacy*, 40(2), 7–11.

Diamond, A. and Lee, K. 2011. How can we help children succeed in the 21st century? What the scientific evidence shows aids executive function development in children 4–12 years of age. *Science*, 333(6045), 959–964.

Ewing, R., Callow, J. and Rushton, K. 2016. *Language and literacy development in early childhood*. Melbourne: Cambridge University Press.

Feez, S. 2007. *Montessori's mediation of meaning: a social semiotic perspective*. PhD thesis. University of Sydney, Australia.

Feez, S. 2008. Multimodal representation of educational meanings in Montessori pedagogy. In: Unsworth, L. ed. *Multimodal semiotics: functional analysis in contexts of education*. New York: Continuum, 201–215.

Feez, S. 2010. *Montessori and early childhood*. London: SAGE.

Feez, S. 2011. Discipline and freedom in early childhood education. In: Christie, F. and Maton, K. eds. *Disciplinarity: functional linguistic and sociological perspectives*. New York: Continuum, 151–172.

Feez, S. 2019. Multimodality in the Montessori classroom. In: de Silva Joyce, H. and Feez, S. eds. *Multimodality across classrooms*. Abingdon: Routledge, 30–48.

Gee, J. 2012. The old and the new in the new digital literacies. *The Educational Forum*, 76, 418–420.

Halliday, M. A. K. 2007. *Language and education* (Volume 9 in the Collected Works of M. A. K. Halliday; edited by J. J. Webster). New York: Continuum.

Lawrence, L. 1998. *Montessori read and write: a parents' guide to literacy for children*. London: Ebury Press.

Lillard, A. S. 2012. Preschool children's development in classic Montessori, supplemented Montessori, and conventional programs. *Journal of School Psychology*, 50(3), 379–401.

Lillard, A. S. 2017. *Montessori: the science behind the genius*. 3rd ed. New York: Oxford University Press.

Lillard, A. S. 2018. Rethinking education: Montessori's approach. *Current Directions in Psychological Science*, 27, 395–400.

Lillard, A. S. 2019. Shunned and admired: Montessori, self-determination and a case for radical school reform. *Educational Psychology Review*, 31(4), 939–965.

Lillard, A. S. and Else-Quest, N. 2006. Evaluating Montessori education. *Science*, 313 (5795), 1893–1894.

Lillard, A. S. and Heise, M. J. 2016. Removing supplementary materials from Montessori classrooms changed child outcomes. *Journal of Montessori Research*, 2(1), 16–26.

Lillard, A. S., et al. 2017. Montessori preschool elevates and equalizes child outcomes: a longitudinal study. *Frontiers in Psychology*, 8, 1–19.

Marshall, C. 2017. Montessori education: a review of the evidence base. *npj Science of Learning*, 2(11), 1–9.

Montessori, M. 1955. *The formation of man*. Madras: Kalakshetra Publications.

Montessori, M. 1964 [1909 Italian/1912 English]. *The Montessori method*. New York: Schocken Books.

Montessori, M. 1965 [1916 Italian/1918 English]. *The advanced Montessori method: scientific pedagogy as applied to the education of children from seven to eleven years, Volume 1 Spontaneous activity in education*. Madras: Kalakshetra Publications.

Montessori, M. 1967/1948. *The discovery of the child*. New York: Ballantine Books. (A revision of *The Montessori method* first published in 1909.)

Montessori, M. 2012. *The 1946 London lectures* (edited by Annette Haines). Amsterdam: Montessori-Pierson Publishing Company.
Painter, C. 1999. *Learning through language in early childhood*. New York: Continuum.
Palaiologou, I. 2016. Children under five and digital technologies: implications for early years pedagogy. *European Early Childhood Education Research Journal*, 24(1), 5–24.
Rioux, J., Ewing, B. and Cooper, T. J. 2019. The Montessori method, Aboriginal students and Linnaean zoology taxonomy teaching: three-staged lesson. *The Australian Journal of Indigenous Education*, 1–11.
Ruijs, N. 2017. The effects of Montessori education: evidence from admission lotteries. *Economics of Education Review*, 61, 19–34.
Vygotsky, L. S. 1978/1935. *Mind in society: the development of higher psychological processes*. Cambridge, MA: Harvard University Press.
Vygotsky, L. S. 1986/1934. *Thought and language*. Cambridge, MA: The MIT Press.
Whitescarver, K. and Cossentino, J. 2008. Montessori and the mainstream: a century of reform on the margins. *Teachers College Record*, 110, 2571–2600.

5 Teaching writing in digital times
Stories from the early years

Clare Dowdall

Introduction

Supporting young children as they become writers can be regarded as a major undertaking for early years educators, who work in contexts that are informed by a range of evolving forces. As Marsh outlines in the foreword to Burnett and Merchant's call to 'Rethink Primary Literacy' (Marsh in Burnett and Merchant 2018), we are living in an age of acceleration; an age where teachers in particular might question how to adequately prepare children for an unknown future, amidst rapid technological and social change. This chapter presents the views and experiences of two early years teachers as they endeavour to support young children's writing development within this evolving context. Drawing from one focus group conversation, the particular field of cultural production (Bourdieu 1993) in which they work, and the forces that impact their practice are considered. The chapter reports specifically on the teachers' views about use of digital technologies as they help children to find their voices and embark on schooled forms of composition.

The increased emphasis on accountability and performativity within literacy education has been well documented in recent years. Vivid accounts of the impact of testing and high stakes accountability on the pedagogy for children's literacy are articulated in literature originating from a range of settings, including the United States, Australia, and England (see, for example, Cremin and Myhill 2012, Moss 2017, Peel 2017, Simpson 2017). In England, in early years education, accountability-driven practice and policy continues to grow. Statutory testing in the form of phonics screening for Year 1 children (aged 5–6) has been conducted annually since 2012, and a statutory baseline assessment for all children, to be completed within six weeks of starting school (aged 4–5), is to be introduced in 2020. The content domain for this test includes 'literacy, communication and language', and will assess children's vocabulary, phonological awareness, early reading, and early comprehension (Standards and Testing Agency 2019).

While the baseline test does not include content relating to mark making or writing, statutory requirements for young children's writing are introduced in the English national curriculum programmes of study at Year 1 and 2 (ages 5–7) (DfE 2013), listed under the headings: transcription, handwriting, composition, vocabulary, grammar, and punctuation. These facets are assessed using a 'Teacher Assessment Framework' at the end of Key Stage 1 (children aged 6–7 years). This framework contains a series of 'pupil can' statements that support teachers to judge whether children have achieved an 'expected standard' for writing in relation to the national curriculum statutory requirements (Standards and Testing Agency 2018). Together, these curriculum and accountability measures have the potential to frame the possibilities for young children's learning and, in particular, the writing curriculum and associated pedagogies. These measures are regarded by many in England as pervasive and unwarranted, and in response to their uptake, a growing coalition of teachers, parents, subject associations, clinical specialists, professional bodies, trade unions, and research associations (amongst others) have launched an online campaign entitled *More Than A Score*[1] to express their concern at the possible negative impact of such pressing formal assessment on young learners.

Alongside this accountability context, the increasing uptake of digital technologies in formal learning environments can be seen to be impacting education policy and curriculum. This is evidenced by the publication and implementation of numerous policy documents and advisory frameworks designed for local, national, and international audiences, to support educators as they prepare young people and adults for living and participating in digital times.[2] In Ireland, for example, the Digital Learning Framework for Primary Schools (Department of Education and Skills (Ireland) 2018) has recently been introduced and evaluated for its efficacy in impacting teachers' practice in this area. Accompanying the framework, case study exemplars have been made available, featuring teachers using digital technologies to promote literacy. The label 'Digital School of Distinction' has been created and is awarded to schools identified as leading the way in implementing the use of technology to support learning (see www.digitalschools.ie).

It can be observed that each digital policy document and framework, regardless of its genesis and context, aims to promote the integration of digital technologies and related skills into people's everyday lives, with the intention of securing better and more successful futures for individuals and the economies in which they operate. Part of this remit necessarily involves the development of digital literacies amongst young children and their educators. However, the guidance found within policy documentation is often generated to apply across the total population, rather than for young literacy learners, and the aims are necessarily broad-based. The European Union's DigComp 2.1 Digital Competence Framework for Citizens (Carretero et al. 2017) is a good example of this.[3] The framework outlines eight levels of proficiency against five competences, namely: information and data literacy; communication and collaboration; digital content creation; safety; and problem solving (Carretero et al. 2017, p. 11). Digital competence is illustrated using classroom-based examples; yet how digital literacy is to be achieved, or how these digital competencies can serve as a conduit for the promotion of the literacy and writing skills that are stipulated in associated local curricula, is not stated.

For educators attempting to develop young children's writing, this lack of specificity is problematic, and teachers can struggle to embed the digital practices that they recognise as being supportive, especially within a context that is so securely bounded by accountability measures (Dowdall 2019). A tension between the interpretation of literacy as a set of discrete skills (as presented in curriculum) and literacy as part of a much larger digital 'becoming' can be observed. This is an argument that resonates with scholars who have adopted the perspectives of the New Literacy Studies, and in particular, the foundational work of Brian Street (Street 1998) to define autonomous and ideological models of literacy in relation to their work. From this perspective, the autonomous model can be adopted to construct literacy as a 'set of decontextualised self-contained skills or sub-skills … prevalent in accountability cultures'; whereas the ideological model conjures a context dependent model that:

> recognises the diversity and complexity of children's literacy practices that … are everyday, situated, multiple, and that … make use of a range of tools (pencils, paper, touchscreens, keyboards) and multiple modes of expression e.g. words, spoken and written, drawings, digital designs and so forth.
>
> (Cremin et al. 2015, p. 12)

This tension introduces challenge into the working practices of early years educators as they attempt to reconcile the potential for the use of new technologies with a curriculum that is locked into traditional paper and skills-based versions of literacy. Recent work by scholars involved in the European DigiLitEY COST Action[4] recognises that there is an urgent need for a unified research approach to develop educational provision for our youngest learners in a digitally mediated era. In their White Paper composed for this COST Action, Marsh et al. (2017) argue that two binaries affect the abilities of early years educators to integrate digital technologies into their classroom practices: a binary that sets conventional and new conceptions of early childhood literacies against each other; and a binary that separates teachers' own use of digital technologies from the integration of these technologies into the classroom. They conclude that to equip the youngest learners for a digitally mediated future, teacher continuing professional development (CPD), conducted in supportive communities of practice, is needed. However, Burnett and Merchant (2018) argue that while much has been written about how technology might or should change schooling, and how children's literacies and lives are inflected and transformed by digital media, little practical guidance for those working with the youngest learners exists to actively enable teachers to empower children's creative and critical engagement with digital media.

To underpin this argument and frame this chapter theoretically, I draw from Pierre Bourdieu's considerations of power, positioning, and social (re)production in art, literature, education, and the social world more generally. Along with their homes and communities, the early years settings that children inhabit can be described as complex textual landscapes that contribute to their literate identities (Carrington 2005). These landscapes significantly impact the experience of becoming a writer, and therefore the attitudes to writing and proficiencies that children and their teachers develop. The identities and positions that are formed within these textual landscapes can be framed from numerous 'positional' perspectives: as culturally bounded; as negotiated; and as discursively constructed through place and time (see Golden and Pandya 2018). Given any or all of these framings, in these textual landscapes, a range of social, material, and political forces interplay to construct a unique learning environment. These forces include: the pedagogies and values of the teaching and learning communities who inhabit the landscape; the material resources including the paper and screen-based texts and digital technologies that are utilised in the environment; and the curricula and pervading accountability measures that are imposed on the landscape from within and beyond the setting (Carrington 2005).

These forces can be collectively constructed as a field of cultural production where positions and dispositions mutually constitute each other (Bourdieu 1993). In this 'field', constitutive structures produce individual habitus or 'systems of durable transposable dispositions' that in turn operate as structuring structures (Bourdieu 1977, p. 72). In the account above, these constitutive structures might include interplay between the accountability context as grealised in the early years curriculum for writing; the impact of technological change upon the settings in which children's writing is developed; the histories of the educators and the learners; and the subjectivities of the teachers and young learners who 'struggle' as they themselves co-construct and are constructed by the field (Bourdieu 1993).

Bourdieu argues that these structuring structures are generative of practice (Bourdieu 1977); so, for example, while an individual teacher may desire to work in ways that they perceive to be 'new' and free from the accountability and curriculum agenda, or while they might aspire to use digital technologies to promote contemporary literacy for the digital age, they may in fact be unable to break away from inculcated skills-based, target driven instruction to give children free reign in their creative writing using paper or screen-based resources as the past conditions and experiences of their practice are always present through the teacher's and children's habitus. This determines, to an extent, the activity within the field – or in this example, the writing classroom.

In this field, the individual habitus of the agents (including the teachers and the children in their care) works together with the social structures implicit in the educational and historical context of the writing classroom – or early years setting – to recursively converge and generate a complex and collaborative community of learning. In Bourdieu's terms, this field will impact the opportunities that it affords the participants. It will be structured by the choices that the participants make. It is therefore a site of contestation and symbolic violence (Bourdieu and Passeron 1977, p. 4) where a teacher's beliefs about their legitimate practices are imposed in such a way that the power relations at play can actually be obscured from the teachers and children, and the opportunities to evolve pedagogies are circumscribed in ways that the teacher may not be aware of. In a setting where teachers hope to introduce and respond to new ways of being and becoming, as young writers in digital times for example, an explicit awareness of the forces that impact teachers' beliefs and practices can therefore be regarded as essential.

Moving forward in this chapter, I aim to explore the experiences of two early years teachers as they support young children's writing development in their particular fields of cultural production. Through a consideration of the forces that are impacting the teachers' practices, I will aim to understand how they help children to become writers in fields that are subject to accountability and technological change. Following an analysis of the teachers' stories about how they use technology to promote children's writing, I will consider whether an evolved understanding of how to support young children's writing development might be articulated in digital times. This consideration will aim to present an expanded view of the writing process, where digital resources and practices can be regarded as supportive and even central to helping children to become engaged and proficient writers.

The study

The discussion in this chapter draws on data that was collected as part of a small-scale qualitative study, funded in 2016 by the United Kingdom Literacy Association. The study, entitled *Children's 'writing' in the 21st century: composition, crafting and design*, was comprised of five focus group conversations with teachers of children aged 4–11 in three primary school settings in the South West of England. This chapter will refer to data constructed from one of the focus group conversations that was conducted with three teachers who work together exclusively in the early years phase of their school (with children aged from 3–7) in the autumn term of 2017. The conversation included the Foundation Stage Leader (also the reception teacher), a Year 1 teacher, a Year 2 teacher, and myself. Informed consent was sought via email and given in line with the University of Plymouth Research Ethics and Integrity Committee guidelines, which in turn are derived from the British Educational Research Association (BERA) *Ethical Guidelines for Ethical Research* (2018).

In this chapter, I use the term 'focus group conversation' to acknowledge that my method is derived from a number of complementary accounts of the focus group interview method (see for example Flick 2006, Denscombe 2010, Krueger and Casey 2015, Cohen et al. 2018), but to particularly signal the distinctive methodological emphasis that is presented by Cathy Nutbrown in her and Peter Clough's discussion about the importance of voice in social science research (Clough and Nutbrown 2010). Central to this account is the notion that the voices of the participants and researcher(s) are evident in the construction of the stories that are built (Clough and Nutbrown 2010). My role within this focus group conversation was as an informed moderator (Cohen et al. 2018), who – due to insider knowledge and understanding about the topic of promoting children's abilities as writers within the 21st-century context – was able to contribute to the discussion (Flick 2006). As such the data presented is positioned as a co-construction, whose value derives from the collaboration afforded by the conversation. In the next section of this chapter, extracts of the conversation are presented and analysed for the forces that are playing on them.

At the outset of the conversation, I invited the teachers to talk to me about how they were helping children to become writers in the digital age; and to tell me about the paper-based and screen-based writing, composing and mark-making activities that the children enjoyed. The teachers had recently participated together in CPD with a teacher-trainer who develops teachers' and schools' use of technology to raise standards across the curriculum. This CPD had clearly impacted the teachers' views and practice, and they were positive about the potential for technology to be used to inspire and engage children.

In between paper and screen in Year 1

In our conversation, the Year 1 teacher described how his children had collaboratively composed their own retelling of the *Owl Babies* story (Waddell and Benson 1992), using the movie-making app Puppet Pals 2.[5] Subsequently they transcribed the words from their screen-based composition to create an individual paper-based textual outcome for assessment. As the teacher described the two-stage process, he explained how the teaching team work in between paper-based and screen-based approaches, to support their young children (aged 5 and 6) to become writers:

> I think at the moment we kind of work in between the paper-based and the screen-based. We're using both methods to create high-quality outcomes. So before we had the iPads and stuff, you might have just had a story mountain.[6] Now we're using Puppet Pals to actually have the children make a story; and when they write it they'll be able to play and pause, so the actual plan is kind of, it goes at their pace, and it's less abstract, than like a mountain on a piece of paper; when actually thinking about it, when I have used story mountains before, although they're quite good, it's very rare to actually see a child self-refer to a story mountain, whereas with a video they can play and pause.

The teacher's description illustrates how the use of digital technology can expand the children's composition process beyond the national curriculum requirement: to compose a sentence orally before writing it (DfE 2013). In this example, having shared a picture book, the teacher and/or children upload original images of key characters and backgrounds, photographed from the book, to create a wordless animation in the Puppet Pals 2 app. The children then narrate over the animation in small groups, to compose a multimodal story which can be played back and watched or listened to in real time. Of significance here is that the children collaboratively compose their story, without being hampered by the transcriptional challenges of spelling and handwriting. Their collaborative composition is followed by a second 'writing' stage, where children individually transcribe their story onto paper, using the multimodal screen-based text for support.

Consideration of this two-stage writing process reveals a range of competing forces and tensions that play out on the field as the teacher helps promote his young children's writing. The use of digital technology can be regarded as one force amongst many used to strategically scaffold (Wood et al. 1976) the children as they compose. Dockrell et al. (2015) draw from Sawyer's account of work in the field of learning sciences (Sawyer 2006, n. d.) to define scaffolding in relation to writing pedagogy as 'the support given during the learning process that is tailored to the needs of the student with the intention of helping the student achieve his/her learning goals'. The use of scaffolding techniques in writing pedagogy has been outlined by Wray and Lewis in their account of children learning to read and write non-fiction in paper-based contexts. These techniques include the use of social, collaborative, meaningful, and situated activities that include demonstration, joint activity, and supported activity leading to eventual independence as writers, as children move from collaborative environments to assume sole responsibility for effective and meaningful reading and writing practices (Wray and Lewis 1997, pp. 21–23).

In the *Owl Babies* example, an expanded scaffolding process that draws on the affordances of the original paper-based text and the involvement of digital technology to help children to compose can be observed. The original text provides a model for the children's own writing, while the selection and use of the Puppet Pals 2 app provides a resource around which their oral compositions – informed by knowledge of the story – can pivot. The use of technology ensures that the children are scaffolded socially and dynamically by the app itself, and the dialogue and collaboration that working around the technology with their peers and more able others affords. As the teacher shared one of the group's recordings of their story in Puppet Pals 2, the interplay of the children's voices, as they narrated and interjected with dialogue, was evident.

VOICE 1: Once upon a time, there were three baby owls. They lived with their mother.

(pause)

VOICE 2: Then one night, they woke up and their owl mother was gone.
VOICE 3: 'Where's mummy?',
VOICE 2: said Sarah,
VOICE 4: 'Maybe she's gone hunting?', said Percy.
VOICE 3: 'I want my mummy', said Bill. 'Let's go ahead and try flying somewhere else.'
VOICE 1: So they flew. 'No, she isn't here.'
VOICE 3: 'Where is mummy? I want my mummy.'

This transcript captures the children as they compose and perform their story together, without overt formal direction from a teacher. The children take it in turns to contribute, either in role as a baby owl, or as narrator, while leaning on their knowledge of the story, as well as the visual affordances and the animation provided by the app for prompts, as to when and what to contribute. While this retelling is similar in places to Waddell's original text, there are some distinct differences, illustrating that the children are originating ideas as they step into the role of a baby owl or the narrator, and are not merely recounting word-for-word the memorable text. The engagement of the children, as they tell their story using the app, cannot be represented here; however, in the recording, it is evident from the expression in their voices, and the pacing and pausing of their story, that the use of technology supports engagement and collaboration, as these very young children successfully compose their story harmoniously, fluently, and without the direct intervention of an adult.

Alongside their collaborative composition process with digital technologies, the children's writing is scaffolded strategically by the teacher to help them achieve their learning goals: by his expectations for outcome as informed by statutory curricular requirements; by his compliance with local and national policy; and by the use of targets for success. As an example of this, a formal target for the children's writing is displayed prominently on the screen of the app throughout the animation, stating: *How can we tell a story and improve it?* This carefully positioned target serves as a reminder to the children, and illustrates the claim that multiple, competing forces are acting on the children's writing process. The target apparently establishes and communicates expectations for children's creativity and innovation, encouraging tentative additions to the familiar story text; however, it also constrains the potential for children's composition through an implied value judgement and requirement to improve. Later in the conversation, the teacher illustrates this complexity as he describes how the children's innovative story making with digital technology is in fact guided by explicit teacher modelling and direction in relation to beliefs about what children 'need':

> We started off and we found the children **needed** some sentence opener prompts. They **needed** some conjunctions, and it still **needs** to be modelled like a piece of writing would ... Using the puppets, I made my own kind of version to show them how it could look.

These explicit modelling and demonstration strategies build from genre-based writing pedagogy as developed by Australian scholars in the Sydney School in the 1980s (Rose 2009, p. 151). They were formally introduced in English state education in the 1990s (DfE 2011) using interventions such as the National Literacy Strategy (DfEE 1998) and the Primary National Strategies Framework for Literacy and Mathematics (DfES 2006). The legacy of these interventions has persisted through significant reform to the national curriculum and associated assessment practices implemented in 2013 by the then coalition government.[7] This reform introduced new statutory requirements for children's writing, with a particular emphasis on the demonstration of proficiency in the use of prescribed vocabulary, grammar, and punctuation, and an increased focus on the use of testing and teacher assessment in these specific areas.

Despite the teacher's innovative use of technology, and aim for creativity, the conversation reveals the ongoing impact of the improvement agenda for children's writing, and the inculcation of a shared metalanguage for describing genre-based writing pedagogy, involving the joint construction of text with the ultimate aim of children taking control of their writing following exposure to models of writing and scaffolded practice (see Rose 2009, pp. 151–154 for a detailed account of genre writing pedagogy and its genesis). In the conversation, the teacher expresses his view that the children 'need' to be provided with a clear model of success, including the use of a range of sentence openers and conjunction use. The model provided by the teacher is highly ambitious. It reflects the statutory expectations for children's writing by the end of the second year of their formal education, rather than the requirements for Year 1, which do not demand the same level of proficiency.[8] His description of what his children 'need', in order to achieve a 'high quality outcome', can be regarded as highly aspirational for writers in Year 1 (in the first, autumn term of their education); and symptomatic of the high-stakes accountability context within which he is working. While introducing innovative digital practice to promote children's early writing, the teacher is driven by the accountability context, and what can be described as a skills-based view of literacy. His approach is framed extensively by the local and national accountability context, even though the children in his setting are younger than it is intended for. In this example, the use of digital technology – as engaging, motivating, and 'cutting edge' as it might appear to be for these young writers – is still primarily harnessed to support success in relation to notions of grammatical competence within this accountability context, rather than to foster the creative composition of children's stories and the development of their authentic voices as storytellers of short narratives – as required by the statutory curriculum.

However, despite the visibility of the accountability frame in the *Owl Babies* example, which could be regarded as a force that narrows children's experiences as writers, the introduction of digital technologies into the composing activity does enrich the children's experience. As their teacher explains, the use of technology allows the children to find success as 'writers', as their oral multimodal textual composition is transcribed into a paper-based textual artefact with form and structure; one that can be held, read back, and used as evidence of their compositional and transcriptional skills. As an initial stage in the writing process, it can be observed from the recording that the use of technology has introduced genuine enjoyment, authenticity, collaboration, and complexity as the children work together to compose their story and participate meaningfully with each other through this technologically mediated literacy event. In this way, their writing process is expanded and enriched. As their teacher explains, it is a process that sits in between the paper and the screen, in the way that it is framed, as well as in the way that children experience it.

This view is reiterated by the Year 2 teacher in his story, when describing the use of another app, ChatterPix Kids,[9] and the role it can play in scaffolding the process of writing as children develop their skill as storytellers.

Not just writing in Year 2

In ChatterPix Kids, users import a photo of a story character and draw a line on its face to make a mouth that can move. Users can then record a voice-over for up to 30 seconds. When the voice-over is replayed, the character's mouth moves, as if the character is talking. The Year 2 teacher had taken a photograph of Augustus the tiger, the central character in the storybook, *Augustus and his Smile* by Catherine Rayner (2006). In this book and in digital versions of it, the story of how Augustus tries to find his lost smile is narrated in the third person.

Following familiarisation with the text, the Year 2 teacher asked his children to retell parts of the story into the app, using a collaboratively constructed timeline of the story for plot support. The following extract demonstrates how technology supported two children of different abilities in different ways: one composing in role as Augustus and requiring the adoption of the first-person narrator; and the other recounting the story in the third-person and in the style of the original text. The children were given a target to introduce adjectives into their compositions.

TEACHER 2: ... what you do is literally draw a line where the mouth is and it makes the character talk. It brings the character to life, so they love that and then they re-tell the story. I set mine the task of trying to rehearse using adjectives because this would be used as a prompt, and I did this with my highers the afternoon after they did this. They then used this to help them. Millie is good but her mouth is tiny.
MILLIE ON RECORDING: My name is Augustus the tiger. One day I lost my smile. First I done a huuuuge tigery stretch and I set off to find it. First, I ...
TEACHER 2: [over the recording]: She's using the timeline now ...
MILLIE ON RECORDING: ... climbed up the biggest tree and I saw tiny blue airbirds, then I climbed in the biggest, biggest houses and I looked in the cupboard ...
TEACHER 2: That's it, that was like 30 seconds, but ...
INTERVIEWER: Is it helping her? She is getting into role as a tiger?
TEACHER 2: Yes it gets her into role, allows her to rehearse using the skills we are trying to get them to use. So she was using adjectives and time adverbs and so on in there, but it also – she's a high writer which allows her to do that, but it's more so for someone like Alice who's a lower writer. It allows her to actually – she can't write very much without a lot of support and it allows her to tell the story because there it is in action, because I had to film this one off an iPad. Now it probably allows her to actually tell the

story like – you know when her mum comes in, I can say, 'Well, she's not just writing, this is what she's doing to develop her English.'
ALICE ON RECORDING: He looked under the bushes.
TEACHER 2: ... Someone like Alice wouldn't necessarily be able to read to a story mountain to herself, so she can play that and actually have a go at writing it and keep remembering what it is, and pause it and seeing it back and that's what we're using them for.

Within this extract, there is evidence that the children are helped to find success as writers, using digital technologies. While Alice does not achieve her teacher's objective of using adjectives, she nevertheless uses the affordances of the app to scaffold her ability to recount the story in the third-person. She enters the role of the narrator to do this and experiences the opportunity to move from retelling a personal story to narrating the story of a character who is brought to life by a simple animation. In her teacher's words, 'she's not just writing' as she is doing this, she is becoming the owner of the story as she narrates it.

Millie moves beyond this. She uses the app, in conjunction with a timeline of events, to develop the role of Augustus, fulfilling the teacher's objective of using adjectives, as well as creating an original first-person account with events that differ from the original story. She experiences the intensity of entering the text and writing in role, through the creation of her voice-over. For both children, the use of digital technology scaffolds the development of genuine authorial intent and engagement, as they possess their own story making process.

Flower and Hayes' (1981) *Cognitive process theory of writing*, while derived from protocol analysis of proficient adult writers, offers a useful frame for considering how these teachers support their young children's writing, in the light of the pervasive accountability context. As Flower and Hayes have described, the orchestration of the writing process involves managing the task environment, drawing up from one's long-term memory, and mastering the processes of planning, translating, and reviewing; whilst also managing the series of overarching goals that are driving the process (Flower and Hayes 1981, p. 366). I suggest that the teachers' use of digital technologies in these examples is altering the writing process for these very young 'writers', as they grapple with the orchestration of all the elements involved with writing their stories and recounts to meet aspirational imposed targets. The Puppet Pals 2 app provides an engaging, collaborative, multimodal composing experience that supports recount and innovation; the ChatterPix Kids app supports composition in role, helping the young writer to enter the text and experience a vivid degree of authorial engagement, intent, and purpose.

From an accountability-framed perspective and from a cognitive process perspective, it is possible to argue that the use of digital technologies in these examples expands and evolves the children's writing process. The teachers' practices are informed by the accountability and performativity context, and underpinned by the expectation that the children will meet the prescribed curriculum targets. Equally, the teachers' practices are driven by their desire to engage and motivate their children to write in authentic, collaborative, and meaningful ways, through the planned use of digital technology. This purposeful use of technology alters the writing process by both simplifying and intensifying it. Children are not only engaged visually and multimodally; and through the adoption of writing in role; they are supported by the separation of the composing and transcription elements of the writing process, and the removal of the potential for the child to be overwhelmed as they attempt to orchestrate all the elements involved.

I suggest here that the both teachers' practice can be regarded as an evolved, hybrid pedagogy for writing, where activities using technology are being introduced to build upon and embellish existing, established scaffolding techniques and embedded practice to give purpose to the literacy event and to engage learners more intensively. This *in between* practice is *not just writing*; it sits somewhere between an approach that is established in many English state schools, known as Talk for Writing (TfW) (see Bignell 2013, Dockrell et al. 2015, for accounts of this), and the multifarious possibilities offered by the integration of technology into the children's writing process.

From the outset of both teachers' stories, the legacy of performativity, within which the TfW approach was originally implemented, and in which young children's writing continues to be developed, is tangible. The teacher's description of the creation of *high-quality outcomes*, as the product of the teachers' and children's labour, reflects what Bearne has described, in relation to writing assessment, as the 'tyranny of the technical' (Bearne 2017, p. 74). In this scenario, what is countable and observable as high-quality becomes the content of the curriculum, and children's learning is measured in relation to this (Moss 2017). In addition, the introduction of digital technology supports the more context-dependent and situated qualities of young children's writing, for example, development of authorial intent and purpose; awareness of the reader; the ability to select and use powerful vocabulary for effect (see Bearne 2002, 2017). In these examples the possibilities offered by composing in a digital context are embellished by this framing. From an outcome-driven perspective, the teachers' views are that a blend of technology and traditional methods can support children (and themselves) to find overall success, in relation to the existing frameworks for assessment that are used to measure and compare children's progression towards expected *high-quality outcomes*; from a writing process perspective, the use of technologies can be observed to promote the more desirable elements of the writing process, such as development of authorial confidence, intent, and audience awareness. Using Bourdieu's framing, it can be observed that the field and practice co-constructed by the teachers and children impacts the opportunities afforded to them; and that the opportunities for the development of responsive pedagogy are circumscribed by the structuring structures, including the accountability context and the availability of technologies and access to them. Melding these powerful structuring forces allows teachers to integrate digital technologies into their writing pedagogy. In turn, the process is altered and enriched, and made more relevant for children learning to compose in digital times.

Conclusion

The teachers' articulations of working 'in between the paper-based and the screen-based', and children 'not just writing' seem to capture the experience of teachers as they attempt to meld existing, new, and evolving forces that play on their pedagogies for writing. These forces include the accommodation of policy and associated accountability structures for writing; conformity to recognised and valued pedagogies; and the harnessing of new possibilities for composing in the 21st century. These new possibilities are outlined by Burnett and Merchant in their Charter for 21st Century Literacies, where they argue for an 'expanded view of literacies' that recognises that children's communication repertoires must broaden beyond what they describe as 'old' models of literacy education to develop criticality and creativity, as appropriate for the digital age that learners inhabit (2018, p. 3). Within this view, Burnett and Merchant argue that children should be encouraged to be collaborative, playful, and allowed to take the lead in their learning. Teachers in turn will understand that children's situated activity may be spontaneous and unpredictable; outcomes may be experimental; and new meaning may be created as resources are explored and traversed.

In this chapter, I offer a contribution to sit within this view. I would like to propose an expanded view of the writing process that melds the affordances of digital and paper-based technologies to support children to become engaged and intentful composers within an accountability-framed context. In so doing, the task of introducing digital technologies into early years writing pedagogy, and building on home experiences with the screen, becomes more justifiable – in curriculum and professional development terms. Digital screen-based technologies are increasingly used collaboratively in formal and informal playful learning contexts (Flewitt et al. 2015, Kucirkova et al. 2019). These technologies can also be harnessed to promote the production of written outcomes that are valued by current accountability frameworks (Cremin and Myhill 2012), finding a kind of synthesis (albeit skewed towards curriculum and accountability forces) of autonomous and ideological models of literacy and approaches towards helping children become literate in digital times. In turn, the field of cultural production that plays on how young children are supported to become writers in the 21st century is enriched; and the role of digital technologies can be valued as a key scaffold in an evolving and expanded process that builds from and moves beyond paper-based accountability-driven articulations of writing process.

Notes

1 See www.morethanascore.org.uk/what-we-do/.
2 See for example: Australia's Digital Technologies curriculum (ACARA 2015); Canada's Use Understand and Create Digital Literacy Framework for Canadian Schools (MediaSmarts 2019); the UK's Digital Capability Framework (JISC 2016); The recently updated European Digital Competence Framework, known currently as DigComp2.0 (Vuorikari et al. 2016); British Columbia Government's Digital Literacy Framework (n.d.); the Irish Government's Digital Learning Framework for Primary Schools (Department of Education and Skills (Ireland) 2018); and UNESCO's ICT Competency Framework for Teachers (2011).
3 For DigComp 2.1, see http://publications.jrc.ec.europa.eu/repository/bitstream/JRC106281/web-digcomp2.1pdf_(online).pdf.
4 See the DigiLitEy website for information: http://digilitey.eu/about/.
5 Find Puppet Pals 2 at www.polishedplay.com/support-pp2.
6 A stage model or flow-chart used for plotting story structure.
7 See www.gov.uk/government/speeches/education-reform-new-national-curriculum-for-schools.
8 In Year 1 the requirements state that children should be taught to 'write sentences', 'sequence sentences to form short narratives', and 'join words and join clauses using and' (DfE 2013, p. 15). It is not until Year 2 (age 6–7) that children are required to 'write narratives about personal experiences and those of others' and learn how to use 'subordination (using when, if, that or because) and co-ordination (using or, and, or but)' to form multiclause sentences (DfE 2013, pp. 21–22).
9 For ChatterPix Kids, see www.duckduckmoose.com/educational-iphone-itouch-apps-for-kids/chatterpix/.

References

Australian Curriculum and Assessment Reporting Authority (ACARA). 2015. *Australian curriculum: digital technologies*. Available from: www.australiancurriculum.edu.au/f-10-curriculum/technologies/digital-technologies/pdf-documents/ [Accessed 30. 03. 19].
Bearne, E. 2002. *Making progress in writing*. London: Routledge.
Bearne, E. 2017. Assessing children's written texts: a framework for equity. *Literacy*, 51 (2), 74–83.
Bignell, C. 2013. Talk in the primary curriculum: seeking pupil empowerment in current curriculum approaches. *Literacy*, 46(1), 48–55.
Bourdieu, P. 1977. *Outline of a theory of practice*. Cambridge: Cambridge University Press.
Bourdieu, P. 1993. *The field of cultural production*. Cambridge: Polity Press.
Bourdieu, P. and Passeron, J. C. 1977. *Reproduction in education, society and culture*. 2nd ed. London: SAGE.
British Columbia Government Education and Training: BC's Digital Literacy Framework n.d. Available from: www2.gov.bc.ca/assets/gov/education/kindergarten-to-grade-12/teach/teaching-tools/digital-literacy-framework.pdf [Accessed 25. 07. 19].
British Educational Research Association (BERA). 2018. *Ethical guidelines for ethical research*. Available from: www.bera.ac.uk/wp-content/uploads/2018/06/BERA-Ethical-Guidelines-for-Educational-Research_4thEdn_2018.pdf [Accessed 05. 03. 19].
Burnett, C. and Merchant, G. 2018. *New media in the classroom: rethinking primary literacy*. London: Sage.
Carretero, S., Vuorikari, R. and Punie, Y. 2017. *DigComp 2.1: The Digital Competence Framework for Citizens with eight proficiency levels and examples of use*, EUR 28558 EN,

doi:10.2760/38842. Available from: http://publications.jrc.ec.europa.eu/repository/bitstream/JRC106281/web-digcomp2.1pdf [Accessed 02. 04. 19].

Carrington, V. 2005. New textual landscapes, information and early literacy. In: Marsh, J. ed. *Popular culture, new media and digital literacy in early childhood*. London: Routledge Falmer, 13–27.

ChatterPix Kids. Available from: www.duckduckmoose.com/educational-iphone-itouch-apps-for-kids/chatterpixkids/ [Accessed 20. 03. 19].

Clough, P. and Nutbrown, C. 2010. *A student's guide to methodology: justifying enquiry*. London: SAGE.

Cohen, L., Manion, L. and Morrison, K. 2018. *Research methods in education*. London: Routledge.

Cremin, T. and Myhill, D. 2012. *Writing voices: creating communities of writers*. London: Routledge.

Cremin, T., et al. 2015. *Researching literacy lives*. Oxon: Routledge.

Denscombe, M. 2010. *The good research guide for small-scale social research projects*. 4th ed. Berkshire: Oxford University Press.

Department for Education (DfE). 2011. *The national strategies, 1997–2011*. London: DfE. Available from: https://assets.publishing.service.gov.uk/government/uploads/system/uploads/attachment_data/file/175408/DFE-00032-2011.pdf [Accessed 19. 03. 19].

Department for Education (DfE). 2013. *National curriculum in England English programmes of study: key stages 1 and 2*. London: DfE.

Department for Education and Employment (DfEE). 1998. *The national literacy strategy framework for teaching*. London: DfEE.

Department for Education and Skills (DfES). 2006. *Primary national strategy: primary framework for literacy and mathematics*. London: DfES.

Department of Education and Skills (Ireland). 2018. *Digital learning framework for schools*. Available from: www.education.ie/en/Schools-Colleges/Information/Information-Communications-Technology-ICT-in-Schools/DLF.html [Accessed 30. 03. 19].

Dockrell, J., Marshall, C. and Wyse, D. 2015. *Talk for writing evaluation report and executive summary*. London: Education Endowment Fund. Available from: https://educationendowmentfoundation.org.uk/public/files/Projects/Evaluation_Reports/EEF_Project_Report_TalkForWriting.pdf [Accessed 07. 03. 19].

Dowdall, C. 2019. Young children's 'writing' in the 21st century: the challenge of moving from paper to screen. In: Erstad, O., et al. eds. *The Routledge handbook of digital literacies in early childhood*. Oxon: Routledge.

Flewitt, R., Messer, D. and Kucirkova, N. 2015. New directions for early literacy in a digital age: the iPad. *Journal of Early Childhood Literacy*, 15(3), 289–310.

Flick, U. 2006. *An introduction to qualitative research*. 3rd ed. London: SAGE.

Flower, L. and Hayes, J. R. 1981. A cognitive process theory of writing. *College Composition and Communication*, 32(4), 365–387.

Golden, N. A. and Pandya, J. Z. 2018. Understanding identity and positioning for responsive critical literacies. *Language and Education*, 33(3), 211–225.

JISC. 2016. *The digital capability framework*. Available from: www.jisc.ac.uk/rd/projects/building-digital-capability [Accessed 30. 03. 19].

Krueger, R. and Casey, M. A. 2015. *Focus groups: a practical guide for applied research*. Thousand Oaks: SAGE.

Kucirkova, N., et al. 2019. Systematic review of young children's writing on screen: what do we know and what do we need to know. *Literacy*, 53(4), 216–225.

Marsh, J., et al. 2017. *Developing digital literacy in early years settings: professional development needs for practitioners. A white paper for COST Action IS1410*. Available from: http://digilitey.eu/wp-content/uploads/2017/01/WG2-LR-jan-2017.pdf [Accessed 01. 04. 19].

MediaSmarts. 2019. *Use, understand and create: a digital literacy framework for Canadian schools (K-12)*. Available from: http://mediasmarts.ca/sites/mediasmarts/files/pdfs/digital-literacy-framework.pdf [Accessed 30. 03. 19].

Moss, G. 2017. Assessment, accountability and the literacy curriculum: reimagining the future in the light of the past. *Literacy*, 51(2), 56–64.

Peel, A. 2017. Complicating canons: a critical literacy challenge to common core assessment. *Literacy*, 51(2), 104–110.

Puppet Pals 2. 2018. *Polished play*. Available from: www.polishedplay.com/support-pp2 [Accessed 12. 03. 19].

Rayner, C. 2006. *Augustus and his smile*. London: Little Tiger Press.

Rose, D. 2009. Writing as linguistic mastery: the development of genre-based literacy pedagogy. In: Beard, R., et al. eds. *The SAGE handbook of writing development*. London: SAGE, 151–166.

Sawyer, R. K. n.d. *Optimising learning implications of learning sciences research*. Report for OECD/CERI International Conference 'Learning in the 21st Century: Research, Innovation and Policy'. Available from: www.oecd.org/site/educeri21st/40554221.pdf [Accessed 15. 04. 19].

Sawyer, R. K. 2006. *The Cambridge handbook of the learning sciences*. New York: Cambridge University Press.

Simpson, A. 2017. Teachers negotiating professional agency through literature-based assessment. *Literacy*, 51(2), 111–119.

Standards and Testing Agency. 2018. *Teacher assessment frameworks at the end of key stage 1*. Available from: https://dera.ioe.ac.uk/31093/1/Teacher_assessment_frameworks_at_the_end_of_key_stage_1_for_use_from_the_2018_to_2019_academic_year_onwards.pdf [Accessed 20. 03. 19].

Standards and Testing Agency. 2019. *Assessment framework: reception baseline assessment*. Available from: https://assets.publishing.service.gov.uk/government/uploads/system/uploads/attachment_data/file/781766/Reception_baseline_assessment_framework.pdf [Accessed 01. 04. 2019].

Street, B. 1998. New literacies in theory and practice: what are the implications for language in education? *Linguistics and Education*, 10(1), 1–24.

UNESCO. 2011. *ICT competency framework for teachers*. Available from: https://en.unesco.org/themes/ict-education/competency-framework-teachers [Accessed 18. 07. 19].

Vuorikari, R., et al. 2016. *DigComp 2.0: the digital competence framework for citizens. Update phase 1: the conceptual reference model*. Luxembourg Publication Office of the European Union. Available from: http://publications.jrc.ec.europa.eu/repository/bitstream/JRC101254/jrc101254_digcomp%202.0%20the%20digital%20competence%20framework%20for%20citizens.%20update%20phase%201.pdf [Accessed 30. 03. 19].

Waddell, M. and Benson, P. 1992. *Owl babies*. London: Walker Books.

Wood, D., Bruner, J. and Ross, G. 1976. The role of tutoring in problem solving. *Journal of Child Psychology and Psychiatry*, 17, 89–100.

Wray, D. and Lewis, M. 1997. *Extending literacy: children reading and writing non-fiction*. London: Routledge.

6 Developing textual competence
Primary students' mastery of noun groups in two factual text types

Helen Lewis

Introduction

This chapter presents a small study which explores the way that primary aged school children develop textual competence in one area of writing. It focuses on linguistic resources children use to make meaning in two schooling text types – Information Reports and Expositions – and contributes to understanding about particular institutional writing across different stages of schooling in the primary years.

One of the self-evident yet fascinating things about children's writing is that it improves over time. Interest in describing that improvement and the development of textual competence has led to many studies, especially of writing in the early years. Despite this, there is still relatively little understanding of writing development, and a need for more research into how genres develop over time (Wray and Medwell 2006, Donovan and Smolkin 2006, Kent and Wanzek 2016). As a brief overview of studies into writing by the 9- to 12-year-old age group, early studies in the United States that included primary school writing were carried out by Hunt (1965), who examined texts written by students in Grades 4, 8, and 12, and Loban (1976), who examined grammatical structures in writing of students in Kindergarten through Year 12. Similarly in the United States, Fang (1998) studied the writing of first graders according to some grammatical features in relation to their meaning-making potential, and found a lack of growth. In the United Kingdom, Harpin (1976), in a large-scale study, looked at structural components in the writing of children aged 7–11 years, considering syntax, vocabulary, and word count, and found general indications of development; however, in this study, little account was taken of contextual factors, which in the present study are foregrounded in distinguishing between text types and the purposes for which meaning is crafted. A significant study in primary years' writing in the United Kingdom was conducted by Perera (1984, 1985) into the interaction between the speech and writing of 8- and 12-year-olds, finding that there are constructions specific to each, and that the more complex ones occur in writing. In later UK-based studies researchers have looked at the usage of the form of specific features, such as subordination in the mainly narrative type writing of

5- to 9-year-olds (Allison et al. 2002) and features of sentence and word structure at different key junctures of education (Hudson 2009). Beard and Burrell (2010) examined narrative writing in 9- and 11-year-olds, focusing less on linguistic features than on organisation and overall effectiveness. Early high school students (13- and 15-year-old adolescents) were studied in England (Myhill and Jones 2006, Myhill 2008, 2009), producing detailed analysis of texts to determine linguistic patterns that may indicate a trajectory of development. Furthermore, working with Australian data, Christie and Derewianka (2008), using a systemic functional linguistic approach, presented a comprehensive study of development in chosen curriculum areas, providing in short compass a broad sweep across four age periods spanning from childhood to adolescence. The present study aims to elucidate development in one of Christie and Derewianka's (2008) age groups – the upper primary school level.

Social semiotic theory of language

This chapter draws on Systemic Functional Linguistics (SFL) which espouses language as a meaning-making system intimately related to its context of use and is concerned with theorising and researching language as social practice, especially educationally. SFL has had a significant influence on curriculum development and literacy practices in Australia, including the distinctive genre-based literacy programs in schools and tertiary education (Christie 1992, Martin 1993, 1999, Cope and Kalantzis 1993, Hasan and Williams 1996, Rothery 1996) and has informed many associated pedagogical resources (Gray 1985, Macken et al. 1989, Derewianka 1990, 2011, Hammond 2001, Humphrey et al. 2011, Derewianka and Jones 2016). It informs the Language Strand of the national curriculum for English in Australia (Derewianka 2012). This concerted work has had a substantial impact internationally, feeding into and informing research, curriculum development and teaching practices, particularly through the uptake of the use of genre (in the form of 'text types') (e.g. Hyland 2002, Johns 2002, Schleppegrell and de Oliveira 2006).

An overview of the SFL model will contextualise the important place of the noun group in the meaning-making process. Starting with a very broad perspective, the SFL model sees that language varies between cultural contexts and develops differently within those contexts to satisfy particular purposes. Hence, within the schooling culture, different schooling text types are recognised as appropriate for learners to encounter. The overarching cultural context provides the purpose for the text – whether to write for entertainment or to argue a point of view or to provide information and so on. A choice at this level determines genre. A second layer of specific contextual factors comes into play in any given instance of textual creation – the situational factors. As these situations vary, so do the choices available in the language system, clustering into three dimensions of the situation in which the text is produced: (1) the way in which language represents our experience of the world, the experiential, or *field*; (2) the way in which language realises roles and relationships in interaction, the interpersonal, or *tenor*; and (3) the way in which language forms coherent and cohesive texts, the textual, or *mode*. While all three are essential to explaining the meaning in any given text, the experiential captures the 'subject matter' meaning, and has a wide reach in terms of accounting for the contribution of most items in a clause; and the meanings are structured segmentally. In contrast, interpersonal meaning develops prosodically and textual meaning builds up cumulatively, both over the whole text, so that less can be said at clause level.

This chapter examines the noun group in terms of its expansion potential and the way in which children grow into exploiting the potential to develop their textual competence. In SFL, our experience of the world is construed by the different processes in which people participate, such as physical actions (*playing, eating, hiding*); mental activity (*seeing, believing, wishing, knowing*); verbal utterances (*speaking, announcing, imploring*); and creating or explaining relationships between bits of information (*Cicadas* **are** *insects; the female* **has** *a little sting at the end of its abdomen*). Each 'Process' represents its own slice of experience and is the centre of a single clause. These Processes are all realised by verbs, carrying the central action of the experience, and act on or are acted upon by many diverse entities – the doers and the done-to, and the thinkers and the sayers and the be-ers as well as what is thought and sensed and said. These 'Participants' are typically realised by nouns or noun groups (*Cicadas; insects; the female; a little sting*). To round off the experience, there is often further detail expanding on the processes – when, where, how, why, with whom, about what, and so on. These 'Circumstances' can be realised by adverbs or prepositional phrases (a preposition and a noun group) (*at the end of its abdomen*) (Derewianka 2012). Thus, for two of the three major 'chunks' of meaning in a clause – Participants and Circumstances – noun groups are essential.

Data and explanation of analysis

The data set

Adopting an SFL approach, Lewis (2014) closely examined authentic texts from the second of Christie and Derewianka's (2008) four age periods – the upper primary school level. Three key schooling genres were examined – Narratives, written with a purpose of entertaining, Expositions, written to argue a point of view, and Reports, written to provide information about something. These three genres were examined for empirical evidence of meaning-making features in the development of writing which present in different genres. The main concerns were to identify and make explicit some of the linguistic resources primary students use to make meanings in response to the demands of schooling, and to explore how these linguistic resources might vary with age and according to different curriculum requirements. The data consisted of texts produced by students in three socially disparate primary schools in a rural region in Australia. The final corpus contained 48 texts, all considered 'well done' by the teachers of the students. The distribution was evenly over the four school years (48 ÷ 4 = 12 per year) and over the three genres (48 ÷ 3 = 16 per genre). Within the three genre groupings, an experiential analysis was undertaken across the four grades. The texts were analysed from the clause level, the phrasal/group level, and the word level. The analysis examined how the deployment of experiential clausal elements differed according to the three genres and the four grades (Lewis 2014). The data reported on in this chapter concerns 32 of those texts, covering two genres – Reports and Expositions – in order to compare usage in two factual genres, and concentrates on an indispensable meaning-building resource – the use of the noun group.

Analysing the noun group

A review of the grammar of the noun group will explain the constitutive elements looked for in the texts, describing how meaning is made in the various components. First, a note about the label 'noun group'. The groups considered in this study are technically 'nominal' groups. A nominal group is a group of nominal words – nouns (proper nouns, common nouns, and pronouns), adjectives, numerals, and determiners. 'Noun' is a subclass of nominals, as is 'adjective' (Halliday and Matthiessen 2004). Adjectival groups are therefore considered a type of 'nominal' group, and, relatively few though they are, are included in the overall group counts. But, for ease, the term 'noun group' will be used throughout. Second, why 'group'? The simplest form of noun group is a single word – a noun or a pronoun. However, the commonest form is more than one word; the nomenclature 'group' covers the single word as well as the group that is the expansion of the word. In building meaning, the 'group' can be extended from one word – usually a noun – and amplified in several ways to yield detailed and full information about the entity that is the Participant in the clause or part of the Circumstances. In order to look at the way the noun group amplification takes place, the noun groups were firstly viewed and categorised according to their 'univariate' structure. This perspective involves identifying a 'nucleus' word – the Head noun – which is either free-standing or modified in some way. The modification can be before or after the 'Head', as indicated in Table 6.1. All examples are taken from the collected texts and presented under pseudonyms.

To examine the pre-modifying elements of the noun group more closely, it is helpful to use a second perspective, one which foregrounds the functions within the noun group. It is multivariate in that each univariate structural component is considered through an experiential lens and can be named according to its function. The pre-modifying elements are particularly specific, as can be seen in Table 6.2. Now the nucleus noun is identified as the particular 'Thing' to which the other elements refer, each modifying it in a particular way, providing information about the Thing according to the sorts of questions asked in brackets. As writing develops, the choices made to fill each of these 'slots' are increasingly appropriate to

Table 6.1 Univariate view of the noun group

Pre-modifier	Head	Post-modifier	Source
	molochs		Year 3 (Annie)
these amazing	animals		Year 5 (Kim)
the possom {sic}	family		Year 5 (Ginny)
two tiny	antennae		Year 4 (Nobby)
fantastic and brilliant marine	animals		Year 6 (Lily)
the most extreme	weather	[in the world]	Year 6 (Jack)
the only	animals	[[that breed in winter]]	Year 6 (Belle)

Table 6.2 Uni- and multivariate views of the noun group

Univariate structure	Pre-modifier				Head	Post-modifier
Multi-variate structure	Pointer (which?)	Quantifier (how many?)	Describer (like what?)	Classifier (what type?)	Thing (what are we talking about?)	Qualifier (anything else?)
Examples					molochs	
	these		amazing		animals	
	the			possom	family	
		two	tiny		antennae	
	the		most extreme		weather	[in the world]
	the	only			animals	[[that breed in winter]]

meaning, and teachers can be specific in helping students recognise where the desired meaning can be built into the noun group. It should be noted that the function of post-modifier – adding information that in some way qualifies the 'Thing' – is filled by an embedded element, that is, a finite or non-finite clause or a prepositional phrase, conscripted to be part of the structure of the noun group. These phrases and clauses (denoted by single [] and double [[]] square brackets respectively) have all the meaning potential of any clause or phrase: any nouns present have the capacity to be modified. As children progress with their writing, the addition of any extra information to the Thing indicates development in meaning making, particularly the presence of a 'Qualifier', which is an indication of large noun group, and has the potential to be developed by a writer into an intricate component (see Table 6.5 for examples of embedded clause types acting as Qualifier/Post-modifier).

The multivariate view of the noun group also enables us to account for noun groups where the Head and the Thing are not the same. This happens in two situations. First, it happens when the noun group is incomplete – the Thing is ellipsed and the Head is another element in the noun group. The Head could be the Pointer (e.g. *this* in … ***this*** *is regarded as unhelpful* (Seth, Year 5)); a Quantifier (e.g. *most* in … ***most*** *like to fly around* (Mike, Year 3)); a describer (e.g. *nocturnal* in … *The Toucan is not **nocturnal*** (Cassie, Year 5)) or a Classifier (e.g. the *Emperor* in … *the **Emperor*** *has a different stratige* {sic} (i.e. the Emperor Penguin) (Kay, Year 6)). Not much will be made of this case in this chapter, but the second reason for the dissociation of the Head and the Thing is relevant here. In the second situation, the noun group is complete, but the Head noun does not in fact represent a Thing; it is an elaboration or extension of another Thing, as in *the **flock*** *of colourful toucans*. Univariately speaking, '*flock*' is the Head, with '*of colourful toucans*' a Qualifier. Multivariately, experientially, the Thing being referred to is '*toucans*'; see Table 6.3.

This is a common structure having a quantifying function – and commonly analysed as 'Quantifier'. One advantage of separating it out is that it clarifies how the full potential of the noun group can be drawn on after the first choice of Quantifier (for example, *a flock of the most colourful toucans ever photographed* [made-up example]). Martin et al. (2010) posit the use of the multivariate function of 'Focus' to identify these structures. In most forms, 'of' is a structure marker, though this may be missing in some 'selecting' items. This terminology is adopted here and the noun groups analysed for the use of the Focus types presented in Martin et al. (2010), summarised and exemplified in Table 6.4.

Table 6.3 Structure of noun group with extended quantifier (Focus)

Example	a	flock	of	colourful	toucans
Multivariate	extended Quantifier – Focus			Epithet	Thing
Univariate	(pre-modifier)	Head	(post-modifier)		

Table 6.4 Types and subtypes of Focus

Focus subtype	Examples Head (… of):	Examples in data	Source
perspective	side; top; peak; start; picture	the **end of** its abdomen	Year 4 (Nobby)
re-counting	cup; glass; litre, set; flock	a **group of** Killer Whales	Year 6 (Lily)
partitive	bit; component; arm, chapter	the **lowland of** New Guinea	Year 5 (Ginny)
selecting	five; some; bigger; first; next; all	**one of** the few birds	Year 6 (Kay)
dimensional	size; height; feel	the **surface of** the water	Year 6 (Lily)
evaluative	fool; genius	(not in the data)	
classifying	kind; type; class; species	a **part of** the possum {sic} family	Year 5 (Ginny)

There are two other ways that Participants are realised that are found in the texts in this data. These other two Participant structures have to do with the make-up of the Head/Thing. In the first instance, sometimes the Participant consists of more than one noun group – there may be two or more, commonly a list of things, as illustrated in the earlier example from Maisie's text. In the second instance, illustrated below in Table 6.5 (rows 2 and 3), a clause functions as the entire Head of a noun group – that is to say, it is embedded and is functioning as an entire noun group (Halliday and Matthiessen 2004). This is a form of 'nominalisation' and increasing use of it may be a sign of development. Nominalisation is the conversion of non-nouns – especially verbs – into noun forms, so that the expansion potential of the noun group can be tapped into (see Derewianka this volume). This particular form of nominalisation (using a clause as a noun group) is recognised as a forerunner of grammatical metaphor, where alignment between a particular meaning and its grammatical expression is shifted. True grammatical metaphor manifests in early adolescence (Christie and Derewianka 2008), and thus these embryotic instances are noted in the study. The examples shown in Table 6.5 (rows 2 and 3) are along with examples of the other situation in which embedded clauses are used, that is, as Qualifiers (rows 4 and 5).

Measuring complexity

The great deal of information carried in the noun groups used as examples above show that the place of noun groups in the recording of experience and information is key (see Halliday 1989, chapter 3, for a full discussion). Noun groups are used in both Participants and Circumstances, two of the three major 'chunks' of meaning in a clause.

An initial measure of the complexity of the Participants and Circumstances involves taking into account the fact that, due to the way the noun group expands (illustrated above), there are more noun groups than there are Participants and Circumstances. To begin with, complex noun groups often contain embedded clauses which contain their own Participants and Circumstances, both sites of noun groups. For example, Maisie in Year 3 writes: *The birds [[that live in water]] (Participant) are (Process) ducks, swans and pelicans plus much more (Participant)*. This

Table 6.5 Embedded clauses as/in noun groups

Clause function	Clause type	Noun group with clause as Head	Source
Head	finite	That is [[what I know about the spotted Cuscus]]	Year 5 (Ginny)
Head	non-finite	When it comes to [[keeping the Egg warm]]	Year 6 (Kay)
Post-modifier	finite	someone [[you hardly know]]	Year 3 (Jasper)
Post-modifier	non-finite	a chance [[to have fun]]	Year 6 (Travis)

clause contains two Participants, both realised as noun groups: (1) *The birds [[that live in water]]* (2) *ducks, swans and pelicans plus much more*. The first Participant (*The birds [[that live in water]]*) is a noun group that contains an embedded clause as post-modifier (*[[that live in water]]*). In that embedded clause is a Circumstance (*in water*) containing a noun group: (3) *water*. Maisie's second Participant in this clause is *ducks, swans and pelicans plus much more (Participant)*. This is a group complex comprising four noun groups: (4) *ducks*, (5) *swans* (6) *and pelicans* (7) *plus much more*. This one clause thus contains seven noun groups in two Participants.

The use of noun groups in Reports

Turning now to look at the specific text types under study, the example above taken from Maisie's report illustrates how meaning in the noun group is carried. A simple count of all nouns and noun groups associated with Participants and Circumstances will give an indication of the complexity of Participants and Circumstances – the more nouns that make up the Participant or Circumstance, the more complex and lexically dense the writing is. Table 6.6 shows the data on total noun groups for the 16 Reports in this study.

In Table 6.6, for Reports, a percentage calculation of the increases (see the second column from the right) traces where development happens. This '% increase' is the ratio of the total additional noun groups (fifth column) to those noun groups realising Participants and in Circumstances (second column). Between Year 4 and Year 5, there is a leap of almost 20% in the total number of nouns/noun groups used. This gives a sharper picture, a larger step, than the calculation of lexical density (see the final column) for these texts. This suggests that by Year 5, students writing Reports are becoming adept at exploiting the meaning potential of the noun group for informative purposes. The rest of this section looks at how young writers employ the structure of the noun group when writing Reports and locates features of the noun group which are particularly conducive to Report writing.

The noun groups that realise Participants and contribute to Circumstances in the Year 3 to Year 6 Reports were examined first according to their univariate structure (pre-modification, Head, post-modification), as tabulated in Table 6.7. The figures shown are percentages of total number of noun groups. Participants/ Circumstances comprising single noun groups are in the majority, with the

Table 6.6 Noun groups in Reports

Single noun groups ...	realising Participants and in Circumstances	in embedded clauses	in group complexes	Total additional noun groups	% increase	Lexical density
Year 3	141	16	36	52	36.9	3.16
Year 4	256	18	76	94	36.7	3.58
Year 5	202	16	95	111	55.0	4.22
Year 6	242	19	116	135	55.8	4.64

Table 6.7 Univariate view of noun groups in Reports (percentage)

		Year 3	Year 4	Year 5	Year 6
Single noun group	Head only	49.2	43.7	38.7	34.2
	Pre-modification + Head	38.3	43.7	45.0	49.6
	with Post-modification	7.8	6.3	9.3	10.6
noun group complex		3.6	5.4	5.8	4.2
(Head=whole clause)		1.0	0.9	1.3	1.3
total %		100.0	100.0	100.0	100.0

remaining realisations being group complexes or whole clauses that are down-ranked to become themselves the Participant. The breakdown of these is unpacked in the bottom two rows but one of the table.

The third and fourth rows show a general increase of the use of modification across the Year groups. There is about an 11% increase in the use of pre-modification, and about a 3% increase in post-modification.

Pre-modification

There is approximately an 11% increase in the use of pre-modification across the years of Report writing (Table 6.7, row 3). Using a multivariate view, the components of the pre-modifier are visible, and to examine the way noun groups are expanded in the pre-modifier, the different patterns and configurations of the individual elements were collected, and a list compiled of those used. In summary, there were 12, 13, 14, and 17 different combinations of elements respectively used across the years, all in the particular sequence outlined above (Pointer, Quantifier (including Focus), Describer, Classifier, Thing – see Table 6.2 for representative examples), but including multiple use of some elements, especially Describers and Classifiers (e.g. *warm yet not scorching burrows* (Jack, Year 6); *the average adult Emperor* (Belle, Year 6); *the male killer whale* (Lily, Year 6)). The following table, Table 6.8, shows how the increase of pre-modification manifests with respect to the way three elements are used – the structure functioning to 'focus' attention as described above, and the lexical classes of Describers and Classifiers, all pertinent to the purpose of Information Reports – to describe and classify.

The Focus structure (shown in Table 6.8, row 2) is used across years as a classifying function, and in all but Year 3 as for selecting a subset of the Thing. Different functions are used as the writing matures and different aspects of the entities under report are being developed, and different 'patterns' are used for presenting the information – for example, presenting an angle of something, perhaps the perspective of whole/part relationships; or a descriptive quality of some dimension of the entity. The use of Focus increases from 1.3% of the noun groups in Year 3 to 12.6% of the noun groups in Year 6. Table 6.9 gives examples of the wide range of use of Focus in Reports.

Developing textual competence   103

Table 6.8 Use of pre-modification in Reports

Pre-modification + Head	Year 3	Year 4	Year 5	Year 6
% + Focus	1.3	8.6	5.0	12.6
% + Describer	10.7	15.2	23.6	21.3
% + Classifier	6.7	19.9	22.1	29.0

Table 6.9 Examples of use of Focus in Reports

Year	Focus type	Examples from data
3	classifying	all the **kinds of** birds in the world *(Mike)*
4	classifying	the **only kind of** tree [[they like]] *(Joe)*
4	selecting	**one of** the most harmless beetle bugs *(Janet)*
4	selecting	**some of** the world's biggest beaks *(Cassie)*
4	perspective	on the **sides of** there {sic} abdomen *(Nobby)*
4	partitive	the **roots of** any plant *(Nobby)*
5	classifying	around **40 spieces** {sic} **of** Toucans *(Cassie)*
5	classifying	any **type of** animals {sic} blood *(Seth)*
6	selecting	**one of** the few birds [[that can't fly]] *(Kay)*
6	perspective	the **middle of** the circle *(Belle)*
6	classifying	in the **different types of** deserts *(Jack)*
6	perspective	**top of** the food chain *(Lily)*
6	dimensional	the **size of** a young child *(Kay)*
6	re-counting	any **number of** partners *(Lily)*

It is in the Reports genre that we find a systematic use of this structure. In a genre where the purpose is to focus on entities themselves and particular aspects of the entities in classifying and describing, different ways of identifying entities and parts of entities are useful. The fact that a variety of these forms is shown to appear in this genre may encourage teachers to consider this genre for developing this feature.

Using Describers and Classifiers in pre-modification (shown in Table 6.8, rows 3 and 4) involves lexical choices, where the writer builds meaning into the Head. Describers answer the question, 'What is it (the Thing) like?' and provide an objective, factual property or a subjective, evaluative sense. In the case of Information Reports, the objective properties dominate as students build up factual descriptions of Things being reported on. Classifiers denote the type of Thing, and lexis tends towards technical, specialised field language. Examples are given in Table 6.10. Configurations of noun groups involving one or more Describers increase by 10% across the years, as do those involving one or more Classifiers by 22% across the years. By Year 6, close to 30% of the noun groups involve a Classifier.

104 Helen Lewis

Table 6.10 Describers and Classifiers in Reports

Year	Function	Examples from data
3	*describing*	a **long stiky** {sic} tounge {sic} *(Annie)*; a **special** place *(Jasper)*
3	*classifying*	**mother** birds *(Maisie)*; **webed** {sic} feet *(Mike)*
4	*describing*	**long, thick**, beaks [[that are held between there {sic} legs]] *(Janet)*; a **calm** time *(Ned)*
4	*classifying*	**hawthorn** berries *(Janet)*; **adult** cicadas *(Nobby)*
4	both	**organic vegetable** gardens *(Janet)*; the **low air** presure {sic} *(Ned)*
5	*describing*	**strong and sturdy** branches *(Kim)*; the **blood sucking** bats *(Seth)*; a **short conical** muzzle *(Seth)*
5	*classifying*	**emergent** layer *(Cassie)*; **Vertibrata** {sic} phylum *(Ginny)*; **temperate and subtropical** rainforests *(Seth)*
5	both	**razor sharp front** teeth *(Seth)*; **warm tropical** trees *(Kim)*
6	*describing*	**fierce** storms *(Belle)*; the **most extreme** weather in the world *(Jack)*; **striking black and white** colourations *(Lily)*; an **excellent** swimmer *(Kay)*
6	*classifying*	the **scientific** name for killer whale *(Lily)*; little or no **organic** matter what so ever *(Jack)*; the **Gentoo** penguin *(Kay)*
6	both	**cold basin** deserts *(Jack)*; a **small food** source *(Belle)*; **fantastic and brilliant marine** animals *(Lily)*

Post-modification

Although there is only a slight increase in the use of post-modification across the years of Report writing (Table 6.7, row 4), Table 6.11 shows that this increase manifests itself through the use of qualifying phrases rather than clauses; in fact, the use of embedded clauses in post-qualifiers decreases.

Embedded clauses

Another perspective on the use of noun groups may be given by looking at the embedded clauses. Clause embedding occurs in two situations, and both have been referred to already. First, the use of the clause as the whole noun group.

Table 6.11 Use of post-modification in Reports

with Post-modification	Year 3	Year 4	Year 5	Year 6
% with qualifying phrase	2.1	3.7	6.4	7.2
% with qualifying clause	5.7	2.6	2.6	3.2
% with multiple post-qualification	0.0	0.0	0.3	0.3

Table 6.12 Use of embedded clauses in Reports

	Year 3	Year 4	Year 5	Year 6
% of clauses that contain embedded clauses	13.2	8.1	13.1	8.7

For example, *That **is** what I know about the spotted Cuscus* (Ginny, Year 5), where the clause *[[what I know about the spotted Cuscus]]* fills the role of the noun group being the information linked to *That* in much the same way as *insects* are linked to *cicadas* in the earlier example, *Cicadas **are** insects*. See Table 6.7, row 5, for the use of this structure. Second are those clauses that qualify the Head/Thing in the normal noun group structure, as for example in the following: *long, thick, beaks [[that are held between there {sic} legs]]* (Janet, Year 4); (see Table 6.11, row 3). Table 6.12 compiles these uses and shows how these clauses are deployed across the years. The frequency of embedded clauses seems inconsistent and fluctuates across the years.

The use of noun groups in Expositions

The rest of this section examines how young writers employ the structure of the noun group when writing Expositions, suggesting which features of the noun group are particularly suited to focus on when teaching Exposition writing. In Table 6.13, for Expositions, the situation is different to that shown in Table 6.6, for Reports. The percentage calculation of the increase (column 6) shows there is a larger, 25%, jump, and not between Years 3 and 4, but between Years 5 and 6. This suggests that students writing Exposition are, by Year 6, more and more distinguishing the meaning potential of appropriate components of the noun group for use in persuading.

The noun groups that realise Participants and contribute to Circumstances in the Year 3 to Year 6 Expositions were examined first according to their univariate structure (pre-modification, Head, post-modification), and are tabulated in Table 6.14. Figures are percentages of total number of noun groups. Participants/Circumstances comprising single noun groups are in the majority, with

Table 6.13 Noun groups in Expositions

Single noun groups ...	realising Participants and in Circumstances	in embedded clauses	in group complexes	Total additional noun groups	% increase	Lexical density
Year 3	141	8	16	24	17	3.39
Year 4	137	11	18	29	21.2	3.15
Year 5	180	19	40	59	32.8	3.54
Year 6	162	42	51	93	57.4	4.15

Table 6.14 Univariate view of all noun groups in Expositions (percentage)

		Year 3	Year 4	Year 5	Year 6
Single noun group	Head only	69.7	42.2	42.3	43.1
	Pre-modification + Head	23.6	48.2	45.6	39.2
	with Post-modification	3.6	7.8	8.8	12.5
noun group complex		3.0	0.6	1.7	1.2
(Head=whole clause)		0.0	1.2	1.7	1.9
total %		100.0	100.0	100.0	100.0

the remaining realisations being group complexes or whole clauses that are down-ranked to become themselves the Participant. The breakdown of these is shown in the bottom two rows but one of the table.

The third and fourth rows show that, with respect to Expositions, the use of modification is varied. There is a jump of about 25% after Year 3 in the use of pre-modification, after which usage steadies and even falls by about 6% to Year 6. Post-modification, on the other hand, shows a constant increase of use, with about a 9% increase from Year 3 to Year 6.

Pre-modification

Table 6.14, row 3, indicates an approximate 15% increase in the use of pre-modification across the years of Exposition writing. The use of the individual elements of Focus, Describer, and Classifier is shown in Table 6.15.

These three elements are used differently in Expositions to in Reports. While the use of the structure of Focus increases across the years in both genres, more increase and more variation are evident in Reports. Here, in Expositions, the Focus structure is used almost exclusively as a selecting function, with the emphasis on amassing persuasive evidence (e.g. **all** *these very important reasons* (Nola, Year 4); **a lot of** *waste* (Maddy, Year 5)). There is only one instance in Year 6 of the structure being used to classify, where it identifies the subset of transport methods as a point to mention in the argument. Table 6.16 shows examples of the use of Focus in Expositions.

Use of Describers and Classifiers also differs. In Expositions, configurations of noun groups involving one or more Describers increases (by 10% across the

Table 6.15 Use of pre-modification in Expositions

Pre-modification + Head	Year 3	Year 4	Year 5	Year 6
% + Focus	2.6	3.8	4.6	6.0
% + Describer	20.5	11.3	13.8	30.0
% + Classifier	28.2	10.0	12.8	19.0

Table 6.16 Examples of use of Focus in Expositions

Year	Focus type	Examples from data
3	selecting	**all** the time *(Mike)*
4	selecting	**all** the catholic schools in Australia *(Joe)*
4	selecting	**most of** the children *(Nola)*
4	selecting	**all** these very important reasons [[that I have just given you]] *(Nola)*
5	selecting	**all** the money [[that the community gets]] *(Dane)*
5	selecting	**a lot of** waste [[that would have to be buried underground]] *(Maddy)*
6	selecting	**2 of** the islands *(Jess)*
6	selecting	just **some of** the reasons [[why I think // that more people should play soccer]] *(Travis)*
6	classifying	very **different methods of** transport *(April)*

Table 6.17 Describers and Classifiers in Expositions

Year	Function	Examples from data
3	describing	**good** company *(Maisie)*; **very loud** sound *(Maisie)*
3	classifying	**computer** games *(Jasper)*; **digestive** system *(Josh)*
3	both	**healthy food** groups *(Mike)*
4	describing	your **favourite** shows *(Allen)*; a **popular** teacher [[that most of the children choose]] *(Nola)*; all these **very important** reasons *(Nola)*
4	classifying	three weeks **Easter** holiday *(Joe)*; **soccer or dancing** lessons *(Allen)*
4	both	a **thick chapter** book *(Joe)*;
5	describing	**better** fasillaties {sic} *(Dane)*; many **older and uneducated** people *(Zizi)*; the **extremely high** risk *(Maddy)*
5	classifying	their **local** rainforest *(Dane)*; a **nuclear power** plant *(Nathan)*; **lung, mouth and throat** cancer *(Zizi)*; the **toxic** gases *(Maddy)*
6	describing	a **fun** sport *(Travis)*; a **great and fun** way [[to get fit and healthy]] *(Travis)*; a **great** leader *(Jack)*; a **fantastic** experience *(April)*
6	classifying	the **Indian** Rupee *(April)*; the **prime** minister *(Jack)*; the **Bullet** train *(Jess)*
6	both	a **wonderful island** country [[located in Asia]] *(Jess)*

years), so that in Year 6 a large proportion (30%) of noun groups uses Describers. In this genre, the use of evaluative Describers is high, contributing to the build-up of the author's stance (e.g. **healthy** *food groups* (Mike, Year 3); *many **older and uneducated** people* (Zizi, Year 5); *a **great and fun** way [[to get fit and healthy]]* (Travis, Year 6)). However, there is not such an increase in the use of Classifiers; use of this function decreases by 18% after Year 3, then increases slowly from Year 4 by 9% to 19% of the total noun groups in Year 6. Examples of different configurations of Describers and Classifiers in noun groups used in Expositions are found in Table 6.17.

Post-modification

Table 6.14, row 4, shows that there is an approximate 9% increase in the use of post-modification across the years of Exposition writing, and Table 6.18 below shows that this increase manifests in the use of both qualifying phrases and clauses. Both qualifying phrases and qualifying clauses tend to increase in frequency year-on-year.

In contrast to post-modification in noun groups in Reports (an increase wholly in using phrases), writers using noun groups in Expositions are increasingly post modifying their nouns using both phrases and clauses. When looking at where these noun groups occur, they show in packaging up arguments. For example, April in Year 6 writes, *Below I will state my points on why I strongly believe that India would be a fantastic place to visit.* The Head word *points* is followed by an intricate post-qualifying phrase (beginning with preposition *on*) containing two embedded clauses, one of which itself contains an embedded clause: *[[why I strongly believe // that India would be a fantastic place [[to visit]].]]*.

Embedded clauses

Table 6.19 compiles the uses of embedded clauses in Expositions and shows how these clauses are deployed across the years.

The tendency is for the use of embedded clauses to increase across the years, with a substantial increase in Year 6. This increase in Year 6 is compatible with two other features already noted, the increase in post-modification using embedded clauses as well as with the use of nominalisation in employing a whole clause as the Head of a noun group (examples of the latter can be seen

Table 6.18 Use of post-modification in Expositions

with Post-modification	Year 3	Year 4	Year 5	Year 6
% with qualifying phrase	0.6	3.6	4.6	6.3
% with qualifying clause	3.0	4.2	4.2	5.9
% with multiple post-qualification	0.0	0.0	0.0	0.4

Table 6.19 Use of embedded clauses in Expositions

	Year 3	Year 4	Year 5	Year 6
% of clauses that contain embedded clauses	6.9	10.0	14.9	25.6

incidentally present in Tables 6.16 and 6.17). This usage in Expositions contrasts with that in Reports, where, although embedded clauses are used to some extent, there is no discernible development across the age groups.

Discussion and conclusions

The data presented in this chapter has been collated to provide tentative explanations of the development of textual competence in the noun groups used by young writers of Reports and Expositions. Although the data set is relatively small, it does seem to suggest that noun groups become more complex with maturity, albeit at different ages and in different ways according to the text type.

A difference in the complexity of the noun groups in the two genres is evident (Tables 6.6 and 6.13). The noun groups in Reports of students in Years 3, 4, and 5 present as more complex than those in Expositions, with the complexity evening out in Year 6: the meaning making involved in building up descriptions of entities that are characteristic of Reports appears to lead to more complex noun groups at an earlier age. The nature of the complexity, however, is not uniform across the different noun group components.

The complexity in the noun groups employed in writing Reports appears to develop most discernibly in the construction of the pre-modifying elements. The use of Focus (summarised in Tables 6.9 and 6.16, with examples in Tables 6.10 and 6.17), seems to be a feature of noun groups in Reports. It appears across the years for classifying a subset of something (*classifying*) and is used increasingly through to Year 6 for a range of other purposes, such as selecting a subgroup (*selecting*), showing an angle on something (*perspective*), and describing a quality of something (*dimensional*) (Table 6.9). It appears much less frequently in Expositions, where it is used almost exclusively to *select* in order to group together persuasive evidence (Table 6.16).

The other feature of pre-modification in noun groups that seems to develop in Report writing is the use of Classifiers (overview in Tables 6.8 and 6.15, with examples in Tables 6.10 and 6.17). This is unsurprising in a text type whose purpose is to provide information on different types and subclasses of entities. In this data, the use of noun groups that contain Classifiers increases from 7% in Year 3 to nearly 30% in Year 6.

By Year 6, the complexity of the noun groups used in Expositions is similar to the complexity of those used in Reports (Tables 6.6 and 6.13). These noun groups are marked by development in different elements of the noun group. The use of the pre-modifying Describer is more pronounced in Expositions by Year 6; these Describers are usually related to a comment by the author, reflecting the purpose of building a stance (Table 6.17). However, the sample further suggests that the use of post-modification in noun groups may be a marker of development in Expositions (Table 6.18). As a structure, it appears much more evident in noun groups in Expositions, with the use of embedded clauses as post-modification especially increasing steadily across the years; in Reports, the slight increase is accounted for by use of phrases in the post-modification.

Use of embedded clauses as a measure of development in these years does not seem justified when looking at where embedded clauses are used in Reports (Table 6.12). There is no discernible pattern of use across the years. In contrast to the case with Reports, the occurrences of embedded clauses may serve as an indication of development in Expositions (Table 6.19). In the Expositions there is a marked increase across the years. Years 4 and 5 show a gradual increase in the overall use of embedded clauses. There appears to be quite a consolidation by Year 6, with 26% of clauses containing embedded clauses, perhaps indicating that these features of the noun group are particularly suited to focus on when teaching Exposition writing.

In conclusion, a close study of the noun groups used in a small sample of Reports and Expositions written by students in Years 3, 4, 5, and 6 shows an interesting difference in deployment, providing empirical evidence that the way noun groups are expanded and used contributes to discriminating between the meaning-making resources for these two genre types. The social purposes for writing provide the key requirements for meaning making, and the resources of the noun groups may be exploited in different ways to fulfil those purposes.

References

Allison, P., Beard, R. and Willcocks, J. 2002. Subordination in children's writing. *Language and Education*, 16, 97–111.

Beard, R. and Burrell, A. 2010. Investigating narrative writing by 9–11-year-olds. *Journal of Research in Reading*, 33(1), 77–93.

Christie, F. 1992. Literacy in Australia. *Australian Review of Applied Linguistics*, 12, 142–155.

Christie, F. and Derewianka, B. 2008. *School discourse: learning to write across the years of schooling*. London: Continuum.

Cope, W. and Kalantzis, M. eds. 1993. *The powers of literacy: a genre approach to teaching literacy*. London: Falmer.

Derewianka, B. 1990. *Exploring how texts work*. Rozelle, NSW: Primary English Teaching Association.

Derewianka, B. 2011. *A new grammar companion for teachers*. Marrickville Metro, NSW: Primary English Teaching Association.

Derewianka, B. 2012. Knowledge about language in the Australian curriculum: English. *Australian Journal of Language and Literacy*, 35(1), 127–146.

Derewianka, B. and Jones, P. 2016. *Teaching language in context*. 2nd ed. Oxford: Oxford University Press.

Donovan, C. A. and Smolkin, L. B. 2006. Children's understanding of genre and writing development. In: MacArthur, C., Graham, S. and Fitzgerald, J. eds. *Handbook of writing research*. New York: The Guilford Press, 131–143.

Humphrey, S., Love, C. and Droga, L. 2011. *Working grammar: an introduction for secondary English teachers*. Frenchs Forest, NSW: Pearson Education Australia.

Fang, Z. 1998. A study of changes and development in children's discourse potential. *Linguistics and Education*, 9(4), 341–367.

Gray, B. 1985. Teaching oral English. In: Christie, M. ed, *Aboriginal perspectives on experience and learning: the role of language in Aboriginal education*. Geelong, Victoria: Deakin University Press, 87–97.

Halliday, M. A. K. 1989. *Spoken and written language*. 2nd ed. Oxford: Oxford University Press.

Halliday, M. A. K. and Matthiessen, C. M. I. M. 2004. *An introduction to functional grammar*. 3rd ed. London: Routledge.

Hammond, J. ed. 2001. *Scaffolding teaching and learning in language and literacy education*. Newtown, NSW: Primary English Teachers Association.

Harpin, W. 1976. *The second R: writing development in the junior school*. London: Allen & Unwin.

Hasan, R. and Williams, G. eds. 1996. *Literacy in society*. London: Longman.

Hudson, R. 2009. Measuring maturity. In: Beard, R., et al. eds. *Handbook of writing development*. London: SAGE, 349–362.

Hunt, K. W. 1965. *Grammatical structures written at three grade levels*. Champaign: NCTE.

Hyland, K. 2002. Genre: language, context and literacy. *Annual Review of Applied Linguistics*, 22, 113–135.

Johns, A. M. ed. 2002. *Genre in the classroom: multiple perspectives*. Mahwah: Lawrence Erlbaum.

Kent, S. C. and Wanzek, J. 2016. The relationship between component skills and writing quality and production across developmental levels: a meta-analysis of the last 25 years. *Review of Educational Research*, 86(2), 570–601.

Lewis, H. 2014. *Mapping the development of children's writing: a functional perspective*. PhD thesis, University of Wollongong, Australia.

Loban, W. 1976. *Language development: kindergarten through grade twelve* (Research Report 18). Urbana: National Council of Teachers of English.

Macken, M. et al. 1989. *Factual writing: a teaching unit based on reports about sea mammals*. Sydney: Literacy and Education Research Network, Directorate of Studies, NSW Department of Education.

Martin, J. R. 1993. Genre and literacy: modelling context in educational linguistics. *Australian Review of Applied Linguistics*, 13, 141–172.

Martin, J. R. 1999. Mentoring semogenesis: 'genre-based' literacy pedagogy. In: Christie, F. ed. *Pedagogy and the shaping of consciousness: linguistic and social processes*. London: Cassell, 123–155.

Martin, J. R., Matthiessen, C. M. I. M. and Painter, C. 2010. *Deploying functional grammar*. Beijing: Commercial Press.

Myhill, D. A. 2008. Towards a linguistic model of sentence development in writing. *Language and Education*, 22(5), 271–288.

Myhill, D. A. 2009. Children's patterns of composition and their reflections on their composing processes. *British Journal of Research Education*, 35(1), 47–64.

Myhill, D. A. and Jones, S. 2006. Patterns and processes: the linguistic characteristics and composing processes of secondary school writers. Technical Report RES-000-23-0208 to the Economic and Social Research Council.

Perera, K. 1984. *Children's writing and reading: analysing classroom language*. Oxford: Blackwell.
Perera, K. 1985. Grammatical differentiation between speech and writing in children aged 8 to 12. Paper presented at the annual meeting of the International Writing Convention, Norwich, England.
Rothery, J. 1996. Making changes: developing an educational linguistics. In: Hasan, R. and Williams, G. eds. *Literacy in society*. London: Longman, 86–123.
Schleppegrell, M. J. and de Oliveira, L. C. 2006. An integrated language and content approach for history teachers. *Journal of English for Academic Purposes*, 5(4), 254–268.
Wray, D. and Medwell, J. 2006. *Progression in writing and the Northern Ireland levels for writing: a research review undertaken for CCEA*. Warwick: University of Warwick.

7 Apprenticing authors
Nurturing children's identities as writers

Teresa Cremin

Introduction

In classroom contexts young people are taught to write and given opportunities to practise and apply their developing knowledge and skills. The extent to which they are positioned or position themselves as writers however, alongside the degree of authorial agency offered or taken, varies. This chapter, in foregrounding the salience of children's identities as writers, documents the socially situated nature of writing, and drawing on two projects examines the nature of their apprenticeship as authors in two particular contexts.

The authorial identities of many groups of writers have been documented. Through autobiographical and biographical accounts, literary writers' identities (e.g. Heaney 1990), academic writers' identities (e.g. Lillis and Curry 2010) and the identity enactments of professional writers have been examined (e.g. Cremin, Lillis et al. 2017). This body of empirical work reveals the significance of conceptions of self as a writer and writing as a form of identity work. It is complemented by research exploring both teachers' and students' identities as writers (see, for example, Cremin and Locke 2017). In relation to teachers, a systematic review suggests a tendency towards negative attitudes to writing and low self-esteem as writers (Cremin and Oliver 2016). Studies of adolescent writers also highlight the challenges and opportunities of claiming a writer identity in secondary phase classrooms (e.g. Elf 2017). By contrast, the writer identities of younger children, who are on their early journeys towards 'becoming writers' (Hong 2015), have received relatively little attention (Collier 2010).

This chapter, in examining data from two UK studies in which children seized or were afforded authorial opportunities to write, considers the shaping influences of these opportunities on the young creative writers' identities. The first study, 'Storytelling and Story-acting', an instantiation of Paley's (1990) narrative approach to learning, involved child storytelling, adult scribing, and later dramatisation of the tale by the class and the author. It offered the 3–6-year-olds a strong sense of agency and in half the settings observed, prompted self-initiated authoring, co-authoring of their own tales with friends, and scribing of each other's tales for dramatisation (Cremin et al. 2018). The second study, 'Teachers as Writers', prompted practitioners, newly positioned as writers themselves, to foreground choice and agency in their writing classrooms (Cremin, Myhill et al. 2017). The students found this engaging and some, including the class of 7–8-year-olds whose identity enactments are explored here, were repositioned and positioned themselves as authors. Through an examination of selected literacy events, both studies reveal the motivational effect of offering authorial opportunities to children, and the influence of ideational freedom and 'voicing writing' on the construction and negotiation of the children's identities as creative writers.

The chapter commences by discussing children's early authoring and the relationship between writing and identity from a sociocultural perspective. Next, the data collection methods of the studies are detailed, this is followed by a reflective account of each study in relation to the themes of ideational freedom and voicing writing aloud. The chapter concludes by considering the challenges of apprenticing young authors in performative cultures and offers recommendations for research and practice.

Becoming writers: exploring writing and identity

This chapter recognises the plurality of children's literacies across the different domains of home and school and the significance of identity in literacy practices. The way in which literacy is viewed has consequences for conceptions of identity, such that identity is viewed as multiple, relational, situated, and always in flux (Moje and Luke 2009). Writing and identity are thus entwined.

Young children's sense of themselves as writers is constructed by the literacy activities in which they engage, both those required in the context of schooling and those in which they volitionally participate in school or beyond. The social environment, their literacy histories, others' perceptions of them as writers, and teacher, parent, and peer interactions around writing also influence their attitudes to and understanding of what it might mean to be a writer in particular contexts (Bourne 2002). Who defines what a good writer is and what counts as good writing is therefore highly context-dependent and constructed, negotiated, and instantiated through interaction. In this sense each writer is always a 'becoming writer', shaping and reshaping their identity and being positioned by others, as well as adopting particular identity positions in the moment.

This dynamic process of identity construction and enactment is influenced by both teachers' and children's conceptions of writing. Studies indicate that teachers tend to conceive of writing practices hierarchically and frequently associate writing with 'creative writing', perceiving this to be literary in nature, related to published works (e.g. McKinney and Giorgis 2009). Pre-service teachers too voice such views, and some perceive children's ability as creative writers as innate or 'fixed'; responsive neither to instruction nor feedback (Norman and Spencer 2005). Such exclusive conceptions of writing and writers fail to recognise the breadth of everyday writing practices in which children and adults engage purposefully.

Teachers' views of writing in the classroom are additionally framed by institutional and assessment discourses and by prescribed curricula, which in contexts of high stakes accountability, tend to profile spelling, grammar, and punctuation, and side-line writing as communication and meaning making (Ryan and Barton 2014). Arguably, the national policy in England, where the studies reported in this chapter were undertaken, is underpinned by an autonomous model of literacy (Street 1998, 2008) which fails to recognise that literacy is ideological and that the 'ways in which people address reading and writing are themselves rooted in conceptions of knowledge, identity, being' (Street 2008, p. 7). Some studies indicate that teachers hold hybrid views about writing and are at least intuitively aware of writing as social practice (McCarthey et al. 2014). Such teachers tend to reflect a combination of Ivanič's (2004) discourses of teaching writing: skills, creativity, process, genre, and social practices. Many practitioners report tensions between their beliefs about writing and their classroom practice, which they consider is institutionally framed and insufficiently aligned with their views or experience (Cremin and Myhill 2012).

Research suggests that teachers may come to ascribe writer identities or essentialist labels to children, ascribing them 'below average' writer identities in response to their apparent school 'readiness' and capacity to identify letters and write letters for instance, reflecting a somewhat mechanical conceptualisation of writing (Yoon 2015). Collier (2010), in a literature review of research about children's identities as writers critiques the field more generally, noting that:

> Narrow ways of describing writer identities are akin to labels. Writers tend to be described in static ways by teachers, by students about themselves, and by researchers who investigate writer identities. Narrow definitions of writers and writer identities preclude the consideration of writing as learning and writing as play, in which new ideas and possibilities are considered.
>
> (Collier 2010, p. 150)

Limited conceptualisations and the practice of labelling can have negative consequences, potentially constraining children's access to certain writing opportunities and shaping teacher feedback. They are also likely to restrict the possibilities of children being offered or taking up certain roles and identities and may in part explain why so many English children express indifference to or report disliking writing (Clarke 2016). Several US studies in this area focus on young people who struggle as writers, whose self-perception is strongly negative (McCarthey 2001, Yoon 2015). Young people's lack of self-esteem and negative identities as writers may also be influenced by their own conceptions of writing as a mechanical activity (Auguste 2018), and by their experience of 'ability' grouping.

Children's identities as writers in school are constructed/re-constructed through classroom writing events, both those they invest in personally and those in which they participate with less interest or commitment. The figured worlds (Holland et al. 1998) in which children's writer identities are constructed and change, build their understanding of what it means to be a writer and the kind of writer they are perceived, or perceive themselves, to be. Studies from the United States (Compton-Lilly 2006), the United Kingdom (Dobson and Stephenson 2017), and Turkey (Seban and Tavsanli 2015) explore figured worlds as contexts in which literacy practices and identities develop. In addition, other researchers explore the ways in which children's identities as writers evolve, and, drawing on Bakhtinian dialogism (Bakhtin 1981, 1986), argue that as they write, children enter into a dialogue with themselves and others. Since writing is a dialogic process, they borrow others' words and create new texts which echo or reflect others' utterances. As Bakhtin observes, we 'live in a world of others' words' (1986, p. 143). Through a study of 19 English language learners in a US kindergarten, Hong (2015) further argues that 'the dialogic becoming processes opened possibilities for young writers to discover and bring their different voices and selves to their writing and enhanced their motivation relative to learning to write and writing to learn' (Hong 2015, p. 301).

Also employing the work of Bakhtin as a theoretical backdrop, Jesson et al. (2016) consider the role and interaction of children and teachers in supporting children's authorial identities. They foreground talk about writing as a mediational tool in becoming a writer, arguing this dialogic space 'can give voice to the silences, the tacit understandings, and the multiple discourses that surround learning to be a writer' (Jesson et al. 2016, p. 155). Whilst such metatalk about writing is not examined specifically in Kissel and Miller's (2015) ethnographic work, the role of peer interaction and feedback from teachers and peers is demonstrated as significant in challenging and shaping young writers' identities. This connects to earlier work by Bomer and Laman (2004) who show that the social and emotional dimensions of peer interactions can lead to enhanced understanding about writing. As Dyson's work (1997; Dyson and Dewayni 2013) has also shown, even in highly structured school activities, writing is socially rooted in playful peer dialogues often of an unofficial nature. Other studies also indicate that children may seek to exercise their agency as authors, thus contributing to the shaping of literacy practices in classrooms (Rowe and Neitzel 2010, Cremin 2017). Taken together, this body of work underscores the potency of interaction and the ways children actively work to take up or reject the roles on offer from teachers and peers; their identities as writers are co-constructed in and through their relationships in school.

The two research projects upon which this chapter draws, whilst respectively focused on the practices of storytelling and story-acting, and the impact of professional writers' engagement on teachers, both took a social practice approach to literacy and acknowledged the social construction and enactment of children's and adults' literate identities. Revisiting literacy events within these projects, this chapter seeks to understand how particular classroom practices positioned children and enabled them to negotiate their identities as authors, apprenticed to the craft. The agency of the young writers and the space to select their ideas and follow their own pathways as writers, as well as the role of voicing their writing aloud appeared to be salient in these contexts, and served, it is argued, to support the children as becoming writers. The methodologies of these studies are now examined before the data are presented.

Methodology

Both the studies were naturalistic in nature, and ethnographic tools (Green and Bloome 1997) were employed to document the social practices of writing and writers' engagement in everyday settings. These were early and primary phase classrooms in the narrative based study, and a residential writing centre and school classrooms in the 'Teachers as Writers' study. In both, children were observed to engage agentically as writers, and positioned themselves and were positioned as authors. The studies did not, however, seek to track children's developing identities as writers, nor understand their 'lived histories' (Hicks 2002) as young authors. The chapter, mainly although not exclusively, draws on data from two classrooms (one per project), in order to consider the influence of the authorial opportunities afforded children in particular literacy events. For this purpose, a literacy event is defined as 'any occasion in which a piece of writing is integral to the nature of the participants' interactions and their interpretive processes' (Brice-Heath 1983, p. 3). The chapter examines how through their interaction in these events, the children were enabled to construct and negotiate their writer identities as they played with ideas and with each other and experienced their writing (and that of others) voiced aloud.

The 'Storytelling and Story-acting' study

In this study (2012–2013), undertaken in six early/primary school settings, adult-focused data included observation, interviews, and video stimulated review, whilst child-focused data included observation, video recording, and the collection of children's stories. The latter encompassed those scribed by adults, those children themselves wrote, and those children scribed for others. Three children in each setting were case studied, but since the young people who were engaged in self-authoring and scribing were not case study children, data were collected opportunistically. In line with the qualitative approach, the dataset was scrutinised, and open, then axial codes identified. These encompassed: children's agency; confidence; sense of belonging and identity; communication, language and literacy; and creativity in stories and performance. The data presented connect to the axial themes of agency and language and literacy and are drawn from several settings, in particular a Reception class (which in the UK is school-entry level), was purposively selected for re-examination since children scribing their own and others' stories became prevalent there. The study used British Education Research Association (BERA 2011) ethical guidelines, and offered and applied principles of confidentiality, including the use of pseudonyms as deployed here.

118 Teresa Cremin

The 'Teachers as Writers' study

This project (2015–2017) set out to build teachers' confidence as writers through their engagement in a five-day residential led by Arvon (a UK creative writing foundation). The extent to which teachers' identities as writers influenced their pedagogy was a key focus. Additionally, the 16 teachers who were allocated to the intervention (half primary and secondary phase) worked in a co-mentoring relationship with another professional writer (post Arvon), both outside and then inside the classroom. This mixed methods study, which focused on the teachers as writers and the consequences for student outcomes in writing, included a Randomised Control Trial of 32 teachers (16 of whom were allocated to the comparison group) and a complementary qualitative data set of observations and interviews of professional writers, teachers, and students. Only the second dataset are drawn upon in this chapter with reference to one primary school teacher's practice and the consequences for the writer identities of her class of 7–8-year-olds. As with the narrative research, inductive coding was deployed and BERA (2011) ethical guidelines were followed.

Becoming writers in the 'Storytelling and Story-acting' study

This approach, advanced by Paley (1990), positions the teacher as the scribe. Yet in England, in half the settings observed, on days when the visiting artist came to facilitate the approach, children spontaneously began to initiate their own related writing activities (Cremin et al. 2018). Many authored and co-authored their own tales with friends and scribed their peers' stories, some of which were later dramatised alongside the ones scribed by their teachers.

Few studies attend to the relationship between this approach and writing (Nicolopoulou et al. 2006, 2015, Cremin 2017). The two US studies, which are largely quantitative, examine the approach as a language intervention and show through hierarchical linear modelling analysis that it is associated with increased print and word awareness. In Nicolopoulou et al.'s (2006) study, it was also noted that many of the participating pre-schoolers became more interested in their journal writing activities (those of a drawn and a dictated nature), and that over time, the length and complexity of their dictated stories increased. In the Cremin, Flewitt et al. (2017) qualitative study, the agency and intentionality shown by the young writers was again noted; they too grasped opportunities to draw their own narratives. In addition, and significantly, many of the children engaged unprompted in writing their own stories and several began to scribe each other's tales for later enactment.

The approach itself is arguably an agentic one, framed around children's own stories which adults scribe verbatim. At the end of the tale (which can take no more than a page), the adult underlines the nouns which will be used for the performance and the child storyteller chooses their own character to inhabit when they enact their tale. In the dramatisation, children make individual decisions as to how to act 'as if' they are a giant, soldier, or lion, for example, or how to create a forest or a frying pan as a group. The practitioners frequently observed that the approach fostered children's volition, as one noted 'it's their stories so they can make it be how they want it to be' and 'it's been getting the boys more into mark-making'. It appeared that the ethos of accepting whatever the children dictated and not altering a word, nor asking for elaboration was salient. Children were free to choose their own characters, events, and settings and did so with considerable delight. In their told tales and self-initiated written narratives, children incorporated personal interests, drew on life experience, popular culture, artefacts in the classroom, and literature.

This ideational freedom appeared to underscore the potency of the approach which was recognised as highly motivating and served to support the children's authorial engagement (Cremin 2017). No idea was censored, all the children's stories scribed by adults were enacted. The children exercised their agency, self-determination, and decision-making, not just as authors of their own oral tales, but also as dramatists, writers, and scribes. Furthermore, as Faulkner (2017) argues, building on Rogoff's (2003) seminal work on children learning through 'intent participation', the approach appears to foster first, second, and third-party intent participation. It enables them to listen to each other's tales and borrow from, adapt, and appropriate each other's ideas. Alongside the child/adult storytelling duo, there were frequently at least one or two other children present close by; in only 12 of the 90 storytelling sessions captured on video was the child narrator 'alone' with the teacher. Different degrees of participation were evident depending on the proximity of these children, but their presence suggested interest in others' ideas and close listening to the tale itself. For example, beyond the first party participation of the storyteller, some 'second-party' participants sat alongside them, watching and listening, others shifted from indirect to intent participation when the acting parts were underlined by the teacher, perhaps anticipating the enactment. Additionally, 'third-party' peripherally participant children, apparently engaged elsewhere, often reappeared in time to listen attentively to the final read-through.

The data indicate that the children appropriated particular characters, actions, and literary tropes, for example princesses, lions, aliens, and popular cultural heroes such as Spiderman or Harry Potter were common in some classrooms. Performance tropes were also noted: in one setting falling in a 'bin' in an exaggerated manner prompted the inclusion of 'bins' in multiple children's stories, in another setting a common castle construction was developed during enactments. It seemed the children's intent participation not only enabled them to draw on each other's voices and ideas, but supported a degree of 'collective meaning making and the social construction of local community narratives' (Faulkner 2017, p. 99). In sum, whilst there was ideational freedom for these young tale tellers, there was also considerable ideational support from the classroom community of storytellers and story performers.

Another element of the authorial apprenticeship offered to the children through this approach was the frequent voicing aloud of their stories. Four oral versions of the tale were evident: the child's unfolding narrative; the teacher's repetition of the tale as it proceeded; the teacher's re-reading of the whole tale with intonation and expression at the close of the scribing; and the teacher's later oral evocation of the same tale, slowly and with pauses during the dramatisation. The enactment was clearly demarcated as a particular author's story, with the teacher announcing, for example, 'Now we'll hear Nathan's tale'. The young author sat in front of the teacher on the story stage (an area marked out on the floor around which the class sat) and was joined by their peers as the tale was brought to life. The author remained a watcher until they too performed a role as their chosen character. Due weight was given to the author at the close of the enactment also, with the teacher observing, for example, 'That was Nathan's tale, let's show our appreciation'. Eager applause followed. In this way children were recognised and honoured as authors and were, through first-, second- and third-party participation, and the enactment, enabled to hear their classmates' stories.

In one class of 5–6-year-olds, the teacher commented that the act of self-initiated drawing or writing their own or peers' tales, became 'one of the main activities of the classroom'. Children committed their own or others' narratives to paper in various ways: in two story books dedicated to this purpose, in folded instant books at the writing table, and on paper in the 'office' role play area. At the start of free-choice time some children rushed to seize the story books or paper, then settled in their chosen spaces, alone, with friends or alongside adults. Children rarely sought adult advice however; rather they drew/wrote their narratives without support, or gathered in pairs or small groups to scribe each other's tales. However adult approbation was sought out in order to enact their stories.

There were multiple entries in this class's story books: drawn tales with later scribing, long strings of letters or lines and short written texts. It was clear that the children were experimenting with the written word and ascribing meaning to their mark-making. There were multiple reports of children taking to mark-making for the first time: Ethan informed his practitioner that he had written stories at home on his mum's bed and on the wall, and Bill brought in a Scooby Doo tale he had written (a series of S's and D's in lines across the page showing left to right directionality with pictures) that he wanted the class to enact. When Rachel scribed her friend's Holly's story she drew a number of visuals to represent each part of the oral narrative (see Figure 7.1). This enabled Holly as the author to read it to her teacher using the pictures and helped her teacher read it aloud during the dramatisation. The written text is the teacher's later written record.

Another child, Micah, an often-reluctant mark-maker, having dictated a story to an early years practitioner, went straight to the office role play area and created another, working alone for nearly 10 minutes on a picture. A visiting education student reported later that Micah, who tended to be shy, had asked her to 'write my story down, so it can be acted out'. Looking intently at her pictures Micah told her tale. Later when her teacher asked which story she

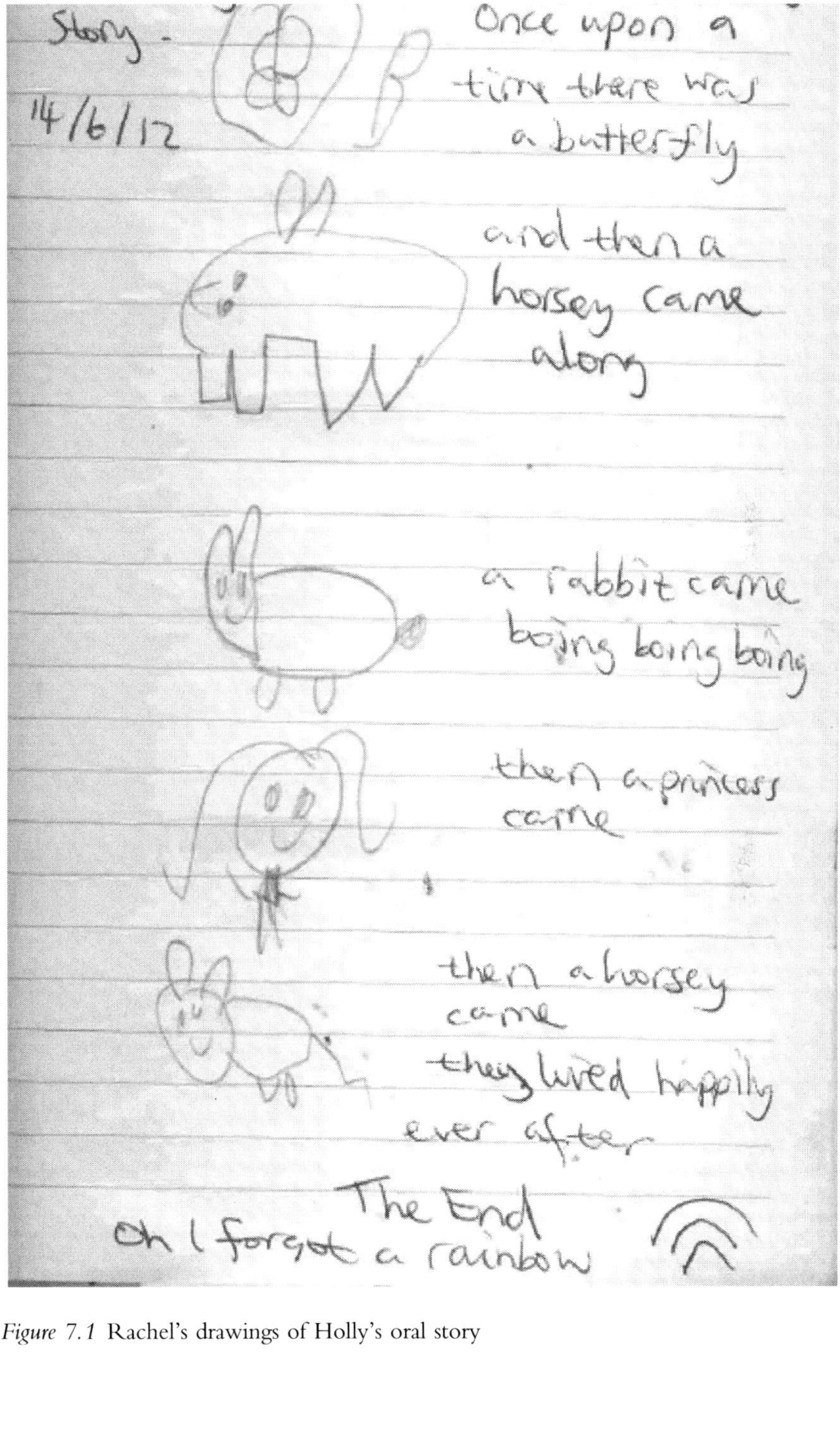

Story.
14/6/12

Once upon a time there was a butterfly

and then a horsey came along

a rabbit came boing boing boing

then a princess came

then a horsey came they lived happily ever after

The End
Oh I forgot a rainbow

Figure 7.1 Rachel's drawings of Holly's oral story

wished to act out, her original narrative scribed by the teacher or her new self-initiated one, Micah chose the latter and hugged it to herself as the class settled around the story stage, clearly proud. Her tale read: '*Once upon a time there was a cat and the mummy put some food in the bowl and then she spitted it out. Then she went to the shops and she got her favourite one. The mummy was cross because the baby cat went on its own.*' In a manner not dissimilar to her protagonist, Micah was known to be a fussy eater, so perhaps her tale was allusive. Micah played the young cat in the performance, literally embodying her own writing and effecting to spit out the food with nervous delight. Her friend Hayley enacted the mummy cat, whilst other children became the bowl and the shops. As the class applauded, Micah returned to her seat on the edge of the circle and whispered to an adult: 'That was my story, I'm a writer'. In doing so she affirmed a sense of herself as a writer in this context and was recognised as such by the early years practitioner and her peers. The fact that her writing had been used as the 'script' for whole class enactment gave real purpose to her early authoring. In the weeks that followed her teacher reported that Micah frequently chose to write her own tales or take dictation of her friends' stories and sought to ensure that these were enacted.

When children initiated their own story-writing or scribed other children's stories, writing was experienced as a meaningful activity, an opportunity to write for themselves and/or their friends about personal and common interests. In many ways their texts operated as 'tools of identity' (Holland et al. 1998). They sometimes scribed in pairs using the same characters creating shared stories, borrowed or swapped ideas and used the opportunity to make sense of experience by entering into a dialogue with themselves. For example, Isabelle who had just moved to a new house due to her parents splitting up wrote: '*One windy day the tree branches were blowing and a little bird shivered in his nest, but mummy was beside him.*' She chose to be the little bird in the enactment and insisted her story was taken home that night. One of Jo's self-initiated tales was a more direct retelling about the challenge of looking after his family's puppies: '*Once upon a time there were two puppies one called Fifi and one called Rose. Rose got out and everyone shouted loud and she didn't come back. Then the next day she did and they played again.*' Through their tales children drew on experience and used writing to make sense, to connect with one another, to explore, understand, and express themselves literally and metaphorically. Their engagement in these writing/scribing opportunities prompted the children to reflect upon and explore their experiences, investigating possible selves and developing and affirming a sense of themselves as writers.

The early years practitioners, realising that this mark-making was meaningful and a form of personal action and reflection, respected the children's self-initiated narratives and sought to ensure space for enacting them, although this was not always possible. As a result, groups of children sometimes acted out one of their written or child-scribed tales in free choice time, emulating the class story-circle routine. The enactment appeared to be a significant driver for the children to commit their self-authored and scribed tales to paper. As a communal social activity, a potential 'textual playground' (Dyson and Dewayani, 2013, p. 258), it gave both context and purpose to writing and perhaps reflected their growing awareness of the relationship between writers and their audiences. The children, energised by the opportunity to create a story that might be enacted publicly, in effect a playscript, seized the opportunity to write and to position themselves as authors. The approach appeared to create a space in which considerable ideational freedom and support was offered, the children's tales were respected, and the continual voicing aloud, attentive listening to, and watching of each other's narratives offered further support. This fostered the children's volitional involvement as young apprentice writers.

Becoming writers in the 'Teachers as Writers' study

This study sought to support teachers on their own journeys as writers with a view to exploring the consequences for children as writers. The residential encompassed workshops, one-to-one tutorials, opportunities to share writing, and space and time to write in the afternoons alone or with others. Whilst few teachers viewed themselves as writers at the outset, gradually they came to accept and, in many cases, embrace the title 'writer'. To some extent this was due to a shift or a broadening in the way being a writer was understood, but there was also a greater commitment to this identity position. The supportive Arvon writing community played a significant role in this transformation. An invitational context for writing was established which enabled the teachers to generate and incubate ideas, and although many were initially anxious about sharing their writing, over time their work was read with interest and responded to with commitment by the tutors, and their assurance grew. Tutors mostly emphasised the teachers' authorial agency, prompting them to make their own choices in response to advice offered, although some teachers found this hard and deferred to their tutors' expertise. The workshops triggered memories and were enriched by the discussion of readings, the use of postcards, objects, and storytelling. Teachers found this engaging and more than a term after the project ended, the interviews indicated that their newly claimed writing identities had been sustained and strengthened, they continued to use the Arvon approach and tried to foreground 'writers not writing'.

There were pedagogical consequences of the teachers' experience as writers, both intended and realised. The teachers wanted to develop the relaxed, supportive ethos back in school, were keen to offer periods of freewriting, and to afford children more autonomy and choice as writers. They also wanted to make more time for revision and supportive feedback, as well as appropriate the Arvon writing activities. Many also intended to write alongside their students in class. Whilst some did, observational evidence suggests that others, concerned about curriculum coverage and potential behaviour problems, did not model being a writer in this way. Nonetheless the data indicate that the Arvon ethos was embraced and more flexible use of time and space for writing, sharing writing, and freewriting opportunities were created. The two features which were much less commonly implemented back in school were explicit teaching and feedback on writing.

Having developed their own assurance as writers and been invited to consider the concept of 'being a writer' at Arvon, the teachers developed more awareness of their students as writers, began to acknowledge identity work in writing, and explore the role of autonomy, agency, and choice. Their practice shifts had an impact on the young people: the focus group interviews (6–8 per focus group in 16 classes) showed that the majority felt the project had a positive impact on their sense of self as writers, their motivation, confidence, ownership of writing, and skills as writers. Commonly the students voiced increased enjoyment and engagement in writing, due in large part, they perceived, to the new creative space being offered, to the chance to make more of their own choices, to freewriting and sharing and discussing ideas. Many observed that their previous experience of writing in school had been less engaging and more routinised, and that now they had increased freedom and the opportunity to use their imaginations. For example:

> I just like being free when I write … I like being in my head when I'm writing. I like writing what I'm thinking, what I like … whatever I want.
>
> (10-year-old)

> The thing I most enjoy about writing is how much you can use your imagination … it really is just something of your mind that will go the reader and say 'wow'!
>
> (11-year-old)

The autonomy offered by freewriting was particularly popular; children reported enjoying being able to let ideas and words have space to form freely without constant review or evaluation. Teachers introduced 'Just Write' notebooks in which students could make their own choices, explore ideas, respond to freewriting prompts, and later choose whether or not to return to their evolving idea. In these books, children noted that they were able to exercise their ownership as writers; for example, two 10-year-olds commented 'you get to choose what to write, what to think and feel and you can say it all' and 'it doesn't matter what other people think, it's about what you think'. During freewriting children often chose to draw upon their lives, and, their teachers perceived, became more invested in this writing as a consequence. As previous research has indicated, choice has salience for writers (e.g. Cremin and Myhill 2012) and students valued this new creative space in which their authorial intentions were respected. This time to 'just write' in un-assessed notebooks, contrasted, many of the teachers commented, with their previous practice which they described as more teacher-led and teacher-directed, 'writing to fulfil specific objectives'. Nonetheless, tensions remained with teachers reporting conflicts between freewriting and curriculum coverage, and in some classrooms, it was framed as an additional isolated extra, limiting its potential efficacy in supporting writers.

A new emphasis on sharing writing developed in some classrooms. Tina, a teacher of 7–8-year-olds, had commented at Arvon that she 'was hyperventilating at the thought of sharing' and was 'afraid of being exposed' as a less than proficient writer. Gradually though she had come to share her writing and back in school she sought to voice her work and invited the children to read aloud their writing to one another, in pairs, small groups, and the whole class. Over time, a new rhythm of voicing writing was established in this class. No pressure was applied, but Tina, attuned to the potential for exposure, sensitively invited children to offer extracts of their emerging compositions: a verse, phrase, image, or closing line and voiced her own. Some examples of the children's story openings heard in one observation include: '*"Promise me" he said sternly, "you will never tell …"*'; '*The night was cold and dark and the mouse knew that if she …*'; '*I remember when I was no bigger than our family dog …*'; '*My mother is a dreamer …*'; '*Once there lived an old man who …*'; and '*Snow fell and Tanja hid, afraid that …*'. These opening extracts were uttered expressively into the classroom sharing space, often with a strong sense of the ellipsis inviting the audience to wonder and imagine. By reading aloud their writing and by listening to each other's, their teacher's and the professional writer's extracts, the emerging authorial voices of this community were heard. By sharing their writing in this public forum (rather than just in the school exercise book for their teacher), children were enacting subtly different identities as authors.

Tina, who commented that she planned to borrow some of their extracts for freewriting prompts, commented, 'We've never heard so much of their work in class', and acknowledged that previously, 'We've marked it and displayed it, but not really focused on sharing it like this, it's different and they're surprisingly interested and really listen'. The children responded enthusiastically, sometimes voting on a favourite line or explaining why they liked it. One noted, 'We get to hear everyone's stories and you can magpie loads', and another that 'You get to know what people are good at, there's some great writers in our class'. Pride and a sense of positive writer identities appeared to be developing for some children. On one occasion a child from another class, sent to work in Tina's room, was told by a peer, 'If you're stuck with your story go and talk to Damon, he's good at hooking the reader in'. Damon, recognised as a writer with particular skills, was asked for his advice, perhaps prompting him to re-negotiate his own and others' views of him as writer. Another child, responding to a friend's poem, conveyed his respect by observing 'It's kinda like music, how do you do that? It's brilliant', affirming his sense of the boy's discoursal voice. Following an emotional reading of her own story (begun at Arvon) to the class, Tina and her assistant tried to write alongside the children during freewriting – she perceived this reduced the traditionally hierarchical teacher–pupil relationships. As one child noted, 'I like it when we all write, it's like we're in it together'.

The observational evidence from this classroom reveals considerable reading aloud, attentive listening, emotional engagement with their own and each other's writing, calm quietness during freewriting, and energised conversation at other times as ideas were discussed. Through offering their writing to each other and through reading aloud each other's writing during feedback sessions, Tina and the children were co-constructing their identities as writers. However, the shaping influence of voicing writing aloud or subvocally on own writing is not known.

Conclusion

The figured worlds in the project classrooms focused upon in this chapter shifted in response to new approaches used by teachers which had consequences for the writerly positions and identities adopted by children and made available to them. In effect children seized or were afforded opportunities within these practices to adopt new positions as authors and some came to self-identify as writers. In the 'Storytelling and Story-acting' project, some children chose to author their own narratives and scribe their friends' stories for the classroom community to enact, and an emerging sense of becoming writers developed. In the 'Teachers as Writers' research, it appeared that, through the new freewriting practices in which the children enthusiastically engaged, and through reading aloud their own and each other's writing, some children reflected an enhanced sense of being a writer. Observational data confirmed this and have been drawn upon to explore the shaping influence of authorial opportunities on young creative writers. Both the younger children's class storybooks and the older children's 'just write' journals enabled them to exercise their latent authorial agency – their rights as writers. This tended to support positive identity enactments as writers.

However, working in the world of school, figured as it is by performative pressures also, caused real challenges. In the class of 5–6-year-olds, the early years practitioner, whilst she considered the young writers' communicative intent deserved to be encouraged and celebrated, expressed concern that their pictures and early mark-making could be seen as 'scribbling' and would not meet national requirements. In the class of 7–8-year-olds, Tina experienced a tension between 'allowing the children to develop as writers and explore what they want to say' and the accountability and assessment regime. She perceived there was a 'deep divide between writing for the curriculum and children as writers' writing for themselves. In both studies some children began to think of themselves as writers and the practice of voicing writing aloud (during scribing of the children stories, dramatisation, sharing extracts, or within feedback spaces), arguably helped the young people construct a sense of themselves as members of a community of authors. In the older class, the adults too were members of this writing community in the time set aside for freewriting and shared their writing as writers.

Looking across studies of writer identity, Collier (2010) concludes that particular writing practices seem 'to foster competent writer identities for a range of students' (p. 161). In addition to valuing talk (in the form of teacher-student dialogues and peer support), she posits that valuing students' preferences offers potential. This was borne out in the two studies examined here. The motivational power of choice was evident both in writing for enactment in Paley's (1990) approach and in freewriting triggered by the Arvon residential – it enabled children to exercise their ownership and authorial agency. Few framing expectations with regard to form, grammar, punctuation, or content were evident, beyond the invitation to share a story in the younger children's classrooms. The younger children chose to write unbidden, and in the older children's classrooms, their compositions, whilst timetabled, remained 'just writing' – without formal restraint. As Dyson (1997, p. 166) observes, 'for children, as for adults, freedom is a verb, a becoming; it is experienced as an expanded sense of agency, of possibility for choice and action'. In both contexts, the writing was undertaken at the children's own pace, in their own way, and on subjects that they chose and cared about. It was, potentially at least, writing that was personally purposeful. These two studies nuance Collier's (2010) conclusion that some writing practices nurture competent writer identities for more students. Together the studies signpost the influence that open opportunities to write can have on fostering children's identities as authors. They also suggest that if such opportunities are underscored by ideational freedom and support, and are buoyed by space and time for voicing writing, this can help nurture young children's sense of self as becoming writers.

Nonetheless, the ways that writing practices that apprentice young authors, such as those described here, change over time deserve increased attention. More longitudinal studies of children's shifting identities as writers are needed to add to those of Compton-Lily (2006), Elf (2017), and Krogh and Jakobsen (2019). In addition, more needs to be known about the extent to which freewriting affords children of all abilities opportunities to self-identify as writers, and whether, and in what ways, voicing writing aloud is influenced by power and status among students, possibly constraining the construction of some children's writer identities. Young children on the journey to becoming writers need support and encouragement. Storytelling and writing for enactment as well as freewriting represent possibility spaces for young apprentice writers, spaces worth further exploration.

References

Auguste, E. 2018. The balancing act of kindergarten writing instruction. *Educational Leadership*, 75(7), 61–64.
Bakhtin, M. 1981. *The dialogic imagination* (trans. M. Holquist). Austin: University of Texas Press.
Bakhtin, M. 1986. *Speech genres and other late essays* (trans. V. W. McGee). Austin: University of Texas Press.
BERA. 2011. *Ethical guidelines for educational research*. London: British Education Research Association.
Bomer, R. and Laman, T. 2004. Positioning in a primary writing workshop: joint action in the discursive production of writing subjects. *Research in the Teaching of English*, 38(4), 420–466.

Bourne, J. 2002. 'Oh what will miss say!' Constructing texts and identities in the discursive processes of classroom writing. *Language and Education*, 16(4), 241–259.

Brice-Heath, S. 1983. *Ways with words: language, life and work in communities and classrooms.* Cambridge: Cambridge University Press.

Clarke, C. 2016. *Children's and young people's writing in 2015.* London: NLT.

Collier, D. 2010. Journey to becoming a writer: review of research about children's identities as writers. *Language and Literacy*, 12(1), 147–164.

Compton-Lily, C. 2006. Identity, childhood culture, and literacy learning. *Journal of Early Childhood Literacy*, 6(1), 57–76.

Cremin, T. 2017. Apprentice story writers: exploring young children's print awareness and agency in early story authoring. In: Cremin, T., et al. eds. *Storytelling in early childhood: enriching language, literacy, and classroom culture.* London and New York: Routledge, 67–84.

Cremin, T. and Locke, T. eds. 2017. *Writer identity and the teaching and learning of writing.* London and New Zealand: Routledge.

Cremin, T. and Myhill, D. 2012. *Writing voices: creating communities of writers.* London: Routledge.

Cremin, T. and Oliver, L. 2016. Teachers as writers: a systematic review. *Research Papers in Education*, 32(3), 269–296.

Cremin, T., Flewitt, R., et al. eds. 2017. *Storytelling in early childhood: language, literacy, and classroom culture.* London and New York: Routledge.

Cremin, T., Lillis, T., et al. 2017. Professional writers' identities. In: Cremin, T. and Locke, T. eds. *Writer identity and the teaching and learning of writing.* London and New Zealand: Routledge, 18–36.

Cremin, T., Myhill, D., et al. 2017. Teachers as writers, for Arts Council England research team. Available from: www.teachersaswriters.org/general/teachers-writers-full-research-report/ [Accessed 24. 02. 19].

Cremin, T., et al. 2018. Storytelling and story acting: co-construction in action. *Journal of Early Childhood Research*, 16(1), 1–15.

Dobson, T. and Stephenson, L. 2017. Primary pupils' creative writing. *Literacy*, 51(3), 162–168.

Dyson, A. H. 1997. *Writing superheroes: contemporary childhood, popular culture and classroom literacy.* New York: Teachers College Press.

Dyson, A. H. and Dewayni, S. 2013. Writing in childhood cultures. In: Hall, K., et al. *International handbook of research on children's literacy, learning, and culture.* Oxford: Blackwell, 258–274.

Elf, N. 2017. Taught by bitter experience. In: Cremin, T. and Locke, T. eds. *Writer identity and the teaching and learning of writing.* London and New Zealand: Routledge, 183–199.

Faulkner, D. 2017. Young children as storytellers: collective meaning making and sociocultural transmission. In: Cremin, T., et al. eds. *Storytelling in early childhood: enriching language, literacy, and classroom culture.* London and New York: Routledge.

Green, J. and Bloome, D. 1997. Ethnography and ethnographers of and in education. In: Flood, J., et al. eds. *A handbook for literacy educators.* New York: Macmillan, 1–12.

Hall, L. A. 2012. Rewriting identities: creating spaces for students and teachers to challenge the norms of what it means to be a writer in school. *Journal of Adolescent and Adult Literacy*, 55, 368–373.

Heaney, S. 1990. *The redress of poetry.* Oxford: Clarendon.

Hicks, D. 2002. *Reading lives: working-class children and literacy learning*. New York: Teachers College Press.

Holland, D., et al. 1998. *Identity and agency in cultural worlds*. Cambridge, MA: Harvard University Press.

Hong, H. 2015. Exploring young children's writer identity. *International Journal of Early Childhood*, 47(2), 301–316.

Ivanič, R. 2004. Discourses of writing and learning to write. *Language and Education*, 18 (3), 220–245.

Jesson, R., Fontich, X. and Myhill, D. 2016. Creating dialogic spaces: talk as a mediational tool in becoming a writer. *International Journal of Educational Research*, 80, 155–163.

Kissel, B. T. and Miller, E. T. 2015. Reclaiming power in the writers' workshop: defending curricula, countering narratives, and changing identities in prekindergarten classrooms. *The Reading Teacher*, 69(1), 77–86.

Krogh, E. and Jakobsen, K. S. 2019. *Understanding young people's writing development*. London: Routledge.

Lillis, T. and Curry, M. J. 2010. *Academic writing in a global context*. London: Routledge.

McCarthey, S. J. 2001. Identity construction in elementary readers and writers. *Reading Research Quarterly*, 36(2), 122–151.

McCarthey, S., Woodard, R. and Kang, G. 2014. Elementary teachers negotiating discourses in writing instruction. *Written Communication*, 31(1), 58–90.

McKinney, M. and Giorgis, C. 2009. Narrating and performing identity . *Journal of Literacy Research*, 41, 104–149.

Moje, E. and Luke, A. 2009. Literacy and identity. *Reading Research Quarterly*, 44(4), 415–437.

Nicolopoulou, A., McDowell, J. and Brockmeyer, C. 2006. Narrative play and emergent literacy: storytelling and story acting meet journal writing. In: Singer, D., Golinkoff, R. and Hirsh-Pasek, K., eds. *Play=learning*. New York: Oxford University Press, 124–144.

Nicolopoulou, A., et al. 2015. Using a narrative-and play-based activity to promote low-income preschoolers' oral language, emergent literacy, and social competence. *Early Research Childhood Quarterly*, 31, 147–162.

Norman, K. A. and Spencer, B. H. 2005. Our lives as writers. *Teacher Education Quarterly*, 32(1), 25–40.

Paley, V. G. 1990. *The boy who would be a helicopter*. Cambridge, MA: Harvard University Press.

Rogoff, B. 2003. *The cultural nature of human development*. New York: Oxford University Press.

Rowe, D. W. and Neitzel, C. 2010. Interest and agency in 2–3-year-olds' participation in emergent writing. *Reading Research Quarterly*, 45(2), 169–195.

Ryan, M. and Barton, G. 2014. The spatialized practices of teaching writing in elementary schools. *Research in the Teaching of English*, 48(3), 303–328.

Seban, D. and Tavsanli, Ö. F. 2015. Children's sense of being a writer: identity construction in second grader writers' workshop. *International Electronic Journal of Elementary Education*, 7(2), 217–234.

Street, B. 1998. New literacies in theory and practice: what are the implications for language in education? *Linguistics and Education*, 10(1), 1–24.

Street, B. V. 2008. New literacies, new times: developments in literacy studies. In: Street, B. V. and Hornberger, N. eds. *Encyclopedia of language and education, volume 2: literacy*. New York: Springer, 3–14.

Yoon, H. S. 2015. Assessing children in kindergarten: the narrowing of language, culture and identity in the testing era. *Journal of Early Childhood Literacy*, 15(3), 364–393.

8 Developing confident writers

Fostering audience awareness in primary school writing classrooms

Honglin Chen and Emma Rutherford Vale

Introduction

The ability to represent, respond to, and connect with audience is fundamental to growing into a confident writer. It is through the writer's interaction with the audience that meaning is created and negotiated (Park 1982). Research into audience has shown that the ability to address readers and meet their needs is a distinct feature of syntactic complexity (Ede 1981) and cognitive development (Kroll 1978). Expertise in writing therefore develops not only with the 'organic growth of form and structure' but also the growing awareness of context including audience expectations (Ramanathan and Kaplan 1996, p. 23).

A highly developed sense of audience is a key learning outcome in English curricula in many Anglophone countries. For example, the Australian Curriculum: English (ACE) highlights the capacity to 'create imaginative, informative and persuasive texts for different purposes and audiences' as a hallmark of becoming a competent writer (ACARA 2015). Similarly, audience awareness is underscored by the National Curriculum in England: English Programmes of Study where all students are required to develop an ability to 'write clearly, accurately, and coherently, adapting their language and style in and for a range of contexts, purposes, and audiences' (DfE 2014). Both curricula stress the need to develop school children's adaptability to different purposes and audiences in learning to write. While the important role of audience has been widely acknowledged, the concept is often understood narrowly by teachers and researchers as a real, concrete person whom the writer can imagine and write for (Magnifico 2010). 'Consider your audience' remains one of the most frequently mentioned but least understood concepts (Ede 1979, Lunsford and Ede 1996, Hyland 2005).

This chapter aims to provide an integrated and principled understanding of the concept of audience by drawing together interdisciplinary perspectives, including rhetorical, cognitive, and social cultural, seeing it as a linguistic and semiotic construct. Through document analysis, we trace developmental changes in audience awareness from early to late primary school years, as are reflected in the ACE. Drawing on interviews and lesson observation data collected from two literacy classes in one regional school in Australia, we discuss some of the ways in which the expectations and needs of the audience differ according to the genre and purpose of the text. The chapter makes suggestions on how teachers may support and foster a clear sense of how to address, engage, and invoke audience in the primary school context.

The concept of audience

The concept of audience emerged as a topic of research interest in composition and communication studies in the late 1970s and early 1980s (e.g. Britton et al. 1975, Ede 1979, Park 1982, Kroll 1984). The concept has different emphases according to different theoretical positions. To date, there are three broad theoretical approaches to audience: rhetorical, cognitive, and social cultural (Ede 1979, Kroll 1984, Magnifico 2010). Those that privilege a rhetorical perspective consider audience as a key element of a rhetorical situation, defining it as 'person(s) rhetorically engaged in a situation' (Bitzer 1971, p. 6). Emphasis is placed on a kind of transactional relationship between the writer and reader where the writer analyses the rhetorical situation and adapts his or her writing accordingly to address the identified needs, expectations, and concerns (Ede 1984, Kroll 1984). Developing into writers from this perspective requires becoming conscious of the audience's convictions and concerns and learning 'how to make choices appropriate to the exigencies of the situation' (Pareitti 2009, p. 167). Many and Henderson (2005) argue that gaining such rhetorical sensitivity is a crucial step in learning to write to persuade and convince others.

The cognitive conception of audience extends beyond identification of the characteristics of the audience to focus instead on the internal representation that the writer makes of the audience in the writing process (Berkenkotter 1981, Flower and Hayes 1981). The representation draws on the writer's ability to 'infer and articulate the knowledge, attitudes, values, and goals of the readers' (Black 1989, p. 232), providing a heuristic for cognitive activities of planning, generating ideas, writing, and revising. The writer must select information and present it in a clear, appropriate, and precise manner to guide and facilitate the audience's comprehension and interpretation (Kroll 1984). This interactive quality of the text which reflects largely the purpose of the writer's thought, transformed and adapted to the audience, is referred to as a reader-based prose (Flower 1981, Carvalho 2002).

The emphasis on rhetorical and reader sensitivity gives primary attention to the dominant role of audience in the creation of meaning. In contrast, a social cultural approach locates audience within the cultural norms and conventions of a discourse community seeing it as a socially constructed concept (Kroll 1984). Instead of just responding to real readers, the writer creates a 'fictional audience' within a text, 'by observing conventions which "imply" or "project" an audience with particular knowledge, assumptions, and attitudes toward the writer and subject matter' (Kroll 1984, p. 182). Park

(1982) suggests that this sense of implied audience is largely informed and shaped by the writer's knowledge of genre and conventions. Ede and Lunsford (1984) expand on the seminal work of Park and others to present a multi-dimensional conception of audience, arguing that the writer both addresses and invokes an audience: an *audience addressed* who reads the text, and an *audience invoked* whom the writer creates through language choices (p. 90). The invocation of an addressed audience, a sense of the ways in which the writer's intention and purpose can be identified and recognised by the reader, has come to be regarded as an essential quality of effective writing (Park 1982, Kroll 1984). However, the current teaching of writing pays inadequate attention to the dynamic relationship between audience, genre, and convention (Park 1982).

An integrated framework

It seems that a nuanced conception of audience must draw attention to the many ways in which students address and invoke audience and meet the audience's expectations and needs. The complex interplay between a writer's ability to address and invoke is vital to considering audience and writing consciously to account for them (also reader awareness Holliway 2010, Hyland 2005). Thus, an integrated understanding of audience awareness encompasses the following three aspects:

- audience addressed: audience involved in a rhetorical situation addressed to achieve the writer's goal and purpose (the rhetorical perspective);
- audience as reader: conceptions or awareness in the writer's mind that shapes the text to be read and comprehended (the cognitive perspective); and
- audience invoked: textual presence (Black 1989) created by the writer and defined by the genre, norms, and conventions (the social cultural perspective).

To date, however, much of the research has not considered how the writer's sense of audience manifests itself in text. A coherent model of language that takes account of the social nature of meaning making is required to draw together conceptions of writer audience relations discussed here and how these are realised in written texts.

Considering audience: a social semiotic perspective

Systemic Functional Linguistics (SFL) offers such a model of language; it connects linguistic form to its function in social contexts. A central premise of SFL is that texts are configurations of meaning construed between speakers or community members in specific situations to achieve their goals within a cultural setting (Rose and Martin 2012). Within this social view of language audience plays a central role, as Hasan (2005, p. 61) aptly points out – 'the possibility of an other is always already there in every linguistic act'. Such an 'other' or audience orientation is towards 'meanings in context' (Martin and White 2005, p. 94) – meanings construed between the writer and reader through semiotic activity in two interdependent social contexts: the immediate context or *context of situation* in which a text is produced and the *context of culture* in the wider discourse community within which communication takes place (Halliday and Hasan 1985).

Within a functional view, context both construes and is construed by text. Audience can thus be considered at two levels of abstraction. In the context of situation, audience can be encapsulated linguistically in the language being used to describe the nature of social activity or *field*, the social relationships being enacted or *tenor*, and the modes of contact or *mode*. Notions of audiences associate most closely with the register variable of tenor, realised through the interpersonal metafunction, which is overtly concerned with realising writer audience relationships, doing much of the linguistic heavy lifting to address and invoke audience in texts. A full conception of audience within this model, though, extends beyond the interpersonal metafunction (Martin and Rose 2008, Martin and White 2005). Increasingly, sophisticated understandings of audience shape writer choices across the three metafunctions. When addressing, conceptualising, or shaping a particular kind of reader, the writer must consider how they position themselves interpersonally in relation to audience (e.g. Do I ask a question or give a command? How forceful can I be in my argument?). Consideration of the age and expertise of an addressed audience will also shape choices of *ideational* or field-related meanings (e.g. How technical can I be with this audience?). Considerations of the audience as reader will shape choices related to the *textual* metafunction (e.g. How can I organise my meanings to be clear, coherent, and to guide the reader through my arguments?).

Within any cultural context, different kinds of meanings are construed and different social goals are realised through genres. In the context of schooling, the practices and bodies of knowledge of each subject or discipline constitute a cultural context or discourse community and the meanings of that group are enacted through *genres* of the classroom (Derewianka 2012). The writer can examine what staging and phasing will engage a reader and enable him or her to fulfil the goal as writer, what kind of play with conventional stages and phases might surprise or delight readers by upsetting expectations, and what room is there to innovate on accepted conventions of staging and phasing within the discourse community.

More recently, development of the *appraisal* system provides further insights into the interpersonal resources that can be deployed to 'write the reader into the texts' (Martin and White 2005, p. 95). A central concern is with dialogistic dispositions (e.g. alignment/disalignment, distance/solidarity), the various ways in which the writer engages with the audience in text. Each dialogic positioning construes a sense of audience that invokes and allows for identification and recognition of prior utterances, alternative viewpoints, and anticipated responses (Martin and White 2005). Such nuanced and increasingly sophisticated understandings of audience become more salient to writing success as students progress through school. Fostering young writers' capacity to involve, engage, and respond to audience requires thoughtful consideration of how intricate writer–reader relationships are shaped and realised through language at various levels.

The data

Data informing this chapter draws from a larger study, *Transforming Literacy Outcomes* (*TRANSLIT* 2014–2017), investigating how literacy progresses across the years of school from preschool to high school. The total data set consists of three clusters of schools, selected according to social positioning and student diversity, comprising nine research sites across preschool, primary, and high school. The data reported in this chapter are drawn from one primary school site in the cluster of Portside, a regional city in New South Wales, Australia. At the time of data collection, Portside Primary School was part of a program of targeted additional funding to support improved literacy and numeracy outcomes under a National Partnerships initiative. Additional funding included the appointment of an instructional leader, expert in literacy and numeracy instruction, to work alongside teachers and students in the early primary years (Kindergarten to Year 2). As such, Portside data provide insights into current literacy pedagogy and teaching practices implemented to support writing instruction.

Data from Portside primary comprise lesson observations, interviews with teachers, curriculum documents, and student writing samples. The classroom observation phase involved non-participant observation in the classrooms of sampled teachers and their students. Teachers were interviewed before and at the end of each observed lesson. The initial interview ascertained teachers' perceptions of literacy demands and challenges at the transition points. The follow-up interview explored the literacy teaching practices employed by the teacher to support student literacy development. Observation data selected for analysis here comprises two literacy lessons: Year 2 (2015) and Years 3/4 (2016). The selected lessons were identified as they have an explicit focus on teaching writing and an instructional focus on audience. Anna, an early career teacher, was responsible for the Year 2 class and had been trained in an instructional strategy to support literacy in the early years called L3. Kate, a highly experienced teacher, assistant principal, and school literacy training provider teaches the Years 3/4 class.

For this chapter, lesson observation data were analysed to identify pedagogic practice that fostered the development of audience awareness. In particular, the analysis focused on identifying strategies the teachers used to promote audience awareness and analysing conceptions of audience apparent in identified instances of teacher instruction, modelling, dialogue, and feedback. Teacher interview transcripts were analysed using NVivo software. Text queries were conducted using the search terms 'audience', 'reader', and 'purpose' to locate instances where teachers discussed the role of audience in student writing. These data sources were triangulated with document analysis of the ACE. Curriculum content was analysed for references to 'audience', 'reader', and 'purpose', particularly in the content of the Language and Literacy strands. Audience related curriculum content was reanalysed using the analytical framework of audience as addressed, as reader, or as invoked.

Growing into writers: audience awareness in the curriculum

In this section, we discuss how the concept of audience is approached in the ACE. Analysis centres around ways in which audience expectations are articulated and defined in the Curriculum. The cumulative nature of the Curriculum means that the analysis can shed light on how audience awareness develops as a key learning outcome across the primary years of schooling. An overview of the audience expectations is provided in Table 8.1.

Not surprisingly the description of audience expectations is found in the 'Language for interaction' content organiser of each strand, reflecting a view of texts as realising simultaneously meanings about something, *with someone*, and in some form (Derewianka 2012). Explicit conceptions of audience are apparent in the curriculum content from Year 2, although foundational understandings of audience are evident in the early years. The idea of *an addressed audience* is developed in the Foundation years through consideration of the way language changes 'depending on relationships between people' (ACELA1428). Thus, in the early years considerations of audience raise sensitivity to ways in which language is influenced by whom the speaker interacts with. This focus is developed in the content elaboration 'that we use different tone and style of language with different people' (ACELA1428 content elaboration). Understanding that language choices are adapted in response to audience is expanded in Year 1 where students recognise that there are multiple ways of making meaning and that texts are received and reacted to differently according to audience. For example, students begin to recognise 'the effect of words, symbols, gestures and body language on the ways communications are received by others' (ACELA1444 content elaboration).

Notions of audience are thus underpinned by a view of meaning making as socially negotiated. References to audience are more explicit in the Curriculum from Year 2 and conception of audience widens from interaction with familiar people and contexts to an increasing range of contexts as students move across proficiency levels. For example, students in Year 2 are expected to 'create short imaginative, informative and persuasive texts … for familiar and some less familiar audiences' (ACELY 1668). By the end of Year 3 the Achievement Standard requires that students 'create a range of texts for familiar and unfamiliar audiences'.

It is evident that the ACE conceptualises development of audience awareness as an expansion of a repertoire of audiences and purposes, shifting from an ability to address well-known audiences who are present, familiar or can be imagined and defined easily, to a growing capacity to adapt to a wider range of audiences who are more generalised (Rubin and Rafoth 1986). For example, in Year 4 students are expected to write for 'a widening range of audiences' (ACELY 1694). Increasingly worldly awareness of *an addressed audience* is evident in Years 5 and 6 where the Achievement standard for Year 6 describes students who can 'communicate with peers and teachers from other classes and schools, community members, and individuals and groups'. Thus, at the end of primary school, students develop from writing for a small range of familiar individuals to writing for personal, peer and community addressing audiences of individuals and groups.

Curriculum content addressing the notion of *an invoked audience* begins somewhat later, appearing in the description of audience expectations in Year 3 and is extended in later primary years. The curriculum is specific about language resources and knowledge that can be employed to engage, impact, and influence the intended audience. For example, students in Year 3 are asked to develop understanding of how the author's choices of words are 'intended to persuade ... readers to agree with the view presented', and to choose 'appropriate text structure for a writing purpose and sequence content for clarity and audience impact'.

The relationship between 'text complexity' and the associated purpose and intended audience is most pronounced in the description of audience expectations in the later primary years. A more developed sense of *an invoked audience* is discernible in the description of audience expectations in senior primary years where a more mature sense of audience is marked by the ability to use textual features to position the reader to 'identify' with the text and 'engage the interest of audiences' (Year 5). The curriculum specifies particular textual strategies that student writers should develop to involve the audience: to anticipate 'differing perspectives and points of view', to guide textual participation (ACELA1483) and interpretation (ACELT1610), to connect with the audience through a narrative voice (ACELY1698).

Thus across the years of primary school, students move from an awareness that language changes according to the addressed audience, that is a particular person in a particular context, to a much more refined sense of texts as crafted in the written mode to organise meaning in ways that support and guide a reader, as crafted by the writer to shape the reader's interpretation and influence reader response to texts and as construing a world that meets the needs and expectations of the readership. In this way audience awareness requires students to develop an increasing repertoire across the textual, interpersonal, and ideational metafunctions to shape texts that are purposeful and effective.

Pedagogic practices for fostering a sense of audience: case studies

Our analysis identified a variety of ways in which the two teachers supported a growing sensitivity to audience in their students' writing. A key approach adopted by the school is to foreground a view of writing as meaningful and purposeful. This was strongly evident in discussions about writing pedagogy with the school's instructional leader, Sarah. When speaking about the goal of the writing program, she highlighted audience awareness as fundamental to achievement in writing.

> I think that they understand that writing has to communicate a message and it has to be clear to the people who are reading it that they're writing for an audience, not for themselves, they're writing for somebody else, and that they understand that the message has to be clear.
> (Interview with Sarah, 6 November 2015)

As with Many and Henderson's (2005) finding, children's writing was displayed on walls or hung up on strings. The practice of displaying students' work is both a celebration of achievement and a means to instil audience awareness – writing is written for a specific audience. Similarly, sending a good piece of writing to the principal or other classrooms was common in the two classes we observed. Sharing with an audience in the school context provides an effective means for fostering a sense of audience addressed.

Another commonly observed practice was the writing circle where students, from their desks or seated in a circle, read their writing to the class and teacher as audience members and receive feedback from the teacher. Through such sharing activity, students develop understanding of the presence of *audience as reader* 'as the final cause for which form exists' (Park 1982, p. 247). Such strategies importantly draw attention to the needs of the audience in the written mode, where audience is not physically present and is therefore a more abstract concept for learners. Immediate feedback is not usually available in the written mode so contexts such as the readers' circle take on significance as a tool to scaffold students' transition from the spoken mode where audience feedback is immediate to the written mode where the audience must be imagined and feedback sought.

In the two case studies below, we attend to pedagogical practices the teachers adopt to foster a sense of audience in learning to write in different types of genres.

Teaching audience in Year 2 persuasive writing class

The writing pedagogy discussed here is from a Year 2 class. The goal of the teaching sequence is to develop persuasive writing and Anna focuses students' attention on the ways they can develop reasons to support an argument. Anna shared her broad pedagogic intention to instil in her students a strong sense of purpose: 'It's getting the kids to understand that they're writing for a purpose and they're not just writing to write on lines in a book, that they are an author and they do create pieces of work' (Interview with Anna, 26 October 2015). In addition to the strong focus on purpose, in the literacy episode explored here, Anna develops her students' understanding of the importance of *audience addressed* and *audience as reader* to the writing process. Significantly, she models different aspects of audience awareness at different points in the modelled writing session, scaffolding student understandings of audience.

The class have been reading a mentor text entitled 'Hey Little Ant' by Hannah Hoose. The text is a fictional dialogue between a boy who is determined to squash an ant and the ant who does not wish to die. The mentor text has been selected to model reasoning and different perspectives on an issue in a story which is engaging and accessible to students. Anna used the text to model argumentation as a form of dialogue, drawing students' attentions to the reasons given by each character during the modelled reading session. The lesson begins with a re-reading of this text to provide stimulus for the modelled writing session which follows.

Assigning an audience to the writing

The modelled writing lesson brings different aspects of audience awareness into and out of focus. References to 'the reader' occur at the start of the modelled writing session and refer students to an addressed reader who remains unspecified at this point in the lesson. Students' attention is first directed to the importance of audience and the interdependency of audience and purpose when Anna reads aloud their WALT (We Are Learning To) displayed on the wall near the whiteboard.[1]

ANNA: (reads): We are learning to be authors who can persuade a reader using opinions and reasons. This is because an author needs to explain their point of view to convince a reader.

The significant role of audience for planning text stages and phases and for selecting language forms was emphasised throughout the modelled writing. Anna modelled how to convince the reader through language choices and logical reasoning, arguing for the reader to 'squish the ant' from the mentor text. To make the writing more concrete for students, the teacher clearly identified herself as the *addressed reader* of the student's argument text.

ANNA: (reads model): Who cares about a silly … that's a comma … little ant? I know I don't. I strongly believe the ant should be squished.
STUDENT: NOT squished.
ANNA: I know you don't agree with me but that's why you need to convince me. *You're writing this to convince me … that I should save the ant instead.*

By making the choice of audience explicit to students the teacher helps to define the purpose of the writing task at hand, giving students someone to argue with. Further, she has established an audience who is both familiar, being the teacher, while at the same time provide scope for the Year 3 students to adopt a widened or more generalised sense of the audience as people 'who believe that ants should be squished'. In setting up this audience Anna was reducing some of the challenge of writing for an imagined audience by creating a communicative context where an audience was present. Anna's pedagogic practice recognises the students' developmental trajectory encompassing audience awareness in Year 1 where 'students communicate with peers, teachers, known adults and students from other classes' (ACE Year 1 level description) as well as *community members* in Year 2 and looking ahead to some 'unfamiliar audiences' expected in ACE Year 3 achievement standards.

Demonstrating an active role of the reader

In addition to identifying an audience for students to dialogue with, Anna draws students' attention to the role of audience as reader of their writing, with particular meaning making needs that must be met. Ong observes '(i)t is really quite misleading to think of a writer as dealing with an "audience", even though certain considerations may at times oblige us to think this way. More properly, a writer addresses readers' (1975 in Magnifico 2010, p. 169). While establishing a voice for students to dialogue with, Anna also makes regular reference to the needs of the reader, modelling use of 'think aloud', the conventions of the written mode that organise text that hangs together and makes sense for the reader. Anna focused on elements of the textual metafunction at the rank of grapheme, word and clause complex, explicitly connecting these to 'the reader' who must try to make meaning of their writing.

ANNA: That's right. I *need to show the reader* that I'm leaving a clear line because remember paragraphs separate ideas and if you put all our ideas together *the reader will get a little bit confused* and it's too much information to go all together.

In this way Anna explicitly drew students' attention to the act of writing and the cognitive processing needs of a reader (Kroll 1984). In particular, she drew attention to textual elements that support the reader by modelling the use of punctuation and features of layout. Her modelling provides an understanding of these writing choices as meaningful, realising purpose and functioning to co-construct meaning with a reader:

ANNA: What punctuation could I use at the end of that to make it a more powerful statement?

Anna's skilful integration of rhetorical notions of audience, with more textual awareness of a reader who makes meaning of the students' writing as a message, supports students to view aspects of writing at the rank of word, clause, and text as meaningful and purposeful.

Shaping and positioning audience disposition

Language structures and features that achieve purpose and influence audience are also modelled during the lesson. Anna modelled ideational and logical resources for providing reasons and connecting ideas to form an elaborated argument. In particular she focuses students on the resources from the interpersonal metafunction that express and modulate attitudes and position the reader in relation to the value positions in the text.

ANNA: Who cares about a silly little ant? I know I don't. I strongly believe the ant should be squished.

Anna modelled a range of language resources to express attitudes and graduate force. She demonstrated to students how to dispose the reader negatively to the ant, positioning the reader to view it as insignificant through the negative judgement of capacity and normality as 'silly' and 'little'. Anna provided authority for her argument using self-attribution, 'I strongly believe', but through self-attribution she leaves room for other voices in the argument. She intensified her attitude through the adverbial 'strongly' and use of the verb 'squished' indicating a material process with an inscribed negative attitude with fused upscaled force. Ideationally, the process 'squished' is colloquial, commonsense and childlike, evoking a young audience of equal status to the writer. Further use of resources of attitude to negatively judge ants are modelled in the supporting arguments.

ANNA: Ants are *nothing* but *thiefs* [*sic*] (modelled text).

The teacher further built student understanding of audience and persuasion through her repeated focus on 'reasons' to support an argument. She focused students on the social construction of meaning emphasising that an audience will not simply accept a thesis without supporting information.

In a brief modelled writing session, Anna has demonstrated how to write persuasively, drawing on interpersonal language resources including expressions of attitude, selection of modality, intensification, as well as logical resources to position an audience to agree with the argument. These interpersonal language resources evoke an audience whose response is shaped by the writer's control of interpersonal and logical resources. Through the modelling session Anna invoked an image of a young, confident, careless audience, uninterested in the value of insect life, yet conversely values manners and compliant social behaviour. Although the teacher-modelled text may appear somewhat awkward and forced logically, it provides a voice for the students to dialogue with in their own subsequent writing. Further, it supports students to begin to understand the deeply interrelated nature of purpose and audience and how these may be realised linguistically.

After the modelled writing session students moved to an independent writing session during which Anna conferenced with individual students to provide guided support when she provided both an immediate audience and feedback on the student writing. Anna worked closely with individual students to extend their understanding of audience. In the excerpt following from the second observed lesson, Anna supported the student to enact a dialogue with the reader, by modelling the way a writer can anticipate the reader's reaction and position to the reader to be well disposed to our arguments. She scaffolded her students' reasoning skills and drew specifically on the mentor text to provide the student with a voice to dialogue with in her writing.

ANNA: [reads student writing] Ants are the same just like you. They also have families. Ants need to take care of their families. (Reads aloud twice).

ANNA: *So now you need to put it back on to the reader.* 'If you squish the ant, you're destroying a family.' Okay, so you need to have those strong statements and opinions. You need to *make the reader think* 'Oh, I really shouldn't do this.' Okay, so you can add things like that 'If you squish the ant, you are destroying a family' cause you're talking about families or 'You're ruining a family.' ...

ANNA: [reads another paragraph] So, Ants take breadcrumbs for their families to survive. Good, full stop. One chip can feed their whole town.

ANNA: Okay, what else can you say about that? *So the boy said that the ant was a thief. So you can turn that back around.* Ants aren't thieves, they are just trying to do what?

Through guided support, Anna drew attention to the dialogic nature of argument and modelled both interpersonal resources to position the reader and logical resources to convince the reader.

Persuasive writing is a challenging task for students in Years 2 and 3 and the observed lesson sequence demonstrates the complexity of the teacher's role in developing the skills of argument while scaffolding student understandings about audience. Effective persuasive writing depends on the writer's social awareness. Our analysis has identified strategies which Anna draws on to develop the students' ability to write to address, invoke and guide the audience. Throughout the lesson, Anna regularly returns students' attention to the interests, logic and needs of an external reader. She modelled how the students can organise their ideas cohesively and clearly, align with the reader's view in order to engage the reader, recognise the presence of the reader, and bring them explicitly into their texts (Hyland 2005, Brisk 2012, Holliway 2010).

In the following lesson, Kate similarly foregrounded considerations of audience, in a lesson focused on character development in narrative.

Teaching audience in Year 3/4 narrative writing class

The second case study presented here draws on data collected from Kate's Year 3/4 class. The focus of this writing lesson was on learning how to write an introduction to a novel focusing specifically on characterisation – 'characters that steer the events in the story' (WALT). We see a different kind of orientation to audience consideration – addressing the needs of the reader to comprehend and interpret the character portrayed in the genre of a narrative.

Facilitating active construction of meaning

As an introduction to the concept of characterisation, the teacher invited the students to reflect on the characters portrayed in the recently read text, *A File on Rose Moncrieff* – a story about Armand and Dean who lived in a small town of Rosemount Creek. In this literacy experience, students were encouraged to think about the characters as readers. As demonstrated in the episode below, Kate's queries about the characters invited the students to actively construct meaning as readers. She supported this by modelling her thinking and inferencing about the characteristics and ages of the characters.

KATE: Think back to 'A File on Rose Moncrieff'. There were two main characters. Who are the two main characters?
STUDENTS: …
KATE: Armand and Dean. They were pretty strong people, weren't they? How do we know that *they* were strong people?
KATE: … but right at the beginning, they told us that they were schoolkids and *we found out* that they were school kids. Did they tell us how old they were?
STUDENT: No.
KATE: No, we guessed they were 8, um …
STUDENT 1: No, 17 or 18
STUDENT 2: 17
KATE: No, maybe we'd have to get it again to … *I thought* they were about your age, a little bit older …

Kate continued to facilitate students' active construction of meaning by drawing their attention to visual, observable features of a character. In particular, she encouraged students to make connection with the character by inviting them to take on an active role to develop a rich understanding of the character from the reader's point of view. Using a visual image, Kate encouraged the student to speculate about the characteristics of the character. She insisted that the student cannot simply take what was presented in an image as there were different possible ways of interpreting the character. In so doing, Kate fostered an understanding of audience expectations, attitudes, and preferences.

KATE: So if you have a look here at the character that I've put there … [point to whiteboard]
You can *see* him, but you don't know anything about him.
KATE: Is he nice? … Is he cranky? …

KATE: He's wearing a soldier's uniform. But does that mean he's a soldier? ...
KATE: Not necessarily. It could be Halloween.

Experiencing a sense of audience

Many and Henderson (2005) suggest that social interaction with an audience in the immediate environment is instrumental in the children's development of increasing awareness of the audience. Kate created opportunities where her class participated in the audience/author interactions. In the excerpt included below, Lara was invited to act out the word 'robot' while the class closed their eyes and blind-guessed the meaning of the word. The aim of the activity was for the class to understand the information provided by the actor/'author'. The class worked together to develop a shared understanding of the character being enacted based on the clues provided by the 'author'. The benefits of this literacy experience are two-fold. It enables the 'author' to understand the need to communicate their message clearly for the *audience as reader*. Participation as the audience by class members provides an opportunity for the class to take on an active role which is often invoked by the author's deliberate choice of words. Such 'collaborative interpretation', as argued by Many and Henderson (2005, p. 335), is pivotal to fostering audience consideration and developing growing sensitivity to audience.

KATE: Okay, Lara, my young actor, up you come.

> [Lara gets up and comes to front of class]KATE: Close your eyes [pointing to class].
> [turning to Lara], Not you, them.

KATE: I only want you to *listen to* what she says. Lara, I want you to be a

> [whispers to Lara]
> [Lara starts to act]

LARA: [Lauren moves arms stiffly] – Ev ... ry ... bo ... dy ... [being a robot]
KATE: Open your eyes. Oh ... [some hands are up] Ok, you *heard* what she was saying. You didn't see what she was doing.
KATE: Joanne, what sort of character do you think she was being?
STUDENT: ... um ... a robot?
KATE: Robot. Yes [to Lauren]. Thankyou.
What was it that told you that it was a robot?
–um, the sound that she was making? ...
STUDENT: The sound?
KATE: The sound and ...?
STUDENT: ... how fast she went?
KATE: Yes, she was talking very stilted – one word at a time, which is what *we would expect* a robot to do.

In the second last turn in the excerpt above, Kate stressed the importance of providing details that were expected by the audience – 'what we would expect a robot to do' – to create shared understanding of the character. Scaffolding provided during this modelling episode enabled a deeper connection with the audience as was evident in the enthusiasm demonstrated by the students' response. To a certain extent, it can be argued that pedagogic practice such as this contributes to developing a growing sense of audience.

Fostering awareness of the reader-based writing

Park (1982) argues that writing for audience involves assessing what can be assumed, what can be elaborated, and therefore what should be made explicit and visible to the reader. In this lesson Kate frequently made explicit references to 'our reader'. Kate insisted that a key strategy to consider audience was 'creating shared understanding' by providing the reader with details about characters such as decisions they make – words they say and how they say them, and 'the thoughts which run through a character's mind'. The writer's job is to make the character 'real' – come to life – for the reader.

KATE: (reads from whiteboard): Characters become real life breathing people to *our reader* if we describe decisions they make, what they say and how they say it. (WALT: We are Learning To).
   Sometimes a writer will reveal also the *thoughts* which run through a character's mind.

Kate illustrated the importance of creating shared understanding by drawing attention to the portrayal of the thoughts going through George's mind, the main character of *George's Marvelous Medicine* the class was studying at the time. Through these interactions, Kate led the students in considering aspects of characterisation, which helped build connection with the audience. Audience expectations were alluded to through the constant direct references of 'we' as a participating audience.

KATE: Now in the text that we're reading now, the main character, who is …?
STUDENT: George
KATE: George. He does a lot of thinking, doesn't he?
STUDENT: Yes.
KATE: He talks to himself quite a lot. He likes to talk to himself.
   And when he talks to himself [hands indicating time rolling by] *we* find out all the things he's doing.

In the following excerpt, Kate modelled a think-aloud process – an example of portraying what was going through the character's mind. She provided an example of general and less detailed description of what went on in her mind and the decision she made later on. This contrasting example further reinforces to the students the importance of presenting information that meet the needs of the audience.

> KATE: (think aloud): 'Um. Well, I was, um, thinking this morning when I was eating my toast, that um I was thinking I might um not be so cranky today, but then when I got to school, I saw ... and I thought ... and I went "no". I won't be.'
>
> KATE: Did I give you a really good description of what I was thinking?

Many and Henderson (2005) point out that dialogic author/audience interactions such as those discussed above have the potential to forge 'a valuable link to' audience needs and expectations (p. 25). Through literacy events such as making inferences about a character, guessing a character, and through modelling think-aloud process, visual material, and experiential activities, Kate supported the students to understand the expectation and needs of the audience – to construct a shared understanding in writing through providing details expected and appreciated by the reader.

Teaching and developing audience awareness: some concluding thoughts

This chapter has demonstrated that audience is a multifaceted and dynamic concept. The integrated understanding of *audience as addressed, as reader*, and *as invoked* provides insights into the intricate relationship between audience, reader, purpose, and context. Our document analysis demonstrates such integrated understanding is infused in the ACE. The framework provides a means to understand the specification of audience awareness across different years of schooling as envisaged by the ACE. The analysis shed lights on a possible developmental continuum for audience awareness as moving from writing for *addressing* and *attending to* known and familiar audience to unknown and a broader range of audiences with an increasing expectation of the students to learn to write to influence, impact, and position an *invoked audience* in the later primary years.

This integrated framework provides a better understanding of effective pedagogic practice that promotes and develops the writer's purposeful awareness of others. Our analysis identified many examples of pedagogic practices where the roles of audiences addressed, attended to, and invoked were modelled and demonstrated through many interactive literacy experiences. Developing into confident writers involves developing a strong sense of how to address audience in a rhetorical situation to achieve particular goals and purpose in writing different genres. In both classrooms, teaching audience awareness involved creating an authentic communicative context for students to write for 'real-life readers who take genuine interest in what students write' (Pace 2009, p. 161). We found practices of connecting students' work to an immediate audience – the teacher, the principal, and peers in the classroom. Placing the task in the authentic communicative situation allows the student to envisage a real audience with whom to communicate for a real purpose. Such writing tasks encourage deeper engagement in the writing process and a stronger connection with the reader (Magnifico 2010).

For such transfer to take place, students require portable understandings about the connection between audience, purpose, and the language choices that realise particular meanings in writing (Macken-Horarik 2009, Chen and Myhill 2016). The most central tool in Anna's lessons to model how to convince an audience was language: as a pedagogic tool for mediating student thinking, as a model to be taken up in students' own composing, and as a metacognitive tool to reflect on their own and other's composing during drafting and revisions. Consideration of how teachers can build metalanguage that is portable to subsequent years of schooling may be fruitful in supporting literacy development that is able to be sustained from class to class and teacher to teacher as students progress through primary years (Macken-Horarik 2009).

The teacher's ability to distinguish between different kinds of language that achieve purpose and to draw students' attention to language choices in systemic ways is essential. If students are to develop portable understandings about how the resources of language can be marshalled to impact audience, they need metalanguage to develop shared understandings, to facilitate meta-talk and to become conceptual tools that support students in reflection on the composing process (Chen and Myhill 2016). Without the power of such conceptual tools, understandings about audience observed in these lessons may remain localised for those students who are unable to infer which choices achieved what meanings. A consistent and shared language to support talk about purpose and audience will support literacy learning progression in ways that are explicit and sustained as students transition through primary years of schooling.

Note

1 The acronym prompt is part of a Department of Education NSW initiative drawing on the work of Hattie (2012) which aims to make teaching and learning intentions visible in the classroom.

Appendix 8.1

Table 8.1 An overview of audience expectations mandated in the Australian Curriculum: English

	Audience addressed	Audience invoked	Audience as reader
	Influenced by rhetorical approaches	**Influenced by sociocultural approaches**	**Influence by cognitive approaches**
Foundation	Explore how language is used differently at home and school depending on the relationships between people (ACELA1428)		Recognise that texts are made up of words and groups of words that make meaning (ACELA1434) Demonstrate a growing understanding that handwriting and presentation of work needs to reflect audience and purpose in order to communicate effectively
Year 1	Understand that language is used in combination with other means of communication, for example facial expressions and gestures to interact with others (ACELA1444)		Understand that ideas in texts can be organised to enhance meaning using sentences and paragraphs
Year 2	Identify the audience of imaginative, informative and persuasive texts (ACELY1668) Create short imaginative, informative and persuasive texts using growing knowledge of text structures and language features for familiar and some less familiar audiences, selecting print and multimodal elements appropriate to the audience and purpose (ACELY1671)		

Year 3 | Identify the audience and purpose of imaginative, informative and persuasive texts (ACELY1678) | - identifying the author's point of view on a topic and key words and images that seem intended to persuade listeners, viewers or readers to agree with the view presented

Identify the effect on audiences of techniques, for example shot size, vertical camera angle and layout in picture books, advertisements and film segments (ACELA1483)

- selecting appropriate text structure for a writing purpose and sequencing content for clarity and audience impact | Plan, draft and publish imaginative, informative and persuasive texts demonstrating increasing control over text structures and language features and selecting print, and multimodal elements appropriate to the audience and purpose (ACELY1682)

(Continued)

Table 8.1 (Cont.)

	Audience addressed	Audience invoked	Audience as reader
Year 4	Plan, rehearse and deliver presentations incorporating learned content and taking into account the particular purposes and audiences (ACELY1689)	Understand how texts vary in complexity and technicality depending on the approach to the topic, the purpose and the intended audience (ACELA1490)	Identify features of online texts that enhance readability including text, navigation, links, graphics and layout (ACELA1793)
	Understand how texts vary in complexity and technicality depending on the approach to the topic, the purpose and the intended audience (ACELA1490)	Identify characteristic features used in imaginative, informative and persuasive texts to meet the purpose of the text (ACELY1690) - describing the language which authors use to create imaginary worlds - how textual features such as headings, sub-headings, bold type and graphic organisers are used to order and present information, and how visual codes are used, for example those used in advertising to represent children and families so that viewers identify with them	
	Plan, draft and publish imaginative, informative and persuasive texts containing key information and supporting details for a widening range of audiences, demonstrating increasing control over text structures and language features (ACELY1694)	- they explain how language features, images and vocabulary are used to engage the interest of audiences	

Year 5 students create imaginative, informative and persuasive texts for different purposes and audiences		Understand how to move beyond making bare assertions and take account of differing perspectives and points of view (ACELA1502)
		Use metalanguage to describe the effects of ideas, text structures and language features on particular audiences (ACELT1795)
		orally, in writing or using digital media, giving a considered interpretation and opinion about a literary text, recognising that a student's view may not be shared by others and that others have equal claims to divergent views
		Recognise that ideas in literary texts can be conveyed from different viewpoints, which can lead to different kinds of interpretations and responses (ACELT1610)
Year 6 students understand how the selection of a variety of language features can influence an audience	Plan, draft and publish imaginative, informative and persuasive print and multimodal texts, choosing text structures, language features, images and sound appropriate to purpose and audience (ACELY1704)	Show how ideas and points of view in texts are conveyed through the use of vocabulary, including idiomatic expressions, objective and subjective language (ACELY1698)
		- identifying the narrative voice (the person or entity through whom the audience experiences the story) in a literary work, discussing the impact of first-person narration on empathy and engagement
	Plan, rehearse and deliver presentations for defined audiences and purposes incorporating accurate and sequenced content and multimodal elements (ACELY1700)	Identify and explain characteristic text structures and language features used in imaginative, informative and persuasive texts to meet the purpose of the text (ACELY1701)

Extracts taken from Australian Curriculum, Assessment and Reporting Authority (ACARA). 2015. *The Australian Curriculum English: Foundation to Year 10 v8.1*. Available from: https://australiancurriculum.edu.au/f-10-curriculum/english/ [Accessed 15.04.19].

References

Australian Curriculum and Assessment Reporting Authority (ACARA). 2015. *The Australian curriculum English: foundation to year 10*. v8.1. Available from: https://australiancurriculum.edu.au/f-10-curriculum/english/ [Accessed 15. 04. 19].

Berkenkotter, C. 1981. Understanding a writer's awareness of audience. *College Composition and Communication*, 32(4), 388–399.

Bitzer, L. 1971. The rhetorical situation. In: Johannesen, R. L. ed. *Contemporary theories of rhetoric: selected readings*. New York: Harper & Row, 381–393.

Black, K. 1989. Audience analysis and persuasive writing at the college level. *Research in the Teaching of English*, 23(3), 231–253.

Brisk, M. E. 2012. Young bilingual writers' control of grammatical person in different genres. *Elementary School Journal*, 112(3), 445–468.

Britton, J., et al. 1975. *The development of writing abilities*. London: Macmillan Education, NCTE.

Carvalho, J. B. 2002. Developing audience awareness in writing. *Journal of Research in Reading*, 25(3), 271–282.

Chen, H. and Myhill, D. 2016. Children talking about writing: investigating metalinguistic understanding. *Linguistics and Education*, 35, 100–108.

Derewianka, B. 2012. Knowledge about language in the Australian curriculum: English. *Australian Journal of Language & Literacy*, 35, 127–146.

DfE. 2014. *National curriculum in England: English programmes of study*. DfE: Department for Education, UK Government. Available from: www.gov.uk/government/publications/national-curriculum-in-england-english-programmes-of-study [Accessed 20. 05. 19].

Ede, L. 1979. On audience and composition. *College Composition and Communication*, 30(3), 291–295.

Ede, L. 1984. Audience: an introduction to research. *College Composition and Communication*, 35(2), 140–154.

Ede, L. and Lunsford, A. A. 1984. Audience addressed/audience invoked: the role of audience in composition theory and pedagogy. *College Composition and Communication*, 35(2), 155–171.

Flower, L. 1981. *Problem-solving strategies for writing*. New York: Harcourt Brace.

Flower, L. and Hayes, J. R. 1981. A cognitive process theory of writing. *College Composition and Communication*, 32(1), 365–387.

Halliday, M. A. K. and Hasan, R. 1985. *Language, context and text: aspects of language in a social semiotic perspective*. Geelong: Deakin University Press.

Hasan, R. 2005. Language and society in a systemic functional perspective. In: Hasan, R., Matthiessen, C. and Webster, J. eds. *Continuing discourse on language: a functional perspective*. London: Equinox, 55–80.

Holliway, D. 2010. A literacy task to assist reader awareness in children's informational writing. *Language and Education*, 24(2), 101–116.

Hyland, K. 2005. Representing readers in writing: student and expert practices. *Linguistics and Education*, 16(4), 363–377.

Kroll, B. M. 1978. Cognitive egocentrism and the problem of audience awareness in written discourse. *Research in the Teaching of English*, 12, 269–281.

Kroll, B. M. 1984. Writing for readers: three perspectives on audience. *College Composition and Communication*, 35(2), 172–185.

Lunsford, A. A. and Ede, L. 1996. Representing audiences: 'successful' discourse and disciplinary critique. *College Composition and Communication*, 47(2), 167–179.

Macken-Horarik, M. 2009. Navigational metalanguages for new territory in English: the potential of grammatics. *English Teaching: Practice and Critique*, 8(3), 55–69.

Magnifico, A. M. 2010. Writing for whom? Cognition, motivation, and a writer's audience. *Educational Psychologist*, 45(3), 167–184.

Many, J. E. and Henderson, S. D. 2005. Developing a sense of audience: an examination of one school's instructional contexts. *Reading Horizons*, 45(4), 321–348.

Martin, J. R. and Rose, D. 2008. *Genre relations: mapping culture*. London: Equinox Publishing.

Martin, J. R. and White, P. R. R. 2005. *The language of evaluation: appraisal in English*. New York: Palgrave Macmillan.

Pace, T. 2009. I can take a stance. In: Weiser, M. E., Fehler, B. M. and Gonzalez, A. M. eds. *Engaging audience: writing in an age of new literacies*. Urbana: NCTE, 147–165.

Pareitti, M. C. 2009. When the teacher is the audience. In *Engaging audience: writing in an age of new literacies*. Urbana: NCTE, 165–185.

Park, D. B. 1982. The meanings of 'audience'. *College English*, 44(3), 247–257.

Ramanathan, V. and Kaplan, R. B. 1996. Audience and voice in current L1 composition texts: some implications for ESL student writers. *Journal of Second Language Writing*, 5(1), 21–34.

Rose, D. and Martin, J. R. 2012. *Learning to write, reading to learn: genre, knowledge, and pedagogy in the Sydney school*. Sheffield: Equinox.

Rubin, D. L. and Rafoth, B. A. 1986. Social cognitive ability as a predictor of the quality of expository and persuasive writing among college freshmen. *Research in the Teaching of English*, 20(1), 9–21.

9 Developing a pedagogy of empowerment

Enabling primary school writers to make meaningful linguistic choices

Susan Jones

Introduction

The chapter will explore a functional approach to grammar pedagogy explaining how it is supported by the theoretical literature, embodied in key principles and evidenced by a randomised control trial. In addition, a more nuanced understanding of the challenges faced by both teachers and learners in realising this approach, informed by a three-year longitudinal study, will be discussed using classroom examples to illustrate both the challenges of this approach and possible solutions. For primary school teachers there is a perennial question concerning just how explicit the teaching of grammar needs to be. In Anglophone countries explicit grammar teaching has fallen in and out of fashion: at times seen as the antithesis of creativity, while at others, as the signifier of standards. Thus pedagogy has become the context for conflicting political discourses that place different values on the nature and purpose of grammatical knowledge. The current re-introduction of grammar into the UK curriculum, therefore, leaves teachers exposed to mixed messages regarding the purpose of this change. This chapter explores the evidence for what constitutes useable knowledge, arguing that it is not sufficient to create a rich experience of language in use, assuming that this will be unconsciously absorbed, but that there is a need for explicit teaching that foregrounds the connection between grammar and meaning. The chapter will argue for a functionally oriented approach that: (1) links grammar to the meaning it creates; (2) is taught alongside writing and not as a separate body of knowledge; and (3) adopts a descriptive approach; noticing the grammatical choices that writers make, rather than a prescriptive approach; dictating rules about right and wrong. Such an approach is, in short, concerned with explicitly empowering young writers in making meaningful linguistic choices.

Grammar in the UK curriculum: resolving the mixed messages

The National Curriculum in England and Wales has made the explicit teaching of grammar mandatory (DfE 2014). Nevertheless the discourses of this curriculum draw on different perspectives and so the same curriculum that links grammar with choice; arguing that explicit grammar is 'very important, as it gives us more conscious control and choice in our language' (2014, p. 65), also advocates the decontextualised testing of a specified knowledge base; mandating grammar terminology for each year group assessed through a national test of grammar for all 11-year-olds. Elizabeth Truss MP, the one-time Parliamentary Under-Secretary of State in the Department for Education, defended this test on the DfE website by commenting that:

> many children struggle with the basics of the English language at primary school, then don't catch up at secondary school. That is why employers bemoan the poor literacy of so many school and college leavers. This new test will mean that children are again taught the skills they need to understand our language, and to use it properly, creatively and effectively.
> (Truss 2013)

Mixed messages are also evident in this quote which clearly values both creativity and effectiveness, whilst also articulating the common deficit rationale for the inclusion of grammar as a means of eradicating error, raising standards, and satisfying the demands of the workplace. Implicit in this comment is also the assumption that explicit knowledge of grammatical terminology precedes effective use. In the UK, the existence of a grammar test has somewhat drowned out the discourse of choice; our own classroom observations have revealed how easily teachers can get drawn into 'ticking off' the grammatical features listed in the National Curriculum and focusing their teaching on the definition and labelling of terms in preparation for the test. The prevalence of the test has created a curriculum context that can make it difficult to ground a pedagogy informed by principles that promote the foregrounding of meaningful connections between grammar and writing. What is ambiguous here is what 'being explicit' means; being explicit only about definition can result in incomplete, even redundant knowledge if there is no explicitness about the effect of linguistic choices.

The pedagogy at the heart of this chapter views grammar not as a language hygiene resource, placing the emphasis on the removal of error, but as a semiotic resource, with an emphasis on shaping meaning through conscious choice. Halliday (1993) describes the ability to craft and use vocabulary and syntax for a particular purpose and to carry a particular message as 'learning to mean', a skill described by Carter (1990) as having 'conscious control and conscious choice over language which enables us both to see through language in a systematic way and to use language more discriminatingly' (p. 119). This emphasis is in contrast to a more prescriptive approach, whereby grammar is taught as a separate body of knowledge, focusing on the naming of the word classes often through de-contextualised exercises; parsing sentences created for the purpose of analysis rather than to engage the reader. The functional approach, advocated here, takes a descriptive view of grammar, drawing attention to grammar as it is used, in order to develop knowledge about how language works in different real-life contexts and so opening up a repertoire of available choices. From this perspective, a writing pedagogy should enable the control of language resources to create meaning, thus empowering young writers to control these resources to better articulate their own meaning and intentions.

The informing research

The approach to grammar teaching detailed below builds on research advocating a functional approach (Halliday 1993, Halliday and Matthiessen 2004, Derewianka and Jones 2010). A functional approach explores grammar as having both form and function, but emphasises how grammar shapes meaning through understanding available choices it 'emphasises the intent of the language user: what people need to do with language and what meanings they want to express' (Derewianka and Jones 2010, p. 6). This approach is also informed by research that explores how children develop the metalinguistic facilities that enable them to both recognise and identify patterns of language use in order to make conscious choices to express their own rhetorical intentions. Bialystok's (1987, 1999, 2001) work with bilingual children identified two complementary skills that operate in a symbiotic relationship with each other; the ability to recognise and identify language patterns (analysis) and the ability to manage one's own language use and language choices (control). In the context of the writing classroom, therefore, pedagogy needs to simultaneously develop a habit of noticing what writers do, while playing with language and the possibilities that this 'noticing' offers. The role of teaching, therefore, is in creating activities that foreground these explicit links between grammar as a resource and grammar as a shaper of meaning.

In his study of oral language, Gombert (1992) draws a distinction between two levels of linguistic knowledge; referring to epi-linguistic and metalinguistic levels of understanding: while both might impact on writing choices, Gombert suggests that epi-linguistic knowledge is tacit while metalinguistic knowledge is conscious, referring to this as: 'the control consciously chosen, decided on and applied by the individual' (2003, p. 3). In the context of the writing classroom therefore, pedagogy might create opportunities to talk about writing choices with a view to making tacit choices explicit. In this way the tacit choices made while writing today might increasingly become conscious choices that inform future writing decisions. Van Lier (1998) adds to this understanding, by arguing that conscious control of language is not so much located in the mind, as actionable knowledge, but rather located in social linguistic activity, so that 'meta' awareness needs to account for both stated linguistic commentary and practical linguistic activity. Van Lier suggests that these different forms of linguistic knowledge occur simultaneously, informing each other, which is why he points out that 'conscious control of language is more truly manifested in linguistic performance than in talking about linguistic performance' (1998, p. 132), suggesting that young writers are sometimes better able to shape meaning in a text in line with personal rhetorical intentions than understand how this is achieved. Thus the writing classroom might offer opportunities for understanding to be supported at the unarticulated and implicit level through practical and sometimes playful use of language, that it should further facilitate a more analytical and discursive awareness of how language works, while also encouraging critical awareness of how language can represent or obscure personal meaning, but crucially that this should not be seen as linear because 'all levels of language awareness persist even as metalinguistic knowledge becomes more sophisticated' (1998, p. 135).

Informed by the seminal work of Vygotsky, the role of talk in the classroom is conceived not simply as a means of articulating what is known, but as an important process in supporting the development of that knowledge; as Corden puts it, 'thought is not merely expressed in words – it comes into existence through words' (2000, p. 7). In the UK, the work of Neil Mercer and Robin Alexander has highlighted the role of the teacher in ensuring that talk becomes genuinely exploratory (questioning and speculative) or dialogic (responsive to others and generating new possibilities). An effective writing pedagogy therefore, needs to be mindful of the value of talk in articulating learning about writing (Parr et al. 2009). Parr et al. suggest that classroom talk might usefully focus on 'inter-textual talk' concerned with 'explicit guidance … enabling children to develop more control and awareness in their writing' (2009, p. 255). This explicit guidance addresses the inter-textual links between reading and writing. As young writers develop, it is in the shift towards a wider repertoire of more 'writerly forms' that the difference between able and struggling writers is especially marked (Myhill 2009). In part this is a consequence of the relationship between reading and writing, such that avid readers encounter and internalise a wider range of linguistic possibilities. In addition, there is an advantage conferred by middle-class patterns of speech, that more closely resemble written forms (Kress 1994). Talk about language choices therefore makes explicit for many children what is unconsciously absorbed by a few.

What much of this research reveals is that one consequence of taking a functional approach is that the metafunctional facility, recognising what you are doing and how you are doing it, is key to learning because 'meaning is at once both doing and understanding … All meaning – and hence all learning – is at once both action and reflection' (Halliday 1993, p. 100). Halliday describes this metafunctional principle as a dialectic relationship between engaging in a language act and understanding a language act. Thus a child can construe the language system from an act of meaning while at the same time create meaning from their use of the language system: 'when children learn language, they are simultaneously processing text into language and activating language into text' (1993, p. 105). If no act of understanding in language learning develops alone then the role of pedagogy is to create opportunities to engage in the simultaneous practice of 'knowing that', 'knowing how', and 'knowing why'. Thus, the explicit teaching required needs to give attention not only to grammatical form but also to grammatical function and rhetorical intention.

From research to pedagogic principles

The functionally oriented contextual approach developed by our research at Exeter University builds on this body of research through establishing four key pedagogical principles (the LEAD principles):

LINK: make a link between the writing being taught and a given grammar resource;

EXAMPLE: explain the grammar through examples, not lengthy explanations;

AUTHENTICITY: use examples from authentic texts to link writers to the broader community of writers;

DISCUSSION: build in high-quality discussion about grammar and its effects.

In each case the emphasis is on explicit teaching, what is being made explicit, however, is the effect of grammar in use.

Link: The research highlights the need to make explicit the relationship between grammar and meaning. The aim of this approach is not to learn grammar but to use it purposefully within writing. A very practical illustration of this is that rather than saying '*today we are going to learn about noun phrases*' a teacher might say '*today we are going to see how we can introduce a character using noun phrases to help our reader visualise them and sense what they are like*'. This is also in contrast to signals from the teacher regarding the desirability of deploying certain features by suggesting '*I want to see you using noun phrases*' or even '*good writing includes lots of expanded noun phrases*'.

Example: The research highlights that language learning involves the integration of different kinds of understanding and that an over-emphasis on the definition of terms, for example, does not allow for these different ways of knowing to be mutually informing each other. Teaching through examples reveals the grammatical structure and names it, but does not dwell on it, nor make it the focus of learning: instead it gives learners an opportunity to see a grammatical term in context and so to build grammatical understanding cumulatively. A practical example might be noting a common pattern such as how a sequence of three co-ordinated clauses with a single subject can capture a particular plot sequence and create text rhythm. The examples below come from *The Snow Leopard* by Jackie Morris:

The cat stirred, rose and leapt up to the high wild mountains with the Child clinging tight on her back.

Back in the mountains, the young Snow Leopard looked up at the stars mirrored in her blue cat's eyes, heard the whisper – and began a new song.

A class might find further examples of these patterns to reinforce understanding that is not dependent on lengthy explanations of verb, clause, or co-ordination.

Authenticity: The research highlights the benefits of analysis: of noticing what writers do. The example above illustrates the power of working with authentic texts, not least because the texts were written to engage the reader and for a real purpose, rather than written to teach a grammar principle. The example below offers a rather stark contrast to *The Snow Leopard* and comes from the UK grammar test, where the sentence has been constructed for the test and contrived to include three words that end in 'ly' to really challenge an 11-year-old's grammar knowledge!

Tick the adverb in the sentence below

The lively crowd cheered loudly when the rally car race began.

We believe this makes the case for using an authentic text!

Discussion: The research draws attention to the value of talk and the role of the teacher in managing the quality of this talk for learning. Our observations however, reveal that, perhaps as a consequence of the pressure of assessment, teachers often do most of the talking and that children then offer responses reduced to rehearsed formulas '*a verb is a doing word*', '*I should vary my sentences*', and '*I can make my writing more descriptive by adding adjectives*'. Exploratory talk, that invites discussion about grammar choices, can foreground the relationship between grammar and writing and encourage children to engage more effectively in the decision-making process in relation to their own writing.

The classroom example below comes from our own materials developed in accordance with these four principles; it illustrates all four and reflects the understanding and skills highlighted as important by the research literature. The lesson is from a scheme of work looking at Arthurian legend and the authentic text cited here is from *Arthur, High King of Britain* by Michael Morpurgo. This is the moment in the text where the reader first encounters the Lady of the Lake: the aim of this plot moment is to evoke a sense of mystery. The grammar that is the focus of attention is concerned with the effect of moving syntactical elements within a sentence, in particular; subject verb inversion.

And out of the mists came a figure in flowing green, walking across the water.

The children are asked to discuss the effect of this sentence:

Read this sentence aloud – where will you put the emphasis?
How could you re-order the information in this sentence?
How does this change the effect?

An alternative ordering is then offered to promote discussion:

And a figure in flowing green came out of the mists, walking across the water.

The children are invited to discuss the two sentences by first reading them out loud to hear the different emphasis and then considering the effect of each of the choices.

In this example a *link* is made between the syntax and the effect, the children generate different *examples*, the discussion starts with an *authentic* text and the whole activity is *discussion* based. The example also illustrates the different kinds of metalinguistic thinking required by this task. In order to put grammar knowledge to useful purpose a young writer needs to have something to say and a rhetorical intention, they need to understand the grammatical resources they have at their disposal *which may require them to generate alternatives* and finally they need to be able to evaluate what they write in light of their own intentions. Given the complexity of this task, it is perhaps not surprising that traditional prescriptive approaches to integrating grammar into the curriculum have demonstrated so little impact on writing improvement (Andrews et al. 2006). The dearth of evidence for an effective grammar pedagogy, highlighted by Andrews et al. (2006) in their systematic review, also called for a Randomised Control Trial (RCT) to address this absence. With this call in mind and with a contextualised approach as the focus, we undertook a RCT exploring issues of efficacy.

The randomised control trial

The original trial took place in 2008–2009 and was funded by the UK Economic and Social Research Council (ESRC) with participants from Year 8: the third year of the secondary system in the UK. The team then secured follow-on funding in 2012 to develop schemes of work that built on the original study across different ages and phases. This began a particularly close working relationship with primary school teachers across the UK. The RCT contrasted pre and post-test outcomes for 16 experimental group classes with 16 control group classes. The intervention took place over three school terms using schemes of work designed by the research team. The team devised parallel schemes of work for both the experimental and the control groups that were identical other than the focus on contextual grammar. The RCT was embedded within a qualitative design, which included the collection of classroom observations, teacher and student interviews and the analysis of writing produced from the lessons we observed. The purpose of the qualitative data was to contextualise the statistical claims regarding the effect of the intervention within a more complex understanding of how the intervention was differentially implemented, understood and experienced across the whole sample.

The outcomes indicated a statistically significant positive effect for the intervention group who improved their writing scores by 20% over the year compared with 11% in the comparison group (Jones et al. 2013, Myhill et al. 2012).

This represented some of the first robust evidence for any form of grammar pedagogy and in recognition of its significance and reach within the UK, in 2014, the study was awarded the ESRC Outstanding Impact in Society award. However, there are certain caveats to these findings; first, the intervention had greatest impact on able writers, perhaps because able writers in the comparison group barely improved over the year and also it was shown that teachers' subject knowledge of grammar was an influencing factor, such that those with stronger grammar knowledge were more effective in facilitating improvement. Furthermore, the qualitative data revealed that many teachers struggled not only with their subject knowledge per se but also in both identifying and articulating grammatical effect (Myhill et al. 2013).

While RCTs are valued within educational research, indeed are often viewed as the 'gold standard' determining 'what works' and 'what works best', they are not without their critics. Biesta (2007) has critiqued this approach both for being largely outcomes-driven rather than values-driven and also for undervaluing professional expertise suggesting that 'evidence does not provide us with hypotheses for action but only with possibilities for intelligent problem solving' (p. 17). Our own reflection on how this research had been received led us to conclude that such approaches can place too much weight on the statistical evidence of efficacy and too little weight on the complexity of the different ways in which teachers implement the pedagogy. At times, the evidence of efficacy which this study can legitimately claim has rather over-shadowed the much more important pedagogical principles that were at the heart of this approach, and the complex interaction of subject and pedagogic knowledge. Understanding 'what works' is only partial in what it can tell us: it is equally, or arguably more critical, that we examine how teachers manage the pedagogical intervention and that we engage with both the barriers and the enablers that support effective learning.

The longitudinal study

In 2013, the ESRC funded a new study that built on the pedagogy informing the RCT, but that employed a very different research methodology. The study aimed to understand how metalinguistic understanding developed and how this understanding was linked to development in writing. This was a longitudinal study that followed four student cohorts across a three-year period; two primary (aged 9–11 years) and two secondary (12–14 years). 24 individual case studies, 12 each from the primary and secondary cohort and balanced for gender and ability, were developed. The data for the case studies included classroom observation data (three observations per term), these observations were immediately followed by student interviews (one interview with each focus student each term), and finally, writing samples were collected (written output from each term of the project plus a repeated task at the beginning of each school year). Thus, for each student there were 18 observations, six interviews and nine samples of writing.

Each data set was analysed separately before being used to construct the case studies and so the building of the case studies represents a secondary phase of the analysis process. Each case study report followed the same organisation using the following lead prompts:

- understanding of grammatical terminology;
- articulated metalinguistic choices about their own writing;
- evidence of learning from writing (linked to the scheme of work being taught);
- influence of teaching.

The study followed the students and so each year the teachers involved in the project changed, as the children moved classes. These teachers joined us for three Continuing Professional Development days during each year of the project where we worked with them sharing the pedagogic principles, enabling them to develop their own schemes of work in line with these principles, and keeping them informed about our developing understanding, particularly in how this informed pedagogy.

Some of the nuances of the findings from this study are discussed elsewhere in this book (see Myhill, Lines this volume). Here an overview of the findings will be presented with a particular focus on what we learned to further develop a pedagogy for contextual grammar teaching and in particular to address those things that both teachers and students struggle with, as indicated in the findings of the RCT.

What was clear from the case studies was that the relationship between knowing about grammar and applying that knowledge is a complex one. Within our sample were children who could use grammar competently but not label it; some who could articulate their rhetorical intentions but were unable to explain how they had achieved it; some who could use everyday language to give credible explanations for their linguistic choices, but without use of the grammatical language. There was no indication that there were stages to this development; for example, that labelling always precedes use or that use always precedes an awareness of rhetorical intention, rather metalinguistic awareness of all kinds seemed to flourish or disappear in response to context. What we can comment on, then, are the conditions in which this awareness appears to flourish or disappear. This discussion will be presented in line with three key themes that were evident in the data:

The focus of student understanding is more often on use than purpose (evidenced by writing conversations).

Understanding is most evident in written texts (evidenced by contrasting written texts with writing conversations).

With practice young writers can become more explicit (evidenced by the longitudinal case studies).

The focus is more often on use than purpose

In the time since the RCT was conducted, the renewed emphasis on grammar in the UK curriculum and specifically the impact of the grammar test in the primary phase, does seem to be raising student confidence in the identification of grammar features, but this appears to have developed alongside a tendency to talk about 'putting things in', or simply deploying grammatical features in their writing. In the student interviews, this is often cited as evidence of writing quality. It seems reasonable to assume that the curriculum emphasis has influenced this understanding of 'good writing'. The young writers in the sample were keen to point out what they had done:

'I have used adjectives and connectives'
'I have used different types of sentences'

They were, however, less able to explain why and how these choices impacted on meaning. Similarly, when asked how they might improve their writing, the additive principles still seemed to apply:

'probably add some more adverbs and some verbs as well'
'a bit more adjectives and nouns'

In this respect, the increased emphasis on grammar in the curriculum can be seen to be effective in increasing the use of grammatical language, but not necessarily always conducive to improved learning. Talk that relates grammar to meaning, however, can be found within the classroom observations and the student interviews. Some of these talk responses were generalised and lack precision, and recur repeatedly, and this was particularly true in relation to discussions about word choice. Typical responses about the effect of word choices, such as adjectives or verbs, evoked responses such as:

it's more descriptive – it's more powerful – it's more exciting
it creates suspense – it creates tensions

These examples were heard across the four schools and in both phases, presenting a litany of notional right answers to 'effect' questions from the teacher. What was evident was that both teachers and young writers struggled to articulate the grammar meaning link and that classroom opportunity to talk about personal writing choices needs to focus more on effect than usage. To an extent, our evidence may be signalling an emerging new discourse linking grammatical choice to rhetorical effect, but that this discourse is not yet fully secure or matured (Myhill and Newman 2016, Myhill et al. 2016). In light of this evidence, we developed classroom examples to model the productive discussion about choices and effects that we hope to foster.

164 Susan Jones

Example 1 – primary: the effect of different decisions regarding the use of a comma or 'and'

This example invites discussion which explores the choice that we have as writers about whether to use a comma to separate a list of noun phrases or to repeatedly use the conjunction 'and'. It opens up the idea that punctuation choices relate to meaning and are not simply about compliance with usage rules.

Authentic texts to prompt discussion:

On Saturday, he ate through one piece of chocolate cake, one ice-cream cone, one pickle, one slice of Swiss cheese, one slice of salami, one lollipop, one piece of cherry pie, one sausage, one cupcake, and one slice of watermelon (from *The Very Hungry Caterpillar* – Eric Carle).

Then Mr Gumpy and the goat and the calf and the chickens and the sheep and the pig and the dog and the cat and the rabbit and the children all swam to the bank and climbed out to dry in the sun (from *Mr Gumpy's Outing* – John Burningham).

Discussion questions:

Why do you think Eric Carle chooses to use commas to separate his long list of noun phrases and John Burningham chooses to use 'and'?
Do you read the two sentences differently?
Can you explain the different effect?

Example 2 – secondary: the effect of noun phrases in creating characterisation

This example invites discussion about how writers present characters to their readers for the first time, and how noun phrases can foreground the description of the character and generate inference.

Authentic text to promote discussion:

An extract from Dickens' *Great Expectations*, when Pip meets Magwitch for the first time.

> A fearful man, all in coarse grey, with a great iron on his leg. A man with no hat, and with broken shoes, and with an old rag tied round his head. A man who had been soaked in water, and smothered in mud, and lamed by stones, and cut by flints, and stung by nettles, and torn by briars; who limped and shivered, and glared and growled; and whose teeth chattered in his head as he seized me by the chin.

Discussion questions:

What is Pip's first impression of Magwitch?

Look at the noun phrases used to describe Magwitch (highlight these visually). Which descriptions make him sound frightening? Why? Do any descriptions make him seem someone we might feel sorry for?

Does this description make us afraid of Magwitch or have sympathy with him, or a little of both?

These examples illustrate how discussion about the relationship between grammatical choice and its effect can be opened through careful questioning which encourages both exploration of effects and verbalisation of the link between grammar and meaning. Our data shows that it is precisely this kind of talk that is sometimes missing in classrooms, and which is ripe for further development.

Understanding is most evident in written texts

Findings from the 24 case studies are summarised in Table 9.1. The writing conversations it refers to occurred twice in each year of the study: students discussed samples of their writing produced within each scheme of work to reflect on their own writing choices and on the learning focus itself. The conversations aimed to explore the extent to which students understood the grammar that had been foregrounded, whether it was used in their writing, and whether students could identify their own use of the grammar focus. For each student, we had six writing conversations with a corresponding writing sample. What the table reveals is that the grammar focus is more evident in the text than explicitly understood or identified in the text, but also that explicit awareness appears to develop with age. The data also suggest that the explicit teaching does have an impact on the students' writing, even when they cannot articulate either what they have done or how.

The case studies include some researcher analytical commentary on the data findings, which reinforce the patterns shown in the table above. Below are three examples of researcher commentary from the primary cohort, showing how the writers are drawing on the explicit teaching in their writing, but may not recognise what they have done:

Table 9.1 Summary of case-study findings

	Grammar focus understood	Grammar focus evident in text	Grammar focus identified in the text
Data used	Writing conversation	Writing sample	Writing conversation
Primary	19/72 26%	42/72 58%	12/72 17%
Secondary	30/72 42%	46/72 64%	24/72 33%
Total	49/144 34%	88/144 61%	36/144 25%

Kai (Year 5): the class researched an animal then described it emphasising scientific vocabulary. There is evidence, particularly from the writing that Kai has understood some of this.

> *An egg is laid in early summer … in summer the egg hatches into a butterfly …* On reading this Kai comments '*The caterpillar turns into the chrysalis. I was about to put that but I didn't have enough time*'.

Emily (Year 6): There is evidence in her writing that she has made use of the features that she has been taught (sentence variety), but she does not generally show awareness of this.

> *They were captured by the famous vishos piarots (with wimpy names) Carrot, Muffin, strawberry, orange and grap. They were terrified. The captin of the ship was could Strawberry (he had the wimpiest name.) Then they were told to give them all there belongings but they would not so they were forsed to walk the plank. They were rily scard by this pont.*

Sofia uses co-ordinated clauses to move the narrative forward:

> *The child ran around in the mud and heard his song.*

There are also examples of students borrowing heavily from mentor texts used in the classroom in a way which may not enable growth in learning (see Myhill et al. 2018 for a more detailed discussion of this). Nevertheless, these examples of the implicit uptake of the language use illustrated in the classroom appear to be part of the complex way in which grammar knowledge is transferred into practice. Imitating and borrowing may themselves be ways that learners become increasingly aware of choices and build a repertoire of choices for future reference. These choices, however, may well remain tacit unless students are offered rich talk opportunities to articulate them.

Almost all of the talk we observed in the project classrooms occurred before a writing task took place. This talk included motivating activities to create ownership of a personal writing purpose as well as talk to generate ideas for content. Talk activities also explored the writing choices of others through the use of authentic texts and rehearsed different phrasing choices for student's own writing. Although the teachers in the study were supported in adopting a contextualised approach informed by a descriptive understanding of grammar pedagogy, there was, nevertheless, a considerable amount of talk on definitions of grammar terms and testing of knowledge. This was influenced by the curriculum imperative of preparing students for the national grammar test, evidencing a tension between different rationales for the inclusion of grammar in the curriculum. What was less typical was talk that might occur during and after writing, to explore and evaluate choices either at the point of writing, or shortly after, to consider alternatives and to practise the articulation of the grammar–meaning link. Indeed the most significant talk of this nature was the writing conversations themselves, which were designed for data collection, but our experience of talking with students in this way suggests writing conversations might also be a powerful pedagogic tool in the classroom.

Prompts used in the writing conversations invited children to explain how they wanted their reader to think or feel and then to find an example of where this had been achieved. A similar activity might be to pause a writing task to share examples from each other's writing, or to ask a reader if an intention to frighten or to persuade has been achieved; the aim being to make tacit choices visible.

With practice young writers can become more explicit

The longitudinal study did reveal that young writers sometimes struggle to articulate how their grammar choices shape meaning, and this informed the reviewing and refreshing of the principles that underpin the contextualised approach to give greater emphasis to the importance of discussion. However, there is evidence that young writers can link choices to an effect; but that precision comes with practice. It was also evident that some young writers can talk about their writing intentions before they have a grammatical language to be precise about it. In the following two examples students comment on their own writing (italicised). Emily can describe the effect but makes no comment about language, while Kai can name the grammatical feature and comment on its general purpose but does not articulate the particular effect on his own choices.

Emily (Year 6) *Hannibal appeared* – it makes you think Hannibal came out of nowhere.

Kai (Year 4): *Down a creepy tunnel, under a volcano, he stomps around* – I've learned what an adverbial is and what happens when you put it in a sentence … it's like description that when you stick it in a sentence it tells you where, when or how.

These two examples alone illustrate the complexity of metalinguistic thinking and the demands it places on a pedagogy, to develop and not stifle it. The case studies made it possible to explore the complex development of metalinguistic thinking by following individual children. The example below concerns Fiona, an average attaining primary school writer, and illustrates one instance of this development, drawing pedagogical conclusions for how this thinking might be supported over time.

At the beginning of the study, Fiona's writing appeared highly dependent on classroom examples, borrowing words, phrases, and entire sentences from model texts. Addressing this tendency might involve ensuring that, over time, the same pattern is explored in a range of different texts, to emphasise the varied possibilities of this pattern, rather than a single particular use. Perhaps, as a consequence of the heavy emphasis within Fiona's school on grammatical definitions, one characteristic of her development over the first year of the project was an ability to define and identify grammatical features in her own writing. This was often articulated adopting the deploying discourse identified above:

'It's got description in it: "large frying pan"'
'I've got some different punctuation in here' (points to a comma)
'I've got ellipsis in here'

In the final year of the project, however, the written texts became more sophisticated and less dependent on the model text, though they did draw on language choices that were the focus of teaching. Although these features appeared in the text they were rarely singled out by Fiona for comment, who continued to comment on generic comments about use, rather than picking out examples of how they had been used for a particular purpose. Examples of this transfer into writing include:

noun phrases used to provide concise detail: '*10-year-old Kojo*'
adverbs used for emphasis:

> *He eventually arrived ...*
> *He quickly paid for*

adverbials to structure texts and signal chronology:

> *As a result of this, Noah's father died*
> *a few years later*

When asked if she could find adjectives that indicated how the characters in her story were feeling, however, Fiona did find examples:

'*he was overwhelmed*'
'*Noah is always determined ...*'

This suggests that surfacing this understanding might be dependent on how questions or discussions are framed and that precision in questioning can lead to precision in articulation of the grammar–meaning link.

By the final term of the project Fiona was able to explain her choice of '*barged into the room and pushed the door open*' as using verbs that show the character was in a bad mood. She was also able to explain that the short sentences: '*He immediately jumped on his chair*' and '*Now this caught Harry's attention*' were used at particular points in the text '*to build tension about what's going on*'. What was new in these explanations was a sense of her own purpose as a writer; to indicate a bad mood or to heighten tension at a particular moment in a plot.

The pattern of development, illustrated in this example of a primary aged writer, seems to move from a conscious emphasis on use not purpose, to increasingly sophisticated writing that reflects the teaching focus, through to an emerging ability to explain choices, in terms linked to meaning and personal writing intention. The focus of conscious attention, therefore, might be seen to move from use to purpose. This suggests that talk activities might, over time, focus on (1) generating lots of examples to embed grammatical patterns and highlight choice, (2) including talk at all points of the writing process supported by precise prompts and questions that focus on purpose not use, (3) establishing their own intentions as a writer.

Two key ideas emerged from this study to inform a refining of the pedagogy supporting the contextualised approach: a need for precision in making links between a grammar choice and its rhetorical effect; and a need for practice both in talking about choices and in writing tasks that enable a reflection on choice. As a consequence, we adapted the CPD with our project teachers, to foreground and model what we were learning about effective pedagogy from our observation of their lessons, and to minimise the emphasis on grammatical definitions and labelling, triggered by the national grammar test. We suggest to teachers that repeatedly seeing grammatical constructions and repeatedly hearing the teacher use the correct terminology may help embed grammatical understanding more effectively than definitions, just as repeatedly hearing teachers engage in precise talk articulating grammatical choices might embed an emphasis on purpose rather than use. In this way, we are trying to show that using the grammatical terminology as a natural part of classroom discourse might be a better way to support the growth of grammatical knowledge for the test than exercises and drilling. At the same time, we are underlining that students need to engage in purposeful discussions about grammatical choice which open up their understanding of grammar–meaning relationships.

To illustrate this, we often use the following example from one of our teaching units, exploring narrative writing and Arthurian legend. The students are looking at description of a setting and how careful choice of nouns can create a concrete visual image, and how verb choices can contribute to mood and atmosphere. An extract from this description is reproduced below, and the sentence which is the focus of discussion is underlined:

> The crypt was cold and dimly lit, and smelt musty, of ancient times. Row by row, through the chamber, stood the burial caskets of people long since dead, knights and their ladies. <u>Cobwebs shivered in a shaft of moonlight piercing the gloom</u>. Then, out of the darkness, came a lady, dark-haired and beautiful, wearing a gown of wine-red.

Through exemplar questions, we show teachers how carefully-shaped questioning can use grammatical terminology, without 'identification practice' simply by naming the grammar feature and then showing the examples in the text under consideration. We also show how teachers' questions can be sharply focused on prompting understanding of the grammar–meaning link, in this case by focusing on the student reader's response to the sentence.

Exemplar questions:

Look at the four nouns here – *cobwebs, shaft, moonlight* and *gloom*. They are creating a visual description or picture of the crypt. What images do they create for you of the crypt?

Look at that very descriptive noun phrase: *a shaft of moonlight piercing the gloom*. Can you see that picture in your mind's eye? Could you paint it?

Look at the two verbs – *shivered, piercing*. Is this a nice place to be? Why do you think the author has chosen those verbs? How might she want to make us feel?

What is being proposed here is not replacing an emphasis on form; which was pedagogy we did see, but a stronger emphasis on function; which our data suggests is missing from current pedagogy.

Conclusion

To an extent, all writing pedagogy aims to empower the writer to write texts that engage the reader, or argue for a cause or express feelings and concerns because giving children a voice is about empowerment and enabling them to write in ways that amuse or inform, inspire or persuade. The role of grammar in this wider aim is contested; but our cumulative research has demonstrated how a functionally oriented approach can foreground the function and semiotics of language, but that supporting the metalinguistic understanding that underpins this, is complex. In order to exercise choice a young writer needs to be aware of the linguistic choices available, and evaluate these choices with a rhetorical purpose in mind. Adopting a contextual functionally oriented approach is also demanding of teachers: they need to develop good enough grammar knowledge to notice how texts work and they need to enable talk in classrooms to surface understanding that is not easy to put into words. There are no simple solutions in education without also reducing the curriculum to correspondingly narrow and simple aims. In some respects, the Truss quote highlighted above illustrates how a wider set of aims have been reduced to knowledge that is testable, with an assumption that this knowledge alone is sufficient to support the complexity we have revealed here. Without explicit teaching that enables young writers to articulate their intentions and discuss the effect of their choices, the role of grammar in the curriculum will always be incomplete. Nevertheless, a pedagogy initially shown to be effective has been enhanced through further research with the aim of engaging with this complexity and with the intention of noticing and addressing the challenges of working this way. One final lesson we have learned through these various research initiatives is the importance of researching *with* teachers: our experience is that teachers are keen to be part of a professional research community, and willing to reflect on and adapt their own practice. In this way, we are increasingly able to build a pedagogy that is informed by clear principles, mindful of classroom challenges, and able to generate many examples of activities, lessons, and schemes of work that form the basis of a genuine pedagogy of empowerment.

References

Andrews, R., et al. 2006. The effect of grammar teaching on writing development. *British Educational Research Journal*, 32(1), 39–55

Bialystok, E. 1987. Influences of bilingualism on metalinguistic development. *Second Language Research*, 3, 154–166.

Bialystok, E. 1999. Cognitive complexity and attentional control in the bilingual mind. *Child Development*, 70, 636–644.

Bialystok, E. 2001. Metalinguistic aspects of bilingual processing. *Annual Review of Applied Linguistics*, 21, 169–182.

Biesta, G. J. J. 2007. Why 'what works' won't work: evidence-based practice and the democratic deficit of educational research. *Educational Theory*, 57(1), 1–22.

Carter, R. ed. 1990. *Knowledge about language*. London: Hodder & Stoughton.

Corden, R. 2000. *Literacy and learning through talk*. Buckingham: Open University Press.

Department for Education (DfE). 2014. National curriculum in England: English programmes of study. Available from: www.gov.uk/government/publications/national-curriculum-in-england-english-programmes-of-study [Accessed 21. 03. 19].

Derewianka, B. and Jones, P. 2010. From traditional grammar to functional grammar: bridging the divide. *NALDIC Quarterly*, 8(1), 6–17.

Gombert, E. J. 2003. Implicit and explicit learning to read: implication as for subtypes of dyslexia. *Current Psychology Letters: Behaviour, Brain and Cognition*, 10(1), Special Issue on Language Disorders and Reading Acquisition.

Gombert, J. E. 1992. *Metalinguistic development*. Chicago: University of Chicago Press.

Halliday, M. A. K. 1993. Towards a language-based theory of learning. *Linguistics and Education*, 5, 93–116.

Halliday, M. A. K. and Matthiessen, C. M. I. M. 2004. *An introduction to functional grammar*. 3rd ed. London: Routledge.

Jones, S. M., Myhill, D. A. and Bailey, T. 2013. Grammar for writing? An investigation into the effect of contextualised grammar teaching on student writing. *Reading and Writing*, 26(8), 1241–1263.

Kress, G. 1994. *Learning to write*. London: Routledge.

Myhill, D. A. 2009. Becoming a designer: trajectories of linguistic development. In: Beard, R., et al. eds. *The Sage handbook of writing development*. London: SAGE, 402–414.

Myhill, D. A. and Newman, R. 2016. Metatalk: enabling metalinguistic discussion about writing. *International Journal of Education Research*, 80, 177–187.

Myhill, D. A., Jones, S. and Watson, A. 2013. Grammar matters: how teachers' grammatical subject knowledge impacts on the teaching of writing. *Teaching and Teacher Education*, 36, 77–91.

Myhill, D. A., Jones, S. M. and Wilson, A. C. 2016. Writing conversations: fostering metalinguistic discussion about writing. *Research Papers in Education*, 31(1), 23–44.

Myhill, D. A., Lines, H. and Jones, S. M. 2018. Texts that teach: examining the efficacy of using texts as models. *L1-Educational Studies in Language and Literature*, 18, 1–24.

Myhill, D. A., et al. 2012. Re-thinking grammar: the impact of embedded grammar teaching on students' writing and students' metalinguistic understanding. *Research Papers in Education*, 27(2), 139–166.

Parr, J. M., Jesson, R. and McNaughton, S. 2009. Agency and platform: the relationships between talk and writing. In: Riley, J., et al. eds. *Handbook of writing development*. London: SAGE, 246–259.

Truss, E. 2013. New grammar, punctuation and spelling test will raise children's literacy standards. Press release. Available from: www.gov.uk/government/news/new-grammar-punctuation-and-spelling-test-will-raise-childrens-literacy-standards [Accessed 04. 03. 19].

Van Lier, L. 1998. The relationship between consciousness, interaction and language learning. *Language Awareness*, 7(2&3), 128–145.

Authentic texts

Burningham, J. 1978. *Mr Gumpy's outing*. Harmondsworth: Puffin Books.

Carl, E. 1994. *The very hungry caterpillar*. New York: Philomel Books.

Dickens, C. 2000. *Great expectations*. Ware: Wordsworth Editions.

Morpurgo, M. 1995. *Arthur, high king of Britain*. London: Pavilion.

Morris, J. 2007. *The snow leopard*. London: Frances Lincoln.

10 Writing their futures

Students' stories of development and difference

Erika Matruglio and Pauline Jones

Introduction

The nature of literacy, its role in shaping society, and how it should be taught are much contested ideas in educational systems around the world. Nowhere is this more evident than in Anglophone countries where controversy over the teaching of English literacy appears frequently in the media (Donnelly 2017, McDonald 2010, Munro 2016, Strauss 2016, Douglas 2017) and in educational debate and policy (Green et al. 1997, Burnett and Merchant 2015). Thus, in a sense, an explicit focus on literacy is nothing new. The literacy debate in our own jurisdiction – Australia – however, seems to be drawing to a critical moment, where innovation in the way we conceptualise, teach, and research literacy may be possible. Changes in curriculum and policy in the past several years have created both more opportunity and more urgency for systematic and 'appliable' research into students' trajectories of literacy development across the years of schooling (for example, see Christie and Derewianka 2008 for a discussion of writing development) as well as into the pedagogies that enable successful literacy learning for all students (Alexander 2017).

The advent of the national curriculum in Australia has strengthened the focus on explicit teaching of literacy, with literacy included as a 'general capability' in all content areas (ACARA 2013). Aspirational curriculum guidelines assert that 'all teachers are responsible for teaching the subject-specific literacy of their learning areas' and that 'all teachers need a clear understanding of the literacy demands and opportunities of their learning areas' (ACARA 2017, p. 1). The recent Literacy and Numeracy Strategy 2017–2020 in the state of New South Wales (DEC 2016) calls for a 'relentless focus on explicit teaching and high expectations for all students across all sectors' (p. 2). Under this strategy, students are now expected to meet new minimum literacy and numeracy standards in order to be eligible for the Higher School Certificate (HSC). What is missing from this political and policy focus on literacy teaching in the disciplines is a thorough understanding of how and whether literacy practices differ between disciplines and how they develop and change over the schooling years.

Furthermore, while a focus on literacy teaching and learning is being strengthened in policy and curriculum, Australian school students' academic performance as measured by the Program for International Student Assessment (PISA) has been in decline in comparison to other OECD countries since 2000 (DET 2018). In addition, the National Assessment Program – Literacy and Numeracy (NAPLAN) results indicate that literacy achievement has stagnated, particularly with respect to writing in upper primary and lower secondary years (National Assessment Program 2018). This indicates that there is currently a need to develop pedagogies to enhance literacy development and overcome the apparent stasis of recent years.

There is therefore now an important opportunity for research which provides insights into the trajectory of literacy development across the years of schooling, in different disciplines, and the facilitating pedagogical factors and barriers to students' achievements. This chapter reports on a section of data from a larger project[1] in order to explore one group of students' experiences of the demands of disciplinary literacies across the changing contexts from later primary to middle secondary. The larger project investigated the nature of literacy transitions in the years from preschool to junior secondary in three school communities belonging to a larger coastal region in New South Wales, Australia. Driven by the research question: 'What is the nature of students' literacy experiences at critical transition points in schooling?', the study involved more than 30 teachers, followed 70 students for three years (interviewing them twice per year) and recorded over 50 hours of classroom literacy lessons at key transition points of preschool to school: Year 2 to Year 3, Year 6 to Year 7, and Year 8 to Year 9. In this chapter, our focus is on one school community; in particular, a selective high school and its associated primary school. Here, we investigate the nature of the students' literacy experiences as they move from the last days of primary school (Year 6) into the early years of secondary school.

Research background

There is a research tradition reaching back to the 1980s in Australia and elsewhere investigating both literacy pedagogy in schools and the differences in disciplinary practices of literacy. This research has often involved both educational linguists and professional educators working together and has investigated various aspects of primary and secondary school literacy (Martin and Rose 2008, Rose and Martin 2012) and literacy beyond school contexts (Veel 2006, Iedema et al. 2008). While we recognise that there has been important research into the disciplinary literacies of many more subjects (such as, for example, Mathematics (Veel 1999), Geography (Humphrey 1996), Music (Weekes 2014), Business Studies (Weekes 2014), Legal Studies (Kompara-Tosio 2014), Society and Culture (Matruglio 2014), and Community and Family Studies (Matruglio 2014)), of particular relevance to the case study we present in this chapter is the research into the disciplinary literacies of Science (Morgan 2013, Veel 1993), History (Coffin 2006, Matruglio 2016), and English (Perera 1985, Rothery 1994, Myhill and Jones 2006). This research has focused on the purposes and genres of reading and writing favoured in these subjects and the language features that are typical (Christie and Derewianka 2008, Achugar and Carpenter 2012, Fang and Schleppegrell 2010, Goldman et al. 2016, Humphrey 2017).

There is also a body of research into the concept of transition generally at key institutional points (Perry et al. 2014, West et al. 2010); however very little of this research investigates what critical literacy transition points might look like across the years of schooling. The concept of transition has more traditionally been explored from perspectives including social and emotional impacts (Evangelou et al. 2008), impact on 'at risk students' (Luke et al. 2003), and institutional and social adjustment (Waters et al. 2012). In this chapter we begin to tease apart how transition occurs between primary and secondary years with respect to literacy expectations and practices.

Approach to the data

The chapter draws on data from the classroom and beyond it. The classroom data were collected in lessons identified by teachers as having a particular literacy focus. Classroom data relevant here included approximately 8.5 hours of lesson observations from ten literacy related lessons, together with associated printed material and student work samples. The observations comprised two primary English lessons, together with eight secondary lessons from English, History, Geography, and Science classrooms. An overview of the data is presented in Table 10.1. Each lesson was observed by two members of the research team, one researcher capturing raw data in the form of video, audio, and still images; the other researcher describing events using a proforma designed by the larger team.

Data from beyond the classroom help triangulate the classroom data and include interviews with both teachers and students. Space prevents us from including the

Table 10.1 Overview of classroom observation data

Lesson #	Year level	Month of year	Curriculum area	Topic/focus	Teacher
1	6	October	English	Poetry	Andrew
2	6	November	English	Poetry	Andrew
3	7	May	English	Poetry	Caroline
4	8	June	English	Poetry	Dianne
5	8	November	English	Writing dialogue	Dianne
6	7	June	Science	Writing for exams	Emily
7	7	November	Science	Group projects	Emily
8	9	May	Geography	Study skills	Dianne
9	10	June	History	Human rights	Hannah
10	10	June	History	Human rights	Hannah

full interview schedules here, but we include indicative interview questions in appendices 2 and 3. Importantly, the same students were followed from the primary to the secondary school, allowing the researchers to trace their development across educational sites as well as across subjects and year levels within individual schools. The discussions below focus on interviews with six teachers (one primary and four secondary as above) and six students (four from Year 7 and two from Year 9). In the interviews, both teachers and students are given the opportunity to talk about their experiences of literacy teaching and learning, and their understandings of their future literacy trajectories.

Our methodological approach for the work described in this chapter included an initial analysis of the video-recorded classroom observations by author 1 of the ten lessons described above. This analysis involved developing a description of each lesson as a pedagogic event and identifying (a) the types of reading evident, (b) the types of writing, (c) the purposes for reading where these were made explicit, and, similarly, (d) the purposes for writing. This analysis was supported by the detailed field notes taken of each lesson. We were also particularly interested where purpose was related to the changing nature of writing; for example, when students were told that this skill would be important for writing later, or when a current task was contrasted with a previous one. These instances were then listed with relevant illustrative dialogue. From these lists, two major themes related to continuities and discontinuities emerged: disciplinary differences in writing (e.g. How did the writing demands of English classrooms differ from that in Science and History?) and writing trajectories (e.g. How did writing demands change over time for students? How did they manage these shifts?). Descriptive summaries of the lesson observations were then developed and shared with author two who cross-checked the detail with raw observations materials including the videos and field notes.

Transcripts of teacher and student interviews were then scrutinised by author 2 looking for points at which the two themes – disciplinary differences in writing and the trajectory of writing development – were inflected. While there were interview questions designed to elicit participants' accounts of these matters, both teachers and students often referred to changing demands, hopes, fears, and challenges as the interviews unfolded and participants were able to reflect upon their experiences of literacy transitions. These responses were then threaded through the descriptive summaries and checked by both authors. From here, we worked to integrate the observations and interview sources into a more nuanced account of disciplinary differences and writing trajectories, considering student experiences and the implications for literacy pedagogy while doing so.

Discussion

Disciplinary difference in writing in secondary school

From the perspective of disciplinarity, there are a number of discernible differences in the classroom literacy practices in English, Science, and History/

Geography. One of the most striking of these is that in Science literacy-focused lessons, students are sometimes engaged in writing about non-science content. This contrasts with the English and History/Geography lessons observed in which students were engaged with knowledge from inside the discipline: poetry writing in English, recounting significant events and producing informative reports in History and Geography. The use of non-science content to teach literacy in Science also appears to result in some students taking the lesson less seriously. For example, in a Year 7 lesson introducing ALARM (A Learning And Responding Matrix) (Wood 2013) to a Science class, the students are introduced to the meanings of some of the verbs used in examination questions:

TEACHER: … so IDENTIFY do we think this sort of verb would be something that requires a little bit of 'thinking'?
STUDENT: No
TEACHER: No why not?
STUDENT: it's basically just saying the same thing
TEACHER: Yeah excellent yeah so we're just identifying it. We're naming it and we're giving a definition of what it is. Okay?

The students were then asked to work in groups to construct brief answers (one or two lines were provided) to several verb-prompts. While some groups in the class engage seriously with the task (as shown in Table 10.2), several boys can be heard joking to each other commenting that 'chocolate is a salad' or 'chocolate is a fruit made of milk'. The teacher must several times check that they are on task and direct them to the work they should be doing.

Table 10.2 Writing in the ALARM lesson

Prompt	Sample responses
Assess: make a judgement of value, quality, outcomes, results, or size	'Chocolate is not necessary for teenage diets'
Identify: name and define	'Chocolate is a brown, sugary substance. Teenager: person older than 12 and younger than 20'
Describe: provide characteristics and facts	'Chocolate has high sugar levels and is a processed food. It is made of coco beans and processed ingredients'
Explain: relate cause and effect/ provide why and/or how	'Teenagers don't need chocolate because it is unhealthy. Chocolate can cause tooth decay and general unhealthiness. It also helps against stress'
Analyse: identify components and the relationship between them	'Teenagers eat chocolate to satisfy their tastes. If teenagers eat to [sic] much they get hyper'
Assess: make a judgement of value, quality, outcomes, results, or size	'Chocolate has small value because they can eat other foods with less sugar and that are more healthy'

After their practice with the non-science content, the teacher introduces another question for them to practice, saying, 'I'd like to give you one more example, one more question, but we're actually going to start linking some Science into there'. The next question, 'Analyse the relationship between elements and compounds', which is linked to the content they have recently been learning, is then shown on the screen and the students must again write answers to the question in groups. The group who produced the above answers completed this task with the following brief but successful response: 'Elements – pure substances that cannot be separated. Compounds – substances composed of two or more elements.'

Despite differences in the writing demands of different high school subjects, teachers' concerns with supporting students to manage the increasing writing demands is evident in all of the teachers' accounts of their practice. For example:

> my focus, particularly with year, with all the juniors, is always to really build their ability to write.
>
> (Hannah, Year 10 Science teacher)

> they use words well … but in high school when you come to that side in terms of being able to read and that understanding, that critical sense, rather than just being good with language in a creative way.
>
> (Caroline, Year 7 English teacher)

Students, for their part, were also conscious of the importance of writing in the secondary school from early on but their concern was often on particular aspects of writing such as the increased volume but the need to be selective at the same time (sometimes expressed rather colourfully):

> Yeah, we've done a bit more writing. We've done a lot more writing actually.
>
> (Lewis, Year 7)

> You have to know not to vomit all the information down.
>
> (Nico, Year 7)

> Mr C. said something about 'kill your darlings' or something and that's probably when you write too much and you don't know what to keep in and what to pull out, so that's probably something I would work on.
>
> (Antonia, Year 7)

While students in the Science lessons observed were often asked to write in groups, the students in the observed lessons of the other disciplines wrote as individuals solely. This has important implications for the amount of actual real experience students have in writing. For example, in Science classes where students were asked to write in pairs or threes, one student would usually dictate the sentence while all the students in the group wrote their group answer in their books. A different strategy was used in the Year 10 Geography class, however, where students were given time to discuss their thoughts in groups but there then asked to write their own answers individually.

TEACHER: What I want you to do is take a couple of minutes now, and if it's so complex to identify solutions, how do we achieve human rights and reconciliation for indigenous Australians … you can talk to the people around you, and then I'd like you, and you're gonna know what I'm going to say! What am I gonna say?
STUDENTS: TEAL!
TEACHER: Construct one last response for me! … You've got two minutes of talking and then you're going to work quietly.

A third significant disciplinary difference in the writing practices in the observed classes has to do with the purpose for writing, sometimes glossed by the teacher as 'depth'. Speaking of the 'ALARM verbs' (identify, describe, explain, analyse, interpret, critically analyse, and evaluate), which are presented to the students as a hierarchy from more to less complex, the teacher explains to the students:

> These verbs will tell you how much depth you need to go into … If you were in a subject like English or something like that, you might even go a bit beyond this. They might look at critically evaluate … In Science though, a lot of our content is sort of, maybe a little more black and white, um right and wrong answers … and, when you write your answers, even in the HSC, you can use dot points, ok, you don't have to have structured sentences and all that sort of thing, um as long as you're getting the information down on the page, you don't really have to have, you know in English and things like that … they look at your sentence structure, well in Science you can just simply use dot points.
>
> (Emily, Year 7 Science teacher)

This extract demonstrates that the teacher understands writing in Science to be different from writing in 'English and things like that' in two important ways. The purposes for writing, that is whether students must be able to write to analyse or to critically evaluate, are different, and the structure of the writing is different, in that students may use dot points in Science but not in English. In other words, the teacher is aware of disciplinary difference in writing at the level of purpose and whole text, and also at lexico-grammatical level.

In their interviews, the teachers articulated what was distinctive about writing in their curriculum disciplines. English teachers discussed the need for students to produce writing which critically analysed other texts. The role of creativity and the relationship between critical analysis and creativity or imagination, however, was a matter for speculation:

> Like we expect them to know what those two words mean [critical analysis], but it's really a process of trying to learn what that is and it's a high level of refinement and creativity and imagination that accompanies that ability to analyse something.
>
> (Ben, Years 7 and 9 English/Drama teacher)

With respect to writing forms or purposes, teachers described writing in English to be analytical or persuasive, drawing on textual evidence to mount arguments in favour of particular interpretations of text. In contrast, Geography requires students to produce reports that incorporate events, facts, and evidence:

> report writing and how to write about a particular topic in a formal manner with statistics and with facts … An extended response in geography is definitely not the same length or form as an English one. An extended response in English is almost like a mini essay where you need to be proving a point. You need to have a thesis and whatnot, whereas the report needs to be well structured.
>
> (Dianne, Year 7 English and Geography teacher)

Students were also keenly aware of the differences in writing demands of the curriculum disciplines although this was often expressed in terms of topics and volume with English frequently nominated as requiring more extended written texts:

> Well yeah, the topics we do are completely different, so what we're going to write about and what we're learning about going to be different.
>
> (Nico, Year 7)

> Mainly English we've done more writing in … A lot of history is note-taking. Not much writing in Science.
>
> (Lewis, Year 7)

Older students were often better able to articulate the differences demanded by subjects and the effect of these differences on students' subject choices:

> Different subjects have different requirements. Not everyone is going to appreciate one subject as much as the others, probably partly because of those different things. The different subjects contrast each other a lot.
>
> (Odette, Year 9)

In summary, our data has illustrated a comprehensive picture of disciplinary difference in the nature of writing in the school subjects of Science, History/Geography, and English. These differences appear to be both in the pedagogies used to teach writing and the actual types of writing that students are required to do. Both students and teachers are aware of these differences between subjects to a certain degree and a significant amount of work goes in to preparing the students for the future demands of their studies.

Navigating transitions in learning to write

Turning now to consider trajectories of writing development across the transition point of primary to secondary school, the writing that students do within subjects differs from primary or even junior secondary years to later secondary. These differences are not simply limited to the types of writing that students do, but also can be seen in the flexibility students are given about what and when to write, the degree of scaffolding they receive for their writing, and the way writing is used to regulate their behaviour. These differences combine to result in a literacy landscape that looks much different in Year 10 than it does in Year 6.

Students in Year 6 appear to have some degree more flexibility about what they write than the secondary students. This flexibility pertains not only to whether or not they have to write down the notes on what they are discussing in class, but also to the content of their own creative writing. For example, the Year 6 English poetry class has been given three questions to answer in groups and report back to the class. The teacher tells them that if they 'want to write on this booklet any ideas or any things that you think of, you can on that page. You don't have to though, it's just more of a, um, just a discussion activity'. Later in the lesson he reiterates several times that they can jot something down during their discussions on the poem, but they don't have to. When it comes to the point that the students are writing written answers to the poem, they are again given a certain amount of flexibility to choose what they write. They are told:

> You don't have to write the questions but if you choose not to write the questions you have to answer in a way that I know what you are talking about. So then if, when it says what is the poem about don't just write it is about this, you need to say the poem is about, and your answer.
>
> (Andrew, Year 6 English teacher)

Later in the lesson the students are asked to write their own poem, and they are given free rein to write whatever type of a poem they like, on whatever preferred topic of interest they like. Students produce many questions about this instruction in an attempt to clarify exactly what the requirements are, and the teacher spends a great deal of time fielding these questions individually as students check whether their ideas are acceptable. One student asks if they are allowed to write about Minecraft, and the teacher replies, 'Let's try and keep it on a serious note. It's up to you what you write about'. The instruction to write a 'serious' poem and not one about something 'made up' is repeated several times in the class, as is the fact that they are 'not doing any specific type of poem'. The one instruction that is not negotiable is that the students must produce 'a poem that is easy for your reader to visualise, and it has multiple poetic techniques' in whatever form and whatever (serious) topic the students like.

In his interview, the teacher explains that his intention is to 'immerse' the students in models of good poetry so that they will take up similar techniques in their own poetry writing – a task that was challenging for the students but one that he hopes will extend their poetry writing and performance:

> So, my focus has been to expose the kids to those [literary devices such as metaphors, similes, etc.] so then when they do some – the idea is they all have to recite a poem either an original or one they've learnt in class and then the top three will go to a stage recital competition in the hall.
>
> (Andrew, Year 6 teacher)

Andrew's comments reveal something of the persistence of progressivist views (Christie and Macken-Horarik 2007) of literacy in the primary school (despite the scaffolded approach advocated in current English curriculum), particularly when compared to the more structured approach to literacy taken by his secondary colleagues. Students also comment on the loose framing of many literacy tasks in the final years of primary school compared with secondary school:

> I've done stories before in primary school and in other classes, but it's interesting to learn the proper techniques. I think in primary school, all they tell you is draw the four windows and then fill them up – paragraph 1, 2, 3, 4 – but it's interesting now to go into more of the techniques.
>
> (Antonia, Year 7)

> We have to repeat the aim and the hypothesis. Back in primary school it was told that you didn't have to, but it would get you more marks if you did. But now it is a requirement to put … not rewrite the aim but say about it in the conclusion.
>
> (Lewis, Year 7)

In the Year 7 lesson on poetry, however, there is both more restriction in and more guidance for what students should write than in primary school. Similar to the Year 6 students, the Year 7 students are first given a poem to read and talk about before writing their own. However, in the Year 7 class, the poem is more obviously and explicitly used as a model for their own writing. There is a clear link between the mentor poem, the teacher's choice for grammatical focus and those that students produce individually (see Table 10.3). The poem they read is explained by the teacher as containing 'strong verbs' which appeal to the reader's sense of hearing. The students are shown a list of similar verbs on the screen which are intended to inspire their own writing and they are then told that they are going to write their own poem.

> I want you now to imagine that you've got to write a poem, you've got this, this sensory kind of hearing ... Using the poem as a model you can start with those two words I hear and think about that outside of the space, ok, and a nice strong use of verbs that indicates the sound ... starting with that out of frame, what's outside. Open up your books, start a new section.
>
> (Caroline, Year 7 English teacher)

In this case, students are told to use a particular type of vocabulary, and write a particular type of poem, which focuses on the sounds the poet hears from outside the building they are in, then moves closer to inside the building then even closer to the immediate context of the poet. The students are still given some freedom in their choice of particular scenario in that they are allowed to write 'in relation to your own home environment or alternatively just the room that we're in now' but the task is both much more restricted and also much more supported than the observed Year 6 class. There are no questions about the requirements of the task and the students are able to begin writing their own poetry without delay or distraction. Most students successfully completed this task, producing poetic texts similar to that depicted in Table 10.3. The mentor text provided students with not only the initial sensory

Table 10.3 Scaffolding poetry writing in Year 7

Mentor poem	*Student's poem*
EAVESDROPPING I hear the wrench my brother smashes on the garage floor as he tries to put a Norton engine back together, the Bells whisky my father slops into a tumbler, followed by ice, a tap turned on, my other brother imitating machine gun fire in the loft where he plays war games. I hear my mother typing in the new room making the dining table shudder as she punches each key, our dog, Steve, barking at the kitchen door, Penny, my cat miaow for supper – and myself on the phone again, straining for background noise, anything familiar. **Jackie Wills** From *Fever Tree* (Arc Publications 2003)	I hear the rush of the wind, the distant, endless roar of the waves, a skitter of a twig from a careless bird the clang of hammers on concrete and steel the rush of wind in the windows, the rustle of paper, the clunk of panels moved by the wind, the flick of pens, the slam of a book, closed too soon, a voice advising, the dropping of a pencil, the flick of pens, again, much louder, my ears straining, my breath.

stimulus, but also a strong pattern for the rhythmic soundscape of the remainder of the poem. This example seems to indicate an almost contradictory developmental trajectory in the literacy pedagogy from more freedom of expression to more constraint, the latter assisting the students towards success within the bounds of poetics.

In a Year 8 poetry class, the students are also given instruction on what they are to write when they are analysing a poem. Rather than being permitted to 'jot ideas down' if they want to, in Year 8 they are required to write specific types of information on their sheets.

> So word choice, the specific word choice is going to often determine the tone or the mood of the poem so … so there on your sheet you need to put mood and tone and you need to say what are we gonna call it? We're gonna say sombre.
>
> (Dianne, Year 8 English teacher)

Similarly, in Year 10 Geography, there is also an explicit focus on students getting the correct notes and making sure they have all written them down. During a brainstorming session, for example, the teacher writes words and dot points on the board, instructing the students to 'write these down if you haven't got them please' and later in the lesson reiterates again for the students to write the points on the board down if they haven't already got them. She also often checks with the students if she can rub off parts of the board, in other words, whether they have written that particular collection of notes or points in their own books. This explicit and repeated focus on making sure everyone has the correct notes contrasts markedly with the observed Year 6 English class, where the students are sometimes left to copy notes from their classmates while the class moves on to another activity.

> Just give us a couple of more minutes and if you're not finished before we move on you might just have to look at somebody else's book while we're going through. I know some people write quicker than others so that's fine.
>
> (Andrew, Year 6 Teacher)

Thus we observe that there is apparently more freedom and consequently less support for both the creative writing and note-taking in primary than in secondary school, at least in the lessons observed in this cluster or schools. While the sample is small, the pattern holds for different teachers in different year levels (7, 8) and in different disciplines (English, Geography), making the pattern worthy of further research. This trajectory from less to more specification in the task seems counter-intuitive to us; however, it may stem from a mismatch between the teacher's expectation about how self-directed students need to be in secondary school and what the actual classroom practice looks like. The teacher in Year 6 may be attempting to prepare students to take more responsibility for their own learning, while the secondary teachers may be reacting to a crowded curriculum increasing in technicality and disciplinary specificity.

However, while students in Year 6 appear to be given some freedom to write on the one hand, the writing that they do appears also to some degree to fill a regulatory function. Their written work is used as a type of display of industriousness and compliance with the instructions they have been given. For example, at one stage in the lesson, the students have been given the task of writing answers to questions about a poem. The teacher circulates around the class while the students work in groups and checks how much they have written. A particular group of boys are perceived by the teacher to be unengaged in the task and the teacher asks 'where are you up to? Don't hide your work! Show me!' The boys are then castigated for being too slow and are told that they might be doing their work at lunch time and that some other groups are already finished. We did not observe any instances of the teacher using the students' written work in such a regulatory way in the secondary school context.

Students' accounts of the transition from primary to secondary school provide some useful and different insights into their experiences; including a perceived demand for longer texts, to produce a greater variety of texts, and, for specialisation:

> They really just expect you to be ready to do longer pieces of writing and also the ability to do short stories as well.
>
> (Lewis, Year 7)

> With English, it seems like it's much more historical, I guess, and a lot of it has a historical background. But that was the same with Year 6 and beforehand, because we had etymology and all that. But that was just looking it up online and then putting it down. You weren't really learning about all the history. While with this, it's much more integrated into history, so I guess it was preparation, that ... at the start of the year, we had to write a review of a story and it needed to be 1,000 words and I only did, I think, 400. I couldn't write any more. But I've developed how much I can write.
>
> (Gino, Year 7)

The issue of prospective literacy demands emerged as part of the students' enculturation into high school. As we have seen above, teachers referred to the importance of writing techniques to the high stakes exam undertaken in Year 12. The students we interviewed were keenly aware of the trajectory of skills from Year 7 to Year 12:

> And since we've started essay writing, it's really interesting to go, oh this is how you actually do this, and this is what you would do in Year 12. That's definitely come up in pretty much all of our classes.
>
> (Antonia, Year 7)

Students varied in their attitudes to the different demands of high school writing. Some students recognised their growing skills as writers as well as the ongoing nature of the curriculum demands:

> I have a much larger vocabulary and I can articulate my words much clearer, but as my English teacher says, I still have to do much harder. So it's just an ongoing process for me. It's never-ending … I've got a tutor.
> (Nico, Year 8)

Others, however, relished the opportunities offered by a broader, more demanding curriculum:

> I've been waiting for something this good, stimulating, so it's been great to be doing it. It hasn't been a problem at all really. It hasn't been a hard transition. It's just jump smoothly in and get into it and you go on.
> (Gino, Year 7)

In summary, when it comes to trajectories of writing development, a transition from more freedom in primary education towards more constraint in secondary writing is noticeable, with a corresponding movement towards more technicality in writing and a higher demand for certain writing techniques. There is also a greater focus on ensuring that students have written the 'right sort' of notes in secondary school, and that they have comprehensive and full notes, perhaps motivated by high stakes testing. Secondary writing is focused squarely on disciplinary knowledge, never appearing to serve a regulatory function as it sometimes does in primary school. The implications of these differences and the disciplinary differences outlined in the previous section will be discussed below.

Conclusion

The experiences and perspectives of the students and teachers explored above clearly demonstrates both the importance placed on disciplinary literacy development and the effort expended on it at all levels of schooling and across all the disciplines included in this study. It also demonstrates an often-insightful ability of students to be able to talk explicitly about their different experiences of literacy transitions into secondary schooling, their own trajectories of literacy development, and the demands of the future with respect to school writing. We have also demonstrated teachers' awareness of some of the disciplinary differences in writing practices and a strong commitment to teaching their own subject's writing practices so that students can succeed both in their present learning situations and in future high-stakes examinations.

Despite this disciplinary orientation to writing, we also observed unexpected episodes in Science, for example, where teachers used non-Science content to teach writing in their discipline. This could result from a tension between what the teachers know either implicitly or explicitly about the distinctiveness of writing in their discipline and the whole-school application across subjects of generic frameworks like ALARM. While these frameworks are generally understood to be transferable across curriculum areas and years of schooling, their application may actually conflict with teachers' understandings of the different purposes for and methods of writing between their discipline and others. Writing frameworks which emphasise links between discipline content, purposes for writing, and the resultant structures and language of writing in specific disciplines, we believe, will in the long term be more beneficial in assisting disciplinary teachers to teach the specialised literacy practices of their discipline than a one-size-fits-all approach which necessarily lacks sophisticated disciplinary nuance.

In other words, our research suggests the need for an integrated language pedagogy in which a full range of linguistic resources are harnessed in the service of discipline specific activities. Importantly, this pedagogy should be integrated in two ways. First, it should take an integrated approach to the teaching of language and content, such that 'teaching language' is not viewed as a separate activity from 'teaching content' and vice versa. This would enable the use of subject-specific technicality and a metalanguage to talk about writing to be used together, facilitating the building of strong disciplinary understandings of how language is used to make meaning in the disciplines. Such pedagogies could be tailored specifically to both discipline and year level, so that students are gradually apprenticed into the most valued meaning-making practices in each discipline as they advance through the years of schooling. We recognise the critical role here of the teacher who is both discipline specialist and literacy expert. We are also cognisant that much of this work is currently achieved via collaborations between subject teachers and literacy experts (where they are available). However, we argue that sensitivity to discipline literacies is part of the discipline expert's unique 'insider-knowledge' and that there is an urgent need to recognise and support subject teachers who are both discipline and literacy savvy.

Second, and relatedly, an integrated language pedagogy should focus on teaching disciplinary communication across what are generally understood to be the 'macroskills' of reading, writing, listening, and speaking. The observed lessons included students engaged in tasks which traversed these skills (discussion and research in group tasks, writing poetry in a spoken-like voice, reading from worksheets, listening to whole class discussion, watching students perform oral tasks, etc.); yet we only ever observed the explicitly named, scaffolded teaching of writing. Oracy and reading skills were usually tacit aspects of the lessons. Our conjecture is that it is often taken for granted that students know how to communicate orally or learn from reading by the time they reach high school, or it may be that teachers realise the importance of sophisticated control of written communication for high stakes examination and so place their focus there. However, the development of oral language skills is a feature of curriculum documents across all curriculum disciplines (ACARA 2017) and students are increasingly being required to produce multimodal artefacts combining spoken and written language, and image for assessment at the highest levels of education (Jones et al. forthcoming). An integrated language pedagogy which makes explicit how oral and written language vary for different communicative purposes would benefit students at every level of schooling.

Our results also suggest the need to better understand the relationship between flexibility, restriction, and guidance across the trajectory of schooling years and across disciplines. While 'freedom' is perhaps often understood as necessary to foster creativity, especially in progressive approaches to pedagogy, years of linguistic research into more guided approaches to pedagogy have shown that a teaching and learning cycle which moves through stages of more tightly controlled, explicit guidance and ones of gradual release of responsibility to the learner (Martin 1999) result in improved outcomes in terms of both literacy and content learning (Rose and Martin 2012). While on the one hand it is often seen as advantageous to give students increasing amounts of freedom in the management of their own learning (seen in the frequent use of Self Organised Learning Environments and Problem Based Learning in schools) it is nevertheless visible from teachers' practice that there is also an understanding that there are certain 'expected' and 'appropriate' ways that students must engage with knowledge in order to do well in exams. This tension between individual freedom and creativity on the one hand and constraint in terms of meeting expectations on the other is one that needs much more research in educational settings.

Notes

1 This work was supported by the University of Wollongong and the Australian Government (through the Transforming Literacy Outcomes (TRANSLIT) project ($400,000 2014–2017/2018)). Investigators: Jones, P. T., Chen, H., Derewianka, B., Freebody, P., Kervin, L., McKenzie, B., Mantei, J., Matruglio, E., Mehorter, B., Rutherford Vale, E. and Turbill, J. Technical assistance provided by Josef English, Adele Beck, Helen Lewis, Trish Weekes, Lily Klasson, and Lydia Zhang.
2 Questions varied to account for teachers' different subject areas and whether primaryor secondary setting.
3 Questions varied according to whether students were in primary or secondary school, and the time of year at which the interview took place.

Appendix 10.1

TRANSLIT indicative teacher interview questions[2]

Pre-observation

- I'd like to start by finding out about what you're planning for the lesson today. Please would you share your goals for the lesson, particularly those to do with literacy? What do you hope the students will know or be able to do at the end of the lesson?
- Can you tell me, how do you think you will know if you have achieved the lesson goals?

- And why do you believe that aspect is important for your students at the moment?
- We're interested in exploring how students experience the literacy strategies and activities and expectations in the classroom (for example how they perceive Les son aims, how challenging they find tasks, etc.). Tell me about the kind of approach you will take in this lesson to teach [LITERACY FOCUS IDENTIFIED IN Q1]?

Post-observation

- Would you mind telling me a little bit about how you felt the lesson went? Were you happy that students learned what you wanted for the lesson? (If possible, try to have a work sample of one of the case study students here.)
- What might you teach next to follow up from and build on this lesson? I'd like to focus on the students' literacy development now. Talk to me about how you feel the students are progressing with their literacy this semester in [INSERT SUBJECT].
- What kinds of factors do you think affect their progress in your class?
- Tell me a bit about how you see your role in relation to your students' literacy development.
- What do you want or hope your students will know and be able to do by the end of this term/at the end of this semester? [Including reading/writing/oral language]?
- What do you see as the most important literacy skills for students to gain control of this year in [INSERT SUBJECT]?
- What about more broadly, looking ahead to their future studies, what literacy skills and knowledge do you see as really important to develop for success in [INSERT SUBJECT]?

General questions re: transition

- Please would you share a bit of your own impression of what the challenging transition points are for students as they progress through [INSERT STAGES AS RELEVANT]? Why do you think those points present challenges for students? *(Alternative: Can you tell me what you think are the times when you students can start to falter in their literacy and learning? What do think might be some of the causes of this?)*
- What do you see as challenging aspects of literacy learning in [INSERT SUBJECT IF RELEVANT] for this year group?

Appendix 10.2

TRANSLIT indicative student interview questions[3], Initial interview and Reading-related questions:

- What kinds of things do you have to read in English? And how do you find this kind of reading? What about Science? What sorts of things do you need to read for school science? And how do you find this kind of reading? And History? What do you have to read for History and how do you find this reading?
- Do you have textbooks for each of these subjects? What is the textbook like?
- I'm curious about whether you have to research in any of your subjects. Do you have to do research assignments for any of these subjects either at home or at school? What kinds of things do you read when you are doing research for [INSERT SUBJECT]?
- What are some of the things that your teacher thinks are important when you read in the classroom?

Writing-related questions:

- What kinds of things do you have to write in English? And how do you find writing [STORIES/ESSAYS AS APPROPRIATE]? What about Science? What sorts of things do you need to write for school Science? And how do you find this kind of writing? And History? What do you have to write for History and how do you find this kind of writing?
- Can you tell me what you think counts as successful writing in ENGLISH? And what about SCIENCE? And HISTORY?
- Tell me about the feedback you get from your teacher about your reading and writing? What's helpful? What's not?
- As a kind of summary for this section of the interview, I'd like to ask you to think about whether you think that reading and writing is the same for every subject?
- And finally, what is easy about reading and writing in your different subjects? And what can make reading and writing hard in different subjects?

Student writing sample questions:

- Let's start with [INSERT SUBJECT], tell me what you think your teacher wanted you to show in this writing?
- What do you think you did well in this piece of writing?
- What do you think you could do better?

Questions asked in later interviews

- To begin, can you talk a bit about an area of reading and writing in [INSERT SUBJECT], where you think you have improved lately? How do you know that you have improved in this area? What would you like to be able to do next in reading and writing for [INSERT SUBJECT]?

What aspect of reading or writing would you like to improve in for [INSERT SUBJECT]?
- What does your teacher expect from you now in [INSERT SUBJECT] compared to the expectations for [INSERT SUBJECT] earlier in the year/last year? Tell me about the assignments and class work and how they are different or similar. Do you still have to do the same types of reading and writing or have these changed?
- When we spoke earlier in the year [OR LAST YEAR] you said you wanted to work on X in your writing. How is that going now? What are some new writing goals you have set yourself?
- What do you think the teachers' expectations for reading and writing in [INSERT SUBJECT] next year will be like compared to this year?

References

Achugar, M. and Carpenter, B. D. 2012. Developing disciplinary literacy in a multilingual history classroom. *Linguistics and Education*, 23(2), 262–276.

Alexander, R. 2017. Developing dialogue: process, trial, outcomes. Paper presented at the 17th Biennial EARLI Conference, Tampere, Finland.

Australian Curriculum and Assessment Reporting Authority (ACARA). 2013. *The Australian curriculum: history*. Australian Curriculum Assessment and Reporting Authority.

Australian Curriculum and Assessment Reporting Authority (ACARA). 2017. *Australian curriculum v8.3 F-10 curriculum: literacy*. Available from: www.australiancurriculum.edu.au/generalcapabilities/literacy/introduction/in-the-learning-areas [Accessed 21. 03. 18].

Burnett, C. and Merchant, G. 2015. The challenge of 21st century literacies. *Journal of Adolescent and Adult Literacy*, 59(3), 271–274.

Christie, F. and Derewianka, B. 2008. *School discourse: learning to write across the years of schooling*. London: Continuum.

Christie, F. and Macken-Horarik, M. 2007. Building verticality in subject English. In: Christie, F. and Martin, J. R. eds. *Language, knowledge and pedagogy: functional linguistics and sociological perspectives*. London: Continuum, 156–183.

Coffin, C. 2006. *Historical discourse: the language of time, cause and evaluation*. London: Continuum.

Department of Education and Communities (DEC). 2016. *Literacy and numeracy strategy 2017–2020*. Department of Education and Communities, NSW.

Department of Education and Training (DET). 2018. *Through growth to achievement: report of the review to achieve educational excellence in Australian schools*. Commonwealth of Australia. Available from: www.appa.asn.au/wp-content/uploads/2018/04/20180430-Through-Growth-to-Achievement_Text.pdf [Accessed 27. 08. 18].

Donnelly, K. 2017, 10 December. Australian literacy standards falling, basics the key. *Herald Sun*.

Douglas, J. 2017. How do we solve England's literacy crisis? One community at a time. Available from: www.huffingtonpost.co.uk/jonathan-douglas/child-literacy_b_14630444.html?guccounter=1&guce_referrer_us=aHR0cHM6Ly93d3cuZ29vZ2xlLmNvbS8&guce_referrer_cs=FLa2B4xAx5NzhZqucZHg2A [Accessed 10/12/18].

Evangelou, M., et al. 2008. *What makes a successful transition from primary to secondary school?* Nottingham: Department for Children, Schools and Families.

Fang, Z. and Schleppegrell, M. 2010. Disciplinary literacies across content areas: supporting secondary reading through functional language analysis. *Journal of Adolescent & Adult Literacy*, 53(7), 587–597.

Goldman, S. R., et al. 2016. Disciplinary literacies and learning to read for understanding: a conceptual framework for disciplinary literacy. *Educational Psychologist*, 51(2), 219–246.

Green, B., Hodgens, J. and Luke, A. 1997. Debating literacy in Australia: history lessons and popular f(r)ictions. *Australian Journal of Language and Literacy*, 20(1), 6–24.

Humphrey, S. 1996. *Exploring literacy in school geography*. Sydney: Metropolitan East Disadvantaged Schools Program.

Humphrey, S. 2017. *Academic literacies in the middle years: a framework for enhancing teaching knowledge and student achievement*. London: Routledge.

Iedema, R., et al. 2008. *Media literacy*. Surry Hills, NSW: NSW Adult Migrant Education Service.

Jones, P. T., et al. (forthcoming). Assessing multimodal literacies in science: semiotic and practical insights from pre-service teacher education. *Language and Education*.

Kompara-Tosio, J. 2014. Literacy in legal studies: writing evaluation essays. Paper presented at the Legal Studies Association of NSW 2014 Conference.

Luke, A., et al. 2003. *Beyond the middle*. St Lucia, Brisbane: School of Education, the University of Queensland.

McDonald, T. 2010. Australian students' literacy levels declining. ABC News. Available from: www.abc.net.au/news/2010-12-08/australian-students-literacy-levels-declining/2366804 [Accessed 21. 03. 18].

Martin, J. R. 1999. Mentoring semogenesis: 'genre-based' literacy pedagogy. In: Christie, F. ed. *Pedagogy and the shaping of consciousness: linguistic and social processes*. London: Cassell, 123–155.

Martin, J. R. and Rose, D. 2008. *Genre relations: mapping culture*. London: Equinox.

Matruglio, E. 2014. *Humanities' humanity: construing the social in HSC modern and ancient history, society and culture, and community and family studies*. PhD thesis. University of Technology Sydney, Sydney.

Matruglio, E. 2016. Objectivity and critique: the creation of historical perspectives in senior secondary writing. *Australian Journal of Language and Literacy*, 39(2), 124–134.

Morgan, A.-M. 2013. 'Proof of concept': beginning to use design-based research to improve science literacies for middle years learners. *Australian Journal of Language and Literacy*, 36(1), 3–16.

Munro, K. 2016. NAPLAN: half of NSW students would fail first HSC test. *The Sydney Morning Herald*.

Myhill, D. A. and Jones, S. 2006. Patterns and processes: the linguistic characteristics and composing processes of secondary school writers. Technical Report RES-000-23-0208 to the Economic and Social Research Council.

National Assessment Program. 2018. *NAPLAN results 2018*. Available from: www.nap.edu.au/information/faqs/2018-naplan-results [Accessed 21. 04. 18].

Perera, K. 1985. Grammatical differentiation between speech and writing in children aged 8 to 12. Paper presented at the annual meeting of the International Writing Convention, Norwich, England.

Perry, B., Docket, S. and Petriwskyj, A. eds. 2014. *Transitions to school: international research, policy and practice*. New York and London: Springer.

Rose, D. and Martin, J. R. 2012. *Learning to write, reading to learn: genre, knowledge and pedagogy in the Sydney school*. Sheffield: Equinox.

Rothery, J. 1994. *Exploring literacy in school English*. Sydney: Metropolitan East Disadvantaged Schools Program.

Strauss, V. 2016. Hiding in plain sight: the adult literacy crisis. Available from: www.washingtonpost.com/news/answer-sheet/wp/2016/11/01/hiding-in-plain-sight-the-adult-literacy-crisis/?utm_term=.c96bfa6dd752 [Accessed 20. 12. 18].

Veel, R. 1993. *Exploring literacy in school science*. Research Report. Metropolitan East DSP. Sydney.

Veel, R. 1999. Language, knowledge and authority in school mathematics. In: Christie, F. ed. *Pedagogy and the shaping of consciousness: linguistic and social processes*. London: Cassell, 185–216.

Veel, R. 2006. The write it right project: linguistic modelling of secondary school and the workplace. In: Whittaker, R., et al. eds. *Language and literacy*. London: Continuum.

Waters, S., et al. 2012. A theoretically grounded exploration of the social and emotional outcomes of transition from primary to secondary school. *Australian Journal of Guidance and Counselling*, 22(2), 190–205.

Weekes, T. 2014. *From dot points to disciplinarity: the theory and practice of disciplinary literacies in secondary schooling*. PhD thesis, University of New England, Australia.

West, P., Sweeting, H. and Young, R. 2010. Transition matters: pupils' experiences of the primary-secondary school transition in the west of Scotland and consequences for well-being and attainment. *Research Papers in Education*, 25(1), 21–50.

Wills, J. 2003. *Fever tree*. Todmorden: Arc Publications.

Wood, M. 2013. ALARM: a learning and responding matrix an introduction. Available from: www.youtube.com/watch?v=gnZ2TiBh-QY [Accessed 21. 05. 18].

11 Wordsmiths and sentence-shapers
Linguistic and metalinguistic development in secondary writers

Debra Myhill

Introduction

Research on writing and the teaching of writing has typically paid notably less attention to the learning and development needs of older writers, aged around 11–16, despite the significant body of work on younger writers, particularly in the early years. This chapter will place a spotlight specifically on this older group of writers, who may well have mastered basic writing fluency and accuracy, but still need focused support in developing expertise as writers. Indeed, in Anglophone countries at least, there is current widespread concern about standards in writing in these older writers (e.g. ACARA 2017, DfE 2017, MoE 2017). The capacity to write well is fundamental to educational success: Graham and Perin argue that 'writing skill is a predictor of academic success and a basic requirement for participation in civic life and in the global economy' (Graham and Perin 2007, p. 3). Understanding the learning needs of this group of writers is critical if we are to understand how best to address this concern about writing proficiency, and this chapter will focus particularly on the linguistic and metalinguistic development of these older writers, and on how metalinguistic understanding is crucially dependent on the nature of the pedagogical strategies used and the management of metalinguistic talk used by teachers in the writing classroom.

Linguistic development in writing

Over the past 50 years or so there have been a number of studies investigating linguistic development in writing with a view to identifying whether it is possible to describe increasing maturity as a writer in linguistic terms. This has been motivated by the idea that teachers could meet children's learning needs and set more appropriate tasks if there were 'some understanding of the stages that children pass through in their development as writers' (Perera 1984, p. 2). Indeed, Perera's (1984) own study is a particularly rich and elaborate analysis of writing development and looks in depth at the difference between spoken and written language – but its focus is on children in the middle years, aged 8–12. A small-scale pilot study by Hunt (1965) in the United States looked at linguistic development across three age groups, 10-, 14-, and 18-year-olds. He found that clause and T-unit length (a main clause and all subordinate clauses or non-clausal structures linked to it) increased in length with age, and also that older writers used many of the same linguistic structures as younger writers but with greater frequency. A subsequent study by Loban (1976) found that writing from older students tended to have longer clauses and sentences, more elaboration in subject and predicate, and greater use of a variety of other structures such as embedded clauses – echoing Hunt's findings that linguistic development may be less about the appearance of particular linguistic structures at particular ages, but about greater use of them. A substantial cross-linguistic study, the Spencer Project, led by Ruth Berman, looked at development in speech and writing across four age groups and across seven languages. To an extent, their findings resonate with those of Hunt and Loban: they found increased clause length (Berman and Verhoeven 2002), increased use of the passive (Ragnarsdóttir et al. 2002), increased syntactic complexity (Verhoeven et al. 2002), and more lexical subject noun phrases (Ravid et al. 2002). Of relevance to this chapter are the findings of Stromqvist et al. (2002, p. 53) that between the ages of 13 and 17 there was a significant increase in lexical diversity and lexical density, a finding also evidenced by Derewianka in Chapter 12 of this book.

What is evident from this overview is that no studies focused specifically on secondary school learners and that older writers are under-represented in this body of work. One exception to this is the Qualifications and Curriculum Authority study (QCA 1999) which analysed examination scripts of 15–16-year-olds in subject English. The sample comprised 144 scripts, stratified by grade, and the analysis considered syntax, word class, spelling, punctuation, textual organisation, and Standard English. This highlighted different characteristics of lower or higher-attaining writers, such as more simple sentences and fewer finite verbs in the writing of the most able writers. These findings were largely replicated in a similar study (Massey et al. 2005).

Our own research has addressed this lacuna in the research in three major studies. Our first study in this area, *Patterns and Processes*, funded by the Economic and Social Research Council (2003–2005), investigated both the linguistic characteristics of secondary-aged students' writing and the composing processes that produced them, although it is the former we are concerned with here. Samples of writing ($n = 718$) were gathered from students in UK secondary schools. The students were stratified by age (13- and 15-year-olds), by gender, and by writing attainment (low, average, and high as measured by UK assessment processes at the time). Each student wrote a narrative piece and an argument piece in a normal English writing lesson, and this was used to form the sample.

The writing was analysed systematically using an analytical framework which considered sentence length, clauses, and syntax of sentence-openers (for more detail, see Myhill 2008), and used inferential statistics to determine where differences were statistically significant. The key findings were:

- *Sentence length*: this increased with age: high-attaining writers' longest sentences were longer than other writers'; low-attaining writers often lost control of grammar of expression in their longest sentences.
- *Clause types*: low-attaining writers used more subordination, more co-ordination, and had more finite verbs in their writing than average and high-attaining writers.
- *Variety in sentence openers*: no age-related difference in sentences beginning with a subject but the proportion of subject sentence-openers declined with increasing attainment; adverbial sentence-openers increased with both age and attainment.

Following this, we moved from the statistics to a qualitative analysis of the texts to understand better what these patterns were telling us about writing development. The finding that subordination decreased with age was counter to previous research (predominantly in primary age groups) and we wanted to understand how these patterns played out in the writing. This analysis led us to conclude that the trajectories of development by age were less significant than those by attainment, though they often mirrored each other. We also concluded that high-attaining (and older) writers were crafting and shaping their writing more deliberately, writing as designers (Myhill 2009). This meant, for example, that they made greater use of short simple sentences for clarity or effect, and they elaborated more within their sentences to provide explanatory or descriptive detail for the reader.

More recently, another study, *Growth in Grammar*, funded by the Economic and Research Council (2015–2018) adopted a corpus linguistics approach to linguistic development, making use of the increasing power of software packages to analyse texts. This study created a corpus of 2,988 writing samples from 983 children, aged 6 to 16 years old, representing a range of text types in different curriculum subjects. One strand of the corpus analysis involved hand annotation of texts for noun phrase expansion and patterns of subordination, whilst another looked at vocabulary (Durrant and Brenchley 2019). The analysis of subordination found that use of subordination increased markedly in the primary age range (ages 6–11) but remained relatively stable thereafter; this finding has some alignment with our earlier study which showed able writers in the secondary age group used less subordination than lower-attaining writers. The analysis of noun phrase expansion is particularly interesting as our earlier study did not look at this, but did find in the qualitative analysis that there was more expansion and elaboration in high-attaining writers, which was often in the noun phrase (see also Derewianka, Chapter 12 of this book). In this study, we found that there was no significant difference in pre-modification of the noun across the age groups. However, post-modification increased significantly with age, with 16-year-old writers using twice as many post-modified noun phrases as 7-year-olds. You can see this pattern exemplified in the examples below:

- Rosie fed them <u>rotten bananas</u> and <u>rotten oranges</u> (age 7).
- The dragon has <u>two flaky long wings</u> and <u>a lot of wiggly heads</u> (age 7).
- It was <u>a man: a man in a long white robe</u> (age 11).
- <u>The strategies this species used to survive</u> was mainly thanks to his own body structure (age 11).
- They had <u>the biggest brains compared to body size</u> (age 11).
- I took a few steps forward to come across <u>an abandoned car with weeds growing out of it</u> (age 14).
- It had been eating <u>the remains of a rat on the floor</u> (age 14).
- <u>An icy wind that tears tall trees up from its roots and tosses them away</u> (age 16).
- <u>Dangerous rocks with dagger-like edges and deadly intentions</u> led the way down (age 16).
- Initially, before the play even begins, we are met by <u>an onslaught of stage directions in which we are met by the antithesis of, 'half shy, half assertive'</u> (age 16).

Our final set of data about linguistic development draws from a four-year longitudinal study, *Writing Conversations*, also funded by the Economic and Social Research Council (2013–2018). This was principally an in-depth qualitative study where we tracked a cohort of 57 primary students, age 9–11, over the last three years of primary schooling, and a cohort of 52 secondary students (aged 12–14) over the first three years of their secondary schooling. Our central focus was how their metalinguistic understanding about writing was manifested but as part of this, we set a narrative writing task at the start of the project, and repeated this at the beginning of each academic year. From this data set, we conducted a linguistic analysis on these writing samples from a sub-sample of students who formed a case study group within the project. We used a modified version of the analytical framework we had used in *Patterns and Processes*, but which included an analysis of the noun phrase.

In terms of syntactic complexity in writing, this analysis echoed earlier research, including ours, in showing that the use of co-ordination decreased with age, with an even more significant difference between high-attaining writers and weaker writers. The number of finite verbs used also decreased with age, and particularly in high-attaining writers in secondary. However, in this data set, the use of subordination increased with age and with attainment, including in the secondary phase, which is counter to the findings of earlier research. A qualitative look at the secondary-aged writers indicates greater variety in both sentence length and syntactical structure, greater use of non-finite subordination, and a sense of more deliberate designing and crafting of sentences:

- The feelings all came back. It was her. My only. Beth…My heart had turned to stone after my wife, Beth, died. Taken from cancer, she was (age 13).

- One night I lay awake wondering what punishment I would get for not handing in my homework, when I heard the faint sound of music (age 14).
- Focusing more and more it looks as if my imagination has become a reality. His arms are starting to shake, knees starting to bend and body starting to transform. Lifting his head and bending over me, he whispers … (age 14).

The results relating to use of the noun phrase are unclear by age, but there are strong patterns indicated by attainment. High-attaining writers in both primary and secondary used longer noun phrases, used less pre-modification, and used markedly more post-modification, mirroring the results from the corpus study.

From our own research into linguistic development in secondary-aged writers, and from earlier research, we would conclude that although there are trajectories of development marked by age, it is the difference between high-attaining and lower-attaining writers which seems to be more significant. Older and more high-attaining writers tend to write longer sentences, with more syntactical variety and with greater noun phrase elaboration through post-modification. They also use more simple, short sentences, drawing attention to the rhetorical emphasis of a short sentence, but also to the way textual rhythm can be altered through sentence length variation.

Common to many of these studies is a quantitative approach to the research: they all rely on frequency counts of the presence of predetermined linguistic structures. This approach has not been without its critics. Writing is a socially determined, meaning-making process and effective writing is far more than the mere usage of particular grammatical constructions. Weaver highlighted that syntactic maturity as measured by frequency of usage does not necessarily equate to better writing:

> Relatively mature sentences can be awkward, convoluted, even unintelligible; they can also be inappropriate to the subject, the audience and the writer's or persona's voice. Conversely, relatively simple sentences can make their point succinctly and emphatically. Often, of course, sentence variety is best.
>
> (Weaver 1996, p. 130)

Indeed, Applebee argued that the pursuit of syntactical developmental patterns marking progression in writing competence is somewhat pointless as what is more important is 'the student's ability to manage an increasing degree of structural complexity – that is, to include more structures effectively within a single sentence' (2000, p. 97). In other words, linguistic development may be partially evidenced through analyses of usage, but it is crucial also to consider the effectiveness of that usage, and how writers are increasingly able to make choices which match audience, purpose, and authorial intention. The qualitative element of our own studies has particularly highlighted the importance of looking beyond the mere *presence* of a linguistic feature to *how it is used* in the writing.

Linked to this is that our studies adopt a form-focused orientation towards the written text. Adopting a Hallidayan functional perspective towards linguistic development (Halliday 1975) permits the integration of form and meaning, and recognises that linguistic choices are rhetorical, meaning-making choices. Such a perspective also recognises that writing is not simply a question of linguistic mastery but that it is a social act, where language is 'a meaning-making system through which we interactively shape and interpret our world and ourselves' (Derewianka and Jones 2010, p. 9). The pedagogical implications of this are that linguistic development might be more effectively enabled if we connect linguistic choice and rhetorical purpose. In the classroom, we can encourage 'writers to recognise and use the grammatical and stylistic choices available to them and to understand the rhetorical effects those choices can have on their readers' (Kolln and Gray 2016, Introduction).

Metalinguistic understanding of writing

This emphasis on *choosing* linguistic structures for meaning-making purposes implies that writers have control, or may need to develop better control, over the linguistic choices they make. In other words, metalinguistic understanding may be a crucial factor in enabling older writers to increase their expertise. Supporting secondary-age writers to become more confident in making linguistic choices to suit their rhetorical intentions is, in essence, a process of making them more metalinguistically aware. Whilst research has signalled the importance of metacognition in writing, that is, thinking about how we write (Berninger and Swanson 1994, Kellogg 1994, Hacker et al. 2009), and particularly self-regulation (Graham and Perin 2007, Graham et al. 2014), the concept of metalinguistic understanding of writing is less well-developed, and particularly so in relation to secondary-aged writers. A review of the research on metalinguistic understanding reveals, first, that it is addressed much more commonly in the context of second language learning, and second, that it tends to be both more form-focused, and concerned with grammatical accuracy and the avoidance of error (see, for example, Aydin 2018, Sun et al. 2018).

There are some ambiguities in the research literature regarding the definition of metalinguistic understanding, from a rather technicist view of it as 'the ability to correct a grammatically incorrect structure in English and explain why it is incorrect, and identify and explicitly state the grammatical role of parts of speech in L2 sentences' (Aydin 2018, p. 172) to views of metalinguistic understanding as fundamentally concerned with looking objectively at language (Camps and Milian 1999). Common to many definitions, however, is a sense that metalinguistic understanding is explicit, reflective, and verbalisable – 'explicit knowledge about language that can be brought to conscious awareness, articulated, and used reflexively as a cognitive tool to construct knowledge about language' (Gebhard et al. 2014, p. 107). In other words, this represents a view that metalinguistic understanding relates to reflection on language and its use, and that it is intentional. In the context of teaching writing, therefore, a pedagogical approach which encourages reflection on linguistic choices in writing and verbalisation of the reasons for making those choices is likely to develop metalinguistic understanding which is directly supportive of writing development. This highlights the pedagogical importance of metalinguistic talk, as it makes visible a learner's metalinguistic understanding about writing.

Our own research on metalinguistic understanding of writing draws on two different data sources. The first is data from audio-recorded lesson observations of classroom talk, collected as part of a randomised controlled trial, funded by the Education Endowment Foundation, where we were exploring how teachers manage effective classroom metalinguistic talk about linguistic choices in writing. The second data set is from the *Writing Conversations* study, referred to above, where we audio- and video-recorded writing lessons, and interviewed students through writing conversations about their own writing and the choices they had made.

Our explorations of classroom metalinguistic talk (Myhill et al. 2016, Myhill and Newman 2016) underline the professional skill required to lead high-quality metalinguistic discussion. In professional development sessions with teachers we have emphasised that this kind of talk is dialogic, in that it is not attempting to elicit predetermined right answers, but that it is trying to open up a consideration of the relationship between a linguistic choice and its particular effect in the writing. Wegerif (2013, p. 32) has argued that dialogic talk is 'the space of possibilities that opens up in dialogue', a metaphor we have found useful because the goal of metalinguistic talk is to enable writers to understand the choices they make and to recognise the repertoire of linguistic possibilities that are available to them. Our analysis of classroom metalinguistic talk revealed three patterns of talk:

- Talk which closed down metalinguistic thinking rather than opening it up. Typically, in this kind of talk, teachers were telling students what kind of linguistic structures they should put in their writing, rather than generating discussion about why. The structures referred to frequently reflected curriculum and assessment requirements, such as advising students to use fronted adverbials; or they reflected rather narrow views of what constitutes 'good writing', such as recommending putting in more adjectives.
- Talk which appeared to invite rich metalinguistic discussion but in which an opportunity to develop this was missed. Here teachers often asked a question which invited an open response, and which was not concerned with eliciting a particular answer. But in managing the interaction between teacher and student, the discussion episode did not develop students' responses and did not exploit the opportunity their answers provided for further probing of their metalinguistic thinking.
- Talk which opened up the dialogic space for metalinguistic discussion. In these occurrences, both the initiating question and subsequent teasing out of responses in a sustained sequence of interaction led to metalinguistic talk which was firmly oriented towards metalinguistic thinking about writing.

An important further finding was that these three patterns were less likely to be the particular style of a particular teacher: very often a teacher would exhibit all three patterns, to varying degrees, in one lesson. Of course, these teachers, who were committed and enthusiastic professionals, were learning a new kind of classroom talk and it may be unreasonable to expect complete mastery of this approach so quickly. Certainly, the second talk pattern, relating to missed opportunities, may well have been part of a professional learning curve, which in time would evolve into the more productive patterns of dialogic metalinguistic talk. It is also the case that teachers' subject knowledge may have constrained their capacity to manage this kind of talk. Many of our teachers are not confident with grammatical knowledge (Myhill et al. 2013) because they themselves were not taught grammar at school, and managing difficult student questions about grammar sometimes led to teachers closing down the discussion. More relevant, however, to our intentions of fostering classrooms where metalinguistic talk represents a functionally oriented approach to language, and which generates exploration of the links between linguistic choices and rhetorical effects, requires a particular kind of subject knowledge. For many of our teachers, and sometimes for ourselves too as planners, verbalising this link is not always easy, and represents a new way of thinking about writing.

In the light of this cumulative set of research findings, the next sections consider the practical, pedagogic implications of knowing trajectories of linguistic development, and of creating classrooms where metalinguistic thinking about writing supports that development, and young writers' capacity to make writerly decisions about language choice.

Developmental patterns in writing

One benefit of knowing what typical developmental patterns are in writing is that it facilitates thinking about appropriate teaching interventions to support looking at a learner's written text to identify the writer's needs are. To illustrate this, below are two pieces of narrative writing from our *Patterns and Processes* project archive. Both are written by 13-year-olds, but they are at different points in their individual developmental trajectories.

Box 11.1 The boat incident

It was about 6'clock and I was waiting to get off at Calais in France from the ferry. I was waiting in our Mazda with my family. I couldn't wait to get to the campsite and begin our vacation. The sun was bright and the whole family just wanted to get off the boat.

I had the door open as it was so hot, when a man with a trailer on his car latched on to my door. There was a loud crash and as I stared in shock as it bent all the way backwards. This was not good. The man

> stopped and got out of his car. He also stared in shock. My mum did not. She was not pleased.
>
> They ranted and raved for a long time and were not getting anywhere. We were the last ones on the boat. Why couldn't we just go? The man's wife was now upset as she knew who was in the wrong. The man finally gave in (to my great relief) and gave my mum and dad some details and we were off. The door did not work properly but it did close. In the end it was only a minor holdback to an overall great holiday.
>
> (13-year-old average-attaining boy)

This is the full piece of writing from this boy. A narrative structure is evident in a rather simple way: there is an opening, a problem, a resolution, and an ending or coda. There is some sense of the narrator's reflection on events (e.g. 'I couldn't wait'; 'to my great relief'), but overall, the narrative structure is very basic, there is limited development and detail, and it is largely plot-driven. A closer look at the language choices indicates a preponderance of co-ordinated clauses, with only three examples of subordination, which contributes to the sense of a plot-dominated sequence. There is relatively little variation in sentence length or structure, with heavy use of subject starts (e.g. 'I'; 'It'; 'The door'), creating a somewhat monotonous textual rhythm – although the short sentence, 'My mum did not', and the rhetorical question do successfully alter the rhythm and emphasise those two sentences. The noun phrases are unelaborated (e.g. 'the man'; 'his car'), offering no visual, emotional or inferential detail to support the reader in engaging with the narrative.

So what might a teacher usefully consider addressing next to support this writer's progression? The developmental patterns identified in our study would suggest that looking at how to manage plot development might be appropriate, focusing on:

- building on the writer's emerging sense of textual rhythm through more strategic variation of sentence length and syntactic shaping;
- exploring different ways to connect ideas and plot events, rather than relying on co-ordinated clauses, perhaps considering how subordinated clauses can slow down the pace of narrative portrayal through giving additional explanatory information or authorial reflection, and provide additional information about context or character reactions;
- elaborating noun phrases to provide more specific concrete detail which will help the reader to visualise the scene, or engage with the sensory aspects of the plot.

The second example is only the first section of a narrative of 1,848 words, and comprises the opening and the narrative problem. The remaining narrative, not reproduced here because of space issues, develops the story of a Gemma's transportation to a new world, with a clear, if somewhat abrupt, resolution.

Box 11.2 The opening of Gemma's narrative

It was a lovely, summer's day in April. The people at 17 Massey's Crescent had just woken. The street was quite a dull street. It had weeds growing through the gaps in the pavement and thorn bushes growing up the side of people's garden walls. The houses towered over you, staring at everyone who walked passed. Especially number 17, the tallest house in the street. At number 17 lives a person I'm sure we all know someone like, and she's called Gemma. She's a quiet, little girl say some people. But has a cunning, mischievous secret side that only a few people have seen. She has the most evil, little eyes I've ever seen. She stares down at you, her devious smile sending a shiver up your spine.

Gemma has a long mass of black hair that shines in the sun. She's always in with the latest fashions. Her horrid, nasty side has not yet been seen by the people she's very popular with. Gemma was at home, after school, watching the television whilst getting ready for bed. She had already had a bath, brushed her teeth and was in the middle of putting her hair up in a bun after drying it. Now she was ready for bed. She turned her television and light off, got into bed and started to go to sleep. What was going to happen next was unthinkable ...

Gemma was suddenly woken by a loud banging noise below her. It was getting louder and louder. She slowly sat up in her bed, cautiously watching everything around her. The light from the moon was streaming in through her window, lighting up the scared expression on her face. The banging got louder. Gemma cautiously slipped on her slippers, quietly opened her bedroom door and bravely crept down the stairs. She opened the door leading into the front room, where the banging was loudest. In front of her was a sensational, gleaming whirlpool that looked as though it was made of glass. It lit up the whole room including the astounding look on her face. She slowly walked towards it, as if it was pulling her in and she couldn't pull away. Then unexpectedly Gemma was being sucked in, and in less than a minute she was gone.

(13-year-old high-attaining girl)

A closer look at this opening section reveals a much slower introduction to the story than in the previous example. Before the plot begins, there is more careful scene-setting and the introduction of the character, Gemma. Similarly the narrative problem builds cumulatively over a paragraph rather than in one sentence. There is some textual rhythm create by more varied clause structures, particularly non-finite clauses ('lighting up the scared expression on her face'), sequenced co-ordinated clauses ('Gemma cautiously slipped on her slippers, quietly opened her bedroom door and bravely crept down the stairs.'), and the freestanding verbless sentence ('Especially number 17, the tallest house in the street'). There is limited syntactic variation with a majority of subject starts for sentences although the fronted adverbial and subject-verb inversion in 'In front of her was a sensational, gleaming whirlpool that looked as though it was made of glass' disrupts this pattern at a key moment in the plot, creating an appropriate delay before the whirlpool is revealed. Perhaps most significantly, this writer has many elaborated noun phrases, providing visual detail about character ('a long mass of black hair that shines in the sun') and setting ('weeds growing through the gaps in the pavement').

To support developmental progression for this writer, it might be helpful to focus on:

- building on the writer's apparent confidence with noun phrase elaboration by choosing specific details which 'show not tell' in relation to character, making the reader infer, rather than telling the reader directly, for example, that Gemma has 'a horrid nasty side';
- exploring syntactic variation in sentences more, and how this can alter both the rhythm of the text and how information is foregrounded or delayed within a sentence;
- considering whether there are alternatives to the use of adverbs, such as the choice of verbs which convey more descriptive detail or adverbial prepositional phrases; or indeed whether all of the adverbs are necessary (e.g. 'unexpectedly').

Supporting metalinguistic thinking and writerly decision-making

Knowing the linguistic developmental needs of writers is an important element in planning purposeful teaching about language. It allows for teaching to more appropriately match learners' needs and to strengthen their understanding of the linguistic demands of writing different genres. Our own research has demonstrated how the explicit teaching of grammar adopting a functional approach has helped students to become better writers (Myhill et al. 2013). This has led to the development of a theoretically informed pedagogical approach, using what we have called the LEAD principles, an acronym referring to making a Link between grammar and writing, Explaining the grammar through examples, using Authentic texts, and building in high-quality Discussion about grammar and choice (for further detail see Chapter 9). This approach is appropriate across the age ranges and for all text types, but in the interests of illustrating this coherently, the examples below will focus on characterisation and setting in narrative writing in the context of secondary-aged classrooms. We know, for example, that a weakness in some secondary students' narrative writing (Myhill et al. 2018) is an over-emphasis on plot, resulting in plot-driven narratives with much weaker characterisation, and establishment of setting. At the same time, more able writers often do not develop character and setting in depth. The two examples of writing discussed earlier exemplify these patterns well. Thus a learning focus on character and setting could be a useful strategy for improving narrative writing in this older age group.

The three activities below draw on authentic texts as models to stimulate reflection and discussion on the linguistic choices made by these professional writers and to consider three aspects of setting and characterisation. They would be integrated into a unit of work on narrative, and young writers would be given opportunities to draft their own descriptions of characters and settings before beginning to write the full narrative. Indeed, a well-developed character or an evocative setting can be a more productive way into developing a narrative, rather than the more conventional way in via plot.

Establishing a setting

This activity draws on the opening paragraph of Steinbeck's *Of Mice and Men*, where he establishes the setting for the story, creating a strong visual and geographical impression of the scene.

Box 11.3 Establishing a setting

A few miles south of Soledad, the Salinas River drops in close to the hillside bank and runs deep and green. The water is warm too, for it has slipped twinkling over the yellow sands in the sunlight before reaching the narrow pool. On one side of the river the golden foothill slopes curve up to the strong and rocky Gabilan Mountains, but on the valley side the water is lined with trees – willows fresh and green with every spring, carrying in their lower leaf junctures the debris of the winter's flooding; and sycamores with mottled, white, recumbent limbs and branches that arch over the pool.

(*Of Mice and Men* – John Steinbeck)

A teaching sequence [with the LEAD principles in square brackets] looking at this description might:

- invite students to think about where their own story might be set;
- ask students to look at a version of the Steinbeck text [Authentic text] with all the prepositional phrases removed and to discuss what this tells them about the setting, or sketch a rough map. Then look at the original version and talk about [Discussion] how the prepositional phrases are strongly locational, providing topographical detail [Link between grammar and writing];
- invite students to consider the visual details provided by the noun phrases inside these prepositional phrases (e.g. 'the yellow sands'; 'the hillside bank' [Examples]) and look especially at the detail in the two long appositional phrases describing the willows and the sycamores [Link between grammar and writing];

- talk about [Discussion] the Proper Nouns and how they make this a specific place, not a generic setting, and how the names may help us begin to infer where it is set if we do not know where the Salinas River is [Link between grammar and writing];
- invite students to write just one paragraph describing the setting for their own narrative, evoking a strong sense of place.

Creating character using specific, concrete detail

One skill in characterisation is to make your characters believable as individuals – not *any* woman, but *this particular* woman. One way to achieve this is to pay attention to the specific, concrete details you use to describe them and to evoke a visual image of them. In this activity, a comparison is drawn between our first impressions as a reader of Fagin and Mr Brownlow in Dickens' *Oliver Twist*.

Box 11.4 Establishing character

[Fagin] … standing over them, with a toasting-fork in his hand, was a very old shrivelled Jew, whose villainous-looking and repulsive face was obscured by a quantity of matted red hair. He was dressed in a greasy flannel gown, with his throat bare; and seemed to be dividing his attention between the frying-pan and the clothes horse, over which a great number of silk handkerchiefs were hanging.

[Mr Brownlow] The old gentleman was a very respectable-looking personage, with a powdered head and gold spectacles. He was dressed in a bottle-green coat with a black velvet collar; wore white trousers; and carried a bamboo cane under his arm. He had taken up a book from the stall, and there he stood reading away, as hard as if he were in his elbow-chair, in his own study.

(*Oliver Twist* – Charles Dickens)

A teaching sequence addressing this might:

- invite students to visualise a key character in their narrative, thinking closely about physical appearance, stance, what they are wearing, where they are, etc. Ask them to write a list of images as noun phrases which capture this visualisation;
- read Dickens' description of Fagin and Mr Brownlow [Authentic text] and discuss first impressions of these two characters (you might want to address here how Dickens' description of Fagin might be viewed as anti-Semitic today and thus unacceptable);
- ask students in pairs [Discussion] to extract a list of images of the two characters from the text, then discuss how many of these are noun phrases with very

concrete details which make the two characters very different and specific (e.g. 'a greasy flannel gown'; 'a black velvet collar' – [Examples]) [Link between grammar and writing];

- ask students in pairs (Discussion) to change the noun phrases in the description of Mr Brownlow to make him a more unpleasant character, using concrete detail to do this [Link between grammar and writing];
- invite students to revisit the list of images written earlier about their own character – can they now add to or amend these so there is concrete detail which contributes to the characterisation [Link between grammar and writing];
- in pairs, explain one of the changes made to the noun phrase images, and why it is better at evoking the character you want to convey [Link between grammar and writing].

Showing characters' inner reflections

Another strand of characterisation which is not always confidently developed is revealing how characters are thinking and seeing things through their eyes. Providing moments of inner reflection in a narrative is one way to slow down the plot and avoid action-driven narratives. In this example from Morpurgo's *Private Peaceful*, we are shown as readers how Tommo, the main character, feels about his first day at school.

Box 11.5 Showing a character's inner reflection

Charlie is taking me by the hand, leading me because he knows I don't want to go. I've never worn a collar before and it's choking me. My boots are strange and heavy on my feet. My heart is heavy too, because I dread what I am going to. Charlie has told me often how terrible this school-place is: about Mr Munnings and his raging tempers and the long whipping cane he hangs on the wall above his desk. I don't want to go with Charlie. I don't want to go to school.

(*Private Peaceful* – Michael Morpurgo)

A teaching sequence to explore this might:

- ask students to discuss in groups [Discussion] how we know that Tommo [Authentic text] does not want to go to school, and what language choices are helping us to understand Tommo's feelings [Link between grammar and writing];
- as a class, look at the use of the first person voice, with first person pronouns and determiners which emphasise the 'I' of this piece, and directly show his thinking;

- then look at the use of negatives ('not'; 'never'), negative verbs ('choking'; 'dread') and negative adjectives ('strange'; 'heavy'; 'terrible'; 'raging') – [Examples]: how they convey his sense of fear and reluctance, and how this is reinforced by repetition [Link between grammar and writing];
- invite students to underline in their own narratives any points where they reveal characters' inner thoughts or reflections. If there is none, or very little, they might like to consider whether this would be a worthwhile revision.

Each of these activities looks explicitly at linguistic choices made in authentic texts, promotes metalinguistic discussion about those choices, and gives students an opportunity to try out these structures in their own writing. As noted earlier, the emphasis is on grammatical choice for meaning-making and rhetorical effect.

Concluding reflections

This chapter has outlined what research has shown us about linguistic development in writing in secondary school writers and has considered the role of metalinguistic thinking and talk in supporting progression in writing. The chapter has also illustrated some pedagogical strategies for fostering metalinguistic talk, drawing on a fully theorised set of pedagogical principles. To support students in 'becoming writerly', and in having more control of their own writing decisions, teachers need to enable writers to develop this metalinguistic understanding as a key tool for thinking and reflecting upon shaping and crafting meaning in a written text. And because writing is learned, not acquired, unlike talk, explicit teaching which opens up older writers' awareness of the repertoire of linguistic choices available is particularly important.

At the same time, our own research has highlighted not only the benefits of metalinguistic talk in generating metalinguistic understanding, but also the challenges. Managing metalinguistic discussion about linguistic choices requires both confidence in grammatical knowledge and how grammatical choices shape meaning in texts, and skill in orchestrating high-quality talk about those choices. Practical activities, such as composition (usually of a short element of a text), comparing two versions of a text, discussing or writing about gaps in a text, and explaining linguistic choices to peers are part of a repertoire of strategies which facilitate metalinguistic talk because they make the writing process and decision-making visible. Equally, the teacher's direct role in creating space for metalinguistic discussion can be achieved when teacher questioning extends students' reflection on writing, going beyond initial first-level responses to probe for great explanation, elaboration and verbalisation. The goal of metalinguistic talk is first and foremost to foster rich metalinguistic understanding about the power of linguistic choice:

> We need to understand the possible power effects of our choices. We need to understand how our ideational choices construct participants, processes,

and circumstances from a particular perspective; we need to attend to our choices of mood and modality, which encode relations of authority and agency between writers and readers; we need to think about how textual choices work to foreground and background ideas, to construct cause and effect, to position information as old or new.

(Janks 2009, p. 130)

Finally, as the chapter has focused on linguistic development and metalinguistic understanding, it has necessarily foregrounded grammar. But of course an effective writing pedagogy is more than just the grammar: it supports students in understanding and self-regulating their management of the writing process; it creates space for playfulness, experimentation, and constructive failure; and it seeks to give students voice within a creative community of writers. The grammar should be naturally integrated within this at relevant points in the learning sequence. If we hope to 'enable pupils to make choices from among a range of linguistic resources, and to be aware of the effects of different choices on the rhetorical power of their writing' (Lefstein 2009, p. 382), then we have to heighten students' sense of agency in the writing classroom. It is impossible to think fruitfully about the power of linguistic choice if the writer has little or no sense of authorial intention, of how he or she wants the reader to think or feel. Linguistic development represents an increasing facility to adapt what is written to accommodate authorial intention, the needs of the reader, and the demands of the form of writing: in other words, to become more 'writerly' as an author, more agentic in decision-making, and more metalinguistically aware of the power of choice.

References

Applebee, A. 2000. Alternative models of writing development. In: Indrisano, R. and Squire, J. R. eds. *Perspectives on writing: research, theory, and practice*. Newark: International Reading Association, 90–110.

Australian Curriculum and Assessment Reporting Authority (ACARA). 2017. *NAPLAN achievement in reading, writing, language conventions and numeracy: national report for 2017*. Available from: www.nap.edu.au/results-and-reports/national-reports. [Accessed 16. 03. 19].

Aydin, F. 2018. L2 metalinguistic knowledge and L2 achievement among intermediate-level adult Turkish EFL learners. *Journal of Language and Linguistic Studies*, 14(1), 28–49.

Berman, R. A. and Verhoeven, L. 2002. Cross-linguistic perspectives on the development of text production abilities: speech and writing. *Written Language and Literacy*, 5 (1), 1–43.

Berninger, V. and Swanson, H. L. 1994. Modifying the Hayes and Flower model of skilled writing to explain beginning and developing writing. In Butterfield, E. C. ed., *Advances in cognition and educational practice* (vol. 2) *Children's writing: toward a process theory of skilled writing*. Greenwich, CT: JAI Press, 57–82.

Camps, A. and Milian, M. eds. 1999. *Metalinguistic activity in learning to write*. Amsterdam: Amsterdam University Press.

Department for Education (DfE). 2017. *National curriculum assessments at key stage 2 in England, 2017* (SFR 69/2017). Available from: www.gov.uk/government/uploads/system/uploads/attachment_data/file/667372/SFR69_2017_text.pdf. [Accessed 21. 03. 18].

Derewianka, B. and Jones, P. 2010. From traditional grammar to functional grammar: bridging the divide. Special issue of *NALDIC Quarterly*, 6–15.

Durrant, P. and Brenchley, M. 2019. Development of vocabulary sophistication across genres in English children's writing. *Reading and Writing*, 32, 1927–1953.

Gebhard, M., et al. 2014. 'Miss, nominalization is a nominalization': English language learners' use of SFL metalanguage and their literacy practices. *Linguistics in Education*, 26, 106–125.

Graham, S. and Perin, D. 2007. A meta-analysis of writing instruction for adolescent students. *Journal of Educational Psychology*, 99, 445–476.

Graham, S., Wilcox, K. and Early, J. 2014. Adolescent writing and writing instruction: introduction to the special issue. *Reading and Writing*, 27(2), 969–997.

Hacker, D. J., Keener, M. C. and Kircher, J. C. 2009. Writing is applied metacognition. In: Hacker, D. J., Dunlosky, J. and Graesser, A. C. eds. *Handbook of metacognition in education*. New York: Routledge, 154–172.

Halliday, M. A. K. 1975. *Learning how to mean: explorations in the development of language*. London: Edward Arnold.

Hunt, K. W. 1965. *Grammatical structures written at three grade levels*. Champaign: NCTE.

Janks, H. 2009. Writing: a critical literacy perspective. In: Beard, R., et al. eds. *The Sage handbook of writing development*. London: SAGE, 126–136.

Kellogg, R. T. 1994. *The psychology of writing*. Oxford: Oxford University Press.

Kolln, M. and Gray, L. 2016. *Rhetorical grammar: grammatical choices, rhetorical effects*. New York: Pearson.

Lefstein, A. 2009. Rhetorical grammar and the grammar of schooling: teaching powerful verbs in the English national literacy strategy. *Linguistics and Education*, 20(4), 378–400.

Loban, W. 1976. *Language development: kindergarten through grade twelve* (Research Report 18). Urbana: National Council of Teachers of English.

Massey, A. J., Elliott, G. L. and Johnson, N. K. 2005. Variations in aspects of writing in 16+ English examinations between 1980 and 2004: vocabulary, spelling, punctuation, sentence structure, non-standard English. *Research Matters: Special Issue 1*, Cambridge: University of Cambridge Local Examinations Syndicate.

Ministry of Education (MoE). 2017. New Zealand education profile 2015–2016. Available from: www.educationcounts.govt.nz/__data/assets/pdf_file/0010/181981/NZ-Education-Profile-2016.pdf [Accessed 13. 06. 18].

Myhill, D. A. 2008. Towards a linguistic model of sentence development in writing. *Language and Education*, 22(5), 271–288.

Myhill, D. A. 2009. Becoming a designer: trajectories of linguistic development. In: Beard, R., et al. eds. *The Sage handbook of writing development*. London: SAGE, 402–414.

Myhill, D. A. and Newman, R. 2016. Metatalk: enabling metalinguistic discussion about writing. *International Journal of Education Research*, 80, 177–187.

Myhill, D. A., Jones, S. and Lines, H. 2018. Supporting less-proficient writers through linguistically-aware teaching. *Language and Education*, 32(4), 333–349.

Myhill, D. A., Jones, S. and Watson, A. 2013. Grammar matters: how teachers' grammatical subject knowledge impacts on the teaching of writing. *Teaching and Teacher Education*, 36, 77–91.

Myhill, D. A., Jones, S. M. and Wilson, A. C. 2016. Writing conversations: fostering metalinguistic discussion about writing. *Research Papers in Education*, 31(1), 23–44.

Myhill, D. A., et al. 2012. Re-thinking grammar: the impact of embedded grammar teaching on students' writing and students' metalinguistic understanding. *Research Papers in Education*, 27(2), 139–166.

Perera, K. 1984. *Children's writing and reading: analysing classroom language*. Oxford: Blackwell.

Qualifications and Curriculum Authority (QCA). 1999. *Improving writing at key stages 3 and 4*. London: QCA.

Ragnarsdóttir, H., et al. 2002. Verbal structure and content in written discourse: expository and narrative texts. *Written Language and Literacy*, 5(1), 95–126.

Ravid, D., et al. 2002. Subject NP patterning in the development of text production: speech and writing. *Written Language and Literacy*, 5(1), 69–93.

Stromqvist, S., et al. 2002. Toward a cross-linguistic comparison of lexical quanta in speech and writing. *Written Language and Literacy*, 5(1), 45–68.

Sun, B., Hu, H. and Curdt-Christiansen, X. 2018. Metalinguistic contribution to writing competence: a study of monolingual children in China and bilingual children in Singapore. *Reading and Writing*, 31(7), 1499–1523.

Verhoeven, L., et al. 2002. Clause packaging in writing and speech: a crosslinguistic developmental analysis. *Written Language and Literacy*, 5(2), 135–161.

Weaver, C. 1996. *Teaching grammar in context*. Portsmouth, NH: Boynton Cook.

Wegerif, R. B. 2013. *Dialogic: education for the internet age*. London and New York: Routledge.

12 Growing into the complexity of mature academic writing

Beverly Derewianka

Introduction

It is often said that in the early primary years students are *learning to read and write* and in following years, they are *reading and writing to learn*. This implies that, having mastered 'the basics', students simply need to apply those skills as they progress through school. This chapter would argue that, as tasks become more challenging in the move into adolescence, students still need supported expansion of their language and literacy resources if they are to meet the expectations of secondary schooling.

The increasing complexity relating to students' writing as a tool for deep learning is well-documented (among others, Perera 1985, Christie and Derewianka 2008, O'Dowd 2010, Myhill this volume). Secondary students are writing more extended texts for a wider range of social purposes across a number of discipline areas. They are dealing with the language of abstraction, formulating general principles, and forging sophisticated logical relationships between ideas. They need the linguistic resources for tasks involving clarifying problems and designing solutions, responding to issues, devising hypotheses, analysing and interpreting data, integrating and manipulating information, explaining how systems work, identifying causes and effects, reasoning with evidence, critically evaluating and forming judgements, considering alternative perspectives, and critiquing against criteria. This results in texts that are conceptually rich, information-dense, and compact, yet composed with clarity, precision, coherence, and sensitivity to the reader's needs.

This is a major leap from most students' experience of writing in the primary school. In response to concerns over students' writing in the transition to secondary, a number of schools in Australia have implemented inquiry projects into students' writing in the middle years (Years 5–9), with funding support from their local or state system. The author has participated as academic partner in a number of such initiatives as part of the Transforming Literacies Project (TransLit) – a long-term study of key transition points in students' literacy development as they move through the years of schooling (Jones et al. forthcoming). These projects typically involve a cluster of schools bringing together the lower secondary years and the upper years of their primary feeder schools over a period of two to three years. During that time, the teachers attend workshops, implement new practices between workshops, keep a journal reflecting on their developing insights, collect data such as student texts, and meet as Professional Learning Teams to analyse the data and develop resources. Teachers and students are interviewed and surveyed at intervals as part of the formative evaluation.

Here we will present a case study of how an upper-primary teacher from a remote rural school in Tasmania, Mandy King, prepared her students for the challenges of writing as they transitioned into secondary education.

A problematic transition

The transition from primary to secondary education has long been a fraught issue in terms of students' writing. For the past decade or so, the literacy space in primary schooling has been dominated by reading – and particularly the teaching of decoding skills in the early years. Observations from the Transforming Literacy project indicate that primary students in Australia do not do much extended writing – and if they do, it tends to be in the form of personal expression or recording information.

In the same period in Australia, the National Literacy and Numeracy Assessment Program (NAPLAN) has had an impact on the quality of students' writing. Because it is high stakes, schools feel compelled to teach to the test (Queensland NAPLAN Review 2018). For several weeks before the test, students are primarily taught to write persuasive and narrative texts – the two genres assessed by the program. Furthermore, these are taught at a relatively low level, providing students with strategies for producing texts on demand, within a time limit, on bland topics, and with no opportunity to undertake research or to engage in authentic composing processes.

With the move into secondary school, students are confronted by the reality of writing in a range of genres across a number of curriculum domains. Secondary teachers often make the assumption that, because students have been taught to write in primary school, they can just get on with teaching 'content'. Generally untrained in literacy pedagogy, they tend to focus on the word level – the teaching of specialist vocabulary.

It is no surprise, then, that NAPLAN results for 2017 revealed a dramatic increase in the percentage of students performing below the benchmark in Years 7 and 9 compared to this cohort in Year 3 and a corresponding drop in the percentage of high achievers in Years 7 and 9 compared to the same cohort in Year 3, as illustrated in Figure 12.1 (Adoniou 2017).

Goss and Sonnemann (2018) similarly report an observable and worrying trend, with writing achievement results declining substantially between 2011 and 2018. It is evident that significant measures need to be taken to improve students' writing capacity in secondary school. But it is also incumbent on teachers in the upper years of primary schooling to ensure a smoother transition into the demands of secondary writing.

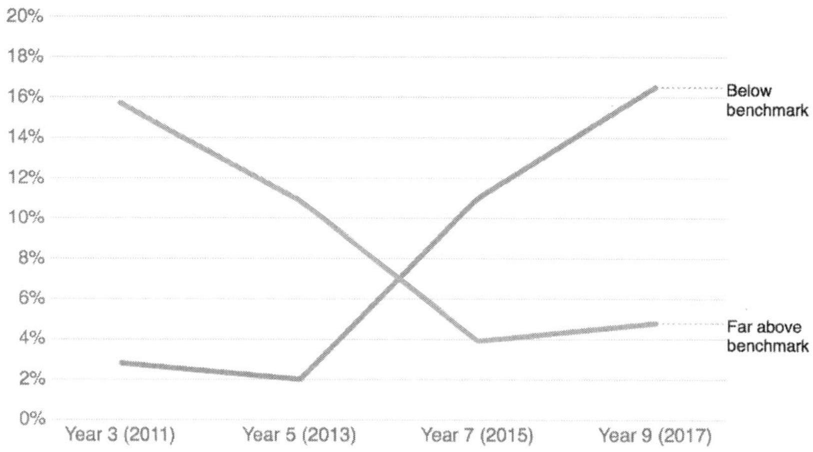

Figure 12.1 NAPLAN writing results of student cohort over time

Preparing for the transition to secondary writing

As part of the TransLit study, Mandy had attended a number of workshops presented by the author. The focus of the school's middle years project was to embed students' writing in authentic curriculum tasks (Myhill et al. 2012), following a teaching and learning cycle (Rothery 1994). The cycle is based on a Vygotskian approach that views learning as a social process where students engage in collaborative interaction with high levels of scaffolding and explicit teaching in the context of shared experience (see Figure 12.2).

The cycle moves in and out of a number of stages where the activities are carefully selected to build up students' knowledge and abilities so that they can experience success (Gibbons 2015). Throughout the cycle, students' understanding of the topic (or 'field') is gradually developed through a range of activities, including the supported reading of selected texts (Lines, this volume). At certain points, students are introduced to relevant features of the genre – its purpose, organisation, and typical language features. Their writing is scaffolded by such practices as the class deconstructing a model text or the teacher jointly constructing with the class a text similar to the one they are working on. At the heart of the cycle are multiple opportunities for formative assessment, with students receiving feedback on their progress and the teacher responding to observed needs.

Mandy chose a history topic – the discovery of gold in Australia – and identified a relevant genre: a consequential explanation, dealing with the multiple effects of the Gold Rush on Australian society. This in itself was a challenging task involving sophisticated explanation and argumentation – quite an ambitious undertaking for her composite class of 9–12-year-old students. To make the inquiry more manageable, Mandy broke it up into a number of 'mini-tasks' over several weeks, which together contributed to the culminating task.

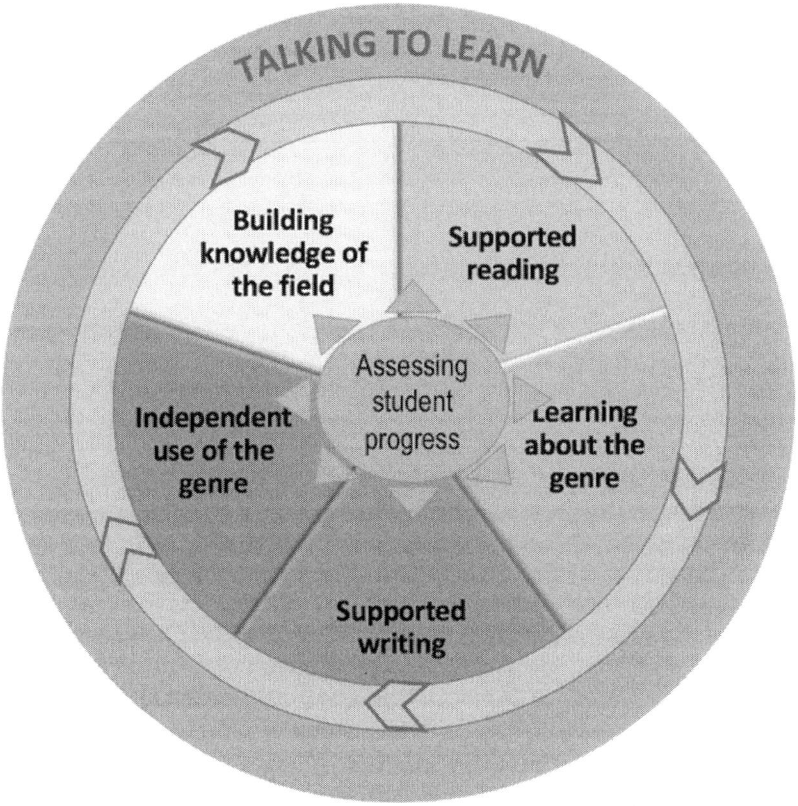

Figure 12.2 Teaching and learning cycle (after Rothery 1994)

Initial field building

Mandy began by building knowledge of the field: engaging students, arousing their curiosity, finding out what they knew of the topic under focus (the Gold Rush), and beginning to build shared understandings (see Figure 12.3). This field building continued throughout the other stages of the teaching learning cycle so that students' understanding of the field accumulated and became increasingly refined over the ten-week unit.

This initial stage included such activities as class discussions, examining images from the period, identifying relevant online materials, constructing a time-line, and watching videos. Importantly, the activities were interactive so that students had opportunities to hear and use the language associated with the topic.

A particular emphasis of the middle-years project was viewing writing as a cumulative process. At each point in the cycle when students learned something

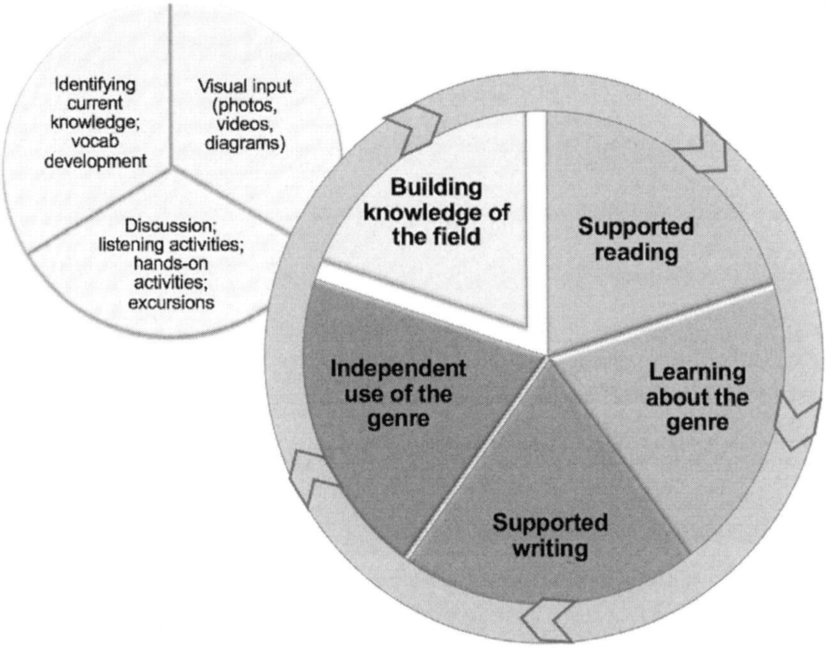

216 Beverly Derewianka

Figure 12.3 Initial building of knowledge of the field

new about the topic or the genre or a language feature, they incorporated these insights into their evolving draft, as illustrated in Figure 12.4.

Following the initial field-building stage, Mandy asked the class to write their first rough draft. This became the raw material that they would continue to revise and craft as they worked through the unit.

The following is typical of an early draft, written by an upper primary student, Xander:

> ### Box 12.1 First Draft
>
> *Was the discovery of gold a significant event for Australia's development or ~~wasn't it~~ it might not be. I think it ~~was~~ is important and here is why.*
>
> *Firstly ... gold and other stones are important in our day's. So if gold wasn't here we couldn't have coins and other cent ~~peciespiceses~~ pieces for buying stuff.*
>
> *On the other hand, years ago there was a very big fight about gold, and that was an impacted about the discovering.*
>
> *So in conclusion the ~~discovering~~ finding of gold had a big impact on our country.*

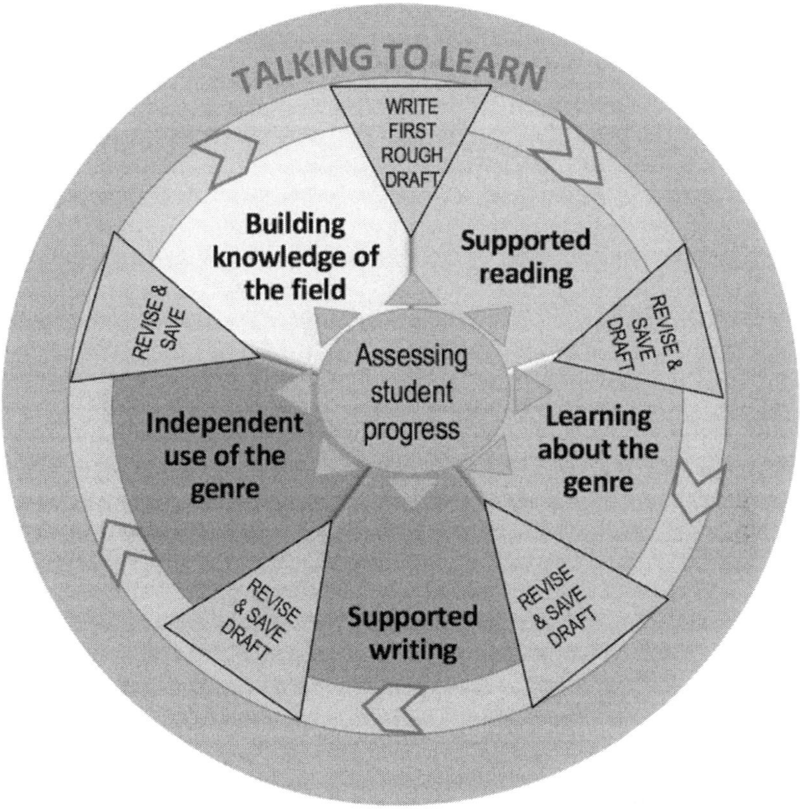

Figure 12.4 Ongoing incorporation of new learning into evolving draft

This rough draft (and subsequent drafts) provided the teacher with insights into student strengths and weaknesses and potential teaching points. By starting the writing process early and revisiting the evolving text often, with input and guidance, the writing task was not as daunting as when the writing is all left to the end.

Supported reading

During the supported reading stage, Mandy continued to build students' knowledge of the field, but now with an emphasis on reading carefully selected texts or text extracts in the topic area. This stage recognises that even older students need to be taught how to read texts on unfamiliar topics that are becoming more challenging, dense, and abstract.

The teacher would typically start by orienting the students to the genre and the content of the text before guiding the class to skim the text to get an idea of how it unfolds by looking at such features as contents pages, headings, sub-headings, images, and so on. The teacher would then focus on key paragraphs, helping the students to gain meaning from the text, particularly in relation to the task at hand. The teacher would support the students in vocabulary development, scanning for specific information, employing comprehension strategies, practising research skills, taking notes using graphic organisers, annotating the text with questions and comments, and answering text-dependent questions (Figure 12.5).

The following graphic organiser (Figure 12.6), representing a consequential explanation, was used by the students to make structured notes from the texts they were reading. Mandy then projected the graphic organiser on the board and guided the students to jointly construct a class version from the student's notes.

Students then drew on these synthesised notes to revise their early draft by extending their representation of the topic.

Learning about the genre

Now that students had started to generate ideas for their writing, the emphasis turned to the composition and crafting of the students' written texts (Figure 12.7). Mandy began by reinforcing the purpose for writing – to explain the consequences of the discovery of gold – followed by examining the stages that such a text typically goes through in achieving its purpose.

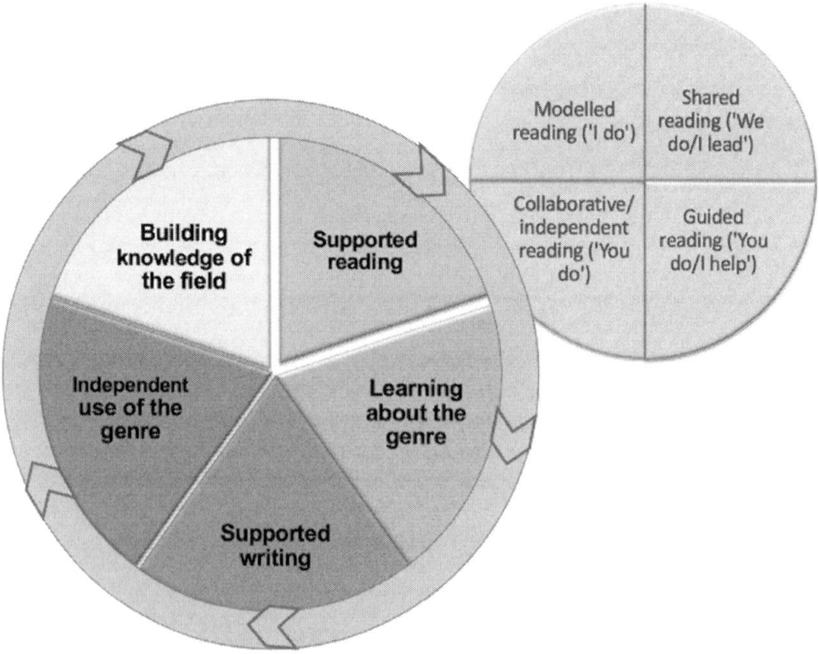

Figure 12.5 Supporting students to read relevant texts

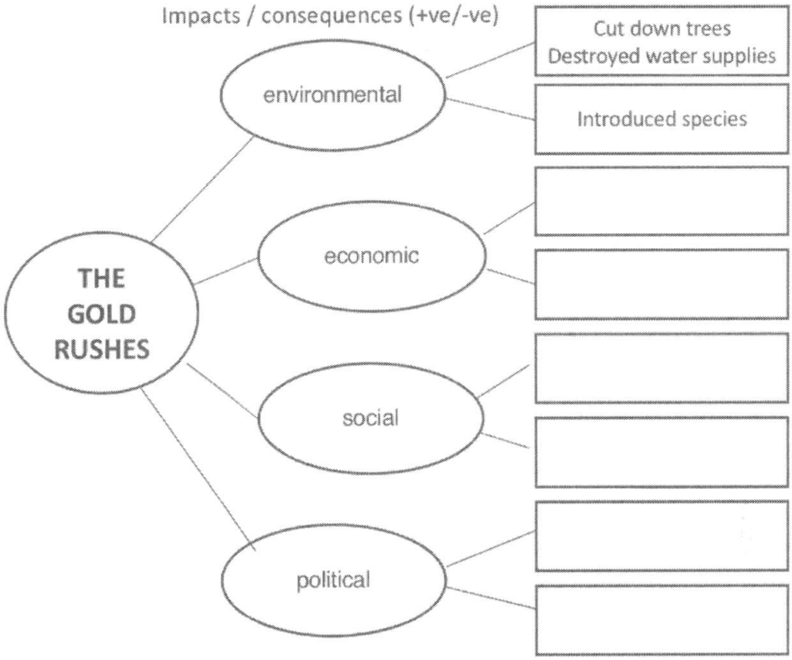

Figure 12.6 Graphic organiser for consequential explanation

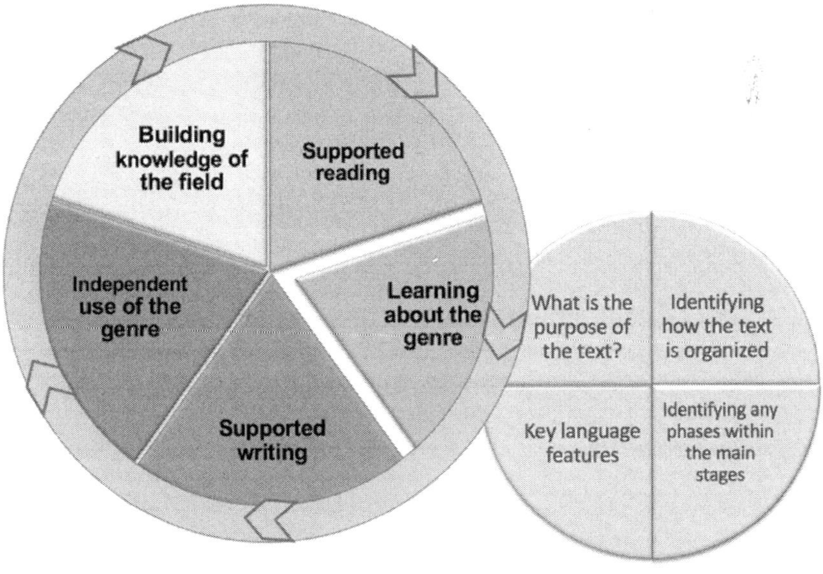

Figure 12.7 Teaching the organisation and language features of the genre

Students were now asked to revise their evolving draft, focusing on organising their text into coherent stages, as in one of Xander's later drafts:

> **Box 12.2 Later draft**
>
> *The 19th century brought many important discoveries. But a very ~~import~~ significant discovery in Australian history was the discovery of gold. The revolutionary discovery led to huge changes in the development of the colonies and here is the reasons why:*
>
> *Firstly it had a economical impact. The high mining fees added a lot of money into the economy and due to the increased rate of immigrating settlers more businesses were started.*
>
> *Secondly it had a social impact. From China to America, lots of people travelled to Australia in search of luck and fortune. Many reached their dreams of fortune and money, but others were not as fortunate.*
>
> *Lastly it had a political impact, since the Eureka Stockate ended with not just reduced mining fees but also the founding of democracy.*
>
> *In conclusion the discovery of gold had social, political and economical impacts due to the immagration of people to Australia and the founding of democracy.*

The focus now changed to selected language features that are characteristic of the genre, and/or the topic/task, and/or observed student needs. Such features might include cohesive devices, multimodal elements, attention to reader needs and interests, expression of attitudes, resources for rich description, the language of cause and effect, and effective sentence structure. Mandy had decided to focus on the overall flow of the text, including topic sentences and paragraph development.

At this point, the class were again guided to revise their evolving draft, highlighting changes they made in relation to the target language feature/s that had been explicitly taught. This allowed for efficient conferencing with the teacher and/or peers, enabling the student to explain why certain choices had been made and their effect.

Supported writing

Class members now participated in jointly composing a text similar to the one they were writing (Figure 12.8). The students came to the activity with knowledge of the subject matter from previous and ongoing field-building activities.

Mandy guided the shared writing of the text, eliciting contributions from the students, writing them on the board, and demonstrating how to shape them into a coherent, interesting written text, drawing on what the class had learnt about the topic, the stages of the target genre, and selected language features. In the process, she extended their suggestions by asking 'how?', 'why?', 'which one?' and explained why a certain choice might be preferable over another. She modelled how to change their

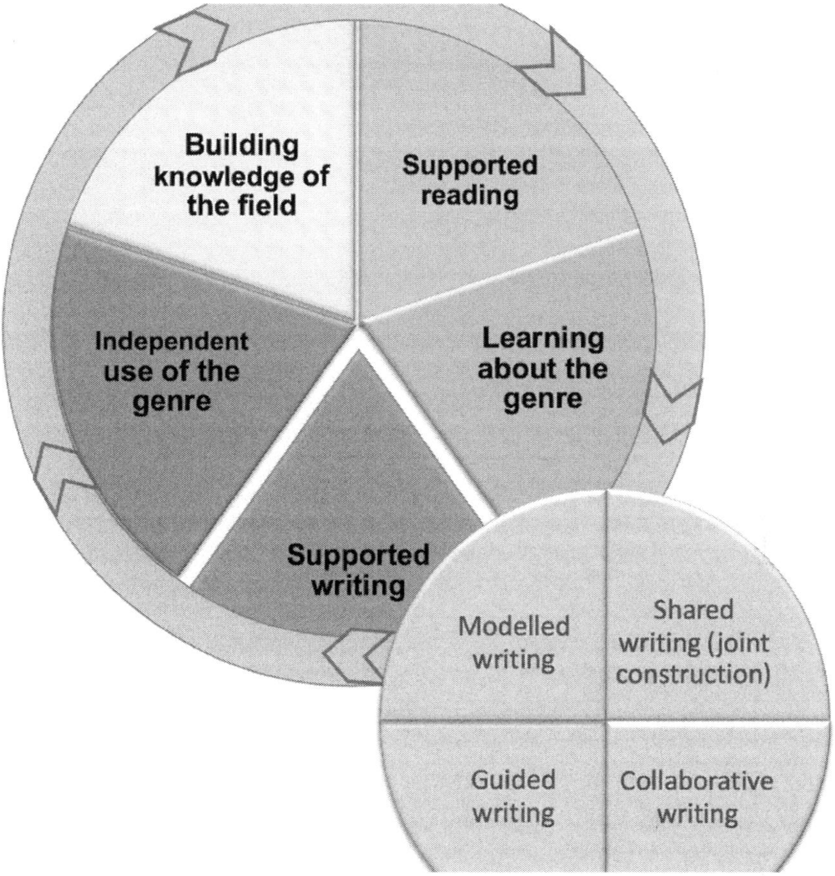

Figure 12.8 Supporting students' writing

spontaneous oral offerings (e.g. 'a lot of people moved to Bathurst'; 'cut down trees') into more 'written', academic language ('mass exodus'; 'forest depletion'). And she prompted them to consider the needs of the reader and the crafting of the language ('Have we made that connection clear?'; 'Could we provide an example?'; 'Is this a good topic sentence?'; 'Could we say that in fewer words?'; 'Could we turn that into a complex sentence?').

The students were thus given an opportunity to experience what is involved in composing such a text and again drew on this to further revise their draft.

Independent writing

At this point, students were in a position to take full control of their own texts (Figure 12.9). They had developed a deep knowledge of the field, they had shaped their text into stages that achieved the purpose, and they had incorporated key

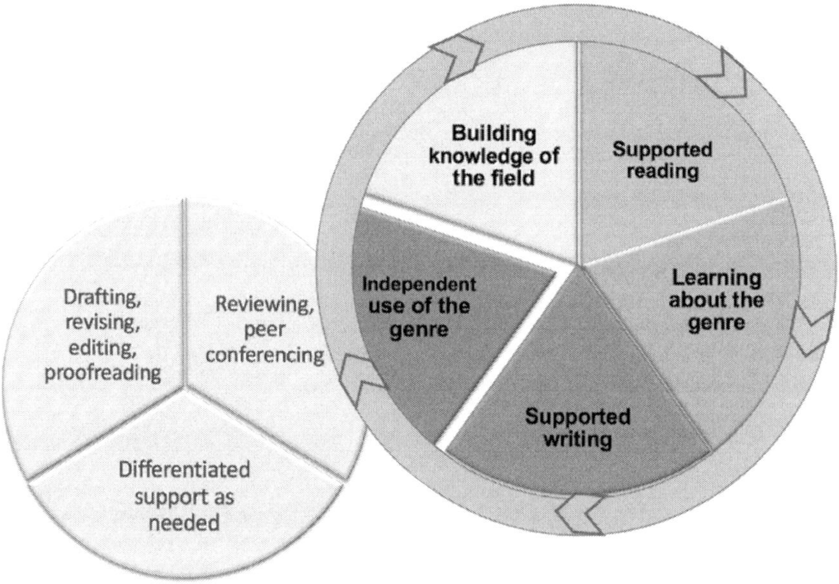

Figure 12.9 Independent use of the genre

language features. They were now at a stage where they could edit the text to flow smoothly, to improve vocabulary choices, and to attend to the needs of the reader before doing a final proofread for spelling and grammatical accuracy.

The explicit teaching about content and language as students moved through the teaching and learning cycle resulted in the final draft below.

Box 12.3 The impact of the discovery of gold

The 19th century had many events of which had a considerable impact on the developing colony of the unknown Southern land. A very significant date in our history was the discovery of gold. The Indigenous people of this land didn't use up the ecosystem, they lived along-side it, the reason why they had a much less eventful effect than the European settlers. The discovery of gold not only had environmental effects, but economic, social and political contributions on the colony that would eventually form into Australia.

The discovery of gold had a large and disadvantaging impact on the unique and endemic wildlife of our beautiful continent. The increasing rate of immigration brought many introduced species, which took out the vital bricks of the ecosystem pyramid and also caused native-vs-new competition. Habitat depletion and deforestation occurred for firewood, timber for housing and buildings and to clear land for farming and living space.

> The discovery of gold also had a considerable effect on the newly forming economy of the developing colony. Due to the mass immigration to Ballarat, businesses raised the wages to stop fleeing convict employees. Also the increased wealth in the economic system led to the improved and increased rate of infrastructure construction, including roads, railways, buildings and telegraph lines. Unlike the environmental impact, the effect on the economy was positive and beneficial.
>
> The discovery of gold caused a tremendous change in the social structure of Australian nineteenth century life. Much of the colony's population was made up of convicts. The new cultures from around the world, including Germany, China, America or just the next state over, joined together to create the immense diversity that Australia is today. But sadly, with the new boomtowns and expanding population, the life of Aboriginal people was changed forever.
>
> Last but not least, the discovery of gold had enormous benefits to Australia's politics. The Eureka Stockade rebellion, of 1854 Ballarat, was formed by miners that had demanded lower or destroyed mining license fees, better treatment by the government forces, and much more comfortable living conditions. Although 30+ diggers and 4 troopers got killed, this 20-minute battle was the first stance of democracy in Australia. The miner's demands were met.
>
> In conclusion, the discovery of gold in NSW and Victoria had beneficial and non-beneficial impacts on the developing colony, by bringing democracy, wealth and decades of a depleting environment. I think, though, although the effect of the eco-system was highly dis-advantaging, the discovery of gold was revolutionary and important.

Even from a quick skim, it is evident that this is an impressive text. If we refer to the characteristics of complex texts as outlined in the Literacy Learning Progression (ACARA 2018), this text would be ranked at the upper end of 'moderately complex texts' bridging into 'sophisticated texts' (Table 12.1).

Let's examine in greater detail the escalation in complexity in this text, drawing on the model of language that underpins the Language Strand of the Australian Curriculum: English (ACARA n.d.) – a bringing together of Martin's genre theory (2012) and Halliday's functional language theory (1985).

Genre: achieving the purpose of the task

We could begin with Martin's (1997) notion of genre as achieving a social purpose by moving through a number of relatively predictable stages. In this case, the purpose of the task is to explain the impact of the Gold Rush on Australian society. The genre is a consequential explanation, which examines the multiple effects of a particular input. The text has been organised into a series of stages that enable it to successfully achieve its purpose.

Table 12.1 Moderately complex > sophisticated texts

Criteria from LLP	Examples from student text
Vocabulary	
• a range of synonyms and antonyms with subtle shades of meaning	synonyms: *impact/effect, reasons/contribution, positive/beneficial, new cultures/immense diversity, indigenous/Aboriginal* antonyms: *endemic wildlife/introduced species, native-vs-new, beneficial/non-beneficial*
• words that appear across academic disciplines • abstract concepts	multiple examples of academic words that are common to all curriculum areas (typically abstractions): *impact, reason, significant, effect, increasing rate, caused, change, benefits, conditions, stance, revolutionary*
• extensive technical and learning area-specific vocabulary	*colony, mass immigration, Australian nineteenth-century life, discovery of gold, Eureka Stockade, diggers*
• subtle evaluative language reflecting author viewpoint	*unique wildlife, beneficial impact, enormous benefits, highly disadvantaging*
• less common affixes	*develop<u>ing</u> colony, <u>de</u>forestation, <u>non</u>-beneficial, disadvantag<u>ing</u>*
Language	
• multiclause sentences with less common constructs	predominance of very dense simple sentences with the occasional compound and complex sentence
• passive voice	*the life of Aboriginal people <u>was changed</u>* *The Eureka Stockade rebellion <u>was formed</u> by miners …* *30+ diggers and 4 troopers <u>got killed</u>* *The miner's demands <u>were met</u>*
• dense language with extensive nominalisation	*disadvantaging impact, increasing rate of immigration, newly forming economy, immense diversity*
• rhetorical devices (metaphor and hyperbole)	*the <u>vital bricks</u> of the ecosystem pyramid* *<u>tremendous</u> change, <u>immense</u> diversity, <u>revolutionary</u>*
• conditional/concessional cohesive devices (although, instead, compared to)	*Although 30+ diggers and 4 troopers got killed, this 20-minute battle was the first stance of democracy in Australia.* *Although the effect of the eco-system was highly dis-advantaging, the discovery of gold was revolutionary and important.*
• extensive noun groups	*a large and disadvantaging impact on the unique and endemic wildlife of our beautiful continent*
• cohesion across text	See 'Cohesion' section below for examples, e.g. using text organisers, text connectives, antonyms and synonyms
Content	
• topics or ideas presented with significant details or elaboration	See 'Compacting ideas' section below, e.g. *economic, social and political **contributions*** *the unique and endemic **wildlife** of our beautiful continent*
• abstract ideas; complex, demanding concepts	*reason; effect; impact; increasing rate; stance*
• complex issues/themes	the injustices of the Eureka Stockade and the impact on the environment and the indigenous population
• experiences portrayed are remote	the experiences are distant in time, removed from the life experience of the writer

The introductory stage begins by locating the explanation in the 19th century and nominating this period as a time of significant change in Australian history. It then narrows the focus to one particular cause of change – the discovery of gold. At this point, the text does a bit of a detour, pre-empting a discussion of one of the effects of the Gold Rush: the impact on the environment. Ideally, this might have been left until later. It then foreshadows how the text will unfold in stages that focus attention on four particular consequences. Following this opening stage, the subsequent stages provide details of each of the selected consequences in turn and concludes by weighing up the positive and negative consequences of the discovery of gold.

The writer has thus demonstrated great skills in developing the overall organisation of the text in response to Mandy's explicit teaching.

Cohesion: managing the flow of information

One of Halliday's (2014) functions of language is to create texts that are made comprehensible through the use of a variety of cohesive devices (the *textual* function).

The most obvious thing to notice is that this is an extended text. As texts increase in length, the demands to shape them into a coherent whole become more challenging. This student's text is highly crafted to make the content accessible to the reader.

Using 'text organisers'

Following Mandy's guidance, the writer has begun by signposting the method of development, identifying four key concepts that will guide the organisation of the text:

> The discovery of gold not only had **environmental** effects, but **economic, social** and **political** contributions on the colony that would eventually form into Australia.

Martin (1997) refers to this as the text's 'macrotheme' (and in the Australian Curriculum it is called the 'text opener'), forging explicit and clear connections between parts of the text.

These categories are then picked up systematically in the rest of the text. They are signalled by the topic sentences of the body paragraphs (Martin's 'hyperthemes'). And the concluding paragraph ties it all together by revisiting the key concepts and their relative impacts (though with the omission of the social category). This organisation is illustrated in Figure 12.10.

Even at the level of the topic sentences – one of the targeted language features – the writer has controlled the cohesive flow by keeping constant the beginning of the sentence (the Theme or 'sentence opener'), reminding the reader that the focus is on 'the discovery of gold'. The end of the sentence is used to introduce the 'new' information – in this case each of the key concepts, as in Table 12.2.

226 Beverly Derewianka

> The discovery of gold not only had **environmental** effects, but **economic, social** and **political** contributions on the colony that would eventually form into Australia.
>
> The discovery of gold had a large and disadvantaging impact on **the unique and endemic wildlife of our beautiful continent.** ...
>
> The discovery of gold also had a considerable effect on **the newly forming economy of the developing colony.** ...
>
> The discovery of gold caused a tremendous change in **the social structure** of Australian nineteenth century life. ...
>
> Last but not least, the discovery of gold had enormous benefits to **Australia's politics.** ...
>
> In conclusion, the discovery of gold in NSW and Victoria had beneficial and non-beneficial impacts on the developing colony, by bringing **democracy, wealth** and ... **environment**. I think, though, although the effect of the eco-system was highly dis-advantaging, the discovery of gold was revolutionary and important.

Figure 12.10 'Text organisers' in student text

Table 12.2 Given and new information focus

Given information	New information
The discovery of gold	**had a large and disadvantaging impact on the ... wildlife.**
The discovery of gold	**also had a considerable effect on the ... economy ...**
The discovery of gold	**caused a tremendous change in the social structure ...**

Using text connectives

Another cohesive device that the student draws on is the use of phrases that link stretches of text and signal transitions in the text (sometimes called 'transition words').
  Text connectives have been used:

- to add information (***Also** the increased wealth in the economic system led to ...*);
- to contrast (***But** sadly, with the new boomtowns ...; I think, **though** ...*);
- to sequence (***Last but not least** ...; **In conclusion** ...*).

Using synonyms

Just as repetition ('the discovery of gold') can be cohesive, so can the use of synonyms. In the topic sentences, the writer has used (near) synonyms to express the consequential relationship between the discovery of gold and the affected entity:

> *The discovery of gold* **had a large and disadvantaging impact** on *the ... wildlife*.
> *The discovery of gold* also **had a considerable effect** on *the ... economy* ...
> *The discovery of gold* **caused a tremendous change** in *the social structure* ...
> Last but not least, *the discovery of gold* **had enormous benefits** to *Australia's politics*.

For such a young writer, this repertoire of abstract causal synonyms is impressive.

Using antonyms

The writer also creates cohesion by using antonyms. These form a cohesive tie by linking two things in a contrastive relationship:

> **endemic** wildlife
> vs
> **introduced** species
> **beneficial**
> vs
> **non-beneficial** impacts
> The discovery of gold had **a large and disadvantaging** impact on the ... wildlife.
> vs
> ... the effect on the economy was **positive and beneficial**.

Field: developing the content

Another of Halliday's functions of language is to depict 'what's going on' – the field. This is referred to as the *experiential* function – representing our experience of the world. In this text there is evidence of a deep engagement with the field of knowledge over a period of time.

Using discipline-related language

In the upper-primary years, the curriculum is becoming more differentiated into discipline areas. Students are being apprenticed into the ways in which scientists, historians, and mathematicians think about the world. This is reflected in the way they use language. The writer of this upper-primary history text demonstrates a sound knowledge of 'what's going on' in the period through language referring to:

- time (*1854; Australian nineteenth century life; a very significant date*);
- place (*the unknown Southern land; the developing colony; boomtowns*);

228 *Beverly Derewianka*

- key events (*the discovery of gold; the Eureka Stockade; this 20-minute battle; immigration*);
- human participants from the past (*convicts; European settlers; the government forces; diggers and troopers*).

Interestingly, much of the discipline-related language comes from other curriculum areas:

Geography: *ecosystem pyramid; environmental effects; the unique and endemic wildlife; introduced species; habitat depletion; deforestation;*

Business: *raised wages; increased wealth; infrastructure; economic system;*

Civics: *immigration; social structure; new cultures; immense diversity; expanding population; comfortable living conditions; democracy; miners' demands.*

This perhaps reflects the way in which History, Geography, Business and Economics, and Civics and Citizenship are all brought together under the umbrella of Humanities and Social Studies in Years 5/6 of the Australian Curriculum.

Using academic language

The writer is also employing academic language that crosses all discipline areas, such as *events; reason; effect; contributions; impact; increasing rate; stance.*

Such language is often abstract and condenses a lot of information. The term 'event', for example, assumes an understanding of all the things that are encompassed in the event: what happened, where it happened, who was involved, why it happened, and so on. It does not have the same kind of 'simple', mono-dimensional meanings as much of the more concrete vocabulary of many primary-level texts.

Expressing causality

History is about change and the causes and effects of change. Because the genre in question is a consequential explanation, we would expect to find language representing causal relationships (as in Table 12.3). What is notable in this text is the range of resources deployed by the writer for expressing causality rather than relying on 'because' clauses typical of the earlier primary years.

Compacting ideas

Particularly striking about this text is the way in which the writer has used lengthy noun groups to represent the various participants (human and non-human). The text packs a lot of information into its noun groups. (The head noun is bolded.)

Table 12.3 Resources for expressing causality

abstract participants	impact, reason, effect, contributions
causal processes	- *The increasing rate of immigration **brought** many introduced species ... and also **caused** native-vs-new competition.* - *... the increased wealth **led to** the increased rate of infrastructure construction.* - *The discovery of gold **caused** a tremendous change*
causal circumstances	- ***Due to the mass immigration**, businesses raised the wages;* - ***With the new boomtowns and expanding population**, the life of Aboriginal people was changed forever.* - *to clear land **for farming and living space***
dependent clauses	- ***[in order] to** stop fleeing convict employees* - ***by** bringing democracy, wealth and decades of a depleting environment*
implied causality	*This 20-minute battle was the first stance of democracy in Australia. > The miner's demands were met.*

- many **events** *[[of which had a considerable impact on the developing colony of the unknown Southern land]]*;
- a very significant **date** *in our history*;
- the **reason** *[[why they had a much less eventful effect than the European settlers]]*;
- economic, social and political **contributions**;
- the **colony** *[[that would eventually form into Australia]]*;
- a large and disadvantaging **impact**;
- the unique and endemic **wildlife** *of our beautiful continent*;
- the vital **bricks** *of the ecosystem pyramid*;
- a considerable **effect** *on the newly forming economy of the developing colony*;
- the increased **wealth** *in the economic system*;
- a tremendous **change** *in the social structure of Australian nineteenth century life*;
- the immense **diversity** *[[that Australia is today]]*;
- enormous **benefits** *to Australia's politics*;
- **miners** *[[that had demanded lower or destroyed mining license fees]]*;
- much more comfortable living **conditions**.

Several of these noun groups include embedded clauses ([[...]]) that provide extra information and often contain additional noun groups: *many **events** [[of which had a considerable impact on the developing colony of the unknown Southern land]]*.

Nominalising

Nominalisation is a key indicator of mature writing that starts to expand in late primary. In earlier years, it is generally a matter of just changing a verb or adjective into a noun (*move > movement; happy > happiness*). In the late-primary text, we can see a few examples of this low-level kind of nominalisation, where the nouns have become so unexceptional that we don't even notice that they have been derived from verbs:

230 Beverly Derewianka

the **discovery** of gold;

the Eureka Stockade **rebellion**.

The writer of the late-primary text, however, is also doing something more sophisticated – collapsing whole clauses into noun groups. That is, where there would have been the option of representing experience in the form of a clause (as in the spoken language), the author has instead transformed the clause into a noun group, thus turning it into a 'thing' that can be played with. In the process, the text becomes more compact and dense, as in Table 12.4.

The fact that there are instances of 'clumsy' attempts at nominalising is a sign of the student experimenting with language.

a large and **disadvantaging** impact;

the effect on the eco-system was **highly dis-advantaging**;

lower or **destroyed** mining license fees;

a **depleting** environment.

Table 12.4 Instances of student's nominalisations

Possible 'spoken' option (as a clause)	>>> Written nominalisation (as a noun group)
many species were introduced by the immigrants	many introduced species
many people migrated to Ballarat	the mass immigration to Ballarat
the settlers depleted the places where the wildlife lived by cutting down the trees	habitat depletion and deforestation
the miners demanded better conditions	the miners' demands for better conditions
in the unknown Southern land a colony was developing	the developing colony of the unknown Southern land
more and more people were migrating	the increasing rate of immigration
the native animals were competing with the new animals	native-vs-new competition
convict employees were fleeing	fleeing convict employees
the economic system made people more wealthy	the increased wealth in the economic system
roads and buildings were being constructed better and more quickly	the improved and increased rate of infrastructure construction
how people lived in Australia in the nineteenth century was changing a lot	a tremendous change in the social structure of Australian nineteenth century life
Australia has lots of people from diverse backgrounds	the immense diversity that Australia is today
the number of people in Australia is expanding	the expanding population
(they wanted) the government forces to treat them better	better treatment by the government forces
the discovery of gold affected how the colony was developing in good ways and bad ways	beneficial and non-beneficial impacts on the developing colony

Mature academic writing 231

Table 12.5 Creating a causal relationship between nominalisations

the increased wealth in the economic system	led to	the improved and increased rate of infrastructure construction
nominalisation	causal relationship	**nominalisation**

Such 'over-reaching' is an important step in learning the language of secondary education, where students need to be able to 'package' ideas efficiently in order to create relationships between the nominalised 'things' (Table 12.5).

This is an alternative to a more 'spoken' sequence of clauses:

Clause 1: People were constructing more houses and roads better than before
Clause 2: because the economic system was producing more and more money.

It is of interest to note that the great majority of sentences in this text consist of a single clause. This is not because the student can't write complex sentences, but because so much of the information has been packed into the noun groups through nominalisation rather than spread across a number of clauses.

It is evident that this student is developing the language resources needed to represent his curriculum knowledge in secondary contexts, from the use of technicality and abstraction through to the compacting of ideas that enables them to be brought into a variety of relationships.

Evaluation: expressing attitudes

Halliday's third function of language is the *interpersonal* – how language enables us to take up roles and create relationships with others. This includes what he calls 'attitudinal lexis', elaborated by Martin and White (2005) as 'appraisal'.

Martin and White propose 'attitude' as part of the appraisal model. Attitudes can be viewed in terms of:

- the expression of feelings ('affect');
- the assessment of the value of something ('appreciation');
- the judgement of human behaviour ('judgement').

Unlike many lower-mid primary texts, the upper-primary text does not rely on affect, with only one expression of emotion:

*But **sadly** … the life of Aboriginal people was changed forever.*

Rather, it is primarily concerned with assessing the quality and attributes of things. These assessments are often 'boosted' to increase the impact ('graduation'):

*a **very significant** date in our history;*

*a **large and disadvantaging impact**;*

*the **unique** and endemic wildlife of our **beautiful** continent;*

*the effect on the economy was **positive and beneficial**;*

*a **tremendous change** in the social structure;*

*the **immense diversity** that Australia is today;*

***enormous benefits** to Australia's politics;*

***more comfortable** living conditions;*

*discovery of gold was **revolutionary and important**.*

The text also makes judgements of human behaviour:

> *Indigenous people of this land **didn't use up the ecosystem**, they **lived along-side it**, the reason why they had **a much less eventful effect** than the European settlers.*
>
> *... as opposed to the **habitat depletion and deforestation** of the settlers.*

Because the task is not to simply explain the consequences of the Gold Rush but to form an opinion about their relative significance, the student has had to draw on the interpersonal resources of appreciation and judgement in order to persuade the reader of his argument.

In sum, this text displays a number of features of mature, complex writing. It achieves the purpose of the task by moving through well-selected stages to explain and argue. It is structured coherently through the use of textual resources such as text organisers and text connectives, along with cohesive devices such as the use of synonyms and antonyms. It represents the student's deep understanding of the field through his use of discipline-related terminology, academic abstractions, and the condensation of meanings into dense noun groups, including nominalisations. And it successfully persuades through its choice of interpersonal strategies.

One might even suspect that Xander's text involved simply cutting and pasting from the internet – but virtually everything can be traced back to the support provided during the production of the text. While Xander's text is particularly noteworthy, all students in the class were able to achieve well beyond previous efforts.

Writing history in the secondary years

While the above text might appear quite accomplished, there is still some way to go when the student has to deal with the challenges of secondary education.

In secondary History, for example, the tasks no longer involve simply recounting and explaining historical events. Now students are being apprenticed into the world of historiography – the study of the methods of historians in examining the writings of and about the past. In the early secondary years, the Australian Curriculum: History requires that students:

- identify the origin, purpose and context of primary and secondary sources;
- analyse, interpret and synthesise information from a range of sources for use as evidence in an historical argument;
- evaluate the reliability and usefulness of primary and secondary sources;
- identify and describe points of view, attitudes and values in primary and secondary sources;
- identify and analyse the perspectives of people from the past (including their own);
- weigh up conflicting interpretations and perspectives;
- develop texts that use evidence from a range of sources that are referenced.

Xander and his classmates are well on the way to transitioning into this new territory.

Participant feedback

When interviewed about the process, Xander commented that he appreciated the opportunity to create multiple drafts as he could see his text improving as he learned more about the topic and he felt a sense of pride in the final draft. Contrary to expectations, this was echoed in interviews with other students:

I really like writing like this because we get to learn new information and put it into our drafts.

I like doing the drafts and putting them in my portfolio because I can look back and see how much better my writing is getting.

I like the way we read information and we can write it in our drafts and have lots of important information in them.

Feedback from the teachers also stressed this aspect, comparing it to when they simply encouraged students to edit and proofread their texts before handing them in:

Students were engaged in the drafting process – and kept looking back to their earlier drafts and commenting how much they had improved and how much extra they had written.

Some students asked to complete extra drafts between to see if they were getting closer to the model text, and they were keen to 'beat' their previous draft and to see how much better they could make the next draft.

Virtually all the teachers commented on the value of cumulatively deepening students' field knowledge over time rather than superficially skimming through a topic. They also linked the focus on field knowledge to greater student motivation and better behaviour in class:

> *The students were so into the topic and their writing really improved.*
>
> *I've noticed that they're more engaged in learning and feel more confident. Their behaviour has improved also, especially the 'strugglers'.*

Others remarked on the importance of providing specific feedback related to what had actually been taught in class:

> *Students loved the feedback, but in particular the specific feedback against various assessment criteria. This really helped show in a timely manner the areas for improvement and where students needed to focus their future efforts. Students absolutely begged me for feedback and some even challenged me on the assessment and their improvement.*

The teachers emphasised the importance of purposefully bringing together reading and writing in the context of a curriculum task to achieve an outcome – as opposed to teaching discrete reading and writing skills as an end in themselves.

> *I've got to the stage now where I'm thinking 'how can you **not** find those cross-curricular connections and how can you **not** link them to literacy' because they're reading, they're writing but they now have to learn how to use them in each of the learning areas.*
>
> *They're seeing more of a purpose for their writing and where it fits in real world contexts.*

They have observed the students' ability to reflect on their work in an informed way and the durability of learning:

> *I've noticed that the language focus, like text connectives from last term, without any further teaching, has carried through into their next piece of writing.*

The genre-based approach is particularly concerned with nurturing the literacy growth of students who come from English as an Additional Language background or who are not yet achieving to their potential, often referred to as 'non-writers' or 'reluctant writers'. It is therefore gratifying to hear from such students how their confidence has improved and how they have experienced success through the support of their teachers. One student with learning difficulties came up to the author following a lesson and volunteered that 'all teachers should be doing this'. When asked to elaborate, she said that 'all teachers should teach us how to do these things', referring to the explicit teaching and targeted scaffolding the teacher had provided. This was also picked up in the comments by one of the teachers:

My student with learning difficulties, he put so much extra work into his essay and wrote a really sophisticated and lengthy text that was so far beyond anything he has previously produced.

In general, teachers felt positive about their own professional growth and their ability to better support their students' learning. In particular, they appreciated the interaction between the primary and secondary teachers in the project, learning from each other how they can better support their students' literacy to cope with the demands of high school.

In conclusion

While initiatives such as the above can serve to prepare students for the rigors of secondary literacy, they assume high levels of teacher professional knowledge in terms of such pedagogical practices as:

- engaging students with substantial content and rich tasks that integrate oral interaction, listening, reading, writing, and visual information;
- teaching students how to read the increasingly complex texts from all areas of the curriculum – not simply in terms of how to decode words and learn new vocabulary, but how to strategically read the text in relation to the task, how to synthesise information from various sources, how to critically analyse and evaluate the text, and so on;
- supporting their writing by deconstructing model texts and jointly constructing a text (or part of a text) similar to the one that the students are writing;
- encouraging students to view writing as a process where they can improve each draft in response to what they have been taught or experienced 'in the thick of it' (eg about the content and about the crafting of the text) and conferencing with them in relation to the current learning intention.

More particularly, however, teachers themselves need to develop a sound understanding of language and the role it plays in mediating learning. This involves such practices as:

- establishing the language and literacy demands of the task;
- selecting a relevant genre to achieve the purpose of the task;
- and identifying focus language features relevant to the task and student needs.

Given the research that points to teachers' lack of confidence in their knowledge about language (Hammond 2008, Routley 2016, Accurso 2017, Schleppegrell 2018), this would underscore the need for intensive professional learning in order to better support students in successfully achieving the writing outcomes of the curriculum, particularly as students move from primary to secondary schooling.

References

Accurso, K. 2017. *Developing disciplinary linguistic knowledge: systemic functional linguistics and the new knowledge base of teaching*. Paper presented at the annual meeting of the American Educational Research Association (AERA), 2017, San Antonio, TX.

Adoniou, M. 2017. NAPLAN results show it isn't the basics that are missing in Australian education. *The Conversation*, 5 August.

Australian Curriculum Assessment and Reporting Authority (ACARA). n.d. *Australian curriculum: English: language strand*. Available from: www.australiancurriculum.edu.au/f-10-curriculum/english/ [Accessed 21. 05. 19].

Australian Curriculum Assessment and Reporting Authority (ACARA). 2018. *National literacy and numeracy learning progression literacy progression appendices 6: text complexity*. Available from: www.australiancurriculum.edu.au/media/3629/literacy-appendix-6.pdf [Accessed 21. 05. 19].

Christie, F. and Derewianka, B. 2008. *School discourse: learning to write across the years of schooling*. London: Continuum.

Gibbons, P. 2015. *Scaffolding language, scaffolding learning*. Portsmouth, NH: Heinemann.

Goss, P. and Sonnemann, J. 2018. *Measuring student progress: a state by state report card*. Australia: Grattan Institute.

Halliday, M. A. K. 1985. *An introduction to functional grammar*. London: Edward Arnold.

Hammond, J. 2008. Intellectual challenge and ESL students: implications of quality teaching initiatives. *Australian Journal of Language and Literacy*, 31(2), 128–154.

Jones, P. T., Matruglio, E. and Edwards-Groves, C. eds. forthcoming. *Transition and continuity in school literacy development*. London: Bloomsbury.

Martin, J. R. 2012. *Genre studies. Vol. 3: Collected works of J. R. Martin*. Edited by Wang Zhenhua. Shanghai: Shanghai Jiao Tong University Press.

Martin, J. R. and White, P. R. R. 2005. *The language of evaluation: appraisal in English*. London: Palgrave.

Myhill, D. A., et al. 2012. Re-thinking grammar: the impact of embedded grammar teaching on students' writing and students' metalinguistic understanding. *Research Papers in Education*, 27(2), 139–166.

O'Dowd, E. 2010. *The development of linguistic complexity: a functional continuum*. Cambridge: Cambridge University Press.

Perera, K. 1985. Grammatical differentiation between speech and writing in children aged 8 to 12. Paper presented at the annual meeting of the International Writing Convention, Norwich, England.

Queensland NAPLAN Review. 2018. *School and system perceptions report and literature review*. Institute for Learning Sciences and Teacher Education, Australian Catholic University.

Rothery, J. 1994. *Exploring literacy in school English*. Sydney: Metropolitan East Disadvantaged Schools Program.

Routley, S. 2016. *Students making meaning through language: case studies of Tasmanian primary school teachers' knowledge of teaching grammar*. Honours thesis. University of Tasmania, Launceston, Australia.

Schleppegrell, M. J. 2018. The knowledge base for language teaching: what is the English to be taught as content? *Language Teaching Research*, 1–11.

13 Articulating authorial intentions
Making meaningful connections between reading and writing in the secondary classroom

Helen Lines

Introduction

A 12-year-old boy in one of our research projects expressed his frustration with writing by saying: 'You're never actually done with it. Whenever you finish a piece of writing, your teacher comes up and tells you, "Improve it, improve it." Oh, it's so annoying!' Writing is a complex, challenging, and effortful activity partly because of its open-ended nature; each task requires new ways of creating and communicating ideas, so that 'the problems of what to include in a text and how to express that content are both numerous and widely diverse … writing anything but the most routine and brief pieces is the mental equivalent of digging ditches' (Kellogg 1994, p. 15). Paradoxically, as learners become more expert as writers, the cognitive challenges increase rather than decrease; once the basics are mastered, writers 'invest more effort and reflective thought in the task' (Kellogg 1994, p. 204), for example by making independent decisions about how a text could be improved, rather than relying on their teacher's advice. By age 16, when students sit national qualifications in England, the complexity of the reflective thought and autonomous decision-making required from them is very evident. As illustration, consider a recent transactional one-hour writing task for the General Certificate of Secondary Education (GCSE) examination in English Language, in which students were asked to imagine themselves giving a talk at a parents' information evening, explaining why all children should study science at school, taking into account others' views and expressing their own opinion. High-grade descriptors for GCSE applicable to the task call for candidates to 'communicate with impact and influence; produce ambitious, accomplished and effectively-structured texts; use a wide range of well-selected sentence types and structures and precise vocabulary to enhance impact; spell, punctuate and use grammar accurately so that writing is virtually error-free' (Ofqual 2017).

Apart from the need to include convincing facts about the role of science in school and society, there are several 'problems' about this GCSE task and its assessment that impact on decisions about content and how to express it. The basic premise is odd, given that science is a core subject in secondary schools, so that students might need to invent a realistic context, such as a change of policy or budget cuts that put science under threat. The task suggests a number of different purposes for the talk, leaving the student to decide which might be privileged, or how they might be hybridised: conveying information about school policy; explaining curriculum time for science; arguing for its inclusion; expressing an opinion, and persuading others to agree with it. Students' personal perspective seems to be required (although directed in favour of studying science), but the task also calls for empathetic imagining of the views of parents. Writing in role as Headteacher or Head of Science could lend authenticity and conviction to the points raised, but might be considered a risky first-person choice in terms of meeting examiners' expectations. The form of the writing itself is an artifice. Presumably the student is positioned as spokesperson for the school to encourage a suitably formal written response, but professional speakers in front of a real audience are more likely to speak from notes than a full written script – as students' experience of 'giving a talk' in the classroom might well have confirmed. Should they try to recreate the spontaneity of an authentic talk, for example by interacting with the imaginary audience within the task, or should they 'play safe' and use a more formal structure and vocabulary? And as all GCSE students know, the real-life recipient of their writing is an examiner who they need to impress with technical accuracy as well as interesting content.

The purpose of this discussion is not to pose examination writing tasks as unscalable hurdles but to outline the kind of 'writerly' knowledge and decision-making expected from students of secondary age. Clearly, a crucial part of the reflective effort required by adolescent writers relates to a confident awareness of authorial intention, with choices over *what* to say and *how* to say it made with a strong sense both of the needs of the implied reader of the text and what the writing should achieve. Current examinations also draw on students' understanding of authorial intention by requiring analysis of how published texts are crafted for impact, specifically, 'how writers use language and structure to achieve effects and influence readers' (DfE 2013, p. 6), while explicit connections are made between students' experiences as readers and as writers:

> GCSE English Language is designed on the basis that students should read and be assessed on high-quality challenging texts from the 19th, 20th and 21st centuries ... the texts, across a range of genres and types, should support students in developing their own writing by providing effective models ... (Students should) use knowledge gained from wide reading to inform and improve their own writing.
>
> (DfE 2013, p. 4)

There are pedagogical challenges here, for example in deciding how pre-twentieth century texts might be used as models of effective writing or ensuring that knowledge gained from reading transfers into writing. But there are also clear opportunities for exploring how language is working in authentic contexts, and for expanding students' own repertoire of linguistic choices, with the aim of 'building students' ability to appreciate and create the texts they encounter in school English' (Macken-Horarik et al. 2011, p. 9).

This chapter draws principally on data from interviews with students of secondary school age to explore their developing awareness of how texts – their own and others' – are deliberately crafted and shaped to achieve their intentions. It outlines some of the challenges involved in articulating this understanding in ways that make meaningful connections between language choices and their rhetorical impact and suggests classroom approaches that might enable such understanding.

Theoretical background

Metalinguistic understanding and authorial intention

Internationally, changes to English curricula have placed greater emphasis on the explicit teaching of knowledge about language (metalinguistic knowledge) in schools, in response to concerns over literacy standards, and, to varying degrees, have foregrounded authentic texts as resources for learning about language. The Australian curriculum has an explicit focus on 'how language works' in a range of texts, including multi-modal, and expressly links capabilities in 'comprehending texts through listening, reading and viewing', with capabilities in 'composing texts through speaking, writing and creating' (ACARA 2017). In England, references to knowledge of how language works in texts are narrower, and more prescriptively tied to the requirement to build learners' 'knowledge of grammar and vocabulary' including the use of grammatical terms: students should be taught to analyse and evaluate 'how vocabulary and grammar contribute to effectiveness and impact, using linguistic and literary terminology accurately to do so' (DfE 2013, p. 4). The approach calls for teachers to pay close attention to the linguistic features of texts as well as the more familiar ground of literary techniques, and to integrate these into coherent instruction that emphasises rhetorical function, although many teachers have had no formal grammar training and lack confidence in their linguistic knowledge (Myhill et al. 2013).

Such curricula initiatives are based on the assumed value of the role of metalinguistic understanding in writing, but in fact we know very little about how secondary-age learners develop such understanding or use it to inform their writing, including the role played by grammatical terminology, which is both under-researched and poorly understood (Myhill et al. 2012). As outlined in the chapters by S. Jones and Myhill, cumulative studies at the University of Exeter have investigated the impact of teaching grammar in the context of teaching writing, considering how an explicit focus on grammar might not only enhance students' writing but also build metalinguistic understanding which learners can draw on independently. Indeed, one clear rationale for a curriculum focus on knowledge about language is that it builds learners' appreciation of the power of linguistic choice so that, 'by understanding how language works, students are equipped to make appropriate language choices and apply them in a range of contexts' (The New Zealand Curriculum 2017, p. 18). Our own theorisation of 'grammar as choice' is informed by Hallidayan functional linguistics which emphasises the meaning-making power of language organised as 'a huge network of interrelated choices' (Halliday 2003, p. 8) and the pedagogy informing our research interventions and professional development with teachers has the aim of expanding young writers' linguistic repertoire and enabling their 'conscious control and conscious choice over language' (Carter 1990, p. 119).

A central question we have been investigating is how adolescent learners consolidate, build, and apply their metalinguistic understanding to improve the reading and writing skills demanded of them by age 16. In this respect, there is limited classroom-based research to draw on and a lack of clarity over key concepts, in part caused by ambiguity over terms (Myhill and Jones 2015), 'metalinguistic' being an adjective that requires a noun for completion – 'knowledge', 'awareness', 'activity', and so on. In Exeter's research, the definition of metalinguistic understanding we have adopted is this:

> the explicit bringing into consciousness of an attention to language as an artifact, and the conscious monitoring and manipulation of language to create desired meanings grounded in socially shared understandings.
> (Myhill 2012, p. 250)

Of particular relevance to this chapter is the emphasis on 'conscious' understanding, which can be verbalised and made explicit and visible to others, aiding reflection on language use (Camps and Milian 1999). Through classroom-based research, we have explored what learners can *say* about language and what they can *do* with language, and how classroom discourses around textual choices and their impact might shape metalinguistic understanding.

Key findings from studies to date are that:

- students are now more confident in identifying grammar structures because of its new emphasis in the curriculum but they find it more challenging to verbalise the relationship between a grammar choice and its meaning-making effect;
- the relationship between articulated and applied grammar knowledge, including use of grammatical metalanguage, is not at all straightforward: for example, some students confidently use language structures they have been taught but cannot explain what they have done using grammar terms; outwardly confident use of terminology can mask weak grammatical understanding, revealed through questioning;
- there is a very strong relationship between what is taught and what is learned, with both positive and negative outcomes.

The focus of this chapter is students' verbalised understanding of authorial choice, in relation to which Lefstein (2009, p. 27) points out that 'without explication of the criteria according to which that choice should be made ... the concept (of choice) remains a mystery to many pupils'. Our research is suggesting that teachers' and students' explicitness about authorial intention is key to informed metalinguistic decision-making, and the purpose of the present chapter is to explore this premise in more depth.

Connecting reading and writing

Consideration of the meaning-making relationships of grammatical choices in writing leads naturally to consider how a focus on the connection between reading and writing might expand students' linguistic repertoire and develop their metalinguistic understanding. Most studies that have considered the symbiosis between reading and writing have tended to focus on developing understanding of the craft of writing through extensive and close reading, learning to 'read like a writer, in order to learn how to write like a writer' (Smith 1983), and taking instruction from expert writers, as author and educationalist Ruth Culham explains:

> As a writer myself, I use models to dig below the surface to notice the moves the writer makes so I can try them in my own work ... this is close reading where reading and writing intersect. I'm reading purposefully and uncovering layers of meaning that I have come to appreciate as a critical part of literacy.
>
> (Culham 2014, p. 6)

Of course, Culham is writing about expert practice, and making explicit processes that have largely become automatised. From our own interviews with learners about their reading and writing practices, it is clear that some students can make insightful connections between the two modes, suggesting how one might impact on the other. For example, one 12-year-old explained how extensive reading helped her revise her writing:

> I listen to it in my head. I always have sort of like reading voices that I can hear someone else telling, then I know when to finish the sentence.

Another student of the same age spoke of trying out techniques encountered in his reading:

> Reading I find helps as well (to) build up your writing skills. I just think of all the different techniques and how they did it and try to put it into my own work.

Enthusiastic readers like these have developed metaknowledge that connects reading and writing, 'knowing about the functions and purposes of reading and writing; knowing that readers and writers interact; monitoring one's own meaning-making' (Fitzgerald and Shanahan 2000, p. 175). However, not all students are keen readers, nor does implicit knowledge gained from reading necessarily transfer into writing or enable clear articulation of writing goals. Although some students do learn through absorbing rhetorical patterns from their reading experiences (for example how a series of short sentences or sentence fragments might quicken narrative pace and intensify the drama of a situation, or how a tricolon might be positioned to emphasise a key point in an argument), most will need explicit teaching of these things, in purposeful contexts.

One instructional practice that has received some attention is the use of text models to examine aspects of the author's craft, where the quality of the 'mentor' text is key. In their meta-analysis of effective writing strategies, Graham and Perin (2007, p. 5) recommend the study of texts 'which provide students with opportunities to read, analyse, and emulate models of good writing', and that these should clearly illustrate 'specific features of effective writing for students' (Graham et al. 2016, p. 58). Our own research shows that text models can be a powerful tool for exploring writers' choices and linking reading and writing, because they are a rich starting-point for exploration of the writerly decisions made by published authors. They also avoid the risks of 'schooled writing' where genres are taught as a set of formulaic techniques to be incorporated into writing, by focusing on the actual choices made by different writers, including how they hybridise techniques from other genres (for example, the use of a short emotional narrative at the start of a persuasive text to compel the reader to feel the problem before the logical argument is presented). However, our research also shows that mentor texts, used with less pedagogical sensitivity, can lead to rather slavish imitation of the model text (Myhill et al. 2018) where it is much less evident that any purposeful learning has occurred. An additional challenge at secondary level is that in a high-quality complex text, its richness comes from the way that different features are interrelated and interlocked, which makes it a difficult, somewhat artificial, task to 'take it apart to see how it is made, how it is held together, and what makes it work' (McKeough 2013, p. 87), without reducing analysis to feature-spotting or imitation to feature-deploying, rather than fostering deep understanding of how text is shaped and meanings made.

The classroom context

Thinking about connections between reading and writing leads naturally to considering students' classroom experiences of being readers and writers, and how these can support or constrain their developing understanding of crafting writing for a reader. This chapter opened with a discussion of the challenges that school writing tasks can present for students, especially in the exam room, where there is little choice over form or genre (narrative and argument being the two dominant text types), where the intended purpose and recipients can be abstract and imaginary, and there is no feedback on the effectiveness of the communication. The complications of deciding for whom students are actually writing in a classroom setting have long been signalled. Flower (1979, p. 63) makes a helpful distinction between 'writer-based prose', with self as the audience – for example when writing notes for an essay – and 'reader-based prose', writing for a real or imaginary recipient, which demands 'the concrete, time-consuming task of thinking about those readers and what they need'. She makes two conclusions: if we are to tap higher rhetorical skills, we need to create realistic assignments centred around a clear reader, or, since this might be cognitive overload for novice writers, pay more attention to defining clear aims for writer-based prose that will help students understand its purpose and build their self-efficacy as readers and evaluators of their own work.

Also pertinent to students' school experience as readers and writers is the substantial body of research that underlines the importance for learner motivation and attainment of authentic reading and writing activities (as opposed to worksheets or text book exercises), especially where these provide students with personal choice (Cunningham and Cunningham 2010, Allington 2012). From a sociocultural perspective, Magnifico (2010) draws attention to how student motivation is considerably heightened by communicating with real audiences for real purposes (for example writing to overseas pen pals, or preparing brochures for a local science centre visited on a class trip) and highlights how internet technologies that are readily accessible in classrooms can provide authentic audiences and writing projects seen as relevant and engaging by teenagers, and which provide feedback essential to their identities as writers. She also emphasises that online forums make the concepts of 'reader' and 'audience' concrete and tangible, thereby focusing linguistic decision-making.

To summarise then, theory suggests the benefits for students' agency as writers of a pedagogy that makes strong connections between reading and writing and is explicit about how language choices work to shape meaning in texts, but it also flags potential classroom constraints on such learning. One clear gap in existing research into writing development is the voices of secondary-age students themselves, and the next section of this chapter considers what might be learned for classroom practice from one-to-one interviews with students aged 12–15 years (Years 7–10 in England) as they verbalise their understanding of authorial decision-making.

Writing conversations with students

Data from two research projects inform this chapter: an ESRC-funded longitudinal study, *Writing Conversations*, which followed a cohort of primary and secondary students to investigate the development of metalinguistic understanding between the ages of 9 and 14, and a three-week intervention, *Grammar at GCSE* (Watson et al. 2014) with students aged 15, investigating whether contextualised teaching of grammar in a non-fiction unit of work might have a positive outcome on students' reading as well as writing, using pre-and post-test measures. Interviews took place after lesson observation with a sub-sample of students from each project class (see Table 13.1) who were teacher-selected to balance for gender and ability, and on the basis they would enjoy and

Table 13.1 Student interview sample

Project details	Age of students	No. in sub-sample	No. of interviews	Totals
Writing Conversations (2013–2018) Longitudinal study in two primary (n = 54) and two secondary schools (n = 57*) over four years.	12-14	15*	6	90
Grammar at GCSE (2013–2014) Small-scale quasi-experimental study with 12 classes in four secondary schools (n = 161)	14-15	12	2	24
Total		27	8	114

benefit from the experience, and they took part on a voluntary basis. The interviews (up to 30 minutes in length) were a semi-structured 'writing conversation' about a piece of students' own writing produced during a teaching unit, and a sample of their peers' writing, with questions prompting discussion of the authorial choices made, for example:

What were you trying to do in this writing? How successful have you been?
What did you want your reader to think or feel?
Tell me about the words/sentences you've chosen. What do you think works well?
Tell me about the writing overall. What would you like to change or improve?

Because these 'writing conversation' interviews were sharply focused on students' own writing and the teaching they had received, student responses proved to be more grounded and revealing than interviews where more generic questions are asked.

In each project, interviews were transcribed and inductively analysed using Nvivo software with codes agreed between researchers. In the discussion that follows I have selected heavily from an extensive data set to focus on comments which show students' understanding of the reader–writer relationship, their awareness of writing for a real or imagined reader, and their comments about the effectiveness of language choices.

Key findings

Awareness of reader

A clear finding from the data is that students' characterisations of the author and the recipient of a text were rarely very specific: 'they', 'them', 'you' and 'people' were frequent terms, applied to both the writer and the reader, as here:

> People use the present tense in like headlines and stuff and they use the present tense to make you feel like it's happening now so you must do something about it.
>
> (age 15)

The student is reflecting on a lesson that looked at the language patterns in authentic newspaper headlines but there is no suggestion she knows these are written by journalists or that she sees herself as a newspaper reader. Non-fiction texts in the *Grammar at GCSE* intervention included a news report, scientific article, and viral email, chosen because they had strong language features for the genre, but students rarely acknowledged genre conventions in relation to the reader–writer relationship. One criticised the scientific article for its technical vocabulary, saying: 'Maybe it wasn't for our age group because the words he was using were like what doctors would understand', signalling the difficulty that students can have in viewing texts objectively or realising their real-world purpose. Since the term 'the reader' is frequently used in assessment objectives and question rubrics, this is perhaps not surprising, but vagueness about author and audience may well have led to statements of intention that were common enough to sound like stock responses, for example: 'hook the reader in'; 'make them want to read on'; 'make the reader feel like it's happening'; 'paint a picture in their head'; 'describe it so they can see it'. A common conception of writer–reader interaction was the need for variety – in use of vocabulary, techniques and especially sentences – to 'keep the reader interested' and 'stop them getting bored':

> varied sentences keeps it flowing and keeps it worth reading because whoever reads it, I don't really want them to be kind of reluctant in reading it.
>
> (age 12)

> I just think varying sentence types is always more interesting for someone to assess or read it.
>
> (age 14)

In contrast to such generalised responses, is this more developed comment from a student discussing the letter she has written to her Headteacher, persuading him to hold a fund-raising event for the students' chosen charity:

> You don't want to be too demanding and you want to be like tactful, but not come across too aggressive and demanding. So I tried to make him feel that like this has happened but you have the chance to do it, you can change their story and you have that power. I used 'please' and instead of like 'must' I used 'could' because they're more I think subtle.
>
> (age 13)

Having a real-life and familiar reader and an authentic purpose for writing (the school was in fact deciding on a charity to support) seems to have made it easier for Zoe to link language choices to a specific intended reader and response. Similarly, students could be more precise about language when they clearly understood the form of the writing and its communicative purpose, as here:

> When we're writing things to friends online, like on emails, we don't necessarily use proper punctuation, like we would extend our ellipsis and our exclamation marks.
>
> (age 15)

Interestingly, although often implicit in the use of 'you', no student referred directly to themselves as reader of their own writing, and there was little recognition of a peer readership. But the idea of writing to impress the teacher as assessor was well established, with several students making linguistic choices on the grounds they would bring better marks or meet success criteria:

> I usually picture Miss reading it because I don't really think anyone else would read it, so I usually try and do different vocabulary and different sentence structures.
>
> (age 12)

> since Year 7 you're always writing for the teacher, you're writing to show your understanding within lessons.
>
> (age 14)

> put in a semi-colon … it's an easy way of getting it marked better, there's more marks.
>
> (age 15)

Comments like these reflect, perhaps, a developing sense of meeting the needs of a real or implied reader, one which has not yet matured into fully-rounded understandings, and because of their prevalence across the schools may be more indicative of teacher discourses than independent understanding on the students' part. Nonetheless, they represent valuable starting-points for learning, and particularly if these kinds of responses are pursued in the classroom through discussion and questioning which explore the ideas more concretely. For example, asking a writer how did they 'paint a picture in their head', and how well do they think they have achieved this, begins to construct a more purposeful learning link between being a writer and attending to reader needs.

Choice of effects

Linked to students' generalised conceptions of the reader–writer relationship was their belief that particular linguistic structures or devices have a generic transformative effect on text, irrespective of context. Notably, comments echoed each other across the age range, suggesting very little development in terms of understanding of applied use. This was particularly true for conceptions of vocabulary, with a premium on unusual or complex choices; sentence variety, where understanding was mostly limited to the choice of long or short sentences, and for rhetorical questions, reflecting a teaching emphasis. Representative comments were:

> if you like use more higher words it makes you look more intelligent.
>
> (age 15)

> use loads of short sentences so it's quick and snappy and you just want to keep on reading.
>
> (age 14)

> make it like a variety of different lengths of sentences. I don't know what impact it has on it but if you have long and small sentences.
>
> (age 15)

> you ask a rhetorical question and it gets them thinking.
>
> (age 13)

> I did two rhetorical questions next to each other to make the reader really think.
>
> (age 15)

Non-contextualised conceptions meant that it was possible for students to hold contradictory views about the same feature or about effects, as with these four 12-year-olds:

'if you end on a long one it doesn't really sound a good sentence to finish on';
'the ending as it is, is OK because it's quite a long sentence';
'they've used like short sentences so that could help the suspense';
'if you're trying to build up tension you could use a long sentence'.

They could also lead students to suggest changes that did not actually enhance the writing:

> I could have changed the words a bit to make them more like persuasive … I could change "I speak" like to "I express".
>
> (age 13)

> I think they might have been able to use a better word than "suddenly" … something about it being quick, something like "rapidly my goggles were hit with a ball of ice" or something like that.
>
> (age 13)

> I don't think the ending is as persuasive as I'd like it to be: "Don't do it for me. Do it for the helpless children." I don't think it sounds like punchy … I'd probably put a rhetorical question on there.
>
> (age 14)

More convincing were explorations of choices linked to specific learning or task contexts. For example, one class of 13-year-olds read extracts from novels set in Victorian times and the First World War and chose one setting for their own narrative, which helped shape writerly decisions:

> I think we were meant to write long sentences to give it authenticity of older writing because we were told that in the past they used longer sentences than we would now, so I think we tried to incorporate that in our work.

In a class of 14-year-olds, arguing for better drug-aware health education for teenagers, a student singled out her use of a taught structure (relative clause):

> 'Leah Betts, who was only 18, died from taking Ecstasy at her own party.' If I take that bit out it would still make sense but it's adding more information and it's quite serious that she was only 18 … when you can throw your life away when you're really young like from one pill.

Here, Rose's comment sharpens the generalised idea that a relative clause 'adds more information' by showing how it strengthens her message about the risks of drug-taking.

The challenge of verbalising writerly choices

One significant finding from these interview conversations is that verbalising the choices made and naming the effect they have is challenging. Some students did not understand interview prompts, so that questions designed to draw out rhetorical intentions drew a literal, content-based response, as in this discussion of vocabulary choices authentic to narrative set in the First World War:

> 'Puttees' – is that a word you used to add authenticity?
> It's what they wore around their legs to keep their ankles stable.

Direct grammatical questions, for example to probe understanding of teacher's feedback, did not secure linguistic discussion. The teacher's marking highlighted effective use of a complex sentence: 'I could feel the cobblestones stabbing my feet':

> So what is making that a complex sentence?
> Like telling you that the floor is cobblestones and that my family is poor.

There were many such responses in the conversations, and it could be that content-based responses to clarify literal meaning in the text are a necessary precursor to linguistic discussion. This seems to be particularly true for weaker and younger writers, but by no means exclusively so.

Analysis of students' writing in our studies shows that many students do appropriate the grammatical choices taught, and very often in an effective manner. But they do not always know that they have made this particular choice – the pattern of transfer from taught input and discussion into writing was not linear. For example, in one school, students had read Mary Shelley's *On Ghosts*, and had discussed language choices that conveyed feelings of fear, including disrupted and one-word sentences. Students then wrote their own account of a strange event, aiming for similar effects. Here, the researcher prompts discussion of Finn's writing:

> Tell me about this: 'I went to the room on the left. Empty. So I got back and went to the room on the right. Nothing.' So you have those single words, 'nothing', 'empty'. What were you doing there? What were you trying to create?
> I can't remember what I was trying to create.
> What do you think the effect of it is?
> Err ... I can't find a word to say. Makes it more scary ... maybe?

Like Finn, many students struggled to find vocabulary for pinpointing the effects of language choices, and there were sufficient examples in the writing conversations to signal this as a significant pedagogical challenge. Classroom 'mantras', as exemplified earlier, are an understandable attempt to define effects in an accessible way, but they can also limit understanding of choices and effects – such as assuming a sole function of rhetorical questions to engage reader interest, when in some texts they might be used structurally to summarise ideas.

Students also struggled with the concept of 'effectiveness', which without exemplification, such as supplying key criteria for evaluation, remains an abstract idea, as revealed in the conversation with Hannah (age 15) about her news report, *Zombie Attack*:

> Instead of putting, 'It started to growl', I put 'The demon started to growl' to make it more effective.
> I wonder if you can say why it's more effective?
> Hannah: I don't know. It's really hard.

The students' struggle to verbalise the grammar–meaning relationship was strongly mirrored in the teaching observed, where teachers frequently chose fruitful grammatical features in rich authentic texts as the focus for learning, but themselves did not articulate the meaning-making effect with clarity. In our subsequent professional development work with teachers we have emphasised this more and generated resources for teachers which model the verbalisation of the meaning-making link between the grammar and its effect.

Framing development in understanding of authorial intentions

The analysis of interview data from the *Writing Conversations* and *Grammar at GCSE* studies has provided insights into what might be looked for as 'evidence' of development in students' articulation of writing intentions and readers' needs. Theoretically, differences between novice and expert writers have been characterised in terms of a more developed understanding and achievement of rhetorical goals (Hayes and Flower 1986), moving from a knowledge-telling model of writing focused on generating content, to a knowledge-transforming model focused on fulfilling communicative goals (Bereiter and Scardamalia 1987). Kellogg (2008) argues that the most expert stage (not reached until at least adulthood) is 'knowledge-crafting' when 'the writer is able to hold in mind the author's ideas, the words of the text itself, and the imagined reader's interpretation of the text' (2008, p. 5) – in other words, when the writer has a very sophisticated understanding of authorial intention. Taking into account the *Writing Conversations* data from the primary cohort, it was possible to see a broad trajectory by age towards an increasing confidence in explaining writerly choices, including grammatical choices, in terms of their impact on meaning, and towards a more developed articulation, both in explanations of effects of particular choices, and in evaluations of their effectiveness. The three examples below illustrate this; all students are talking about their narrative writing:

Example 1 (age 10):

> I like 'her heart hammered' and 'her soul got sucked up like in a tornado'. Some of them, one of them, had an ellipsis, no err, a simile in. And I think that just gives more description so like the reader actually knows like what it felt like.

Here, Ella independently identifies sentence choices she thinks work well and attempts to label them grammatically, although she confuses terms. She is aware of interacting with a reader and the effect she is aiming for, although the explanation of that effect is limited and generalised and common enough to sound an echo of classroom talk rather than independent judgement.

Example 2 (age 13):

> 'Pungent' I put in there, 'rancid', 'intoxicated', very descriptive words, so you get the feeling of what you are describing about, so actually like a picture in their mind. I wanted him to feel the atmosphere; you are going to describe it well so they know exactly what is happening in the story and what it feels like to be the person in the story.

Jack also echoes classroom 'mantras' about effects but has a more developed view of the narrative purpose of description in creating a distinctive mood or atmosphere and in fleshing out plot and character. There is, though, confusion about 'the reader', evident in the mix of pronouns used. 'Him' actually refers to one of the characters in Jack's story about two soldiers in the First World War, while 'you', 'they' and 'them' are generalised references to writer and reader, reflective, perhaps, of how teachers talk about writing goals rather than signalling Jack's authorial agency.

Example 3 (age 14):

> The Year 7 one I think I was less descriptive and more focusing on what the statue was, what he had done, and it wasn't really, it was just more storytelling, but then in Year 9, I was describing the statue more: 'Staring into the distance, beyond the trees, stood a statue, tall, grey and strong with a stern look upon his face', trying to describe what his body looked like and about his face but it doesn't say too much ... I left it to the imagination ... I used more techniques ... like better sentence starters ... I've started it with a verb 'staring' and I could have said, 'Staring into the distance stood a statue' but I'm saying 'beyond the trees' it's like describing it even more ... 'Closer and closer I go, still trying to figure out this mysterious piece of artwork' ... if you're saying 'closer and closer' it's sort of like you're building up to something that is going to happen.

The references here are to the same narrative task (about a statue coming alive) that all students completed at the start of each year of the *Writing Conversations* project; Lucy is comparing her responses at the beginning and end of the project, and the comparison may well have provided greater objectivity to her reflections. She expresses the same intention to 'be more descriptive' but has a stronger sense of the purpose – avoiding over-emphasis on plot – and a more sophisticated understanding of the reader's needs, such as providing sufficient visualising detail but leaving room for interpretation. Lucy recognises that different grammatical choices are possible, including at the level of sentence structure, and explains choices in terms of how they shape reader reaction, for example the fronted adverbial phrase ('closer and closer') to delay revealing subject and action. The function of grammatical structures is understood even though the only grammatical term used is 'verb'; in interview, Lucy did not know the term 'prepositional phrase' but exemplifies one ('beyond the trees') and recognises it as one way of providing descriptive detail.

Although a broad developmental trajectory by age was evident, perhaps unsurprisingly, it was the most able students in the cohorts who showed the greatest awareness of linguistic choices linked to the specific audience, form, and purpose of their writing, and who attempted more developed comments about these. Ability was much more significant than age in this respect. The following example from the *Grammar at GCSE* project represents one of the most fully formed expressions of authorial intention found in the data. The non-fiction unit forming the intervention was titled 'Truth is Stranger than

Fiction' and included a scientific article about astronaut hibernation. Analysis of the text focused on how it was made to sound authoritative, for example by using direct quotations from an expert in the field, specialist technical vocabulary, writing in the present tense, and using subordinate clauses to flesh out details or explain processes, as here:

> Dr John E. Bradford is president of SpaceWorks Engineering, a US-based company that was awarded funds to investigate the pioneering technology. 'In short, we are attempting to put a Mars-bound crew in a deep-sleep stasis during the six to nine-month transfer periods between Earth and Mars,' he explains.
>
> (Will Gater, BBC Focus, 2014)

Students then wrote a scientific article introducing their own invention. Below is an extract from Neil's article about a treatment to make people invisible:

> Invisible. An interesting concept created by amazing writers of fiction and scientists, scientists who stepped out of our norms in past and modern science to help bring us something we have desired for so long now ... Researchers from Cambridge University cracked the code when they were performing experiments with new nano-technology. George Penton, leading researcher, told us: 'We believe that when the molecular structure of isotope 167 is exposed to high levels of SO2, the isotope becomes unstable and "dissolves" into a new substance'.

The influence of the text model is clear here, but it is through reflective discussion that Neil shows how deliberately he has thought about purpose and readership and matched his own language choices to these, rather than just imitating the original:

> When I wrote the piece, I tried to pick out a target audience and I should try to label it for people who like sci-fi because it's quite a science fiction sort of thing. And when I was writing it I had to take into account that I needed to make it look professional and that it was written by someone who knew what they were doing. I used words like 'isotope' and 'SO2' and 'nano-technology', science words that ran off the top of my head. I guess I was trying to sell the product, take more interest in buying it. I also had a very biased opinion. I saw it as a good thing and didn't label any negatives. I was trying to make it more specific to a group ... I don't think it would be a product for everyone ... I wanted to use the words selectively so it sounded more scientific.

Neil's clear conception of his writing intention, and of his 'target audience' and their needs, helped him to frame reasons for specific choices, as here: 'George Penton could be anyone, but by saying he's a "leading researcher", I'm saying that he's part of the group that discovered this ... he's important.' The choice of inverted commas around 'dissolves' was a conscious one that Neil himself drew attention to, saying 'I know a lot of people use them when they take the mick out of things' and explaining: 'It would be "aqueous" if it was scientifically correct I believe' but that he wanted to give 'a loose idea about what is happening'.

In the context of investigating students' verbalised understanding of grammatical concepts, Chen and Myhill (2016), building on an earlier study by Chen and Jones (2012), have suggested a framework for describing development, from identification (naming and labelling of features), to elaboration (explaining or exemplifying), to extension (making a link with writing), to application (articulating how the concept creates meaning in written text). The four student examples above show something of this journey, and the framework might be a useful way of thinking about students' developing understanding of writerly intentions, and how teachers might support this. One clear finding from these authors' studies and those reported here, is that development of writerly knowledge is neither straightforward nor strictly linear, requiring substantial scaffolding and iteration between the 'stages'.

Students of all abilities (and sometimes their teachers) could have confidence shaken by an unfamiliar genre or task, such as a focus on sentence patterning and punctuation effects in poetry. While terminology helped some students identify choices and express intentions more precisely, for others the struggle to remember terms remained a frustration. And as longitudinal data showed, an individual student's sense of agency as a writer could lessen over time, as for Rose, who at age 14 felt herself a less imaginative writer than when younger:

> I just used to love reading and I used to pick up vocabulary just like unintentionally and use it. Now the focus is really on getting a high grade ... you almost have to have a checklist when you're writing so you have to make sure you've got all the techniques you need to have in order to get a high level ... semi colons are always drilled into us.

Concluding comments

Echoing through many of the student responses is the teacher's voice, and the feedback and guidance students have received from teachers. It is important to remember that although these are secondary writers, they are still developing and maturing as writers, and there is a considerable range of expertise in many secondary classrooms. Here, through the student voices, we are witnessing part of that journey, and the growth of emerging awareness of reader needs and authorial intention. Another point to foreground is that both the explicit teaching of how linguistic choices shape meaning in writing, and discussing those choices, are very new ways of working for both teachers and students. In our work with teachers, the key approach taken, whereby analysis of language in the texts that students are reading is accompanied by a strong focus on choices and crafting in subsequent writing, appears to have developed students' understanding of how texts are shaped to meet readers' needs, and empowered their writing decisions. Our studies also show, however, that verbalising authorial intentions can be challenging and is a line of enquiry ripe for further research.

References

Allington, R. L. 2012. *What really matters for struggling readers: designing research-based programs*. Boston: Allyn & Bacon.

Australian Curriculum and Assessment Reporting Authority (ACARA). 2017. *NAPLAN achievement in reading, writing, language conventions and numeracy: 2017 national report*. Available from: www.nap.edu.au/results-and-reports/national-reports [Accessed 18. 11. 18].

Bereiter, C. and Scardamalia, M. 1987. *The psychology of written composition*. Hillsdale: Erlbaum.

Camps, A. and Milian, M. eds. 1999. *Metalinguistic activity in learning to write*. Amsterdam: Amsterdam University Press.

Carter, R. ed. 1990. *Knowledge about language*. London: Hodder & Stoughton.

Chen, H. and Jones, P. 2012. Understanding metalinguistic development: a functional perspective. *Journal of Applied Linguistics and Professional Practice*, 9(1), 81–104.

Chen, H. and Myhill, D. A. 2016. Children talking about writing: investigating metalinguistic understanding. *Linguistics and Education*, 35, 100–108.

Culham, R. 2014. *The writing thief: using mentor texts to teach the craft of writing*. Newark, Delaware: International Reading Association.

Cunningham, P. M. and Cunningham, J. W. 2010. *What really matters in writing: research-based practices across the elementary curriculum*. Boston: Allyn & Bacon.

Department for Education (DfE). 2013. *National curriculum in England: framework for key stages 1–4*. Reference DFE – 00232–02013.

Fitzgerald, J. and Shanahan, T. 2000. Reading and writing relations and their development. *Educational Psychologist*, 35, 39–50.

Flower, L. 1979. Writer-based prose: a cognitive basis for problems in writing. Available from: wac.colostate.edu/jbw/v3n3/flower [Accessed 13. 10. 18].

Graham, S. and Perin, D. 2007. A meta-analysis of writing instruction for adolescent students. *Journal of Educational Psychology*, 99, 445–476.

Graham, S., et al. 2016. *Teaching secondary school children to write effectively (NCEE 2017–4002)*. Washington, DC: National Center for Education Evaluation and Regional Assistance (NCEE), Institute of Education Sciences, US Department of Education. Available from: htpp://whatworks.ed.gov [Accessed 13. 10. 18].

Halliday, M. A. K. 2003. Introduction: on the 'architecture' of human language. In: Webster, J. ed. *On language and linguistics: volume 3 in the collected works of MAK Halliday*. London and New York: Continuum, 1–29.

Hayes, J. R. and Flower, L. 1986. Writing research and the writer. *American Psychologist*, 41, 1106–1113.

Kellogg, R. T. 1994. *The psychology of writing*. Oxford: Oxford University Press.

Kellogg, R. T. 2008. Training writing skills: a cognitive developmental perspective. *Journal of Writing Research*, 1(1), 1–26.

Lefstein, A. 2009. Rhetorical grammar and the grammar of schooling: teaching 'powerful verbs' in the English National Literacy Strategy. *Linguistics and Education*, 20(4), 378–400.

Macken-Horarik, M., Love, K. and Unsworth, L. 2011. A grammatics 'good enough' for school English in the 21st century: four challenges in realising the potential. *Australian Journal of Language and Literacy*, 34(1), 9–23.

Magnifico, A. M. 2010. Writing for whom? cognition, motivation, and a writer's audience. *Educational Psychologist*, 45(3), 167–184.

McKeough, A. 2013. A developmental approach to teaching narrative composition. In: Graham, S., et al. eds. *Best practices in writing instruction*. 2nd ed. New York: The Guilford Press, 73–112.

Myhill, D. A. 2012. 'The ordeal of deliberate choice': metalinguistic development in secondary writers. In: Berninger, V., ed. *Past, present, and future contributions of cognitive writing research to cognitive psychology*. New York: Psychology Press/Taylor Francis Group, 247–274.

Myhill, D. A. and Jones, S. M. 2015. Conceptualising metalinguistic understanding in writing. *Cultura Y Educacion*, 27(4), 839–867.

Myhill, D. A., Jones, S. and Lines, H. 2018. Supporting less-proficient writers through linguistically-aware teaching. *Language and Education*, 32(4), 333–349.

Myhill, D. A., Jones, S. and Watson, A. 2013. Grammar matters: how teachers' grammatical knowledge impacts on the teaching of writing. *Teaching and Teacher Education*, 36, 77–91.

Myhill, D. A., et al. 2012. Re-thinking grammar: the impact of embedded grammar teaching on students' writing and students' metalinguistic understanding. *Research Papers in Education*, 27(2), 139–166.

The New Zealand Curriculum. 2017. Available from: https://nzcurriculum.tki.org.nz [Accessed on 06. 04. 19].

The Office of Qualifications and Examinations Regulation (Ofqual). 2017. English language: grade descriptors for GCSEs graded 9 to 1. Available from: www.gov.uk/government/publications/grade-descriptors-for-gcses-graded-9-to-1 [Accessed 07. 10. 19].

Smith, F. 1983. Reading like a writer. *Language Arts*, 60(5), 58–567.

Watson, A., Myhill, D. and Newman, R. 2014. *Grammar at GCSE: exploring the effects of a contextualised grammar pedagogy on reading and writing at KS4*. Available from: https://qualifications.pearson.com/content/dam/pdf/GCSE/English%20Language/2015/teaching-and-learning-materials/Grammar_at_GCSE_Technical_Report_DC.pdf [Accessed 17. 04. 19].

Index

abilities 7, 9, 30, 32, 69, 73, 87–9, 131, 137, 155–6, 178, 180, 234–5, 251, 253; children's 83, 114; emerging 168; student's 198, 239; teacher's 147; writer's 132–3
ABS *see* Australian Bureau of Statistics
academic disciplines 224
ACARA *see* Australian Curriculum and Assessment Reporting Authority
ACE *see* Australian Curriculum: English
adjectives 31, 66, 71, 73–5, 87–8, 97, 159, 163, 168, 200, 229, 240; good 31; negative 208
adverbs 71, 96, 159, 163, 168, 204
Alexander, Robin 157, 173
Andrews, R. 160, 181–2
antonyms 224, 227, 232
arguments 62, 80, 106, 108, 134, 138, 141–2, 232, 242; historical 233; and readers 134, 141–2, 242; and students 141–2, 242
Arthurian legend (lesson) 159, 169
Arvon (UK creative writing foundation) 118, 123–5, 127
audiences 4, 6, 9–10, 12, 26–7, 123, 125, 131–42, 144–7, 198, 243, 245, 251; addressing 133–4, 136–7; awareness of 10, 89, 131, 133, 135–6, 138–40, 146; expectations of 131, 136–7, 143, 145; importance of 138–9; international 79; role of 136, 140; and the shaping of writer choices 134; target 252; unfamiliar 136, 140
Australia 13, 63, 78, 95, 107, 132, 173–4, 212–14, 220, 222–3, 225, 229–30, 232; and 82% of 13–14 year old's achieve the national minimum standard in writing 13; and the advent of the national curriculum in 173; and the influence of the Systemic Functional Linguistics 9–10, 95–6, 133; multi-site ethnographic project 21; and the National Partnerships initiative 135; and numbers of students struggle with basic writing skills 13; and the impact of NAPLAN on the quality of students' writing 213; and the research tradition reaching back to the 1980s in 174; and the SFL approach 96; and the unequitable access to language of schooling by students from disadvantaged backgrounds 10
Australian Bureau of Statistics 21
Australian Curriculum 225, 228, 239
Australian Curriculum, English 23, 131, 136–7, 140, 146, 223
Australian Curriculum, History 233
Australian Curriculum and Assessment Reporting Authority 13, 21, 23, 131, 173, 187, 194, 223, 239
Australian National Assessment Program Literacy and Numeracy Tests 23, 37, 75, 174, 213–4
authentic texts 11, 158–60, 164, 166, 204–8, 249
authorial identities 113, 116
authorial intentions 5, 7, 124, 198, 209, 238–9, 241, 249–51, 253
axial codes 117

baseline test 78
'becoming writers' 8, 11, 113–14, 117–18, 123, 126–7
benchmarks 13, 213
BERA *see* British Educational Research Association
Berman, Ruth 195
Bourdieu, Pierre 78, 80–1

Bradford, John E. 251
British Educational Research Association use of ethical guidelines 82, 117–18
Burnett, C. 20, 78, 80, 90, 173

case studies 21, 47, 137, 213; groups 197; individual 161
characterisation (concept) 142–3, 145, 164, 204–7, 244
Chen, Honglin 5, 7, 9–10, 12, 147, 252
children 4, 11, 19–24, 26–9, 35–8, 40–5, 47, 55–8, 60–75, 78–90, 113–20, 122–7, 155–7, 159–60; bilingual 156; case study 117; freewriting 124; groups of 67, 75, 122; helping literacy development 57, 82–3, 90; high-achieving 38; identities 113–16, 127; learning and development 58, 79; observing 63; older 67–8, 74, 126; participating 22, 75; pre-school 42; primary aged school 94; stories 86, 117, 119, 122, 126; supporting of 12, 55, 89–90; younger 67, 71, 113, 127
choices 5, 7–8, 95, 97, 123–4, 127, 155–6, 163–4, 166–70, 198–200, 204, 208–9, 220, 241–2, 247–53; authorial 240, 244; author's 137; conscious 155–6, 240; grammatical 154, 163, 165, 167, 169, 208, 241, 248, 250–1; lexical 103; linguistic 5, 9, 154–5, 162, 170, 199–201, 205, 208–9, 238–9, 251; vocabulary 222, 248; word 163, 184
classes 31–2, 34–5, 113–14, 120, 122–6, 135, 137–40, 142, 144–5, 147, 181–5, 214–17, 220, 234, 247–8; composite 214; control group 160; experimental group 160; preschool 73; primary 72; word 155, 195
Classifiers 98–9, 102–4, 106–9; and Describers 98–9, 102–3, 106–9; use of 108–9
classmates 32, 67, 120, 184, 233
classroom examples 163, 167
classroom literacy practices 176
classroom metalinguistic talk 200
classroom practice 19, 22, 80, 115–16, 184, 243
classrooms 19–24, 27–33, 35–8, 61–3, 65–6, 80–1, 115–20, 125–6, 134–5, 146–7, 157, 165–6, 199–201, 242–3, 249–50; community 119, 126; contemporary 4; creating 4; daily literacy sessions 23; early childhood 19–21, 28, 75; and the functional approach to grammar pedagogy 154, 163, 167; Montessori 61–3, 69, 73; primary 19, 21, 23, 25, 27, 29, 31, 33, 35, 37, 72–3; project 126, 166, 243; research 240; secondary-aged 204, 237, 253; where children can collaborate in writing 4; writing 114, 156–7, 194, 209
clauses 8, 71, 96–8, 100–2, 104–6, 108–10, 140, 159, 195, 230–1; co-ordinated 158, 166, 202–3; dependent 229; embedded 100–1, 104–5, 108–10, 195, 229; non-finite 98, 203; single 96, 231; subordinate 195, 202, 251
Clough, P. 82
clusters 23, 32–3, 36–8, 135, 184, 212; developmental 37; lower 28; particular 36
co-ordinated clauses 158, 166, 202–3
coalition government 85–6
Coffin, C. 9, 174
cognitive challenges 237
cognitive processing 88, 140
colony, developing 222–4, 227, 229–30
Comber, Barbara 19
commas 31, 139, 164, 168
communication 1, 40, 47, 56, 78–9, 115, 117, 134, 242; and language 55; oral 1; purposes 4, 8, 188, 246; studies 132; teaching disciplinary 187
communities 3–4, 11, 21, 80, 107, 123, 125–6, 137, 174; collaborative 81; creative 209; members 133, 137, 140; professional research 170; supportive 80
composition 70, 78, 82, 87–8, 127, 132, 208, 218; children's 85; collaborative 84; creative 86; emerging 125; oral 84, 86; screen-based 83; written 70
Compton-Lily, C. 127
computers 74
concepts 6–7, 9, 21, 124, 131–2, 136, 143, 175, 199, 224, 241, 243, 249, 252; abstract 34, 138, 224; cognitive 7; constructed 132; dynamic 146; grammatical 252; multi-dimensional 6, 133
confident writers, development of 131–47
connections 10, 12, 25, 41, 143, 145, 147, 154, 221, 241–2; cross-curricular 234; explicit 238; meaningful 155, 237, 239; preschool 44
consonant sounds 67, 69
content 3, 127, 136, 166, 178–9, 181, 187, 213, 217, 222, 224, 227, 235,

237–8; and the baseline test 78; of the curriculum 89; elaboration 136; generating 249; learning 188; non-science 177–8, 186; and writers 225, 227
continuing professional development 80, 83, 162, 169
conversations 30–1, 33, 63, 82–3, 85–6, 165, 243–4, 248–9; abstract authorial 9; focus group 78, 82; interview 248; oral 4; writing 162, 165–7, 197, 200, 243–4, 249–51
core subjects 237
CPD *see* continuing professional development
creative writers 113–14, 126
Cremin, Teresa 10, 12, 78, 80, 90, 113–16, 118–19, 124
Culham, Ruth 241
curriculum 9, 79–80, 83, 89–90, 126, 136–7, 154, 160, 163, 166, 170, 173–4, 227, 235, 240; agenda 81; areas 72–3, 95, 175, 187, 224, 228; content 136–7; coverage 123–4; crowded 185; disciplines 179–80, 187; documents 135, 187; initiatives 239; mandated 36; policies 40, 55, 57; prescribed 115; statutory 86; subjects 196; targets 89

data literacy 79
deforestation 222, 224, 228, 230, 232
Department for Education 13, 23, 55–6, 78, 83, 85, 131, 154–5, 194, 238–9
Department for Education and Employment 8
Department for Education and Skills 85
Derewianka, Beverly 5, 9–12, 95–6, 100, 134, 136, 156, 173, 175, 195–6, 199, 212
Describers, and Classifiers 98–9, 102–3, 106–9
description 84, 86, 89, 136–7, 140, 170, 176, 205–7, 220, 250
Descriptions 8
developing 37–8, 41, 45, 145–6, 154–5, 157, 159, 161, 163, 165, 167, 169, 225, 227, 230–1; audience awareness 146, 239; confident writers 131, 133, 135, 137, 139, 141, 143, 145; textual competence 94–5, 97, 99, 101, 103, 105, 109; an understanding of how literacy works 42, 162, 241–2, 253; writers in primary and secondary school years 1–13

development 5–7, 10–13, 40–1, 44–5, 55–6, 60–5, 68–9, 74–5, 78–9, 88–9, 94–6, 100–1, 109–10, 167–8, 194–6; character 142; cognitive 131; complex 167; cumulative 12; discernible 109; professional 240
developmental psychology 60, 62
DfE *see* Department for Education
DfEE *see* Department for Education and Employment
DfES *see* Department for Education and Skills
dialogue structures 11
Diamond, A. 61, 65
digital age 81, 83, 90
Digital Learning Framework for Primary Schools 79
digital literacies 75, 79
digital media 12, 80
digital technologies 12, 44, 60, 78–81, 83–6, 88–90; integration of 79–80, 89, 158, 199
disciplinary 9, 62, 134, 173–4, 177–8, 184, 186–8; perspectives 6; understandings 187
Dowdall, Clare 12, 80
drafts 27, 205, 216–17, 220–1, 233, 235; early 216, 218; evolving 216–17, 220; final 222, 233; multiple 2, 233
Dyson, A.H. 3, 20, 37, 116, 123, 127

early childhood 19–21, 40, 62–3, 80; classrooms 19–21, 28, 75; education 20, 40; literacies 80; teachers 20
early literacy development 40, 45, 47
Early Writing Development 45
early years 22–3, 40, 44, 60–1, 63, 65, 67, 69, 71, 73, 75, 78, 90, 94, 135–6; context 11; curriculum 81; educators 40, 78, 80; settings 12, 55, 80–1; teachers 78, 82
Early Years Foundation Stage 55
Economic and Social Research Council 160–1, 195–7
education 23, 47, 79–80, 86, 95, 170, 187; compulsory 13; early childhood 20, 40; formal 37, 43, 86; Montessori 60–2; policies 40, 55, 58, 79; secondary 213, 231–2; tertiary 95
Education Endowment Foundation 200
Else-Quest, N. 61, 75
embedded clauses 100–1, 104–5, 108–10, 195, 229

emergent literacy 40, 43–5, 55; of children 40, 44; movement 40; perspective 43
empowerment 154–5, 157, 159, 161, 163, 165, 167, 169–70
engagement 12, 85, 88, 116–18, 122, 124, 147, 227; children's 41; democratic 1; emotional 126; guided 11–12; self-directed 61
England 13, 55, 78, 82, 95, 118, 237, 239, 243; attainment in reading exceeds that in writing at age 7 and 11 13; and data from national testing 13; and the Early Years Foundation Stage 55; and the growth of accountability-driven practice and policy 78; and the mismatch between current education policy and understanding of writing. 55; and the *More Than A Score* online campaign 79; and the narrow emphasis in current curriculum policy in 55; and the National Curriculum in England: English Programmes of Study 131, 154; and the national curriculum programmes 78, 131, 182, 239; and the national policy underpinned by an autonomous model of literacy 115; schools inspectorate and national curriculum 57; teachers 178–9, 181, 183–4, 186
English (subject) 4, 9, 195, 199, 237–9
English syllabus 23
environment 3, 6, 11, 20, 41, 44, 62, 66, 74, 81, 144; formal learning 79, 81; home 11, 44, 58, 183; (learning) 3, 7, 20, 44, 58, 61–2, 64, 66, 74, 79, 81, 88, 114, 144; literate 44; material 11, 27, 71; print in 44–5; school 58
ESRC *see* Economic and Social Research Council
explicit teaching 5, 8, 19, 23, 154, 157–8, 165, 170, 173, 208, 222, 225, 234, 239, 242
Expositions 8, 94, 96–7, 105–10; noun groups in 105–6, 108, 110; writing 105
EYFS *see* Early Years Foundation Stage

factual (texts) 67, 73, 74; descriptions 103; genres 97
families 21, 36, 44–5, 52, 57, 98–9, 125, 142, 201, 248; children's 75; participating 47; role of 40
Fang, Z. 9–10, 94, 175

feedback 4, 25, 114, 116, 124, 126, 135, 138, 142, 214, 233–4, 242–3, 253; shaping teacher 115, 248; supportive 123
Feez, Susan 8, 10–11, 62–4
Ferreiro, E. 4, 40, 42–3, 51
First World War 247–8, 250
Flick, U. 82–3
framework 12, 45, 79, 85, 133, 146, 252–3; analytical 136, 195, 197
frameworks 38, 79, 89–90, 146, 187, 252–3; current accountability 90
freedom 61, 127, 183–6, 188; children's 62; ideational 114, 119, 123, 127; individual 188
freewriting 2, 123–7
functions 5, 7–8, 10, 64, 71–2, 74–5, 97–8, 102, 108, 170, 225, 231, 241, 249, 251; classifying 102; cognitive 4; experiential 227; grammatical 157; multivariate 99; quantifying 99; regulatory 185–6; selecting 106

games 66–7, 71; challenging 67; classifying computer 107; energetic naming 66; language 66; spoken vocabulary enrichment 71; war 183
GCSE *see* General Certificate of Secondary Education
General Certificate of Secondary Education 237–8, 243–4, 249
genre-based pedagogy 10–11
genres 4–5, 8–12, 37–8, 94–7, 103, 106, 108–9, 132–4, 143, 146, 213–14, 216–20, 222–3, 235, 242; development 8–9; Expositions 8, 94, 96–7, 105–10; groupings 97; Narratives 8, 31, 37, 96, 118, 120, 123, 126, 204, 207–8; Reports 8, 27, 45, 96–7, 101–6, 109–10, 180–1, 213; types 110; unfamiliar 253
Geography 66, 174–5, 177, 179–181, 184, 228
Giovanelli, M. 5
Gold Rush (Australia) 214–15, 223, 225, 232
'good writers' 28, 30–2, 35, 114
Goodman, Y. 40–1
Graham, S. 12, 194, 199, 242
grammar 5, 11, 70, 72–3, 154–6, 158–63, 165–6, 168–9, 196, 201, 204, 209, 239, 243–5, 249; choices 159, 169, 240; contextual 160; explicit 155; features 163, 169; inclusion of 155,

166; knowledge 159–61, 166, 170, 239–40; lessons 73–4; linking to meaning 5, 154; patterns 71–2; pedagogy 154, 161, 166; role of 170; symbols 71, 73; teaching 154, 156, 204, 239; terms 166, 240; tests 155, 163; and writing 11, 155, 159, 204–8
grammatical: choices 154, 163, 165, 167, 169, 208, 241, 248, 250–1; competence 86; constructions 169, 198; definitions 167, 169; structures 4–5, 94, 158, 251; terminology 155, 162, 169, 239; terms 158, 239, 251
graphic characters 42
graphic organisers 218–19
group lessons 62
groups 65, 67, 97, 99, 101, 119–20, 122, 125, 134, 137, 174, 177–9, 181, 185, 252; comparison 118, 160–1; new 68; nominal 97; older 194; recordings 84; settings 44
guidelines (ethical) 82, 117–18

Halliday, M.A.K. 5, 8–10, 62, 97, 100, 134, 155–7, 199, 223, 225, 227, 231, 240
handwriting 19, 67–70, 74–5, 78, 84
Hannon, P. 44–5, 47
Harpin, W. 4, 7, 94
Harste, J.C. 40, 42
Hasan, R. 11, 95, 133–4
Hayes, J.R. 2, 88, 132, 249
Henderson, S.D. 132, 138, 144, 146
high school 95, 135, 174, 178, 185–7, 235
Higher School Certificate 173, 179
History 9, 11, 66, 174–7, 180–1, 185, 227–8, 232–3
historians 227, 232
Hoose, Hannah 139
HSC *see* Higher School Certificate
human behaviour 231–2
Humphrey, S. 8–9, 11, 95, 174–5
Hyland, K. 95, 131, 133, 142

ICSEA *see* Index of Community Socio-Economic Advantage
ideational freedom 114, 119, 123, 127
identities 10, 81, 113–18, 123, 125–6, 243; authorial 113, 116; children's 113–16, 127; children's shifting 127; formative learner 38; literate 81, 116; negative 115; social 9–10, 12; tools of 122; writer 10, 113, 115, 117–18, 126

images 1, 23, 27, 34, 66–7, 125, 141, 143, 170, 175, 187, 215, 218; list of 206–7; noun phrase 207; original 83
Index of Community Socio-Economic Advantage 21
Indigenous people 222, 232
information 74, 95–8, 100, 102, 105, 140–1, 144, 146, 178–9, 202, 204, 225–6, 228, 231, 233; and data literacy 79; explanatory 202; extra 98, 229; important 233; manipulating 212; new 226, 233; reading 74; recording 213; synthesising 233, 235
infrastructure constructions 223, 228–31
integration of digital technologies 79–80, 89, 158, 199
intellectual skills 11, 69, 75
intentions 19, 32, 79, 84, 156, 160, 167–70, 182, 201, 239, 245, 251, 253; authorial 5, 7, 124, 198, 209, 238–9, 241, 249–51, 253; pedagogic 138; rhetorical 156–7, 160, 162, 199, 248; writer's 133; writing 167, 249, 252
interactions 3, 19–22, 37, 45, 57, 66, 74, 94, 96, 114, 116–17, 136, 145, 200, 235; audience/author 144; collaborative 214; micro-level 62; official school 28; oral 235; peer 114, 116; social 4, 10, 65, 144; writer's 131
intervention 25, 85, 118, 160–1, 243, 251; early 23; family literacy 47; groups 160; pedagogical 161; teaching 201
interviews 22, 28, 117–18, 123, 131, 135, 138, 161, 175–6, 179, 182, 233, 239, 241, 243–4; focus group 124; one-to-one 243; prompts 248; questions 176; schedules 176; sources 176; writing conversation 244
inverted commas 252
Ivanič, R. 10, 20, 115

'Jigsaw of Early Writing Development' 45
Jones, Pauline 156, 187
Jones, Susan 160, 174
judgements 43, 64, 177, 212, 231–2
jurisdiction 13, 173

Kellogg, R.T. 4, 199, 237, 250
Kervin, Lisa 11
knowledge 3, 6, 8–9, 31, 66, 84–5, 132, 134, 154–5, 157, 170, 214, 216–17, 220–1, 238–40; acquired 68; actionable 156; disciplinary 8, 186; educational 63, 66; explicit 155, 199; grammatical

154, 169, 201, 208; linguistic 42, 156, 239; pedagogic 161; phonic 56; professional 235; scientific 9; separate body of 154–5; sound 72, 227
Kroll, B.M. 131–3, 140

language 4, 8–11, 63–4, 95, 133–6, 147, 154–7, 187, 199, 212, 220–2, 227–8, 230–1, 235, 238–40; academic 9, 221, 228; children's 62; choices 6, 133, 136, 139, 147, 156–7, 168, 201–2, 207, 239–40, 243–4, 248–9, 252; development 62, 66, 69; discipline-related 227–8; features 8, 175, 214, 216, 219, 222, 225; functions of 225, 231; grammatical 162–3, 167; learning 10, 26, 157–8; and literacy 117; manipulation of 7, 240; model of 133, 223; oral 44–5, 48, 156; oral 44, 45, 48, 156, 187; patterns of 8, 10–11, 245; resources 12, 137, 141, 147, 156, 231; spoken 64–6, 69, 71–3, 230; teaching 187; use 11–12, 156–7, 166, 240; working 155, 157, 239–40; written 41, 44, 63, 64, 67, 69–71, 75, 187–8, 194
laptop computers 27
Leander, K.M. 19, 21
learning 3–4, 8, 10, 19–23, 27–9, 37–8, 40–1, 55–8, 61–2, 64–8, 138–9, 157–9, 176–8, 234–5, 241–3; articulating 157; clusters 23–4, 35; cycle 11, 188, 214–15, 222; disciplinary 8; focus of 158, 165, 204; goals 25, 33–4, 36, 38, 84–5; improved 163; intensive professional 235; new 4, 217; support 79
A Learning and Responding Matrix 177, 179, 187
lessons 63–6, 71, 74, 139, 141–2, 147, 159–60, 169, 175–7, 181–2, 184–5, 187, 195, 200–1, 245–6; classroom literacy 135, 174, 177; English and History/Geography 177; grammar 73–4; group 62; secondary 175; selected 135
letters 6, 42, 44, 47, 51, 55, 57, 64–5, 68–70, 115, 120, 245; cursive 68; formation 27, 54–6, 58; imitating 69
Lewis, Helen 8, 96–7
Lillard, A.S. 60–2, 75
Lines, Helen 12, 162, 214
linguistic choices 5, 9, 154–5, 162, 170, 199–201, 205, 208–9, 239, 251, 253
linguistic constructions 7

linguistic development 7, 10, 12–13, 194–9, 201, 208–9
linguistic forms 7–8, 10, 12, 133
linguistic resources 94
linguistic structures 195, 198–200, 246
literacy 21, 23, 27, 40–5, 47, 55, 57, 78–80, 85–6, 114–17, 135, 173–5, 182, 188, 234–5; children's 44–5, 58, 78, 80, 114; contemporary 81; development of 36, 55, 70, 147, 173–4, 186, 212; disciplinary 8, 174, 187; early 41, 45; education 78, 90; events 10, 89, 117, 146; ideological models of 80, 90; interactive 146; national 23, 213; and numeracy 23, 174; secondary school 174, 235; skills 23, 60; state-based 23; teaching 8, 23, 173–4, 176
literary terminology 239
Loban, W. 94, 195
Locke, John 113
Luke, A. 114, 175
Lunsford, A.A. 131, 133

Macken-Horarik, M. 5, 147, 182, 239
Magnifico, A.M. 9, 131–2, 140, 147, 243
Marshall, C. 60–2
Martin, J.R. 8, 10, 95, 99, 133–5, 174, 188, 223, 225, 231
materials 19–22, 27–8, 34, 38, 60–3, 68, 81, 159; children's 21; online 215; reading 55; visual 146; written 55
Mathematics 61, 66, 174
mathematicians 227
Matruglio, Erika 8, 174
Matthiessen, C.M.I.M. 97, 100, 156
meaning 9, 10, 26–7, 57, 70–72, 90, 157, 163, 208, 218, 248; actively constructed 143–4; as an act 157; and audience 131–3, 136–7, 140–1; in the clause 96; in the noun group 97–8, 100–1, 103; linking to grammar 5, 71, 154, 158, 163, 165–9, 208, 240–1, 243, 249–50, 252–3; linking to punctuation 164; and mark-making 42, 44, 47–8, 54, 57, 120; meaning-making 5, 8–11, 70, 94–8, 109–10, 115, 119, 140, 155–7, 187, 198–9, 208, 240, 243, 249
mental processes 2, 4
mentor texts 139, 142, 166, 183, 242
Mercer, Neil 157
Merchant, G. 78, 80, 90, 173
metafunctions 134, 137, 157

metalanguage 6, 147, 187; grammatical 240; oriented 11; shared 86
metalinguistic 5, 194, 200–1, 208, 240; development 6, 194; discussion 12, 200, 208; knowledge 156–7, 239; thinking 160, 167, 200–1, 204, 208; understanding 6–7, 161, 170, 194, 197, 199–200, 208–9, 239–41, 243
miners 223–4, 228–30
Ministry of Education 13, 194
modelling 4, 135, 140, 142–3, 146; episodes 145; explicit 85; sessions 141
models 2, 11, 45, 57, 75, 84, 86, 90, 123, 134, 139, 147, 163, 169, 182–3; appraisal 231; autonomous 80, 115; clear 86; cognitive 2–3; coherent 133; knowledge-transforming 249; linguistic 4–5; pedagogical 11; socio-cultural 4; supportive 27
MoE *see* Ministry of Education
Montessori 11, 61, 64, 68–70, 72, 75; activities 68, 70; children 61; classrooms 61–3, 69, 73; curriculum 63, 74–5; education 60–2; learning environments 62; pedagogy 60–2; preschools 62, 64, 67, 70, 75; research 61; schools 60; settings 62–6, 68–9, 72; teachers 60–1, 63, 70; tradition 64, 69
Montessori, Maria 60, 63, 68, 70
Morpurgo, Michael 159
Myhill, Debra 5–7, 11, 78, 90, 95, 114–15, 147, 157, 160–3, 195–6, 200–1, 204, 212, 214, 239–40, 242, 252

nano-technology 252
NAPLAN *see* National Assessment Program Literacy and Numeracy Tests
Narratives 8, 31, 37, 96, 118, 120, 123, 126, 204, 207–8; local community 119; self-initiated 119, 122; short 86
National Assessment Program Literacy and Numeracy Tests 23, 37, 75, 174, 213–14
national curriculum 57, 79, 83, 85, 95, 131, 154–5, 173
national grammar tests 166, 169
National Literacy Strategy 85
Newman, R. 6–7, 163, 200
nominalisations 100, 108, 229–32
non-fiction 84, 244–5, 251
noun groups 71, 95–106, 108–10, 228–31; complex 100, 109; configurations of 103, 106; expanded in the pre-modifier 102; in Expositions 105–6, 108, 110; percentages of total number of 101, 105, 108; in Reports 101–2, 108–9; use of 104, 109
noun phrases 158, 164–5, 168, 196–8, 202, 205–7
nouns 71, 73–4, 96–8, 100–1, 108, 118, 169–70, 196, 229, 240
numeracy 13, 23, 174
Nutbrown, Cathy 7, 11, 44–5, 82
Nvivo software 135, 244

older writers 7, 194–5, 199, 208
oral (language) 1–2, 44–5, 48, 84, 86, 119, 120, 121, 156, 187, 189, 221, 225
outcomes 10, 61–2, 83, 89–90, 118, 135, 160–1, 177, 188, 235, 240; improved educational 10; key learning 131, 136; positive 61–2, 243
Owl Babies (story) 83–4, 86

Painter, C. 11, 65, 69
parents 40–1, 44–5, 47, 55, 57–8, 79, 114, 122, 237–8; early years home and school learning environments 58; encouraged to nurture the emergent elements of literacy that young children exhibit 41; imprisoned xvi
Park, D.B. 131–3, 138, 145
Parr, J.M. 157
patterns 13, 102, 159, 165, 167–8, 184, 195–7, 200–1, 204, 248; absorbing rhetorical 242; common 158; developmental 198, 201–2; embedding grammatical 169; of language 8, 10–11, 245; linguistic 95; productive 201
pedagogical 6, 22, 200, 249; challenges 238; conclusions 167; decisions 19; factors 174; principles 161, 208
pedagogies 10–13, 19–22, 37, 60–1, 63, 69–71, 75, 81–2, 85–6, 90, 154–7, 161–2, 169–70, 173–4, 187–8; associated 79; current 170; effective 13, 169; of empowerment 154–5, 157, 159, 161, 163, 165, 167, 169; hybrid 89; informed 10, 162; integrated language 187
peer readership 246
Penton, George 252
Perera, K. 7, 94, 174, 194, 212
Perin, D. 12, 194, 199, 242
phonemes 65, 67, 69
phonetic understanding 52
phrases 29, 71, 98, 104, 108, 125, 167

PISA *see* Program for International Student Assessment
planning 2–3, 12, 20, 27–9, 88, 132, 204; groups 22; process 2; space 29
poems 48, 55, 67, 125, 181–5
poetry 73–4, 177, 182–4, 253
policy 19, 28, 40, 55–7, 78, 90, 173–4, 237
Portside Primary School 135
post-modification (use of) 101–2, 104–6, 108, 110, 196, 198
practices 8–10, 12, 19–22, 37–8, 40–1, 80–2, 84–5, 88–9, 95, 114–17, 126–7, 134–5, 137–8, 173–6, 186–7; disciplinary 174; educational 75; literate 20; new freewriting 126; pedagogical 138, 235; primary school teacher's 118; social 4, 8, 19, 95, 115, 117
pre-modification (use of) 101–3, 105–6, 109, 196, 198
preschools 41, 66, 71–2, 135, 174; children 61, 69; classrooms 70; learning 55; Montessori 62, 64, 67, 70, 75; teachers 41, 43, 63
prescribed curriculum targets 89
primary classrooms 19, 21, 23, 25, 27, 29, 31, 33, 35, 37, 72–3
Primary National Strategies Framework for Literacy and Mathematics 85
primary schools 7, 21–2, 71, 79, 94, 96, 131, 137, 155, 174, 182, 186, 212–13; associated 174; classes 63; sites 135; teachers 63, 154, 160; upper level 95–6; writers 154, 167
print 6, 11, 27, 41–2, 44–5, 118; awareness 6, 41–2; in the environment 44–45; production 27
processes 2–4, 6–7, 9–11, 23–4, 27, 35, 37, 82, 84, 87–8, 90, 96, 145–6, 195, 197; causal 229; cumulative 215; decision-making 159; dialogic 116; drafting 2, 233; expanded 90; material 28, 141; meaning-making 95, 198; social 10, 214; two-stage 83
professional development sessions 200, 249
Professional Learning Teams 213
Program for International Student Assessment 174
programmes 6, 13, 47, 58; conventional school 61; distinctive genre-based literacy 95; English national curriculum 78, 131, 182, 239; family literacy 40, 44–5, 47, 58; high-fidelity Montessori 61; professional learning 23

progression 23, 34, 37, 63, 89, 147, 198, 202, 204, 208, 223; children's 63, 89; supporting literacy learning 147, 204; writer's 202
projects 22, 45, 74, 113, 116–18, 123–4, 132, 161–2, 167–8, 174, 197, 212, 215, 244, 251; classroom 126, 166, 243; family literacy 45; learning to write 21; school's middle years 214; teachers 169; *see also* research projects
pronouns 71, 73, 97, 250
prose 132, 243
punctuation 19, 30, 34, 36, 79, 86, 115, 127, 140, 164, 168, 195, 246

QCA *see* Qualifications and Curriculum Authority
Qualifications and Curriculum Authority 195
'Question Game' 67–8

Randomised Control Trial 62, 118, 154, 160–3
RCT *see* Randomised Control Trial
reader-based prose 132, 243
readers 7, 124–5, 131–4, 136–47, 159, 167, 182, 202, 204, 209, 220–2, 225, 241–7, 249–51, 253; facilitating active construction of meaning 143; first impressions 206; interpretation of texts 137, 250; and relationships with writers 134–6, 140, 142; sensitivity of 132; and students 136, 139–43, 145–7, 212
readership 137, 252
Recounts 8, 32, 67, 88
relationships 95, 114, 116, 118, 123, 136–7, 146, 157–60, 162, 165, 177–8, 180, 188, 231, 240; causal 228, 231; co-mentoring 118; dialectic 157; dynamic 133; social 20, 134; transactional 132
Reports 8, 27, 45, 96–7, 101–6, 109–10, 180–1, 213; annual 21; genre 103; structured 74; writing of 101, 109
research 1–2, 4–8, 13, 21, 40–1, 43–5, 74–5, 113–15, 156–9, 174–5, 187–8, 194–6, 198–200, 208, 241–3; appliable 173; complementary 5; cumulative 170; educational 161; ethical 82; findings 201; highlights 158–9; initiatives 170; linguistic 188; literature 13, 159, 199; narrative 118; projects 21, 116, 237, 243; social science 82; teachers as writers 126

researchers 82, 165, 175, 252; commentary 165; early childhood 20; leading 252
resources 5, 19–20, 22, 27, 37, 84, 90, 110, 141, 156, 213, 220, 228–9, 239; digital 82; grammatical 158, 160; interpersonal 134, 142, 232; linguistic 11, 96, 187, 209, 212; logical 141–2; pedagogical 95; screen-based 81
responses 27, 60, 123, 126, 141, 145, 159, 162–3, 176, 178–9, 200, 235, 246, 248, 251; anticipated 135; formal written 238; influence reader 137; initial first-level 208; qualitative 27; stock 245; student reader's 169
rhetorical intentions 156–7, 160, 162, 199, 248
Rothery, J. 11, 95, 174, 214–15

samples 22, 29, 34, 47, 63, 73–4, 110, 135, 160, 162–3, 165, 184, 195, 244; student interview 244; student text 22
sandpaper letters 68–70
scaffolding 4, 10–1, 84, 87, 89, 139, 142, 145, 181, 214, 234, 253; pedagogic practices 10; process 84; student understandings 139, 142
Schleppegrell, M.J. 5, 9–10, 95, 175, 235
school years 1–13; four-term 63; late primary 131; secondary 1
schooling 6, 9–10, 12, 20, 22, 75, 94, 96, 114, 134, 146–7, 173–5, 186–8, 212; conventional 60, 62; culture 95; formal 40, 44–5, 56; primary 197, 213; primary years of 136, 147; secondary 8, 186, 197, 212, 235; years 173, 188
schools 19–23, 25–8, 31–3, 36–7, 40–1, 45, 47, 54–8, 60–3, 114–16, 123–6, 135, 137–8, 212–13, 237–9; catholic 107; classrooms 117; clusters 135; elementary 61; high-income 36; low-income 36; primary feeder 212; public 61; regional 132; remote rural 213; structured activities 116; suburban Montessori 62; writers in 115
science 66, 174–81, 186, 237–8; classes 177, 179; lessons 178; teachers 178–9
scientists 227, 252
secondary schools 155, 174, 176, 178, 181–2, 184–6, 195, 213, 237, 244
sense exercises 65–6
sentence-shapers 194–209
sentences 29, 71–3, 83, 159–60, 163–4, 167, 169, 179, 195–7, 199, 202–4, 225, 231, 241, 245–7; complex 221, 224, 231, 248; length 7, 195–7, 202; long 196, 198, 247; multiclause 224; short 168, 198, 202, 242, 247; structure 34, 179, 246, 251; structured 179; topics 220, 225–6; *see also* simple sentences
SFL *see* Systemic Functional Linguistics
Sheffield Raising Early Achievement in Literacy Project 45
Shelley, Mary 248
simple sentences 56, 195, 198
single noun groups 101–2, 105–6
skills 12–13, 37, 41–2, 57, 64–5, 68, 79, 87, 113, 115, 155, 185, 187, 206, 208; complementary 156; decoding 213; decontextualised self-contained 80; demonstrating great 225; discrete 80; and Foundation knowledge 64; handwriting 75; intellectual 11, 69, 75; literacy 23, 60; mechanical 60, 70; oral language 187; professional 200; reading 187; transcriptional 86
Social Research Council 160, 195
social structures 81, 223, 226–30, 232
sounds 31, 57, 64–5, 67–72, 107, 144, 165, 183, 245, 247, 250–1; consonant 67, 69; constituent 69; contrasting 67; digraph 67; individual 64; spoken 56
SpaceWorks Engineering 251
Spencer Project 195
spoken language 64–5, 69, 71–73, 230
stories 31–4, 36, 67, 72, 74, 82–9, 117–20, 122–3, 125–7, 143, 182, 185, 202–3, 205, 250; children's 86, 117, 119, 122, 126; dictated 118; extended 34; imaginary 67, 74; imaginative 73; innovative 85; original 88; personal 88; written 120
storytellers 86–7, 113, 119
structures 7, 33, 98–9, 101–3, 105–6, 110, 179, 187, 195, 198, 200, 202, 208, 237–8, 248; appropriate text 137; associated accountability 90; constitutive 81; formal 238; generic 10, 32; molecular 252; normal noun group 105; schematic 8, 11; univariate 97–8, 101, 105
student interviews 160–1, 163, 176
students 7–8, 10–13, 23–5, 27, 32–4, 123–4, 135–47, 165–6, 173–88, 204–9, 212–15, 217–18, 220–2, 230–5, 237–53; early primary years 212; flexibility of 181; individual 25, 141–2;

Index 265

moving across proficiency levels 136–7, 235; primary 94, 197, 213; progress of 23, 135, 147; and readers 136, 139–43, 145–7, 212; responses 244, 253; secondary 181, 197, 204, 212, 243; supporting 147, 208, 238; and teachers 11, 135, 175–6, 213, 253; teaching 25, 235
studies 7–9, 41–2, 47, 61–3, 67, 69–71, 94, 100–1, 113–18, 126–7, 161–2, 165–7, 194–6, 198–9, 240–2; cross-linguistic 195; cumulative 239; family 174; international 61; storytelling and story-acting 117–18; writing conversations 200
subject knowledge 161, 201
syllabus 23
synonyms 224, 226, 232
systemic functional linguistic approach 95
Systemic Functional Linguistics 9–10, 95–6, 133

Talk for Writing 89
teachers 19–30, 32–8, 61–5, 67, 78–90, 113–16, 118–20, 122–6, 135–41, 157–63, 169–70, 173–82, 184–8, 200–2, 233–5; disciplinary 187; early years 78, 82; English 178–9, 181, 183–4, 186; hierarchical 125; individual 19, 81; Montessori 60–1, 63, 70; participating 22, 63; preschool 41, 43, 63; primary school 63, 154, 160; secondary 185, 213, 235; and students 11, 135, 175–6, 213, 253; supporting young children's writing 88
'Teachers as Writers' study 117–18, 123
teaching 1, 5–6, 10, 19, 21–3, 26–8, 55, 63–4, 78–9, 81, 155–6, 173, 204, 213–15, 234; activities 26; children 44–5; formal 44; grammar 154, 156, 204, 239; students 25, 235
Teberosky, A. 4, 40, 42–3, 51
technology 12, 80, 83–4, 86–7, 89–90; digital 88; internet 243; paper-based 90; pioneering 251; print-based 27; use of 79, 83–6, 89
teenagers 177, 243, 248
tests 61, 75, 78, 155, 159, 169, 213; baseline 78; NAPLAN 75; national 155; national grammar 166, 169; new 155; standardised 19
texts 67, 73, 94, 212, 225; connectives 224, 226, 232, 234; models 242, 252; organisers 224–6, 232; types 4, 94–5, 101, 109, 196, 204, 242
textual competence 94, 96, 109; developing 94–5, 97, 99, 101, 103, 105, 109; and research 94
TfW *see* Talk for Writing
topic sentences 220, 225–6
topics 2, 29, 37, 73, 83, 132, 180, 182, 214–16, 218, 220, 224, 233–4; discovery of gold 214, 216, 218, 220, 222–8, 230, 232; preferred 181; unfamiliar 217
Transforming Literacies Project 212
Transforming Literacy Outcomes 135, 213
transition 69, 71, 138, 175, 185–6, 212–14; literacy 174–6, 186; points 135, 174, 181, 212; students 147

United Kingdom 4, 41, 45, 94, 116–18, 155, 157, 160–1, 195; assessment processes 195; curriculum 154, 163; grammar tests 159; studies 94, 113
United Kingdom Economic and Social Research Council 160–1, 195, 197
United Kingdom Literacy Association 82
United States 13, 61, 75, 78, 94, 194; early studies in the 94, 116; and the emergent literacy movement 40; preschool teachers enthusiastic about young children's literacy capabilities 41; and the 'roots' of literacy which developed in young children 41
University of Plymouth Research Ethics and Integrity Committee guidelines 82

Vale, Emma Rutherford 9, 12
verbs 71–3, 96, 100, 127, 141, 159, 163, 168, 170, 177, 179, 183, 204, 229, 251; energetic 71; finite 195–7; negative 208; strong 182
vocabulary 31, 44, 61, 72, 79, 89, 94, 183, 186, 196, 224, 238–9, 245–6, 249, 253; children's 78; choices 222, 248; development 218; scientific 166
Vygotsky, L.S. 3, 10, 64, 70, 157

Woods, Annette 21,
words 41–2, 51–2, 56–7, 66–7, 69–73, 97, 136–7, 140, 144–5, 157, 179–80, 183–7, 198–9, 247–50, 252; academic 224; composing 70; copying 44; decoding 235; functions of 71–2; high

frequency 29–30; practising 54; written 64, 120
workshops 123, 213–14
Wray, D. 84, 94
writer-based prose 243
writer identities 10, 113, 115, 117–18, 126; ascribing to children 115; below average 115; positive 125
writer relationships 244–6
writers 1–6, 8–12, 32, 57–8, 81–4, 113–19, 122–7, 131–7, 140–2, 194, 198–202, 204, 208–9, 224–8, 241–6; academic 113; adolescent 113, 238; community of 6, 158; confident 11, 58, 131, 146; creative 113–14, 126; emergent 11, 13, 47, 58; expert 241, 249; high-attaining 196–8; literary 113; older 7, 194–5, 199, 208; primary school 154, 167; professional 113, 116, 118, 205; proficient 82, 125; secondary 194, 253; secondary-aged 197–9; secondary school 208; student 137; young 82, 86, 88, 101, 105, 109, 116, 118, 154, 156–7, 160, 162–3, 167, 170, 201; younger 194–5, 248
writing 82–90, 113–18, 122–7, 137–42, 154–63, 165–8, 174–83, 185–7, 194–202, 204–9, 212–15, 233–5, 237–9, 241–4, 246–9; choices 140, 156, 165–6; classrooms 114, 156–7, 194, 209; cognitive model of 2, 6; conversations 162, 165–7, 197, 200, 243–4, 249–51; creative 114; culture of 73; development 13, 20–1, 94, 173, 176, 181, 186, 194, 196, 200, 243; intentions 167, 249, 252; pedagogy 84, 90, 138, 156; practices 84, 114, 127, 179, 186, 241; process 85–6, 88–90, 132, 139, 147, 169, 208–9, 217; purpose for 2, 27, 176, 179, 187, 218; samples 161, 165, 195–7; skills 75, 194, 234, 240–1; socio-cultural models of 3–4, 6; tasks 139, 147, 166–7, 169, 217, 237
written language 41, 44, 64, 67, 69–71, 75, 187–8, 194
written texts 2, 4, 29, 40, 42–3, 64, 120, 162, 165, 168, 199, 201, 208, 218, 220

young children 6, 11, 19–20, 22, 40–1, 44, 47, 55–7, 60, 62, 67, 78–80, 82–5, 88–90, 127
young people 8, 79, 113, 115, 117, 124, 126
young writers 82, 86, 88, 101, 105, 109, 116, 118, 154, 156–7, 160, 162–3, 167, 170, 201

Printed in Great Britain
by Amazon